Essential Finance and Accounting
for Managers

Essential Finance and Accounting for Managers

LESLIE CHADWICK MBA FCCA Cert Ed

Head of Work Experience Placements and Senior University Teacher in Finance and Accounting, Bradford University School of Management

FINANCIAL TIMES
Prentice Hall

An imprint of **Pearson Education**

Harlow, England · London · New York · Reading, Massachusetts · San Francisco · Toronto · Don Mills, Ontario · Sydney
Tokyo · Singapore · Hong Kong · Seoul · Taipei · Cape Town · Madrid · Mexico City · Amsterdam · Munich · Paris · Milan

Pearson Education Limited
Edinburgh Gate
Harlow
Essex CM20 2JE
England

and Associated Companies throughout the world

Visit us on the World Wide Web at:
www.pearsoneduc.com

ISBN 0273-64648-6

British Library Cataloguing-in-Publication Data
A catalogue record for this book is available from the British Library

Library of Congress Cataloging-in-Publication Data
Chadwick, Leslie, 1943-
    Essential finance and accounting for managers / Leslie Chadwick.
        p. cm.
    Includes index.
    ISBN 0-273-64648-6 (pbk.)
    1. Financial statements. 2. Managerial accounting. I. Title.

    [HF5681.B2 C413 2002]
    658.15--dc21

                                                    2002020782

10 9 8 7 6 5 4 3 2 1
05 04 03 02

Typeset in Garamond by 25
Printed in Great Britain by Henry Ling Ltd., at the Dorset Press, Dorchester, Dorset

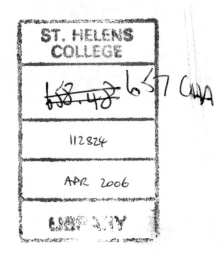

CONTENTS

PREFACE

Welcome to the wonderful world of finance and accounting. Believe it or not, finance and accounting can be both interesting and enjoyable!

Who is this book for?

This book has been designed to meet the needs of MBA and MA students, non-financial managers and executives, and should provide a firm foundation for the future.

- It is the product of research carried out by the publishers and the author into the needs of both students and their tutors and lecturers.
- Students studying on MBA and MA courses, managers and executives do have clear expectations of what a foundation course in accounting and finance should do for them.

What the research told us

The major findings from the research were that many of the foundation-level texts for non-accountants were:

- still to a large extent really designed for professional accounting or undergraduate students;
- too detailed and covering far too much ground;
- difficult to read and understand;
- short of examples and illustrations;
- not relating to the real world of business;
- in need of including more case studies, self-assessments and projects;
- weak in terms of public-sector and service-sector material;
- too UK- or US-orientated;

- ☐ not following a logical flow from one topic to another;
- ☐ lacking in their coverage of certain key topic areas;
- ☐ no use without a solutions manual which in certain cases had to be purchased separately;
- ☐ not addressing the need for a tutor's manual containing suggested answers to questions and outline answers to case studies.

What the users have said they need

People on MBA and MA courses, non-financial managers and executives have said on numerous occasions that they do not want to become accountants or fantastic number-crunchers. They are, however, clear on what they do want, and this was also borne out by the research.

They informed us that they need to:

- ☐ acquire a good grasp of the terminology that is used;
- ☐ understand how the figures, e.g. those in the profit and loss account, balance sheet and cash flow statement have been arrived at;
- ☐ acquire and demonstrate a satisfactory working knowledge of the important concepts, principles and techniques;
- ☐ analyse, interpret and evaluate the accounts, and be able to make comparisons with the financial performance of competitors, e.g. to assess financial performance, or for decision-making purposes;
- ☐ read and understand the published report and accounts of a company;
- ☐ be able to enter into discussions with accountants, e.g. on matters of common interest;
- ☐ know about the drawbacks and limitations of the information that is produced;
- ☐ appreciate behavioural aspects, e.g. how budgets affect people;
- ☐ be able to focus on the key issues;
- ☐ receive material that is clear and concise, that goes into a reasonable depth without going overboard;
- ☐ be supplied with examples and illustrations from various industry sectors, e.g. manufacturing, retailing, services and the public sector;
- ☐ be provided with material that has a more international and European flavour;
- ☐ be supplied with more 'open-ended' case studies which help to integrate with the knowledge gained from other areas, e.g. marketing and strategic management;
- ☐ include projects that involve the production of reports and participation in presentations and discussion sessions;
- ☐ have a selection of appropriate journal articles and extracts from the financial press, e.g. the *Financial Times*;
- ☐ have suggested solutions to the self-assessments within the text and not in a separate manual.

Teaching and learning features

In order to meet the needs of its target audience the book has been designed to include:

- ☐ a concise and user-friendly writing style that is both readable and understandable;
- ☐ learning objectives defined at the start of each chapter;
- ☐ step-by-step examples;
- ☐ a number of self-checks and self-assessment activities, with suggested answers within the text to encourage self-learning;
- ☐ a number of tutor-based assignments, case studies and projects, answers or outline answers to which are supplied to lecturers and tutors in a separate manual;
- ☐ case studies that include a number of 'open-ended' questions and cover various industry sectors and countries;
- ☐ brief chapter summaries that focus on the key messages contained in each chapter;
- ☐ suggested further reading and useful websites;
- ☐ a selection of appropriate readings, consisting of journal articles and extracts from the financial press, e.g. the *Financial Times*;
- ☐ project work of an individual or group nature which culminate in a discussion, written report, verbal report-back and/or presentation.

The design, it is hoped, should help you to develop both your numerical and comprehensional skills, e.g. via the open-ended case studies and reflective learning. It should prove suitable for full-time and part-time students, distance learning, action learning study modes and modular courses.

Lecturer support material

A Tutor's Manual is available for download at http://www.booksites.net/chadwick to adopters of this text. The Manual includes answers or outline answers to the tutor-based assignments, case studies and projects included in the text.

About the author

Leslie Chadwick is currently Head of Work Experience Placements and a senior university teacher at Bradford University School of Management, and is regarded as one of the UK's leading writers on finance and accounting. He commenced his professional career in 1958 with a lengthy spell in local government. He qualified as a Chartered Certified Accountant in 1965 and in 1966 moved into industry as a Management Accountant, followed by two years in professional practice with a firm of Chartered Accountants. He became a lecturer/senior lecturer in accountancy at Huddersfield University in 1971 before taking up his current appointment in 1979. He has contributed numerous articles to many of the UK's leading professional journals. He is the author of several books, some of which have been translated into a number of languages including Chinese or brought out as special editions in Asia and Eastern Europe. He has also written distance learning material for leading UK professional bodies, a chapter for *Management Concepts and Practices* (Financial Times Prentice Hall) and is a co-author of the *Collins Dictionary of Business*. He has lectured and presented papers in the UK, Europe and the Far East.

The assessments

There are three types of assessment, used throughout the text, which are as follows:

☐ self-checks
☐ self-assessments
☐ tutor-based assignments.

Self-checks

When you have completed each individual self-check, you need to compare your attempt with the appropriate section of the chapter concerned.

Self-assessments (the 'A' questions)

On completion of each individual self-assessment, you need to compare your answer with the suggested answer which appears at the back of the book in Appendix 1, and to note the differences and variations.

From a learning point of view, please attempt the self-assessment before you look at the suggested answer. You will then be able to observe and highlight where you could improve your answer, e.g. in terms of the calculations, presentation and layout, and critical comments.

Tutor-based assignments (the 'T' questions)

In addition to reading this text, further research may be necessary in order to complete some of the assignments. The assignments may be used on an individual or group basis, as directed by the lecturer or tutor. They may be discussed in groups, or used as group or individual presentations and/or reports. Feedback will be available from lecturers or tutors.

Lecturers and tutors only will be provided with the Tutor's Manual, which contains suggested and outline answers to all of the tutor-based assignments.

The author welcomes comments from the users of this book which will be taken into account when a new edition is prepared.

ACKNOWLEDGEMENTS

We are grateful to the following for permission to reproduce copyright material:

Figures 7.2, 14.1, 15.1, 15.2, A15.1 from *Essential Financial Accounting*, Financial Times Prentice Hall, © 1991, 1996 Prentice Hall Europe, © 2001 Pearson Education (Chadwick, L. 2001).

Pearson Education Limited for an extract from *Myths and Realities of Accounting and Finance* by Leslie Chadwick; Professional Manager for 'Do you know the score' by Mike Bourne (lecturer at Cranfield School of Management) and Pippa Bourne (Regional Manager, Institute of Chartered Accountants in England and Wales), published in *Professional Manager* by the Institute of Management, November 2000.

We are grateful to the Financial Times Limited for permission to reprint the following material:

Industry spends as much on IT as on equipment, © *Financial Times*, 31 July, 2000; General insurance lifts Royal & Sun, © *Financial Times*, 4 August, 2000; Revamp programme pays off as Nissan shows profit, © *Financial Times*, 31 October, 2000; BP Amoco unveils record $3.8 bn profit, © *Financial Times*, 8 November, 2000; Wiggins shows size of loss, © *Financial Times*, 8 March, 2001; Higher Margins lift AMEC, © *Financial Times*, 8 March, 2001; LVMH profits rise is weaker than expected, © *Financial Times*, 8 March, 2001; Colgate profit puts it further ahead of peers, © *Financial Times*, 20 April, 2001; Daewood racks up record $10 bn loss, © *Financial Times*, 20 April, 2001; Xerox bounces back with better-than-expected results, © *Financial Times*, 20 April, 2001; GE surges to number one spot in FT500 survey, © *Financial Times*, 11 May, 2001; Change in accounting policy hits ITNet figures, © *Financial Times*, 20 February, 2001; Investors set to scrutinise Xerox's core, © *Financial Times*, 7 March, 2001; ING set to pay £125 m for Charterhouse, © *Financial Times*, 31 July, 2000; Intershop in profit but low on funds, © *Financial Times*, 4 August, 2000; Daewood set to be declared bankrupt today, © *Financial Times*, 8 November, 2000; Football clubs, © *Financial Times*, 14 December, 1996; A bigger yardstick for company performance, © *Financial Times*, 16 October, 2000; Daewood executives charged with £23 bn accounting fraud, © *Financial Times*, 20 February, 2001; C&W used swap deal to boost its accounts, © *Financial Times*, 13 February, 2002; Enron accountant may be key witness, © *Financial Times*, 13 February, 2002.

In some instances we have been unable to trace the owners of copyright material, and we would appreciate any information that would enable us to do so.

An introduction to the accounting scene

A child's-eye view of an accountant may picture someone sitting in a tower room of a castle counting money. Adults with a little more knowledge may perceive accountants as being useful in helping to reduce their tax liability or as someone who can fiddle the books! The truth of the matter is that the vast majority of accountants do work within the law, and are very trustworthy, honest and a credit to their profession. You only have to scan the *Financial Times* to appreciate the need and the importance of finance and accounting, as illustrated by the following headlines:

Headlines from the *Financial Times* (*FT*)

Industry spends as much on IT as on equipment *(J. Guthrie, 31 July 2000)*

General Insurance lifts Royal & Sun *(Expressed confidence of achieving performance targets in 2001, A. Felsted, 4 August 2000)*

Revamp programme pays off as Nissan shows profit *(D. Ibison, 31 October 2000)*

BP Amoco unveils record $3.8bn profit *(D. Buchan, 8 November 2000)*

Wiggins shows size of loss *(Loss of £25.2m, C. Batchelor, 8 March 2001)*

Higher margins lift AMEC *(C. Batchelor, 8 March 2001)*

LVMH profits rise is weaker than expected *(J. Johnson, 8 March 2001)*

Colgate profit puts it further ahead of peers *(A. Edgecliffe-Johnson 20 April 2001)*

Daewoo racks up record $10bn loss *(J. Burton, 20 April 2001)*

Xerox bounces back with better-than-expected results *(A. Hill, 20 April 2001)*

GE surges to number one spot in FT500 survey *(Success is measured in market value, GE having a value of $477bn on the snapshot date of 4 January 2001, J. Fuller, 11 May 2001)*

C&W used swap deal to boost its accounts *(D. Roberts and R. Budden, 13 February 2002)*

Enron accountant may be key witness *(P. Spiegel, 13 February 2002)*

The principal aim of this chapter is to introduce you to the accounting scene and to provide you with an appreciation of the purpose and scope of financial accounting, management accounting and financial management.

Learning objectives

When you have completed working your way through this chapter, you should be able to do the following:

- ☐ understand why non-financial managers need to know more about accounting and finance;
- ☐ identify the users of financial accounting information;
- ☐ appreciate the role of financial accounting;
- ☐ appreciate the way in which management accounting attempts to meet the needs of managers;
- ☐ know why predetermined cost and management accounting systems are needed;
- ☐ be aware of the areas of activity covered by financial management;
- ☐ describe how treasury management can generate more money;
- ☐ understand the role of the auditor;
- ☐ explain how taxation affects cash flow and investment and financing decisions.

Beware of accountants!

Accountancy is not an exact science – which means that accountants are often required to exercise their personal judgement, common sense and fairness in a constructive and unbiased way.

Did you know the following?

☐ A company can be highly profitable, but at the same time have serious cash flow problems!

☐ Profits could rise or fall if a company changes its depreciation policy.

☐ Companies could have fixed assets such as equipment, machinery and motor vehicles which do not appear on their balance sheet, e.g. in cases where such fixed assets are rented or leased.

☐ Budgets of income and expenditure are just estimated targets.

☐ Companies have been known to discontinue products or services, simply because of the way in which their costs were worked out!

☐ Where the fixed assets have been revalued the return on capital employed could be affected by a significant amount.

As you continue to study the remainder of this text, the reasons for the above statements should become clear. Our final chapter concludes with a more in-depth look at why all managers and executives need to beware of accountants.

Which managers and executives need to study accounting and finance?

Certain business functions such as marketing, finance and research and development may in certain companies or organisations tend to work on their own, independent of the other functions.

In other companies/organisations personnel are encouraged to find out about other functions. This should help to promote harmony and understanding and encourage mutual co-operation between functions. After all, they are all supposed to be playing for the same team in an attempt to secure long-term survival and prosperity, and the fulfilment of corporate objectives! Individual business functions should not and cannot work in isolation, because they are interdependent on each other.

Who are the users of financial accounting information?

Many of the sets of accounts that are prepared do tend to be drawn up with the taxation aspects in mind. This one factor could dictate how certain figures are to be treated in the accounts. The users of financial accounting information need it for a variety of reasons, such as those which are described briefly below:

- ☐ *The shareholders* need it to see if they are getting a satisfactory return on their investment, and to assess the financial health of the company or business.
- ☐ *The directors and managers* need it for internal and external evaluations and comparisons of financial performance, e.g. in order to highlight their own strengths and weaknesses, or ensuring that they are getting an adequate return on capital employed and/or are able to pay their debts when they become due for payment.
- ☐ *The creditors* want to know if they are likely to get paid, and look particularly at liquidity and cash flow.
- ☐ *Prospective investors* need to assess whether they will get a satisfactory return on their investment, the level of risk attached to their investment, and what could happen if things go wrong.
- ☐ *Tax authorities* need it, e.g. for VAT, income and corporation tax purposes.
- ☐ *The Registrar of Companies* needs it to ensure that legal requirements are being complied with.
- ☐ *The employees* need it to assess their job security.
- ☐ *Society at large* needs it, as we are all would-be investors. They may also be interested in other aspects, e.g. environmental considerations, social responsibility and future plans.

The big picture

It is extremely difficult to define exactly where one area of accounting and finance starts and where it finishes. Figure 1.1 provides you with an overview of the big picture. The top half of the picture refers mainly to *financial accounting* and the bottom half of the picture refers to *cost and management accounting*. The number of qualified accountants and accounting personnel that will be employed will depend upon the size of the company or organisation concerned.

Accountancy is said to be the language of business and cash flow the life blood of business. To succeed, survive and prosper businesses have to make profits, make adequate returns on the capital invested, and generate sufficient cash flow to meet their needs. From a review of Figure 1.1 you can observe that the principal areas of accounting and finance are:

- ☐ financial accounting
- ☐ cost and management accounting
- ☐ financial management
- ☐ treasury management
- ☐ auditing
- ☐ taxation

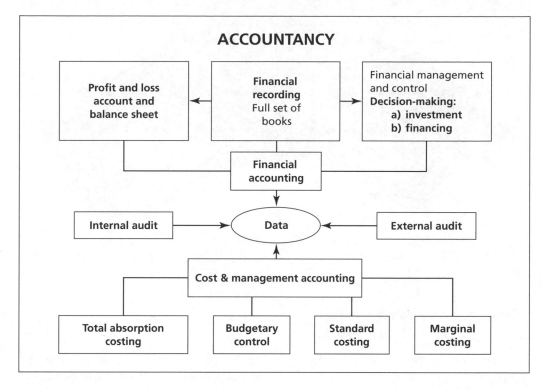

Figure 1.1 – The big picture

In this text we are particularly concerned with certain aspects of financial accounting, management accounting and financial management.

Financial accounting

Financial accounting is concerned with the capture, recording and classifying of data in order to present, report and communicate financial information. The financial information which is presented needs to be clear, relevant, reliable, accurate and consistent, and to meet the needs of the various users, as and when required. The three principal financial statements that are produced, e.g. in a company's annual report and accounts, are:

☐ the *profit and loss account* (which is also called the *income statement*);

☐ the *balance sheet* (which may be described as *a position statement*);

☐ The *cash flow statement* (also called a *funds flow statement*).

Between them, they help to answer frequently asked questions, such as:

☐ How much profit have we made?

☐ How much is the company worth?

☐ What has happened to our cash flow?

The generation of figures for the previous and earlier years enables internal and external comparisons of financial performance to be made and reported on. A variety of useful statistics may be produced using accounting ratios, graphs, charts and tabulations. The *source data* from which the financial statements are prepared include documents such as invoices, credit notes, receipts, copy sales invoices and bank statements.

The figures in the financial statements referred to above are arrived at via a recording system and the application of the accounting concepts and accounting policies. An account is simply a storage location for financial information, e.g. the motor vehicle expenses account; the sales account; the stationery, printing and telephone account; and many more. A separate account is kept for each item or group of items depending on and dictated by the degree of analysis which is required.

Cost and management accounting

Management accounting is very closely linked to cost accounting – so closely that it is difficult to say where each starts and finishes. **Cost accounting** simply aims at measuring the performance of departments, goods and services. **Management accounting**, however, is involved with planning and control; problem solving; motivation; and monitoring, for example:

☐ Providing management information

The management accountant may be described as an *information manager*. The information generated should be designed to meet the needs of the user and help them to control business operations and with their decision-making activities.

☐ Advising management

For example, on matters involving alternative courses of action, different strategies, and what to do in such scenarios as changes in the rate of inflation or interest rates.

☐ Forecasting, planning and control

A vast amount of management accounting is concerned with the future and the *predetermination* of costs and revenues, for example, budgetary control and standard costing. The management accountant should also be actively involved in the *strategic planning process*, including the setting of objectives, the formulation of policy and the development of *planning and control systems*.

☐ Communications

To be effective it needs to be supported by a sound, reliable and efficient communication system. Such a system should produce good, clear and timely communications in a form appropriate to the needs of the user and which will not overload the user.

☐ Flexibility

There is a need for the management accounting section to be involved with frequent monitoring *internally*, e.g. control systems, so that modifications can be made to improve response times, and *externally*, e.g. to help identify threats and opportunities.

☐ Links with other functional areas

There are very strong links with other functional areas, e.g. meeting together as part of the budget preparation process. This promotes a greater understanding between them, problem sharing, improved co-operation and better co-ordination. Their role may also include educating managers from other functional areas about the techniques and benefits of management accounting.

☐ 'Gate-keeping'

The management accounting function tends to sit at a very important information junction. It receives and disseminates information from the external environment, and information which is produced internally, on its way up to higher levels of management or on its way down to lower levels of management and subordinates. This may be described as 'gate-keeping' as it can control the flow of certain types of information in and out of the company and up and down within the company, as indicated in Figure 1.2.

Costs for decision making

You need to remember that although management accounting does provide a lot of very useful information for management it is not an exact science. Just like financial accounting it depends to a great extent on the judgement of the accounting personnel concerned. It also depends on assumptions about the future business environment, e.g. economic factors,

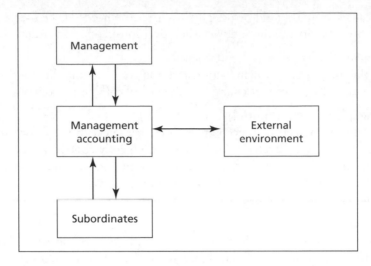

Figure 1.2 – Management accounting: the gate-keeper

political factors, technological factors and social factors. The costs and revenues that need to be used are the relevant costs/revenues, i.e. those costs/revenues that only happen if the project or investment goes ahead.

Financial management

Financial management aims to ensure that companies or organisations survive and prosper in the long term and realise their strategic objectives. It is particularly concerned with the planning, acquiring and efficient use of funds, and the investment of those funds in order to maximise shareholder wealth. If investors are to be attracted to part with their money, they need to be compensated with returns that reward them for the risk they have undertaken. A summary of the key components of financial management is illustrated in Figure 1.3.

We will now take a look at some of the areas that may be classed as financial management.

Sources of finance and financial markets

This is concerned with *external sources* of finance such as ordinary shares, long-term loans and debentures, and *internal sources* such as retained earnings (i.e. 'ploughed-back profits'), and the cost of the various sources, i.e. the cost of capital. It is also concerned with alternative ways of financing assets such as renting, leasing, hiring and employing subcontractors.

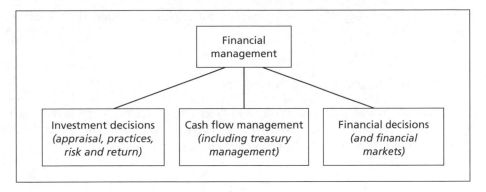

Figure 1.3 – A brief overview of financial management

Capital structure and gearing

Gearing (leverage) is all about the balance of financing from *debt* (i.e. long-term loans and debentures), and the *equity* (i.e. ordinary share capital plus the reserves).

Dividend policy

Dividend policy is frequently described as the 'dividend puzzle'. Why do companies pay a dividend and then borrow money to finance expansion? The short answer to this question is: because of market expectations. Dividend policies have to be formulated and dividend payments budgeted for.

Valuation of assets, shares and companies

Methods of valuation have been developed to value shares in unquoted companies.

Working capital management

This involves the management of: inventory (e.g. stocks of raw materials); credit control (the collection of amounts owing from customers for goods and/or services); cash (including treasury management which concerns itself with the investment of surplus cash short-term, e.g. overnights or for a week or a month); short-term investments; and creditors (suppliers of goods and services on credit).

Capital investment appraisal (project appraisal)

This involves the application of the concept of *relevant cash flows* and a knowledge of investment appraisal methods, e.g. payback, the net present value method, the internal rate of return method. Other considerations include the time value of money, the tax factor and accounting for risk.

Take-overs and management buy-outs

Take-over strategy includes both attacking and defensive strategies. Mergers make sense if *synergy* is present, i.e. one plus one equals three! The new combined enterprise should be more profitable and efficient than the individual companies concerned.

Foreign exchange management

The aim here is to reduce risk, e.g. making use of hedging and/or currency swaps.

Other areas

Other areas of activity include transfer pricing, portfolio theory and strategic investments.

It is impossible in a foundation text such as this to cover all of the areas mentioned. However, in later chapters we will go into greater depth on sources of finance, working capital management, capital structure and gearing, and capital investment appraisal.

Audit

The role of the auditor

The role of the auditor has been described as being that of a watchdog, rather than a blood-hound. The objectives of an audit are: to prevent and detect errors and fraud; and to verify and report upon financial statements and reports, e.g. the statutory audits of companies by external auditors. Organisations, e.g. large multinational companies and metropolitan councils, may also have their own internal auditors. A brief introduction to the role of the auditor is provided in Chapter 9.

Value for money (vfm) audits

This tends to be used quite extensively for public-sector services such as health and education. However, its use can be applied to private-sector organisations. In its assessment of whether or not a service is providing value for money, it looks at the three Es of vfm – *economy, efficiency and effectiveness* – as follows:

☐ *Economy* – cutting costs and reducing waste

☐ *Efficiency* – the efficient use of scarce resources

☐ *Effectiveness* – reaching targets and achieving objectives

Measures ('benchmarks') used for making comparisons between services could be the cost per patient treated, per student, per household.

Taxation

Taxation cannot and should not be ignored. Throughout the world, it can have a dramatic impact on the prices paid for materials, goods and services. It can affect:

☐ *Profits*, i.e. the net profit after tax figure.

☐ *Cash flow*. There is or may be a time lag between earning the profits, paying dividends, paying wages and salaries, and paying the tax.

☐ *Investment*. Governments may give tax relief and/or incentives to encourage investment. In the UK, they do give capital allowances in the place of the depreciation that is charged in the accounts.

☐ *Dividends* are paid net of tax. In private limited companies and family companies decisions have to be taken about whether it is better to pay dividends to the directors or give them higher salaries.

☐ *Finance*. Where interest on loans and bank overdrafts etc. is allowed as a deduction in computing the tax payable, the real cost of the finance is the after-tax cost.

☐ *Tax losses*. One of the reasons for taking over another company could be to acquire and make use of its tax losses.

In addition there are international tax matters and double-taxation provisions that may need to be investigated.

Summary: an introduction to the accounting scene

Beware of accountants

Accounting is not an exact science and depends to a great extent on the way in which individuals/groups of people apply the concepts and accounting policies, e.g. the depreciation policy.

Appreciation of business functions

It is important that personnel understand the role, purpose, problems and needs associated with business functions other than their own, e.g. marketing, finance, research and development, logistics, purchasing.

The users of accounting information

There are many parties interested in the published reports and accounts of companies, e.g. *stakeholders* such as directors, shareholders, bankers, the tax authorities, creditors.

The big picture

Figure 1.1 provided you with an overview of the accounting scene, and included:

Financial accounting

This is concerned with financial recording and financial reporting for both internal and external purposes. It involves the preparation of the three key financial statements (*the final accounts*) from *historic data* which consist of the profit and loss account, the balance sheet and the cash flow statement.

Management accounting

This aims to provide management with information, advice and control systems, and will help them with their planning, decision making and control, e.g. forecasts. Much of the information that is produced has to be estimated, i.e. *predetermined*, e.g. budgets and standards. Management accounting therefore looks to the future, in contrast to financial accounting which looks back at past performance. The management accounting function does have an important communication role and occupies a position of power at a key information junction. This position is described as '*gate-keeping*' and is illustrated in Figure 1.2.

Financial management

Financial management concerns itself with investment decisions, financing decisions and cash flow management. It covers a very wide range of activities, e.g. sources of finance, working capital management, the cost of capital, dividend policy, and capital investment appraisal.

Auditing

Auditors can be external or internal and aim at detecting and preventing errors and fraud. Vfm (*value for money*) auditing is used to assess the three Es, *economy, efficiency and effectiveness*, e.g. for services such as health and education.

Taxation

The tax factor can play a significant part in decision making, e.g. financing decisions, dividend policy and investment decisions.

The role of information technology

The recording systems for both large and small organisations can be handled by computers with the information being stored on the hard drive and/or discs. In addition to tailor-made systems, numerous off-the-shelf software packages are available for recording financial and management accounting information, credit control, inventory control, payroll, etc.

Self-checks

When you have completed each individual self-check, compare your attempt with the appropriate part of this chapter.

1. Explain briefly why managers and executives need to 'beware of accountants'.
2. Why do individuals need to know more about business functions other than their own?
3. From which source data do the accounts and financial statements originate?
4. Why are shareholders and directors interested in the financial information?
5. Explain how each of the following relates to management accounting:
   □ the provision of information
   □ forecasting and planning
   □ communication
   □ 'gate-keeping'
   □ Relevant costs/revenues
6. Describe briefly the key features of:
   □ sources of finance
   □ working capital management
   □ capital structure
   □ capital investment appraisal
   □ value-for-money auditing

7. Explain how taxation can affect cash flow.

8. Explain how taxation may affect capital investment decisions, e.g. whether or not to buy some new high-tech equipment.

Self-assessments

When you have attempted each individual self-assessment, compare your attempt with the suggested solution in Appendix 1.

A1.1   Explain how the role of accounting and finance will differ between an SME (small or medium-sized enterprise) and a large multinational company.

A1.2   (a) How much profit will be made from the following buying and selling activities of product reference 007/XL5?

5 Jan.	bought	400 at £20 each
7 Jan.	sold	100 at £50 each
12 Jan.	sold	200 at £60 each
14 Jan.	bought	500 at £30 each
16 Jan.	sold	200 at £75 each

(b) What will be the value of the closing stock?

This question has been designed to get you to think about profit and valuation.

Tutor-based assignments

These assignments can be used for discussions, reports and presentations as directed by the lecturer or tutor, and will involve further research.

T1.1   (a) What is vfm? auditing?

(b) Explain how its adoption can be of benefit to both public-sector and private-sector organisations.

T1.2   **Mini case study**
The twins
Many moons ago there lived a very wealthy textile mill owner. He and his wife lived in an enormous house with large formal gardens, a lake, stables and parkland.

One day whilst driving home from the golf club in his Rolls-Royce, he was in deep thought about the future of his children. He had a twin son and daughter, Wolfgang and Henrietta, and a younger daughter, Tamsen. He did not want them to be dependent on him, but to make their way in the world using their own efforts, but with perhaps a little help from father. 'That's it!' he exclaimed, as he turned into the drive of his estate, 'that's what I will do, and then the rest is up to them'.

Several years had passed, and the time had come to put his master plan into operation. First, Tamsen, the youngest, was provided with a training contract by her father's accountants, so that she could train and eventually qualify as an accountant. He promised her that if she achieved this goal, and having obtained the required experience, he would put up the finance, either to buy into a partnership or to set up her own practice. Tamsen agreed, and commenced her professional career.

The twins returned from university, both having obtained an upper second-class honours degree on a B.Sc. Business and Management Studies course. Father was very pleased about this, because, to date, the choice had been theirs and theirs alone. The twins had assumed that they would just go on and work in their father's business empire. They had worked in various capacities in the summer vacations, and for a one-year placement, which was part of their degree course, at one of their father's local companies.

Their father invited them to a meeting to discuss their future one sunny evening in July. As they sipped their red wine and toasted the future, their father explained his master plan which he strongly believed would stand them in good stead, as he explained, 'to survive and prosper in the complex and diverse business environment in the long term'. His plan for them was simple: he would provide each of them with a loan of £500,000 on which they would pay him interest at 5% per annum. The twins were surprised but pleased, as the course on which they had studied had fired the enthusiasm within them to be entrepreneurs.

After spending the remainder of the month on holiday, and August and September searching for opportunities, the twins both emerged with detailed but quite different business plans, and started their businesses on 1 November 20X6.

Wolfgang

Wolfgang had always been interested in wine and growing things and also had relatives who were in the wine trade. He set up a company with an ordinary share capital of £500,000 with him as the sole shareholder. For his first twelve-month period, his transactions were:

Bought:	Vineyard	£240,000
	Tools and equipment	£60,000
	Stock of wine	£40,000
Paid out:	Labour	£100,000
	Cost of sales (other than stocks)	£120,000
	Overhead expenses	£80,000
Received	Sales	£340,000

The closing stock of wine at the end of the year was valued at £90,000.

Henrietta

Henrietta decided to set up a financial services company with an ordinary share capital of £500,000 with her as the sole shareholder. Her set-up costs and transactions for the year were as follows:

Bought:	Freehold property (buildings)	£350,000
	Fixtures, fittings and equipment	£48,000
	Motor vehicles	£20,000
Paid out:	Salaries	£72,000
	Overheads	£36,000
	Investments in shares	£82,000
Received:	Commission etc.	£150,000
	Sale of investments	£64,000

The cost of the investments which were sold during the year amounted to £42,000.

Required:

(a) Produce a statement to show the profit or loss for each of the companies, and a statement to show how much they were both worth at the end of the year.

(b) Comment on the results and the outlook for the future.

(c) If they wanted a further £250,000, other than asking father, where would you suggest to them that they look?

Further reading

Atrill, P. and McLaney, E., *Accounting and Finance for Non-specialists*, Financial Times Prentice Hall, 2001

Berry, A., *Financial Accounting: An Introduction*, International Thomson Business Press, 1999

Drury, C., *Costing: An Introduction*, Thomson Business Press, 1998

Hussey, J. and Hussey, R., *Business Accounting*, Macmillan Business, 1998

Knott, G., *Financial Management*, Macmillan Business, 1998

Useful websites

You may find these websites useful throughout your studies:
For all of Pearson's online resources: www.booksites.net
The FT website: www.ft.com
The Virtual School of Accounting and Finance: www.itbp.com

In addition, nowadays, quite a number of authors provide a companion website to accompany their text.

2

Concepts and creativity

In this chapter we review the concepts that are used to determine the figures that appear in the financial statements, how these figures can be affected by creative accounting, and consider financial accounting recording systems.

Learning objectives

Having worked through this chapter, you should be able to:

☐ appreciate how the application of the various concepts affects the profit and loss figures and the valuation of assets and liabilities;

☐ describe and discuss briefly the following concepts:
— money measurement
— realisation
— prudence
— materiality
— matching (accruals)
— cost
— going concern
— entity
— consistency
— disclosure
— objectivity (fairness)
— verifiability
— duality;

☐ understand what is meant by '*creative accounting*' and how it can be used to paint different financial pictures, e.g. in the financial statements;

☐ describe the '*cut-off procedure*' and how it can affect the financial statements;

☐ understand why the way in which the realisation concept is applied could lose an organisation money;

☐ discuss what is meant by '*writing off*' a transaction as an expense and '*capitalising*' it;

☐ appreciate how the financial accounting recording systems work.

The regulation of financial reporting

Accounting standards

Financial Reporting Standards (*FRSs*), and Statements of Standard Accounting Practice (*SSAPs*) are frequently referred to as the *accounting standards* and provide guidelines that cover a considerable variety of accounting issues: e.g. taxation; cash flow statements; accounting policies; government grants; extraordinary items; research and development expenditure; stocks and work-in-progress. Although they are not legally enforceable, company accounts do tend to comply with the standards because their auditors have a duty to state whether or not the accounts give a '*true and fair view*'. There are also International Accounting Standards (*IASs*), which have been designed to promote international harmonisation. The code that is followed in the USA is GAAP (i.e. Generally Accepted Accounting Principles).

The Companies Act 1985/89

The Companies Act incorporates certain EU directives and stipulates numerous legal requirements that must be followed regarding the published reports and accounts of companies.

Financial accounting concepts

The concepts provide the rules and guidelines that govern the way in which the figures that will appear in the financial statements are arrived at. You should note, however, that the application of many of the concepts involves judgement, e.g. as to what is significant. This means that different individuals using the same data could produce two entirely different sets of accounts because of the way in which they applied the concepts. Accounting is not an exact science.

The overriding consideration for companies in the UK is that the financial statements should give a 'true and fair view'. What is true and fair is a matter of judgement and opinion.

The money measurement concept

Only those items that can be measured in monetary terms will be included in the financial accounts. More qualitative factors such as morale, good industrial relations and management ability, cannot therefore be shown in the financial statements. Money is not always stable, e.g. in times of high inflation. It is possible to produce inflation-adjusted accounts, if required.

In recent times, certain items that in the past did not have a monetary value assigned to them now have one, e.g. professional footballers and brands.

The realisation concept

Sales

This concept helps us to answer the question: at what point should we include a sale of goods or services in the profit and loss account?

The answer to this question is: all cash and credit sales for the period should be included in the profit and loss account, irrespective of whether or not the cash has been received.

A good guide as to the date of the sale used in the UK, and its entry in the accounting records, is the VAT tax point. Some businesses sometimes account on a cash basis, e.g. dentists.

The realisation concept could involve profits being earned on the sale of certain goods and services on credit, and tax being paid on those profits, and then finding out in a future accounting period that they are bad debts. The company would have reduced its cash flow by paying tax on a profit that has not been realised! Relief for the bad debt will be given, but it will take some time to affect cash flow.

Purchases

The purchases, e.g. stocks of raw materials, fuels, etc., which should appear in the financial statements is the total cash and credit purchases for the period, irrespective of whether or not they have been paid for.

The prudence (conservatism) concept

One of the reasons why accountants have a thrifty image is the prudence concept, which tends to adhere to the following rules:

☐ Do not anticipate profit.

☐ Provide for all possible losses.

The effect of the above rules is that profits tend to be understated.

The following are some prime examples of the prudence concept in action:

☐ valuing stocks of raw materials, work-in-progress and finished goods at the lower of cost and net realisable value;

☐ taking no profit at all in the early stages of a long-term contract;

☐ making a provision for bad and doubtful debts;

☐ providing for contingent liabilities, i.e. something that may or may not happen.

The materiality concept

The accounting treatment of income and expenditure can be affected by whether or not the item in question is regarded as *significant*, and the answer to this will depend upon somebody's judgement. The decision will affect whether an item is *written off* and charged as an expense in computing the profit or loss for the period, or capitalised and *carried forward* in the balance sheet, e.g. as a stock, or as a prepayment, or as a fixed asset such as office equipment or fixtures and fittings.

In practice, items such as printing and stationery, cutlery, glassware, and cleaning materials tend to be treated as being of insignificant value, and the whole amount is charged in the profit and loss account. However, what is significant will depend upon the size and nature of the business.

The matching (or accruals) concept

This concept may also be described as 'periodicity', as it attempts to charge (or allocate receipts) to the accounting period in which the expense is consumed or the benefit received, i.e. they are matched to an accounting period.

We can, in fact, for the purpose of illustrating the application of this concept, classify costs as expired costs or unexpired costs (subject to the application of the materiality concept).

> ## Expired and unexpired costs
>
> **Expired costs** are those costs that have been used up, i.e. consumed during the current accounting period, e.g. rent paid for the current period.
>
> **Unexpired costs** are those costs that have not been used up and consumed in the current accounting period and that belong to a future accounting period, e.g. the closing stock of raw materials.

In cases where a cost *belongs* to the current accounting period but at the end of the period it is still *owing* and has not been paid, if it is significant it will be treated as an expense for the period, and the amount owing will be shown as an *accrual* in the balance sheet. For example, if at the year-end 30 June 20X6, an amount of £24,000 was owing for building work which had been carried out and completed, it would be *charged* as an expense in the profit and loss account and also shown as an accrual in the balance sheet (as a *current liability due within one year*).

Where expenses have been paid in the current period, any portion that belongs to the next accounting period, if significant, will not be charged as an expense in the profit and loss account for the current period, and should be carried forward to the next period as a *prepayment* in the balance sheet. For example, if during the year ended 30 September 20X8 a company had paid the rent of offices of £160,000 for the year to 31 December 20X8 the prepayment would be £40,000, i.e. for the period 1 October to 31 December 20X8. This amount would *not* be deducted in computing profits or losses of the current period, and would be *carried forward* in the balance sheet as a *current asset*.

> ## Illustration of rent paid in advance
>
> Details. Prepaid rent brought forward from 30 Sept. 20X8 (as above) £40,000.
> During the year to 30 Sept. 20X9 rent of £200,000 was paid out for the year to 31 Dec. 20X9.
>
> The effect on the year ended 30 September 20X9 would be:
>
> Profit and Loss Account   a charge of £40,000 plus £150,000 = £190,000
>
> Balance Sheet   a prepayment shown in the current assets of   £50,000
>
> The prepayment was one quarter of £200,000 for the period 1 Oct. to 31 Dec. 20X9.

Depreciation

The aim of depreciation is to *spread the cost of a fixed asset*, e.g. machinery, equipment, fixtures and fittings, motor vehicles, over its useful life. This is yet another good example of matching. Each year, the organisation in effect uses up a portion of the fixed asset. The depreciation is the expired cost; the book value, i.e. the cost of the fixed asset less the cumulative depreciation, is the unexpired cost. We will look in greater depth at depreciation of fixed assets in Chapter 3.

The cost concept

The amounts shown in the accounts tend to be shown at *historic cost*, or *historic cost less depreciation*, as appropriate. However, accounting standards permit other values to be used, and provide guidance for the revaluation of fixed assets such as land and buildings, machinery and equipment, etc., or the valuation of stocks and work-in-progress etc.

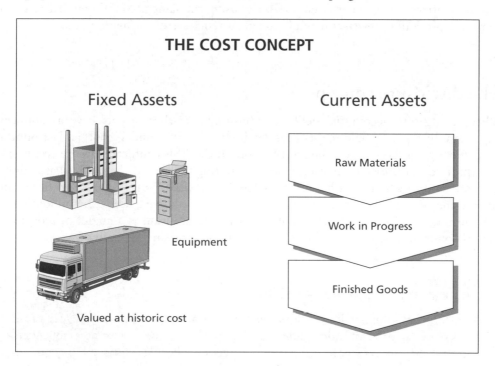

The going concern concept

Accounts have to be prepared on the assumption that the organisation is going to continue, rather than on a winding-up basis, where the assets would be valued at their 'break-up values'.

The entity concept

The company is a separate entity and, therefore, personal transactions of the owners should be kept separate from business transactions, e.g. the personal transactions of partners or directors. The overall aim is to produce financial statements for the organisation. If personal transactions do go through the business books of account, they have to be accounted for. Many companies keep a private ledger for recording the personal transactions of directors, e.g. loans to and from directors.

The consistency concept

To ensure that the financial statements are comparable from year to year, the figures should have been arrived at on a consistent basis, e.g. using the same accounting policies year on year for depreciation, the treatment of foreign currencies, stock valuations, etc.

The disclosure concept

Where changes to accounting policies, or post-balance-sheet events have a significant impact on the reported figures, they must be disclosed in the annual report and accounts of the company concerned. You should have noticed that this conflicts with the consistency concept, in that companies may alter their accounting policies. If the change has a significant impact on the figures it has to be disclosed, e.g. 'If last year's figures had been computed using the new depreciation policy, the profits would have been £2.3million higher' (FT illustration in box). You will recall that what is significant is a matter of judgement, and no doubt the company's auditors will have an opinion on this matter.

Change in accounting policy hits ITNet figures

ITNet, the computer services business, announced a sharp fall in its full-year profits after changing its accounting policy to recognise the risks of some public-sector contracts. The group recently lost a £70m contact to collect revenues and pay benefits to the London Borough of Hackney. Their pre-tax profits before goodwill were £0.4m compared with a figure of £10.2m for the previous year!

Edited extract from: J. Guthrie, Financial Times, *20 February 2001*

The objectivity or fairness concept

Those individuals who prepare the financial statements must eliminate personal bias in order to ensure that the accounts give a true and fair view of the profit or loss and the financial affairs as portrayed in the balance sheet.

The verifiability concept

The financial statements should be capable of independent verification. Hence the need for auditors.

The duality concept

The duality concept refers to the double entry bookkeeping system which is used to record and accumulate the financial information that is used to prepare the financial statements. The golden rule of double entry is: *every debit should have a credit and every credit should have a debit* (see the recording system, when we review it later in this chapter). It is quite mechanical and can nowadays be easily handled by computer systems and software packages. Every business transaction has a dual effect. For example, if we buy a motor vehicle for £15,000 and pay by cheque, the motor vehicles account goes up by £15,000 and the bank account goes down by £15,000, or if we sell a service to a customer on credit for £62,000 the sales account will go up by that amount and the account for the credit customer will also go up by £62,000.

Before we move on to look at creative accounting, it is perhaps useful to have a quick recap via a selection of self-checks. On completion of each, compare your answer with the appropriate section of this chapter.

Self-checks

1. Why do accountants have such a conservative image?

2. Explain and illustrate how each of the concepts listed below can affect the profit and loss figure:

   (a) the realisation concept
   (b) materiality
   (c) matching of accruals and prepayments
   (d) consistency.

3. Why can the application of the realisation concept lead to paying tax on a debt which later becomes a bad debt?

4. List factors on which the success of a business may depend which are not shown in a balance sheet.

5. Explain why the accounting treatment of closing stocks of materials etc. is a good way of explaining and illustrating the application of the matching concept.

Creative accounting

The fact that accounting is not an exact science provides numerous opportunities for creativity. An accounting joke:

> Prospective client (to the accountant): 'Will you prepare my accounts for me?'
> Accountant: 'Certainly, would you like a high or low profit or loss?'

Working within the law, accountants can be very creative, because much of what they do relies to a great extent on their own personal judgement.

So just how can creative accounting take place?

There now follows a series of scenarios which should provide you with an insight into this quite artistic area. Accountants can, using the same figures, paint significantly differing pictures.

The application of the concepts

Applying the materiality concept, if it is decided that an item of capital expenditure is of an insignificant value it will be simply written off as an expense in computing the profit or loss for the period under review, e.g. glassware and cutlery in a hotel (the fact that glasses do get broken and cutlery tends to disappear could be another reason for writing their cost off immediately in the profit and loss account). The decision to *write off*, i.e. charge as an expense in the profit and loss account, or *capitalise*, i.e. treat as an asset and carry it forward into the future in the balance sheet, is not always clear-cut. For example, the legal costs and first year's interest relating to a new building could be added to the cost of the building!

The operation of the 'cut-off procedure'

The *'cut-off procedure'* comes into operation towards the end of an accounting period. It involves setting a date called the *'cut-off date'*. Purchases and sales after this date will not be included in the computation of the current accounting period's profit or loss. Thus, purchases after the cut-off should not be included in purchases, creditors and the closing stock figure. Sales after the cut-off should not be included in sales or debtors, but should still be included in the closing stock figure.

The half a million pound stock deficit

Many years ago BHS (British Home Stores) had a half a million pound stock deficit. One of the principal reasons for this deficit was errors in the 'cut-off procedure' e.g. purchases made after the cut-off date being excluded from purchases, and then included in the closing stock figure.

The operation of the 'cut-off procedure' with or without errors can have a significant impact upon reported profits or losses.

Credit control and inventory control

A vast number of organisations engage in '*window-dressing*' their debtors (amounts owing from customers) and stocks (inventories). This occurs because, in the period leading up to the year-end they may have a special purge in collecting the outstanding debts owing to them. During the same period, they may focus on reducing their stock levels. This means that the debtors and/or stock levels are lower at the year-end than they are throughout the remainder of the year. This will help improve the ratios used for evaluating financial performance associated with credit control and inventory, e.g. debtor days, stock days and the rate of stock turnover. Decisions about writing off obsolete stock or writing down the value of stocks can also affect the picture.

Provisions

The level at which provisions, e.g. the provision for bad debts and the provision for depreciation, are set affect both the reported profits and the value of the assets in the balance sheet. Even though the accounts have to give a true and fair view, the *depreciation policy* for certain fixed assets may not be realistic. For example, equipment that has a useful life of ten years may be written off over five years. This may have come about due to the influence of the *prudence concept*.

The revaluation of assets

If fixed assets such as freehold land and buildings, machinery and equipment are revalued upwards, this does not bring in any extra cash. However, the reserves, e.g. revaluation reserve, will increase, and this in turn increases the capital employed. This could well bring about a reduction in the return on capital employed. The profit after revaluation, even after a slight increase in depreciation, could be quite similar, but it would be expressed as a percentage of a much higher capital employed figure. This is one of the reasons why directors are not always keen on revaluing their company's fixed assets. You should also note that fixed assets could be revalued downwards.

'Off-balance-sheet financing'

In cases where an organisation rents or leases fixed assets (*other than leasehold land and buildings*), the fixed assets concerned do not appear on the balance sheet and, therefore, are not included in the capital employed figure. This means that companies and organisations that have a significant amount of 'off-balance-sheet financing' tend to have lower capital employed figures when compared with companies that have little or no 'off-balance-sheet financing'. Movements in the capital employed figure will affect the *return on capital employed (ROCE)* – this may also be described as the return on investment (ROI). The profits with or without 'off-balance-sheet financing' may be quite similar. With, we charge the rental or hire charge etc. Without, if we buy the fixed asset outright, we charge depreciation. Similar profits expressed as a percentage of a lower capital employed figure would give a higher ROCE.

Extraordinary items

One-off profits or expense items can obscure the true picture, e.g. profits or losses on foreign exchange transactions.

The financial accounting recording system

How the double entry system works

The information from the source data, e.g. *invoices, credit notes, banking records*, from which the profit and loss account and balance sheet are prepared is stored and accumulated in numerous individual accounts: for example, sales account, motor vehicle expenses account, equipment account, salaries account, loan interest account. Although some businesses may still use hand-written systems, vast amounts of this mechanical process is nowadays handled by computer. Irrespective of the method of recording, e.g. various software packages, the output is still arrived at using the *duality concept* and double entry bookkeeping explained earlier. A quick recap may be helpful to illustrate that its operation is quite logical and easy to understand.

☐ Cheque received from the renting out of buildings will be recorded as an increase to the bank account and an increase to the rent received account.

☐ Cash paid into the bank account would increase the bank account and reduce the cash account.

☐ Work performed on credit for a client company will increase the sales/fees received account and increase the amount owing in the personal account of the client concerned.

As you can observe, the double entry bookkeeping system is really a plus and minus system, and an account is simply a storage location for information needed to produce the financial statements and details of debtors and creditors, etc.

The books of account

Non-financial managers do not get involved with bookkeeping. However, they do like to have an appreciation of how the double entry system works and an insight into how the financial statements are arrived at. A typical system will use all or most of the following books of account.

Books of first entry

These are the books in which the business transaction first appears in the accounting recording system. The second part of the dual entry will be completed within seconds, days or weeks depending on software used etc. *Books of first entry* include:

- [ ] A **cash book** records details of the cash and bank accounts usually in an analysed format, e.g. using spreadsheets with columns for various items of income and expenditure and discounts allowed and received.
- [ ] **Day books or journals** provide a record of credit transactions and may also be kept in analysed spreadsheet form, for example, the sales day book for credit sales to customers, and the purchases day book for goods and services received on credit from suppliers. Each will provide a list of all the transactions for the period, e.g. day, week or month. The individual personal accounts of customers or suppliers will be written up from the listing, and the total(s) of the analysis posted to the relevant account, e.g. purchases of raw materials account, stationery and printing account, motor vehicle expenses account.

The ledgers

These include:

- [ ] the **nominal ledger** for the accounts that are used to store the profit and loss account and balance sheet information, e.g. ordinary share capital account, freehold land and buildings account, sales account, and various other accounts;
- [ ] a **sales ledger** for amounts owing from debtors, and **a purchases or bought ledger** for amounts owing to creditors;
- [ ] a **private ledger** for private matters relating to directors.

The preparation of the profit and loss account and balance sheet

At the end of an accounting period, e.g. 6 months or 12 months, **the final accounts**, i.e. the profit and loss account and balance sheet, will be prepared along the lines illustrated in Figure 2.1.

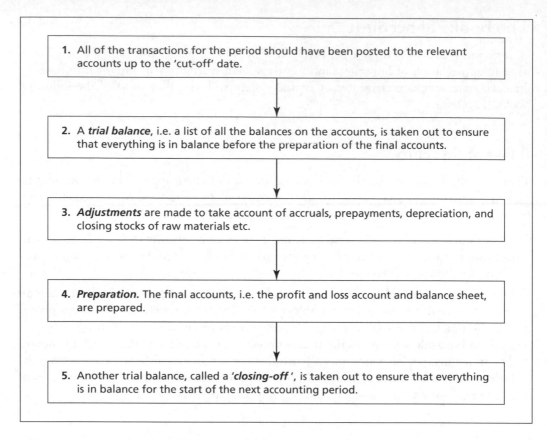

1. All of the transactions for the period should have been posted to the relevant accounts up to the 'cut-off' date.

2. A *trial balance*, i.e. a list of all the balances on the accounts, is taken out to ensure that everything is in balance before the preparation of the final accounts.

3. *Adjustments* are made to take account of accruals, prepayments, depreciation, and closing stocks of raw materials etc.

4. *Preparation.* The final accounts, i.e. the profit and loss account and balance sheet, are prepared.

5. Another trial balance, called a '*closing-off* ', is taken out to ensure that everything is in balance for the start of the next accounting period.

Figure 2.1 – The way in which the financial accounts are prepared

Summary: concepts and creativity

The concepts, accounting standards and company law govern the way in which the figures that appear in the published report and accounts are arrived at. The overriding consideration for external reporting purposes is '*true and fair view*'. For internal reporting purposes the accounts produced can be much more detailed and presented in whichever format is considered to be the most appropriate.

The concepts

From a managerial viewpoint the principal financial accounting concepts are:

☐ *Money measurement* – Only items that have monetary values are shown. Therefore, the calibre of the management, good industrial relations, etc. cannot be shown in the accounts.

☐ *Realisation* – Provides the rule for when sales are to be included in the computation of the profit or loss for the period.

☐ *Prudence (conservatism)* – Provides for all losses. Does not anticipate profit.

☐ *Materiality* – What is significant? Should we write it off as an expense in the profit and loss account for the period, or capitalise it and carry it forward to the next accounting period in the balance sheet?

☐ *Matching* – Aims to match the revenue for an accounting period with the expenditure that was incurred in earning that revenue.

☐ *Cost* – The amount we paid out for a fixed asset is a fact. In most instances fixed assets are valued at cost or cost less depreciation.

☐ *Going concern* – The business is valued on the basis that it is going to continue, and not on a winding-up basis.

☐ *Entity* – The business is a separate legal entity.

☐ *Consistency* – Accounting policies should be employed on a consistent basis, e.g. the valuation of stocks and work-in-progress, depreciation, etc.

☐ *Disclosure* – Events that have a significant impact on the reported figures should be disclosed, e.g. post-balance-sheet events, changes in accounting policies, etc. On the one hand the previous concept says be consistent, and on the other hand disclosure says, if you are not consistent, and it has a significant impact, disclose it!

☐ *Objectivity/fairness* – Avoid personal bias when preparing financial statements.

☐ *Verifiability* – Capability of being audited.

☐ *Duality* – Double entry bookkeeping and the dual effect of every business transaction.

Creative accounting

Accounting is not an exact science. The exercise of judgement may be tinged by a little personal bias which can bring about '*window-dressing*' and '*creative accounting*'. Financial statements prepared from the same original data could portray a number of different pictures. This can come about because of the following:

☐ the way in which the concepts and accounting policies are applied, e.g. depreciation and materiality, as illustrated in Figure 2.2;

☐ the operation of the 'cut-off procedure';

☐ the level at which provisions are set, e.g. depreciation, bad and doubtful debts;

☐ 'window-dressing', e.g. via running down stocks (inventories) and/or having a special effort to collect outstanding debts in the run up to the year-end;

Transaction adjudged to be:	Profit and loss account (income measurement)	Balance sheet (asset valuation)
Significant	Exclude, or write off a portion each year	Carried forward into the future, e.g. in fixed assets
Insignificant	Write off, i.e. charge it all as an expense	Exclude; it has all been written off

Figure 2.2 – The effect of the materiality concept on profits, losses and asset valuation

☐ the revaluation of fixed assets, and stocks of raw materials, fuels and work-in-progress, etc;

☐ extraordinary items, e.g. one-off profits or losses.

The financial accounting recording system

The double entry bookkeeping systems can be hand-written or kept on a computer. They store and accumulate a record of all the business transactions to provide the analysis needed for the preparation of the profit and loss account and balance sheet. This also includes keeping the personal accounts of debtors and creditors, i.e. amounts owing to and by the company or organisation concerned. Figure 2.3 provides you with a concise overview of how the recording system is used to prepare the final accounts.

Self-checks

Here are some more self-checks for you to attempt. When you have attempted each one, compare your answer with the appropriate part of the chapter.

1. What is the purpose of charging depreciation as an expense in the profit and loss account?

2. Explain how a significant change in an accounting policy should be dealt with in a company's annual report and accounts.

3. Describe and explain what is meant by 'window-dressing' in relation to stocks (inventories) and debtors.

4. Why are directors not always very willing to revalue their company's fixed assets?

5. Which accounts are kept in the sales ledger?

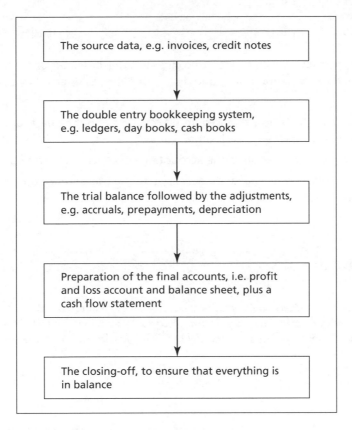

Figure 2.3 – The preparation of the final accounts

Self-assessments

When you have completed each of the self-assessments, compare your answer with the one suggested in Appendix 1.

A2.1   Describe and illustrate why it is difficult to compare the financial performance of a company that has a lot of 'off-balance-sheet financing' with that of a company that has little or no 'off-balance-sheet financing'.

A2.2   Explain briefly which original source data is used to write up the accounts, and why it is necessary to take out a trial balance before preparing the final accounts.

A2.3   Describe and illustrate how the 'cut-off procedure' can reduce or increase profits.

Tutor-based assignments

Further research or study may be needed to complete tutor-based assignments. These may be used for presentations, group discussions, etc., as directed by a lecturer or tutor.

T2.1 Explain and illustrate how the accounting concepts and the quest for a 'true and fair view' may conflict with each other.

T2.2 Discuss how the application of the accounting concepts can be very creative.

T2.3 What is creative accounting, and how can it be used to produce differing results from the same source data?

Further reading

Benedict, A. and Elliott, B., *Practical Accounting*, Financial Times Prentice Hall, 2001

Dyson, J. R., *Accounting for Non-accounting Students*, Financial Times Prentice Hall, 2001

Gillespie. I., Lewis, R. and Hamilton, K., *Principles of Financial Accounting*, Financial Times Prentice Hall, 2000

Pizzey, A., *Accounting and Finance*, Continuum International Publishing, 2001

Useful websites

Support for the users of the books by Benedict and Elliott, and Dyson:
www.booksites.net/benedict
www.booksites.net/dyson

3

The depreciation of fixed assets

The aim of this chapter is to illustrate how depreciation of fixed assets is calculated and how it is shown in the final accounts, i.e. the profit and loss account and the balance sheet.

Learning objectives

When you have worked through this chapter, you should be able to:

☐ understand the reasons why depreciation has to be accounted for;

☐ calculate the depreciation of fixed assets using:
  — the straight line method;
  — the reducing balance method;
  — the revaluation method;

☐ appreciate how depreciation is shown in the profit and loss account and the balance sheet;

☐ follow the way in which disposals of fixed assets are dealt with.

Why charge depreciation?

The aim of depreciation is to spread the cost of the fixed asset over its useful life. To charge the full cost of a fixed asset as an expense in the profit and loss account of the year in which it was purchased would simply not give a true and fair view of the profit or loss. It could in fact be described as a deferred expense; for instance, although the fixed asset is bought in one accounting period it is in effect consumed over a number of accounting periods.

The straight line method of depreciation

To calculate depreciation using the straight line method we need to know:

☐ the cost of the fixed asset;

☐ the life of the fixed asset;

☐ the residual value (if any) of the fixed asset at the end of its life.

Example   The straight line method of depreciation

A machine costs £60,000, and has a life of four years and a residual value of £10,000 at the end of its life. The depreciation to be charged in the profit and loss account will be:

$$\frac{\text{Cost less residual value}}{\text{Life}} = \frac{£60,000 - 10,000}{4} = £12,500 \text{ per annum}$$

However, it is very difficult to estimate what the residual value is going to be in several years' time. The method may therefore ignore the residual value which means that the calculation will be as illustrated below.

Example   The straight line method of depreciation

The cost of some equipment will amount to £160,000, and its life is five years. The depreciation which would be charged to the profit and loss account would be:

$$\frac{\text{Cost}}{\text{Life}} = \frac{£160,000}{5} = £32,000 \text{ per annum}$$

This could also have been expressed in percentage terms, in this particular case at 20% on cost per year, i.e. 20% × £160,000 = £32,000 per annum.

The reducing balance method of depreciation

This method charges a percentage of cost in the first year and then a percentage of the book value (written-down value or WDV) from the second year onwards. Thus, as the asset gets older the depreciation charge gets smaller.

Example   The reducing balance method of depreciation

A car costing £12,000 is to be written off at 25% reducing balance per year. The depreciation figures for the first three years would be:

	Cost or WDV £000	Depreciation at 25% £000	WDV (i.e. book value) £000
Car			
Year 1	12	3	9
Year 2	9	2.25	6.75
Year 3	6.75	1.6875	5.0625

and so on, rounding the numbers as you think fit.

The revaluation method of depreciation

For certain fixed assets, such as contractor's plant and equipment, tools, cutlery and crockery, the revaluation method may be considered more appropriate. The reason for this is the uncertain condition of the asset at the end of the accounting period.

Example   The revaluation method of depreciation

The depreciation under the revaluation method is simply the difference between the opening value of the asset at the start of the accounting period and the closing value of the asset at the end of the accounting period.

At the start of the year a hotel had a stock of crockery and cutlery of £9,400. At the end of the year it was valued at £6,000. The depreciation, therefore, will be £3,400.

Accounting for depreciation

Depreciation is the charge made in the profit and loss account for the use and wear and tear of fixed assets. It does not provide funds for the replacement of fixed assets. Funds can only be provided for the replacement of fixed assets if cash is put on one side for that purpose, for instance paid into a special account that is to be used to replace certain fixed assets. There are two systems for dealing with the depreciation charge, as follows:

☐ System 1
  In the year of purchase charge a full year's depreciation irrespective of the date on which the fixed asset was acquired, and in the year of sale no depreciation at all.

☐ System 2
  The time apportionment system charges depreciation on a time basis from the date it is purchased right up to the date on which the fixed asset is disposed of.

The accounting records for depreciation

The fixed asset account records the cost of the fixed asset, and the provision for depreciation account stores the cumulative depreciation figure, i.e. the depreciation to date. The difference between the two accounts is the book value, i.e. the written-down value, the figure that in a balance sheet may simply be called the *net book value* (see Figure 3.1).

The annual amount of depreciation will be charged as an expense in the profit and loss account and added to the cumulative depreciation to date brought forward from last year in the provision for depreciation account. This figure, i.e. last year's depreciation to date brought forward plus this year's profit and loss charge, is the figure that will be deducted from the cost of the fixed asset in the balance sheet, in order to arrive at the net book value.

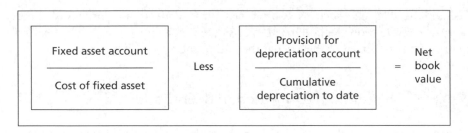

Figure 3.1 – Accounting for depreciation

The profit or loss on the sale of a fixed asset

The profit or loss on the sale of a fixed asset is the sale proceeds of the fixed asset minus its book value.

The reporting standard

The reporting standard in the UK, *FRS 15 Tangible Fixed Assets*, was issued in 1999, and sets out the principles of accounting for the initial measurement, valuation and depreciation of tangible fixed assets, with the exception of investment properties. Some of its provisions worthy of note are, as follows:

☐ Tangible fixed assets should be initially *valued at cost*, and include and capitalise only those costs that are directly attributable to bringing the asset into a condition where it is ready for its intended use.

☐ Where an entity adopts a *policy of capitalising finance costs*, only those applicable to the construction of tangible fixed assets, e.g. buildings, should be capitalised as being part of their cost. Entities do not have to capitalise finance costs, it is an option.

☐ The *revaluation of tangible fixed assets* should only be used if the company has adopted a policy of revaluation. However, such a policy need not apply to all classes of tangible fixed assets.

Summary: depreciation of fixed assets

Depreciation is treated as an expense in the profit and loss account in an attempt to spread the cost of the fixed asset over its useful life. The charge is there to cover the wear and tear of the fixed asset. You should note that charging depreciation does not provide for the replacement of fixed assets.

There are a number of different methods that can be used for charging depreciation in the profit and loss account. Three of the methods are the following:

☐ the straight line method

☐ the reducing balance method

☐ the revaluation method.

The depreciation can be charged to the profit and loss account using one of the following systems:

☐ System 1
Charge a full year's depreciation in the year of purchase and none in the year of sale.

☐ System 2
Time apportionment – depreciate the fixed asset from the date of purchase right up to the date of sale.

The reporting standard

FRS 15 in the UK provides accounting principles covering the initial measurement, e.g. finance costs; valuation such as revaluations, gains and losses on disposal; and disclosure requirements.

Self-checks

1. Explain how each of the following methods of depreciation calculates the depreciation charge for the period:

   ☐ the reducing balance method
   ☐ the straight line method
   ☐ the revaluation method

2. Why do companies charge depreciation?

3. Describe briefly how depreciation may be dealt with using a time apportionment system.

4. How does depreciation tend to get recorded in the accounting system?

5. What does the UK standard FRS 15 have to say about revaluations, and the capitalisation of interest?

Self-assessments

You will find the answers to these self-assessments in Appendix 1.

A3.1 Now see if you can compute the annual charge for depreciation for each of the fixed assets described below:
   1. Fixtures and fittings costing £86,000, life ten years, residual value £4,000.
   2. Office equipment costing £25,000, life eight years.
   3. Plant and machinery costing £120,000, to be depreciated at 20% of cost per annum.

A3.2 Work out the depreciation charge for each of the three years for a car costing £16,000 to be depreciated at 25% reducing balance per year.

A3.3 Details relating to some contractor's plant were as follows:

Plant	Start of year £000	End of year £000
Year 1 valuations	56	49
Year 2 valuations	49	33

You are required to calculate the depreciation for years 1 and 2 using the revaluation method.

Tutor-based assignments

T3.1 Explain how depreciation will affect the calculation of the profit or loss figure, and the value of fixed assets, but not the cash and bank balances.

T3.2 (a) Produce an illustration, in which you buy a motor vehicle, keep it for four years, and sell it in year 5, having depreciated it at 25% per year, using the reducing balance method of depreciation.

(b) Then, use the information produced, to explain why profits or losses arising from the sale of fixed assets can be described as over- or under-provisions for depreciation.

Further reading

Berry, A., *Financial Accounting: An Introduction*, International Thomson Business Press, 1999

Fardon, M. and Cox, D., *Accounting*, Osbourne, 2000

Pizzey, A., *Accounting and Finance*, Continuum, 2001

Wood, F. and Sangster, A., *Business Accounting 1*, Financial Times Prentice Hall, 1999

Useful websites

www.learn.co.uk/default.asp?WC1=Unit&WCU=3103
www.macmillan-business.co.uk
www.bh.com/management
www.booksites.net/wood

4

Sources of business finance

Where does the money come from?

Which type of finance would be most suitable?

Is there any low-cost finance that we ought to know about?

How can the EU help us?

This chapter is designed to give you a concise overview of the principal sources of external and internal finance that are available. The majority of sources apply to all sizes of business. Which source is the most appropriate depends upon the circumstances of each individual organisation.

Costs and risks

The financing of business organisations has been described as a *'system of costs and risks'*. If you are a high risk you pay more for your money via a higher rate of interest. If you are low-risk, you pay less for your money. If you have lots of fixed assets you can reduce your borrowing costs by pledging some or all of them as security, because it reduces the risk undertaken by the provider of the funds. Banks frequently make the comment to loan applicants, e.g. those who are in a start-up situation, 'Why should we risk our money, if you are not prepared to risk yours?' The bankers do expect and like to see commitment on the part of the loan applicant. Here, also, by looking through the *Financial Times* you will appreciate the importance of the various sources of finance and the numerous alternatives that are available.

Financial Times headlines

Investors set to scrutinise Xerox's core *(A focus on whether or not Xerox can improve the cash generation and profitability of its core businesses, A. Hill, 7 March 2001)*

ING set to pay £125m for Charterhouse *(M. Peel, 31 July 2000)*

Intershop in profit but low on funds *(Excellent results, but liquidity is becoming a problem, B. Benoit, 4 August 2000)*

Daewoo set to be declared bankrupt today *(In October their creditors had demanded a new restructuring and cost-cutting package, before advancing $400m in new loans. In early November they defaulted on $40m of debts, J. Burton, 8 November 2000. See also www.ft.com/daewoo)*

Learning objectives

When you have studied the whole of this chapter, together with the self-checks and self-assessments, you should be able to:

☐ appreciate the way in which funds flow within a business;

☐ acquire an insight into how the financial life-cycle theory can help influence and explain financing and take-over decisions;

☐ describe the principal sources of external financing;

☐ discuss the way in which internal financing can be generated;

☐ be aware of the alternative ways of financing assets;

☐ know and be able to illustrate the operation of the *keywords* associated with financing decisions;

☐ understand the importance of:
  ☐ the *cost of capital*
  ☐ *taxation*
  ☐ *dividend policy*

  on the financing decision;

☐ be aware of the simple rules associated with business financing.

The flow of business funds

Business finance can come from a multitude of sources, as illustrated in Figure 4.1. It can come from long-term sources, such as *ordinary shares, loans and debentures*, and short-

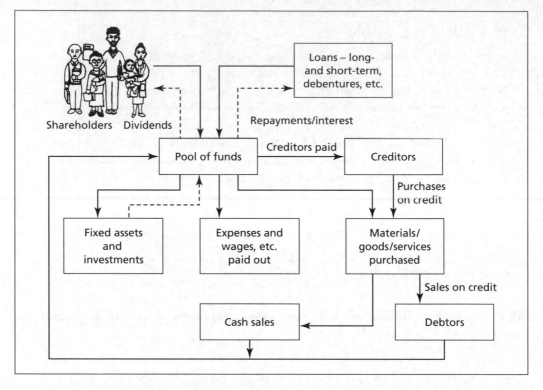

Figure 4.1 – The flow of business funds

term sources, such as *short-term loans, hire purchase, creditors*. It can also come from internal sources, the most important of which is retained earnings, i.e. the *ploughed-back profits*.

Figure 4.1 also shows the *working capital*. This is made up of the *current assets*, e.g. stocks, debtors, cash and bank balances, and the *current liabilities* payable within the next twelve months, e.g. creditors, expenses owing, dividends owing, tax owing. It provides the *circulating capital* which is used to pay the everyday operating expenses, and is particularly concerned with *cash flow*.

The financial life-cycle

Using an amended *Boston Matrix* (the Boston box), Figure 4.2 can help to provide a valuable insight into how and why companies do what they do in relation to financing and take-over decisions. The cash mentioned in the figure refers to the availability of cash in relation to the needs of the business, e.g. a problem-child-type organisation needs all the cash it can

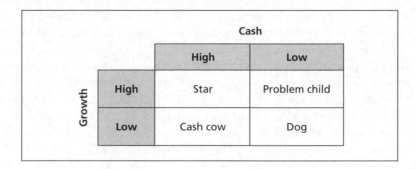

Figure 4.2 – The financial life-cycle and the amended Boston Matrix

get in order to sustain its growth. A dog-type company needs cash to stay alive! 'Growth' refers to growth in the sales of goods and/or services.

What we can learn from a review of the amended Boston Matrix

The position within the life-cycle can help explain the following:

☐ *Why a company finances its assets in a particular way.* For example, a problem child, in addition to funds from self, family and friends, may take out an overdraft or loan secured using their own personal assets, e.g. freehold property, and rely heavily on finance from creditors. A star, however, is rather like a magnet and attracts investors, e.g. ordinary share capital, long-term loans, debentures and convertible loan stock. In the system of costs and risks the star is quite likely to pay less for its finance, e.g. via the interest it has to pay to the providers. The dog, on the other hand, will rely on creditors, and if things go really bad, the creditors will kill it off! They will petition the court to have it wound up.

☐ *The impact upon a company's dividend policy.* The problem child will have a low-dividend pay-out and a high plough-back. It needs the cash. The cash cow will tend to have a high pay-out and a low plough-back. It does not need the cash. The star will be able to formulate the dividend policy it wants, e.g. taking into account stability and growth. The dog is short of cash.

☐ *The way in which a company manages its working capital.* Problem children and dogs may have very good credit control because they are desperate for the cash. However, this could be at the expense of granting over-generous cash discounts for prompt payment. A small percentage cash discount can be a very high *APR* (annual percentage rate of interest)! The star can employ more specialists to manage the working capital for credit control, stock control, treasury management etc., e.g. using *JIT* (just-in-time) and *MRP* (material requirements planning) for dealing with stocks.

☐ *The impact on a company's take-over strategy.* The cash cow needs growth, and could be intending to acquire a problem child. Sometimes, a cash cow invites a problem child to take it over. This is known as a 'reverse take-over'. One possible reason for this could be that the directors of the cash cow are nearing retirement and see it as a way of ensuring future success and survival in the long term. The star can formulate and follow its own take-over strategy, no doubt carefully thought-out and closely associated with its corporate objectives. A famous UK entrepreneur, Sir John Templeton, tended to take over dog-type companies that had low PEs (price/earnings ratios), i.e. those that the market did not expect much of. He then, together with his management team, turned the dog-type companies around over a number of years, and sold them on. In time, as soon as he took over a dog, the market's reaction was an increase in the dog's share price because of improved market expectations.

Financial instruments

A financial instrument is a legal document representing a claim on the company, e.g. ordinary shares, preference shares, debentures. The various rights of the securities in the UK are set out in the company's *Articles of Association*.

Short-term, medium-term or long-term financing?

What is regarded as short-, medium- or long-term finance depends on the size and nature of the business. The figures that follow should provide you with a useful guide:

Current liabilities	Due to be paid within one year
Short-term	1–5 years
Medium-term	5–10 years
Long-term	Over 10 years
Permanent	Usually not repayable, e.g. ordinary shares and convertible debentures

Where companies are engaged in numerous projects it is not always easy or possible to identify the specific source from which the finance has come. In cases where new finance has to be acquired in order that a specific project may go ahead, it may be possible to match the term of the finance to the life of the project, e.g. project loans linked to a project's expected cash flows.

External sources of finance

The principal sources

There are so many sources, and variations of sources, in the market place that it is impossible to cover them all within this text. We will now provide you with a concise review of the principal sources of external finance.

Ordinary share capital

The ordinary shareholders are often described as the '*equity shareholders*'. They usually have one share and one vote. Owning over 50% of the shares will give them a controlling interest, and this is particularly important in small, medium and family-owned companies, e.g. if they issue more shares they could lose control. The shareholders' rewards in this system of costs and risks are twofold. They receive *dividends* and also *capital gains* (*or losses*) on their investment. They do bear the greatest risk, as they are the ones at the back of the queue if *winding-up* or *liquidation* takes place. They get paid out last. If there is nothing left, they get nothing! In certain circumstances, companies are allowed to buy back their ordinary shares. There can, however, be 'A' ordinary shares which do not have voting rights.

Factors that may be taken into account when deciding whether to issue more ordinary shares are:

☐ the issue costs;

☐ control, e.g. in family companies;

☐ market acceptance, e.g. whether the issue can be underwritten, whether it will be successful, or there is negative investor sentiment towards the sector;

☐ the current level of gearing, e.g. the percentage of debt (long-term loans and debentures) to equity (the ordinary share capital plus reserves);

☐ the service costs, i.e. the dividend pay-out and tax implications.

Preference shares

Preference shares tend to be fixed-interest-bearing securities, i.e. the dividend on them is at a fixed rate. There are various other classes of preference share; they can for example be *participating, cumulative or non-cumulative, and/or redeemable preference shares*. The directors may, if they wish, decide not to pay the preference dividend. As a general rule preference shareholders do not usually have any voting right unless their dividend is in arrears. On liquidation, they rank just ahead of the ordinary shareholders. If these shares are issued when interest rates are very low, and interest rates go up significantly, they will have very low service costs, e.g. when compared with new borrowing; and, conversely, high interest rates imply high service costs.

Long-term debt (debt)

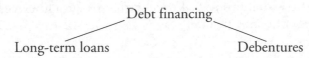

Debt financing

Long-term loans   Debentures

Long-term loans may be *secured* or *unsecured*, and at *fixed* or *variable interest* rates. When problems arise it may be possible to renegotiate or reschedule the repayments of capital and interest, e.g. if the company, organisation or country experiences cash flow problems. Where current interest rates are well below the rate being charged on a fixed interest loan it may be possible to refinance, i.e. pay off the old loan with a lower-rate new loan, depending on set-up costs. For very large organisations, several banks or other financial institutions may join together to share the risk and provide a long-term loan. In many such cases the interest will be linked to LIBOR (London inter-bank offered rate of interest).

BT triumphant as the big investors dash for shares

This was the headline in the *Daily Mail*, 19 June 2001, for an article written by Brett Arends. Some quotes from this article are reproduced here, and make quite interesting reading:

British Telecom defied doomsayers as it closed its record £5.9bn rights issue.

Big institutional investors bid for more than twice the number of new shares up for auction.

The success was a victory for BT's risky decision to save on advisers' fees by not having the issue underwritten.

The background to the BT story was the company's *debt problem*. It needed to reduce it, as it was draining its resources. Over a period of less than two months, it reduced its debt by £15.1bn, and achieved this as follows:

		£bn	£bn
May	Debt mountain		27.80
	Disposals:		
	Stakes in Japan Telecom and Spain's Airtel	4.40	
	Malaysia's Maxis	0.35	
	Yell	2.14	
		6.89	

	£bn	£bn
June Sale and leaseback of property	2.30	
Rights issue	5.90	15.09
Closing balance of debt		12.71

Source: B. Arends, *Daily Mail*, 19 June, 2001

Debentures are usually secured and the holders protected by a *deed of trust*. The trustees have to act in accordance with the deed; to do otherwise would exceed the powers laid down. *The interest on debentures has to be paid whether or not a profit is made.* Where the deed requires trustees to commence legal proceedings to have the company wound up in the event of default in the payment of interest, the trustees are not allowed to arrange a compromise or reschedule the debt. Thus, in periods of adverse trading conditions it is the *highly geared* companies, i.e. those that have a large proportion of debt in their capital structure, that go out of business. If the debt financing includes a significant amount of debentures, this increases the risk to the lender. In the system of costs and risks, the interest cost tends to be lower than secured long-term loans because the risk to the lender tends to be lower.

Convertible loan stock and convertible debentures can only be issued if the market is willing to accept them. Star-type companies have a good chance of being able to issue these successfully. The holder has an *option to convert into ordinary shares* at an agreed price at some *specified future date*. Until they convert, or if they do not convert, the holders receive interest. The interest on convertibles tends to be lower, e.g. in addition to being secured they also have the conversion option. If the holders want to get their money back they have to covert into ordinary shares when the time comes, and sell the shares on the open market. The decision as to whether or not to convert will depend on whether the holders want their money back, on interest rates and on share prices. For example, if the interest rate being paid is much higher than current interest rates, the holders may decide to keep them. On the other hand, if the current share prices are much higher than the agreed conversion price, the holders will be attracted to the conversion option.

If the holders do convert, the earnings per share (EPS) could go down; this is called a '*dilution of earnings*'. The dilution effect is usually caused by having an enlarged cake to share out (made up of profits that have increased because the interest on the convertibles no longer has to be paid out), being divided by an increased number of ordinary shares.

The **security** for long-term loans and debentures can be by a fixed charge, i.e. a charge on specific assets such as land and buildings, or by a floating charge, i.e. a general charge such as a charge over all of the assets.

Bank overdrafts

Bank overdrafts can be either secured or unsecured. One of the reasons why bank overdrafts are so popular and appeal to businesses is because of their flexibility and the speed with which renegotiations can take place, e.g. via a telephone call or face-to-face contact.

Many companies nowadays use their bank overdraft as a long-term source of funds, even though it is still described as being *'repayable on demand'*. Proof of the long-term use comes from the bankers themselves. They encourage their corporate and other business customers to convert a large part of their overdraft into a term loan. This would then commit the customers to regular repayments of capital and interest. Many customers just say 'no, thank you', as they prefer the flexibility that the overdraft affords.

> One SME (small or medium-sized enterprise) had an overdraft of £10 million secured on the assets of the whole group. There was no way that this could be considered as short-term finance and repayable on demand! Bankers do not like killing off good customers, and only tend to call in an overdraft as a last resort.

Venture capital

Start-ups, e.g. problem-child-type companies with good business plans, that are willing to risk their own funds and pledge personal assets may be able to attract finance from a venture capitalist.

Sale and lease-back

This involves selling property, e.g. land and buildings, to a financial institution such as an insurance company, and then leasing it back. For example, this was used by a local authority to finance phase two of a redevelopment plan. Care does need to be taken regarding rent reviews, as this may have a significant impact on future costs, profits and cash flows.

> ## M&S to swap old HQ for rooms with a view
>
> In 2001 Marks & Spencer revealed its plans to quit its old headquarters in London's Baker Street, in favour of new canal-side premises in London's Paddington Waterside development.
>
> The decision, heralded as a break from the past, will see them lease two interlinked triangular buildings, and sublet their Baker Street property to a third party. The reason for this is that, as leaseholder, M&S will continue to pay a peppercorn rent of £500,000 on the Baker Street property, which still has over 100 years to run, and they can sublet it for much more.
>
> *Extract L. Farndon,* Daily Mail, *22 May 2001*

Although the M&S case did not involve an outright sale of the Baker Street property, it does help illustrate how sale and lease-back arrangements work.

Creditors and accruals

Creditors and accruals, i.e. amounts owing for goods and services on credit, do provide short-term finance that can be vital to problem children and dog-type companies. It was finance from creditors that helped to make Honest Ed very rich.

> Honest Ed, a supermarket owner in Canada, received goods on 90 days' credit from his suppliers. He sold the goods within a very short space of time and invested the cash short-term, i.e. by employing a 'treasury function', and then paying for the goods on the due date. That's how he became very rich!

Proposed dividends, owing to shareholders, and tax owing also provide a valuable source of short-term finance in that they are not payable immediately, e.g. there can be quite a time lag between the year-end and the payment being made.

Hire purchase

Hire purchase is considered to be expensive. Wrong! It can be expensive, but it can also be available at rates that are lower than those that have to be paid out for a bank loan. The time period can be for the short or medium term, e.g. up to 5 years or up to 10 years. Assets purchased in this way, e.g. motor vehicles, show up at their full cost less depreciation in the balance sheet. The amount of hire purchase owing at the year-end also appears in the balance sheet.

Free finance

Last, but not least of the principal sources, is free finance – an area which may involve considerable sums of money. This consists of *grants* and *allowances* from local or national government or the EU etc. The ball game changes from year to year in terms of what is available, e.g. there have been grants to support: infrastructure projects; rural areas; tourism; the old iron and steel communities; farming. Information can be obtained from local chambers of trade, the EU, and various other sources. In addition, there may be low-cost loans available and support for exporters.

Other sources of external finance

There are a considerable number of other sources of external finance around, some of which deserve a brief mention here.

Mortgages

A mortgage is similar to a secured loan. The property that is being purchased is pledged as security for the mortgage. Interest rates can be fixed or variable.

Bridging loans

These are used to bridge the time lag between the exchange of contracts and the completion of the purchase or sale of property.

Invoice discounting

Invoicing companies will for a fee advance immediately an amount, e.g. 75% of the value of the sales invoices, to the company. When the debtor pays the company the discounting company will be paid. Notice that the company still has to collect the money owing from the debtors.

Factoring

Here, the company sells its sales invoices to the factoring company, for a fee. The factoring company is then responsible for collecting the debts, *with or without recourse*. In the without-recourse case, the factoring company, for a higher fee, assumes full responsibility for collecting all of the debts.

Accounts receivable financing

In this instance the company pledges its debtors, i.e. the accounts receivable, as security for cash on a continuing basis with, for example, merchant bankers and/or finance companies. In this case, it is the company's own responsibility to collect the debts due.

Bills of exchange

The bill of exchange is sent by the seller to the purchaser. The purchaser agrees to accept the bill and returns it to the seller. On its return, the seller is able to obtain payment immediately by discounting it with a discount house, merchant bank, clearing bank, etc. The periods covered tend to be in the region of 60 to 180 days.

Deposits and instalments

The financing of the goods and services that are being provided could be helped by up-front deposits and/or instalments, e.g. for construction projects extending over a lengthy period of time, ship-building, and the installation of new computer systems.

Internal sources of finance

Retained earnings

> These are, perhaps, the single most important source of finance within the UK and elsewhere.
>
> We have to make profits to survive and prosper in the long term, and reinvest some of those profits in forming our own future.
>
> Problem-child companies do need to have a high 'plough-back'.

The above comments, which may be made from time to time, reinforce the importance of retained earnings, i.e. undistributed profits, as a major source of finance.

Surplus assets

> Lack of concern with cash flow and the productivity of the capital employed can be fatal to a small company. Your best source of capital is often hidden in your balance sheet.
>
> H.N. Woodward, *Harvard Business Review*, Jan./Feb. 1976

Although the above statement was made many years ago, it still holds true today.

Companies, and other organisations engaged in education, health-care, radio and television, etc., may have fixed assets such as land and buildings, machinery, equipment (including office equipment), fixtures and fittings, investments, and stocks of raw materials, etc. which are surplus to requirements. The task of management is to identify these items and, after careful consideration, if required, sell them. This would bring in some cash to improve the cash flow position, and in a number of cases free-up space for other uses or to sell off or sublet. For example, if machines and equipment are sold, cash comes in, and the space occupied is available for other purposes or to sell off or sublet. If we dispose of surplus stocks of raw materials, cash comes in, space is freed up and the associated overheads and holding costs are reduced.

Working capital management

In addition to disposing of surplus assets, efficient stock control and more effective credit control could release cash for other purposes. Woodward, in the quoted article, also pointed out that one of the quickest ways of improving cash flow is to improve credit control.

Alternative ways of financing assets and operations

There are a number of alternatives to buying a fixed asset such as machinery, equipment or motor vehicles outright, e.g. hiring, renting or leasing. There are also alternatives that may be used for producing goods and/or services, e.g. buying finished parts or using subcontractors.

Hiring, renting or leasing

Apart from leasehold land and buildings, fixed assets that are hired, rented or leased do not appear on a firm's balance sheet; as you may recall, this is described as '*off-balance-sheet financing*'. The hire charges and rental payments will be charged for each period in the profit and loss account. For example, a problem-child company would be freed from having to find a lump sum. They would, however, have to find the hire or rental payments out of their profits. The hiring, renting or leasing of machinery and equipment can act as a 'hedge against obsolescence'. The company has the use of the asset for a specified period of time, at the end of which it is free to replace the asset concerned, e.g. with new state-of-the-art equipment.

Subcontractors

Subcontractors may provide all of the fixed assets they need to use, all of the raw materials, all of the labour force, and pay for all of their overheads. This enables the company to devote its own scarce resources to other purposes, e.g. research and development, marketing, distribution.

Financing decisions, a keyword approach

If you possess a good working knowledge of the meaning of the keywords associated with the financing decision, you are in a much better position to make more informed recommendations.

Capital structure and gearing

Equity is defined as ordinary share capital plus reserves. The *existing level of gearing* (leverage), i.e. the ratio of debt to equity, is the starting point when it comes to deciding whether to go for more debt, e.g. long-term loans or debentures, or issue more ordinary shares. For example, if the company is already very highly geared, i.e. it has a very large proportion of debt compared to equity, it may be difficult or impossible to attract more debt. The market may not be interested in supplying more debt when a certain level of gearing is reached.

Retained earnings

As mentioned earlier in this chapter, for many companies this is perhaps their single most important source of finance. Retained earnings, ploughed back and reinvested in the business, increase the reserves figure in the balance sheet. The reserves are part of the figure we described as 'equity'. If the reserves increase, the company will become less highly geared and, therefore, more capable of attracting more debt.

Dividend policy

The policy adopted will affect the retained earnings figure. The higher the dividend payout, the lower the retained earnings. The paying of dividends fulfils the expectations of the market, but it is a puzzle. Why pay out dividends with the one hand, and then borrow funds with the other hand?

Security

In the system of costs and risks, secured borrowing, i.e. pledging assets as security for loans, overdrafts and debentures, will command a lower rate of interest than unsecured borrowing.

Track record

A track record is a record of sound financial performance over a number of years and enables companies and other organisations to attract finance. For example, investors are attracted to invest in star-type companies. In order to become a *public limited company (plc)*, a company has to issue a *prospectus* which includes details of the company's financial performance for the last seven years.

Many of the individuals wanting to start their own business do have a financial track record. Their bankers have a record of how they have conducted their own personal banking matters. This could go a long way towards gaining financial support from their bankers, e.g. via loans and overdrafts.

Shop around

There are lots of financial products around, offering differing rates, terms and conditions, for example:

☐ *loans with repayment holidays*, e.g. no repayments for the first twelve months, but at a higher rate of interest, to compensate the lender for the additional risk that has been undertaken;

☐ *loans with 'strings attached'*, e.g. before making the loan the lender may insist on having one of their own people on the board of directors and/or insist on vetting and approving all new investment plans and/or make the loan in return for an equity stake;

☐ *hire purchase*, which may cost less than a bank loan;

☐ *free finance*, e.g. grants, subsidies and allowances, which may be available at local, national or international level.

The cost of capital

All sources of capital have a cost including an opportunity cost. In addition to the *service costs*, e.g. interest or dividends, there may also be *set-up costs*, e.g. legal fees, underwriting fees, management fees. This is why it is considered better and more economical to obtain finance in large amounts, rather than lots of small amounts. There are a number of different ways of calculating the cost of capital, e.g. weighted average using book values or weighted average using market values. The cost of capital, or the cost of capital plus a risk premium, may be used as a discount rate for capital investment appraisal purposes. This will be covered later on in this text.

Management involved in raising additional finance does have to consider all of the costs involved, and engage in negotiations designed to avoid adverse terms and conditions.

The tax factor

The tax factor affects retained earnings, cash flow, the cost of capital, dividends, and buying and selling investments, e.g. capital gains. Some accounting theories assume a world without taxes. The world is not like that, and the impact of taxation cannot and should not be ignored. For example, the government or other tax authorities may impose an additional surcharge if they so wish.

Financing guidelines

The following general rules help to point any company in the right direction when it comes to raising and managing finance:

☐ A certain proportion of the working capital is a long-term investment, and should really be financed from long-term sources.

☐ Long-term assets, e.g. fixed assets, should not be financed from short-term sources.

☐ Plan ahead and anticipate future needs.

☐ Be prepared to cope with the unexpected.

☐ Develop close relationships with the providers of finance, e.g. bankers, venture capitalists.

It is considered by some that the best time to obtain finance is when you don't need it! However, what this really means is don't leave it too late, and allow plenty of time to assess what you really need before it becomes too urgent.

Summary: sources of business finance

The financing of business may be described as a '*system of costs and risks*'. Businesses that are considered by the market to be high-risk, e.g. because of poor financial performance or a shortage of fixed assets to pledge as security, are more likely to have to pay more for their borrowings.

The *flow of business funds* (Figure 4.1) illustrates the way in which a business obtains finance and how that finance is used within the business.

The *financial life-cycle theory* uses the amended *Boston Matrix* (Figure 4.2) to help illustrate why companies: finance themselves in a particular way; opt for their dividend policy; manage their working capital as they do; adopt and formulate a particular take-over strategy.

External sources of finance

A summary of external sources is given in Figure 4.3.

Type	Characteristics
Ordinary shares	Voting rights; dividends; capital gains (or losses); the control factor; paid out last in a winding up.
Preference shares	Usually a fixed dividend; may be cumulative or non-cumulative; can be redeemable or non-redeemable; usually no voting rights unless their dividend is in arrears.
Long-term loans	May be secured or unsecured, fixed or variable interest.
Debentures	Usually secured. Lender protected by a deed of trust. The trustees cannot agree to a compromise or rescheduling of the debt; interest has to be paid whether or not the company makes a profit.
Convertible loan stock or convertible debentures	The holder has the option to convert into ordinary shares at some specified future date. Until that date, or if they decide not to convert, they receive interest.
Bank overdrafts	May be secured or unsecured; flexible, e.g. easy to get a decision quickly from the bankers. Many small and medium-sized companies use them as a long-term source of funds.

Other principal sources include: venture capital; sale and lease-back; creditors and accruals; hire purchase; and free finance in the form of grants, subsidies and allowances.

Figure 4.3 – The principal external sources of finance and their characteristics

Other sources of external finance

Other sources include: mortgages; bridging loans; invoice discounting; factoring; accounts receivable financing; bills of exchange; deposits and instalments. In the construction industry, instalments paid on account of the work certified are a vital part of financing construction projects.

Internal sources of finance

Companies and other entities tend to look to external sources when they need more money. To improve the productivity of the capital invested in the business, they need to look at their internal sources of finance. In addition to *retained earnings*, additional funds may become available from the sale of *surplus assets*, e.g. buildings, machinery, equipment, investments, unwanted stocks. This will improve cash flow and in certain cases release space for other purposes and cut down on overheads, e.g. holding costs relating to stocks. Sound working capital management can also help to liquidate stocks and debtors and free cash for other purposes.

Alternative ways of financing assets and operations

In addition to the outright purchase of a fixed asset, there is also what has become known as '*off-balance-sheet financing*', i.e. the hiring, renting and leasing of fixed assets (other than leasehold property). Other ways of producing products, components or a service include employing subcontractors or buying the products or components ready-made.

Keywords

The following keywords provide a valuable insight into the considerations that may have to be taken into account when making a financing decision:

☐ capital structure and gearing

☐ retained earnings

☐ dividend policy

☐ security

☐ track record

☐ shopping around

☐ cost of capital

☐ the tax factor

Financing guidelines

Figure 4.4 provides you with some general rules applicable to the financing decision.

> General rules:
>   Part of the working capital is a long-term investment
>   Don't invest long-term with short-term funds
>   Plan ahead
>   Expect the unexpected
>   Develop good working relationships with the providers of finance

Figure 4.4 – Financing decisions – general rules

Self-checks

On completion of each self-check, compare your attempt with the appropriate section of this chapter.

1. Explain briefly the flow of business finance.
2. What can we learn about companies from looking at their position within the amended Boston Matrix?
3. Describe the major characteristics of:
   □ ordinary shares
   □ preference shares
   □ convertible loan stock
   □ debentures
4. Explain why, although the bank overdraft is considered to be short-term financing and repayable on demand, this is not always the case in practice.
5. Describe briefly the sources of internal financing.
6. What alternative ways are there of financing assets?
7. Prepare brief notes on each of the following:
   □ capital structure and gearing
   □ the financial performance record
   □ shopping around
   □ free finance
8. Why are retained earnings considered to be such an important source of finance?

Self-assessments

You will find the suggested answers to these self-assessments in Appendix 1.

A4.1   Explain why obtaining finance has been described as a 'system of costs and risks'.

A4.2   Discuss the factors that would have to be considered by a family company thinking about issuing more ordinary shares.

A4.3   Describe ways in which the stockholding of raw materials, work-in-progress and finished goods may be reduced, so as to improve cash flow and reduce overheads.

A4.4   Companies guilty of 'over-trading' have a tendency not to follow generally accepted financing rules. Discuss.

Tutor-based assignments

For discussion, project reports or presentations, as directed by the tutor/lecturer.

T4.1   Explain and illustrate how the financial life-cycle theory (using the amended Boston Matrix) may affect the way in which companies finance their assets and operations.

T4.2   (a) Contrast the use of long-term loans, debentures and convertible loan stock, from the point of view of the provider and that of the borrower.

        (b) It was reported in the *Financial Times* (31 October 2000) that the Nissan president, Carlos Ghosn, declared 'Nissan is back'. In addition to a focus on profits and efficiency, debt reduction was cited as being a key part of Mr Ghosn's plan, and in the first half-year net debt had been reduced by ¥200bn to ¥1,150bn. Discuss why this is so important to Nissan's long-term success and survival.

T4.3   In relation to internal sources of finance, discuss and illustrate why management need to give a higher priority in terms of:
☐ managerial attitudes
☐ retained earnings
☐ surplus assets
☐ the replacement decision
☐ inventory control
☐ credit control

Further reading

Atrill, P. and McLaney, E., *Accounting and Finance for Non-specialists*, Financial Times Prentice Hall, 2001

Burns, P. and Morris, P., *Business Finance: A Pictorial Guide for Managers*, Butterworth-Heinemann, 1994

Davies, D., *The Art of Managing Finance*, McGraw-Hill, 1997

Knott, G., *Financial Management*, Macmillan, 1998

Useful websites

www.booksites.net/atrillmclaney
www.hw.ac.uk/library/howtoaccounting.html
www.moreover.com/cgi-local/page?o=portal&c=Accounting%20news
www.thisismoney.co.uk

5

The financial statements

Learning objectives

When you have worked through all the material contained in this chapter, you should be able to do the following:

☐ have a working knowledge of the structure, format and purpose of the profit and loss account and the profit and loss appropriation account, as used by a company for internal reporting purposes;

☐ calculate the:
  — cost of sales
  — gross profit
  — net profit
  — retained profit (profit and loss account balance) carried forward;

☐ appreciate that the cost of sales figure depends upon the nature of the business, e.g. retailing, manufacturing, financial services, banking, health, education, maintenance, radio and television;

☐ be familiar with the structure, format and purpose of balance sheets prepared for internal reporting purposes.

☐ define and describe the component parts of the balance sheet, e.g. the balance sheet equation, current assets, current liabilities, fixed assets, ordinary share capital, reserves;

☐ appreciate the effects that business transactions have on the profit and loss account and the balance sheet;

☐ be aware of the limitations of the profit and loss account and balance sheet.

What is a profit and loss account?

The **profit and loss account (P&L)**, can also be described as the *income statement*. Its purpose is to compute the profit or loss for the period in accordance with financial accounting concepts, accounting policies, accounting standards, relevant legislation and generally accepted accounting principles. As pointed out in earlier chapters, accounting is not an exact science and relies to a great extent on personal judgement. It has also been described as measuring business income or the economic activity for a period.

In this chapter we look at the profit and loss accounts which may be used for internal reporting purposes. For internal reporting purposes the formats used can vary significantly – the organisation can adopt the format they themselves prefer. This will also be affected by the nature of their business. A typical profit and loss account tends to be made up of four sections, as illustrated in Figure 5.1.

Profit and Loss account for the period ended ....
Part 1 The trading account section in which the gross profit is calculated
Part 2 Other income For example, rent received, dividends, discounts received, etc.
Part 3 The profit and loss account section in which the net profit before tax is computed
Part 4 The profit and loss appropriation account section in which the net profit before tax is shared up between taxation, dividends, transfers to reserves and retained earnings

Figure 5.1 – The profit and loss account and its component parts

When you look at an actual profit and loss account you will, in the majority of cases, see just one heading, for example, 'Profit and loss account for the year ended 30 June 20X5'.

The headings listed in parts 1–4 of Figure 5.1 are just not used. However, each of these component parts will still be present.

The trading account section

The purpose of the trading account section is to calculate the gross profit, which, in its most simple form, is as illustrated in Figure 5.2.

	£000	£000
Sales		28,400
Less cost of sales:		
Opening stock	500	
Add purchases	16,200	
	16,700	
Less closing stock	300	16,400
Gross Profit		£12,000

Figure 5.2 – The trading account section of a retailer

If the business concerned was involved in manufacturing, then manufacturing wages and associated overheads would be included in the cost of sales figures. The costs of production, i.e. materials consumed, manufacturing labour and factory overheads, would be calculated in a manufacturing account. This information would then be used in the trading account section, as shown in Figure 5.3.

	£000	£000
Sales		120,000
Less cost of sales:		
Opening stock of finished products	800	
Add factory costs of production*	82,000	
	82,800	
Less closing stock of finished products	1,100	81,700
Gross Profit		£38,300

Figure 5.3 – The trading account section of a manufacturing company
*This would have been arrived at in a separate manufacturing account which computes the figure by taking into account stocks of raw materials, stocks of work-in-progress, direct labour and manufacturing overheads.

In the case of a service such as a consultancy, insurance, television, health or education, the trading account could be far more detailed and/or include figures from numerous other accounts. Such a trading account section could be drawn up on the lines illustrated in Figure 5.4.

The other income section

This will include all income, other than trading income, e.g. rent received, dividends received and discount received for prompt payment of debts due.

	£000
Fee income (sales)	7,000,000
Less the direct cost of providing the service*	4,000,000
Gross profit	3,000,000

Figure 5.4 – The trading account of an organisation that provides a service
*The direct costs would include the direct labour, e.g. salaries paid to consultants; direct materials that are used to provide the service, e.g. software; and direct expenses, e.g. the cost of travel to and from clients.

The profit and loss account section

This section tends to include all of the indirect (overhead) expenditure, i.e. the expenditure that is not involved in producing the product or service. The expenditure that appears in this section can be simply listed or subdivided and shown under various headings such as those illustrated in Figure 5.5.

The profit and loss section:

Administration expenses, e.g. general administration, training, personnel department

Directors' remuneration, e.g. fees, salaries, bonus payments and pensions

Selling expenses

Distribution expenses

Financing expenses, e.g. bank charges, bank and loan interest, interest on debentures, discount allowed to customers for prompt payment

Research and development expenses

Other expenses, e.g. canteen, welfare, sports and social

Depreciation, e.g. of non-manufacturing fixed assets

Figure 5.5 – Typical expenses that may be found in the profit and loss account section

You should, however, appreciate that the distinction between which expenses go into the trading account section and which go into the profit and loss account section is not always so clear-cut. As a general rule all those expenses that are direct costs of the product or service go into the trading account section, either directly or via another account such as a manufacturing account. Most other expenses, i.e. the indirect expenses, are dealt with in the profit and loss account section. Examples of direct and indirect expenses are given in Figure 5.6.

Direct expenses (for the trading account section):

☐ The cost of manufacturing labour, or the labour used to provide the service

☐ Materials used to produce the products e.g. components used, packaging

☐ Advertising costs that are specific to the product or service

☐ Depreciation of manufacturing fixed assets

Indirect expenses (for the profit and loss account section):

☐ Administration costs, e.g. staff salaries, stationery

☐ Financial expenses

☐ Advertising to promote the company image

☐ Depreciation of non-manufacturing fixed assets

Figure 5.6 – Direct and indirect expenses

You should note that a published profit and loss account gives the information that is required by the Companies Act 1985/89, and this does not provide as detailed a breakdown and analysis of the figures as are used for internal reporting purposes.

The profit and loss account appropriation section

The appropriation section (account) is the place where the *net profit before tax* (NPBT) is shared out between the stakeholders, as illustrated in Figure 5.7.

Appropriation section

	£000
Net profit before tax	2,400
Less taxation	800
Net profit after tax (NPAT)	**1,600**
Less dividends (paid and proposed)	200
	1,400
Less transfers to reserves (if any)	600
Retained earnings (this year)	**800**
Add cumulative retained earnings brought forward from last year	1,100
Retained earnings (the P&L a/c balance)	**£1,900**

Figure 5.7 – The appropriation section

Points to note from a review of Figure 5.7 are:

☐ That the dividend included will be the amount *paid and proposed for the year*, i.e. the interim dividend paid (if any) plus the proposed final dividend.

☐ The directors may, if they wish, transfer some of the net profit after tax to a reserve account, e.g. a *general reserve account*. This could be an indication that the profits transferred to this account have already been or will shortly be reinvested in the business via the purchase of fixed assets, and not readily available to pay future dividends.

☐ The retained earnings brought forward, in many cases described as *'the profit and loss account balance'*, represent the cumulative profits that have been *'ploughed back'* into the company in earlier years. Adding this to the current year's retained earnings will provide the cumulative figure of retained earnings (profit and loss account balance), which will appear in this year's balance sheet.

☐ The net profit before tax is shared between the tax authorities, shareholders, transfers to reserves and retained earnings.

Profit and loss account for Aberamec Stores plc

We will now take a look at a specimen profit and loss account for a retail organisation that has been prepared for internal reporting purposes, Figure 5.8.

From a review of the profit and loss account (P&L) shown in Figure 5.8, you should note that:

☐ All of the figures just merge into each other and the important figures and headings have been highlighted in bold print.

☐ *Directors' fees, debenture interest and discount allowed* for prompt payment by customers are all charged as expenses in the P&L. *Notice particularly that debenture interest (and interest on loans if there had been any) are not classed as appropriations.*

☐ The increase in the *provision for bad debts* will be added to any existing provision, and then deducted from the debtors in the balance sheet. Its effect will be to revalue the debtors at a more realistic figure. You should note that the increase in the provision for bad debts is not an appropriation.

☐ The effect of a prepayment is to reduce the expense involved, in this case the £10,000 rent, rates and insurance, and to carry it forward into the future, where the benefit will be received (consumed), by showing it as a current asset in the balance sheet.

☐ In this particular example there were no transfers to reserves in the appropriation section. Any transfers to reserves are at the discretion of the directors.

☐ Certain direct costs, e.g. depreciation of equipment, could have been extracted and dealt with earlier in computing the gross profit.

☐ You should note that in the UK the taxation charge is not simply a percentage of the net profit before tax. It has to be computed in accordance with tax law, e.g. adjusting for expenses which are not allowed for tax purposes and capital allowances which are given in lieu of depreciation.

Aberamec Stores plc

Profit and loss account for the year ended 30 June 20X5 (for internal reporting purposes)

		£000	£000	£000
Sales				9,980
Less:	**Cost of sales**			
	Opening stock		940	
	Add purchases		7,000	
			7,940	
Less:	Closing stock		1,060	6,880
	Gross profit			**3,100**
Add	Discount received (i.e. not trading income)			60
				3,160
Less:	**Expenses:**			
	General expenses		151	
	Salaries		1,044	
	Discount allowed (i.e. an expense)		20	
	Directors' fees		723	
	Increase in provision for bad debts		40	
	Debenture interest		100	
	Telephone, stationery and printing		20	
	Rent, rates and insurance	50		
	Less prepayment	10	40	
	Audit and accountancy fees		2	

		£000	£000	£000
Depreciation				
	Fixtures, fittings and equipment	160		
	Motor vehicles	60	220	2,360
	Net profit before tax			**800**
Appropriations:				
	Less corporation tax			250
	Net profit after tax			**550**
Less	Ordinary dividend (interim)		160	
	Ordinary dividend proposed		200	360
	Retained this year			**190**
Add	Balance b/f from last year			300
	Balance c/f this year			**£490**

Figure 5.8 – A specimen profit and loss account used for internal reporting purposes

What is operating profit?

Another profit figure which is used is *operating profit*. This is the same as the net profit before interest and tax, but with non-trading income such as rent received and dividends deducted.

What is a balance sheet?

A balance sheet is *not* an account, it is a *position statement*, as at a *certain date*. It is a statement of assets, capital and liabilities. Assets are what the company *owns*: e.g. fixed assets such as land and buildings, machines, equipment and motor vehicles; and current assets such as stocks (i.e. inventories), debtors (i.e. accounts receivable), cash and bank balances. Liabilities are what the company owes, and include: share capital, e.g. ordinary shares; reserves; and liabilities such as long-term loans.

The balance sheet equation

The balance sheet equation states that *capital = assets less liabilities*. This equation can be used in a variety of ways to produce balance sheets for internal reporting purposes. Figures 5.9–5.11 illustrate some of the more popular formats. All of the formats are demonstrating the same message, which is: this is where the finance has come from, and where it has gone to (i.e. been used) and is represented now.

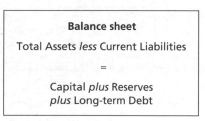

Figure 5.9 – Balance sheet (Format 1)

Balance sheet

Total Assets *less* Current Liabilities

=

Capital *plus* Reserves
plus Long-term Debt

Figure 5.10 – Balance sheet (Format 2)

Figure 5.11 – Balance sheet (Format 3)

The moving balance sheet

Every time a business transaction takes place we could, in fact, draw up a new balance sheet. However, in practice we only prepare a balance sheet periodically. We bridge the gap between balance sheets by preparing the profit and loss account for the period involved. It is, however, useful to appreciate how individual business transactions affect the balance sheet figures. Figure 5.12 should provide you with a good insight into the *dual effects of business transactions* on the balance sheet. It is also useful to understand how a single transaction will affect the profit and loss account and balance sheet, and this is illustrated by Figure 5.13.

Transaction etc. (all £000)	Effect on assets	Effect on capital and liabilities
Fixed assets bought by cheque £600	*Fixed assets* up £600. *Current assets*, bank account down £600	
Bought raw materials on credit £36	*Current assets*, stock up £36	*Current liabilities*, creditors up £36
Received a long-term loan of £2,000	*Current assets*, bank account up £2,000	*Long-term debt*, long-term loans up £2,000
A revaluation of fixed assets £750	*Fixed assets* up £750	*Reserves*, capital reserve or revaluation reserve up £750

Figure 5.12 – Balance sheets – dual effects

Transactions etc. (all £000s)	Effect on profit and loss account	Effect on assets	Effect on capital and liabilities
Sold an investment costing £80 for £65	Profit down by £15	*Investments* down by £80. *Current assets*: bank account up by £65	*Reserves*: retained earnings down by £15
The net effect of this on the balance sheet is a net decrease to assets and a decrease to capital and liabilities of £15			
Sold good costing £16 on credit, for £20	Profit up by £4	*Current assets*: stock down by £16, and debtors up by £20	*Reserves*: retained earnings up by £4
The effect on the balance sheet is a net increase of £4 to assets and an increase of £4 to capital and liabilities			
Motor vehicle expenses owing at the end of the period £2	Expenses up by £2 Profit down by £2		*Reserves*: retained earnings down by £2 *Current liabilities*: creditors up by £2
Depreciation of fixed assets £32	Profit down by £32	*Fixed assets* down by £32	*Reserves*: retained earnings down by £32

An increase in the provision for bad debts of £14	Profit down by £14	*Current assets*: debtors down by £14	*Reserves*: retained earnings down by £14
Proposed dividend of £100	Profit in the appropriation section down by £100		*Reserves*: retained earnings down by £100 Current liabilities: proposed dividend owing to shareholders £100

Figure 5.13 – How a transaction or accounting entry will affect the profit and loss account and balance sheet

Aberamec Stores plc balance sheet for internal reporting purposes

We will now look at Figure 5.14, a balance sheet that has been prepared for internal reporting purposes. A brief description of each of the component parts of the figure now follows. You may find it useful to keep referring back to the actual numbers shown in Figure 5.14.

The employment of capital

The employment of capital section shows how the funds that have been invested in the business are represented, e.g. used to aquire fixed or current assets or investments, but offset by the short-term funding received from current liabilities.

Fixed assets

These are items that are bought for *use* in the business and *not for resale*, for example, land, buildings, leasehold property, plant and machinery, office equipment, fixtures and fittings, motor vehicles. You should note that fixed assets (other than leasehold property) that are *hired, leased or rented* are not shown in the balance sheet because the company does not own them and has not bought them outright. However, details of such '*off-balance-sheet financing*' will appear in a company's published accounts, but only if it is a significant amount.

Investments

'Investments' refers to where a company has used its own funds to invest in stocks and shares of other companies.

Aberamec Stores plc
Balance sheet as at 30 June 20X5

			£000
Authorised share capital			
8,000,000 £1 ordinary shares			8,000

	Cost	Depreciation to date	Net
	£000	£000	£000
Employment of capital			
Fixed assets			
Freehold land and buildings	8,000	Nil	8,000
Fixtures, fittings and equipment	1,600	520	1,080
Motor vehicles	400	220	180
	10,000	740	9,260
Investments			500
Working capital:			
Current assets			
Stock		1,060	
Debtors	850		
Less Provision for bad debts (30 + 40)*	70	780	
Prepayments		10	
Cash and bank balances		110	
		1,960	
Less:			
Current liabilities (due within 12 months)			
Creditors	980		
Taxation	250		
Proposed dividend	200	1,430	530
			10,290
Capital employed			
Issued share capital			
Ordinary shares (800,000 @ £1 fully paid)			8,000
Reserves			
Share premium		800	
Retained earnings (P&L account balance)		490	1,290
			9,290
Long-term debt			
10% debentures (20 × 8/9)			1,000
			10,290

* The £30,000 provision for bad debts was the amount brought forward from last year.

Figure 5.14 – A balance sheet prepared for internal reporting purposes

Working capital

Working capital is sometimes called *the circulating capital*. It represents the difference between the current assets and the current liabilities. In effect it keeps the wheels of business turning by financing the everyday operating expenses.

Current assets

Current assets are shown in the order of liquidity (i.e. in the order of taking the longest time to convert back into cash) and consists of the following:

☐ Stocks £1,060,000
These can be stocks of fuels, raw materials, work-in-progress and finished goods.

☐ Debtors £780,000
Debtors are customers who have not yet paid for goods supplied to them on credit. The figure in the balance sheet may, however, be reduced by the accumulated provision for bad (and doubtful) debts – an accounting process which is very similar to the way in which depreciation of fixed assets is dealt with.

☐ Prepayments £10,000
These can be goods or services already paid for, but which will not be used up until the next (or a future) accounting period, e.g. rent and insurance.

☐ Cash and bank balances £110,000

Current liabilities

Current liabilities are amounts owing that will tend to be paid off within the next twelve months. Some examples of current liabilities are as follows:

☐ Creditors £980,000
The suppliers of goods and services to the business on credit that have not yet been paid for.

☐ Accrued expenses Nil
The expenses for the current period that have not been paid.

☐ Taxation £250,000
The amount owing for taxation.

☐ Proposed dividend £200,000
This is the amount owing to the shareholders for dividends.

☐ Bank overdraft Nil
The bank overdraft is usually considered to be current liability. However, some companies do in fact use it as a long-term source of funds, e.g. small and medium-sized companies.

Intangible assets

In addition to the assets already mentioned above there could also be intangible assets. These are non-physical long-term assets such as the following:

☐ patents

☐ copyrights

☐ trade marks

☐ brand names, e.g. the Ladybird brand (see below)

☐ goodwill

☐ certain types of research and development expenditure.

Woolworths acquires Ladybird brand for £11m

Ladybird, one of Europe's oldest brands in children's clothing, was yesterday sold by Coats Viyella to Woolworths for about £11m.

Coats has owned Ladybird since it bought Adolf Pasold, a clothing manufacturer, in the 1980s. The Pasold family firm originally bought the Ladybird brand in 1938 for £5, and used the brand to develop a trading relationship with Woolworths. Recently, Woolworths, which controls 6.5% of the children's clothing market, has designed and sold clothes under the Ladybird label. Yesterday's acquisition gives the high-street chain more freedom to develop the brand and market it aggressively in foreign countries, including Australia and Cyprus. 'The deal is part of Woolworths' strategy to increase floor space for selling clothing.'

Source: Katherine Griffiths, The Independent, *17 January 2001*

Capital employed

This section of the balance sheet shows the sources from which the long-term capital invested in the business has been provided, such as share capital, reserves and long-term debt. All of these may be described as amounts owing because they are owing to the individuals or institutions that have provided them.

Share capital

This can be divided into two, as follows:

☐ Authorised share capital £8,000,000
  This will only appear as a note on the balance sheet and refers to the maximum number

of shares that can be issued by the company. The shares may be ordinary shares and preference shares. The ordinary shareholders (frequently referred to as *the equity shareholders*) are the real entrepreneurs of a company, i.e. the real risk-bearers. They are paid out last on a winding-up.

☐ Issued share capital £8,000,000

The amounts shown represent the proportion of the nominal (or par, or face) value of shares (ordinary and preference), that has been received to date. In the case of Aberamec Stores plc, Figure 5.14, the ordinary shares have been fully paid up. The amount received in excess of the £1 per share (i.e. the nominal or par or face value) is called *share premium*. The balance, if any, that is to be paid at some future date for the shares is referred to as *calls*. Once shares have been issued and are fully paid and then sold on the open market, the company does not receive any more money, apart from a very small transfer fee.

Reserves

Reserves can consist of the following:

☐ Share premium £800,000

A kind of capital reserve representing the amount received from an issue of shares, over and above the nominal value of the shares. It may also be described as a statutory reserve, i.e. it can only be used for certain specific purposes laid down by company law: for example, to provide the premium on the redemption of shares or debentures. It cannot be distributed as dividends.

☐ Capital reserves Nil

These may be caused by:
— the revaluation of fixed assets
— the acquisition of shares in a subsidiary company
— the redemption of own shares.

☐ Revenue reserves £490,000

These represent the profits that have been *'ploughed back'* into the company, i.e. retained profits or undistributed profits, and tend to comprise:
— the general reserve (nil) is a reserve to which transfers are made from the profit and loss appropriation account;
— the profit and loss account and/or retained earnings (£490,000) is the cumulative balance of profit and loss appropriations built up since the company commenced trading.

Many non-accountants have differing perceptions of what the balance sheet figure of reserves means. They tend to think of a reserve as being cash and/or bank balances that are kept on one side for emergencies. This is not the case. The reason is that reserves are liabilities and not assets. They represent profits that have been retained and reinvested in the business on behalf of ordinary shareholders. Thus, the stake of the ordinary shareholder in a company (sometimes called *ordinary shareholders' interest or equity*) is their *ordinary share capital plus reserves*. The reserves were cash originally but may now be represented by increases in various fixed and current assets.

Long-term debt

Types of long-term debt include the following:

☐ Debentures £1,000,000
A special type of loan, usually secured on an asset or assets belonging to the borrower. A debenture carries with it a legal obligation to pay interest by certain dates and to repay the capital. The lenders, i.e. the debenture holders, are usually also protected, by a deed of trust.

☐ Long-term loans Nil
Obtained from banks and other financial institutions.

How much is a business worth?

It has been said that a balance sheet will answer the question 'How much is the business worth?' *But does it?* The balance sheet does provide a valuation – it tells us what the net worth (or net assets) amounts to. Figure 5.15 shows that the net worth can be calculated by either of the two methods illustrated.

Method 1	Method 2
Total assets	**Capital**
less	*plus*
Current liabilities	**Reserves**
e.g. creditors, etc.	*plus*
= **Net assets**	**Long-term debt**
(net worth)	= **Net assets**
	(net worth)

Figure 5.15 – The calculation of net worth (net assets)

However, we would only really know how much the business was worth if it were sold. The assets would no doubt fetch a lot more, or a lot less, than their balance sheet values, i.e. book values. The amounts received would also depend upon whether or not the business was being sold as a *going concern*. If it was, an additional amount may be received which represents the *goodwill*. Goodwill purchased represents the right to take over the orders, customers, organisation and profit-earning capacity, etc. of the business that has been acquired. If the business were simply being liquidated, the assets would be sold at their *break-up values*, which are likely to be much lower than their going concern values.

The limitations of the profit and loss account and balance sheet

The profit and loss account and balance sheet are *historic* documents. They look backwards, not forwards. In fact they are even more historic than many people realise. The reason for this is that in practice there can be a considerable lead time between a company's year-end and the publication of their report and accounts. The figures that are produced are affected by the way in which the accounting concepts and accounting policies are applied: 'off-balance-sheet financing', the revaluation of assets, the operation of the 'cut-off procedure', and creative accounting. The balance sheet shows the position as at a particular moment in time. A day after, or a week after, or a month after, the position could have changed quite considerably.

Summary: financial statements

The profit and loss account

The profit and loss account is made up of four parts:

☐ the *trading account* in which the *gross profit* is calculated;

☐ *other income* from rents received, discounts received, dividends received, etc.;

☐ the profit and loss section in which the *net profit before tax (NPBT)* is computed;

☐ the *appropriation section* where the NPBT is shared out between taxation, shareholders, reserves and retained earnings.

It is the financial statement that attempts to measure the economic activity and/or business income for an accounting period in accordance with accepted accounting concepts, accounting standards and relevant legislation, etc. An internal profit and loss account of a company was illustrated in Figure 5.8.

You should note that directors' remuneration, loan interest, debenture interest and depreciation are used to calculate the net profit or loss in the profit and loss account. They are not appropriations of profit, but charges that should be deducted in measuring the profit. Dividends that have to be included in the appropriation account are the dividends that have been paid or proposed for the accounting period under review. Sometimes, the *operating profits*, made up of the net profit before tax (NPBIT) less the non-trading income, are used. Note, also, that the profit and loss account can be called the P&L account, or the income statement (or, for a non-profit organisation, an income and expenditure account).

The balance sheet

The balance sheet is an accounting statement of assets, liabilities and capital prepared *as at a specific date*, i.e. a moment frozen in time. It is not an account and is not part of the double-entry bookkeeping system. Figure 5.16 spells out what a balance sheet is, and what it is not.

A balance sheet

Is:
- ☐ a statement
- ☐ prepared as at a certain date
- ☐ usually based on historic cost or historic cost less depreciation

Is not:
- ☐ an account
- ☐ drawn up to cover a period of time
- ☐ always a very good guide as to the value of the assets

Figure 5.16 – What a balance sheet is and what a balance sheet is not

You should also remember, when dealing with the balance sheet, *the balance sheet equation*, which states:

Capital = Assets less Liabilities

You should note that there are various combinations in which the equation may be used, as illustrated by the balance sheet formats of Figures 5.9, 5.10 and 5.11.

A balance sheet can be affected by *'window-dressing'* and other forms of *'creative accounting'*. Window-dressing could cause the balance sheet to portray a different picture from the one that really exists, e.g. running down stocks or having a special effort collecting money from debtors in the period leading up to the year-end.

The component parts of the balance sheet

The employment of capital
The employment of capital, i.e. the uses to which the capital employed has been applied, is made up of the following:

☐ Fixed assets

Assets owned by the company, which have been bought for use in the business and not for resale, e.g. land and buildings, machinery and plant, fixtures and fittings, office equipment, and motor vehicles.

☐ Investments

For example, quoted and unquoted shares that have been purchased in other companies.

☐ Intangible assets

Examples are brand names, patents, copyrights and trade marks.

☐ Working capital

Current assets less current liabilities. This is the circulating capital of the business that is used to finance the everyday-type operating expenditure.

☐ Current assets

These are made up of the following:

— stocks of raw materials, fuels, work-in-progress and finished goods;
— debtors, representing amounts owing from customers who have bought goods or services from the company on credit. To give a more realistic indication of this figure, the debtors may be reduced by a provision for bad and doubtful debts;
— Prepayments, deferred expenditure, i.e. paid out in the current accounting period but not yet consumed. The benefit of the expenditure extends beyond the current account period;
— bank balance;
— cash balance.

☐ Current liabilities

These are simply amounts due to be paid within the next twelve months that are owing to:

— creditors and accrued expenses, for goods and services that have been supplied to the organisation on credit;
— the tax authorities, for taxation;
— the shareholders, for proposed dividends.

Capital employed

The capital employed consists of the following:

☐ Issued share capital

The amount invested in the company by the shareholders by way of ordinary shares, and preference shares (*if any*).

☐ Reserves

There are several types of reserves, as follows:

— share premium – the amount that is received from an issue of shares over and above the nominal (par or face) value of the shares;
— capital reserves – which may result from a revaluation of fixed assets; the acquisition of shares in a subsidiary company or the redemption of the company's own shares;

— revenue reserves – usually a general reserve and retained earnings (i.e. the profit and loss account balance). Both represent profits that have been *ploughed back and retained* in the business, i.e. the undistributed profits.

☐ Long-term debt (or long-term liabilities)
The following are examples of long-term debt:
— *debentures* – a specialised type of loan usually secured by a charge on the assets of the company;
— *long-term loans* – from banks or other financial institutions.

The effect of transactions on the final accounts

Certain business transactions can have a dual effect on the balance sheet: for example, if a fixed asset is bought for cash, cash goes down and the fixed asset concerned goes up (see Figure 5.12).

If a transaction affects the figures in the profit and loss account, it will also affect the balance sheet retained earnings (P&L a/c balance) figure (see Figure 5.13).

Limitations

The usefulness of the balance sheet is limited because of the following:

☐ The *time factor*, i.e. the fact that it only shows the position at a particular moment in time, rather like a photograph.

☐ The *application of the materiality concept, the cost concept and the money measurement concept*, i.e. items tend to be shown at their historic cost or historic cost less depreciation. Also, items that cannot be measured in monetary terms cannot be shown, e.g. morale, excellent industrial relations, management expertise.

☐ *Valuation* – the balance sheet book value of the assets may be much less or much more than their real values. Thus, it is dangerous to say that a balance sheet will show us how much the assets are worth and/or how much the business is worth.

Self-checks

On completion of each self-check, compare your answer with the appropriate part of this chapter.

1. Describe the four component parts of a profit and loss account prepared for internal reporting purposes.

2. Explain how the cost of sales figure would be arrived at in:
   (a) a manufacturing company, and
   (b) a company that provides a service.

3. What are direct expenses?

4. Describe the purpose of the profit and loss appropriation section and its component parts.

5. What are retained earnings?

6. The following data are extracted from the accounts of Aberamec Stores plc:

	£000
Sales	9,980
Opening stock	940
Closing stock	1,060
Purchases	7,000
Discount received	60
Expenses (including depreciation)	2,360
Appropriations (tax and dividends)	610
P&L balance brought forward from last year	300

Calculate from them:

☐ the cost of sales
☐ the gross profit
☐ the net profit
☐ the retained earnings for the year
☐ the cumulative retained earnings (i.e. P&L a/c balance carried forward).

7. How will the following items affect the profit and loss account and balance sheet?
(a) an increase in the provision for bad debts
(b) prepaid rent.

8. What is a balance sheet?

9. What is the balance sheet equation?

10. Explain what share premium is, and how it is shown in the balance sheet.

11. Give two examples of capital reserves.

12. Describe briefly two kinds of long-term debt.

Self-assessments

You will find the suggested answers to the self-assessments in Appendix 1

A5.1 Why is capital shown with the liabilities and not included with the assets?

A5.2 Explain briefly how the net profit before tax is calculated, and how it is shared out in the appropriation section of the profit and loss account.

A5.3 From the following information calculate the cost of sales and the gross profit:

	Opening stock £000	Closing stock £000	Purchases £000	Sales £000
Materials	48	80	460	640

A5.4 From the following data, see if you can work out the net profit before tax.

	£000
Gross profit	320
Expenses	125
Depreciation	40
Dividends paid	12
Loan interest	8
Directors' fees	50
Tax payable	20
Proposed dividend	16

A5.5 Calculate the retained profit figure which will be carried forward to the next accounting period, from the following information:

	£000
Net profit before taxation	240
Taxation payable	68
Dividends paid	20
Dividends proposed	24
Retained earnings b/f	84
Directors' fees	56
Loan interest	30
Transfer to reserves	100

Tutor-based assignments

These assignments can also be used for group discussion, projects and/or presentations.

T5.1 Investigate and describe the limitations of profit and loss accounts and balance sheets.

T5.2 Explain and illustrate how each of the following will affect the profit and loss account and balance sheet:

(a) Prepaid rent amounting to £20,000.

(b) An increase in the provision for bad and doubtful debts of £14,000.

(c) An amount owing for stationery and printing of £7,200.

(d) A proposed dividend of £64,000.

(e) The purchase of equipment costing £1.5m on credit.

(f) The revaluation of buildings by £2m.

(g) Writing down computer equipment by £85,000 because of advances in technology.

(h) The correction of an error. An amount of £42,600 had been entered in the salaries account as £46,200, and this figure had been used to compute the profit in the profit and loss account.

(i) After the profit and loss had been prepared, an amount of stock was discovered in another part of the factory, valued at £36,000.

(j) Advertising literature valued at £245 had not been charged in computing the profit or loss.

Further reading

Britton, A. and Waterston, C., *Financial Accounting*, Longman, 1999

Dodge, R., *Foundations of Business Accounting*, International Thomson Business Press, 1999

Harvey, D., Atrill, P. and McLaney, E., *Accounting for Business*, Butterworth-Heinemann, 2000

Hussey, J. and Hussey, R., *Business Accounting*, Macmillan, 1998

Melville, A., *Financial Accounting*, Financial Times Prentice Hall, 1999

Nobes, C., *Introduction to Financial Accounting*, International Thomson Business Press, 1997

Useful websites

www.thomsonlearning.co.uk
www.bh.com/finance
www.macmillan-business.co.uk

6

Cash flow statements

Learning objectives

The principal objectives of this chapter are that by the time you have worked carefully through it, you should be able to do the following:

☐ appreciate why it is necessary to produce a cash flow statement;

☐ prepare a cash flow statement in line with FRS 1;

☐ deal with problems involving the sale of a fixed asset.

Why a cash flow statement?

The profit and loss account of a business shows how much profit or loss was earned during an accounting period and how the figure was arrived at. However, it does not show what has happened to it. The balance sheet shows the resources of the business at the beginning and end of the accounting period, but it cannot clearly show the movements in capital, reserves, long-term debt, assets and liabilities.

In order to answer the questions 'What has happened to cash or profits?' and 'What has happened to working capital?' we need to draw up a cash flow statement (funds flow statement).

The objectives of the cash flow statement are to show the following over an accounting period:

☐ the way in which the business has financed its operations;

☐ the sources from which funds have been derived, for example, share capital, loans, profits;

☐ the way in which the funds have been used, for instance to buy stocks of raw materials or fixed assets.

In short, the cash flow statement shows how a business has financed its assets, for example, from long-term sources or out of working capital.

In addition to a profit and loss account and the balance sheet, the published accounts of UK companies also include a cash flow statement. However, the information that is used to produce it is in fact a selection or reclassification and summary of information contained in the profit and loss account and the balance sheet.

The flow of business funds

We have already reviewed the sources of business funds in Chapter 4 (see Figure 4.1), but perhaps a brief recap would prove helpful at this point. The funds can come from the following sources.

Share capital

Ordinary shares

The holders of the ordinary shares usually have voting rights and receive dividends. These shares bear the greatest risk in that they are paid out last on a winding-up. They also attract capital gains (or capital losses) and determine who controls the company.

Preference shares

These usually tend to have a fixed dividend and have no vote unless their dividend is in arrears. They can be redeemable or irredeemable.

Debentures

Debentures are a special type of long-term loan: they are usually fixed-interest, repayable at a future date and secured on assets *via a deed of trust*. If the company defaults in paying the interest, the trustees for the debenture holders have to act in accordance with the provisions of the deed of trust, e.g. to start winding up proceedings.

Long-term loans

These may be secured or unsecured and attract fixed or variable rates of interest. In the event of the company being unable to meet its interest payments it may be possible to reach an agreement with the provider to reschedule the debt. The risk to the company is not therefore as high as it is for debentures, as it will be unlawful to arrange a compromise with the trustees for the debenture holders.

Convertible loan stock (or convertible debentures)

The holders tend to receive a fixed rate of interest but have the option to convert into ordinary shares between specified future dates. This frees the company from having to provide a lump sum to repay the capital. When the holders convert there could be a reduction in the earnings per share (EPS); this is called a **dilution of earnings**.

Bank overdraft

Although this is described as being 'repayable on demand' quite a large number of organisations treat it as a long-term source of finance. It may be secured or unsecured.

Other external sources These include: sale and lease-back, hire-purchase, mortgages, and the period of credit received from creditors.

Internal sources of finance

There are also quite a number of internal sources of finance, the most important of which is that which is self-generated, i.e. the *ploughed-back profits* (the profit and loss account balance and general reserve which is shown in the reserves section of the balance sheet). Additional cash flow can also be generated by selling off unwanted assets, e.g. land, buildings, equipment and stocks of raw materials.

The funds received can be used to pay:

☐ dividends to shareholders;

☐ interest on loans, and also to repay existing loans;

☐ creditors and expenses;

☐ for materials;

☐ for fixed assets.

The longer-term funds from share capital and loans tend to be used to finance the purchase of fixed assets and provide a certain portion of working capital.

The working capital shown in Figure 4.1, i.e. the current assets and current liabilities, tends to be used to finance the day-to-day operating expenses, such as wages and various overheads. Thus, you can see why it is also called *circulating capital*. As transactions take place its form changes, for example, if materials are bought on credit, stock goes up and creditors go up.

Alternative ways of financing assets

You should note that there are other ways of financing assets. In addition to outright purchase certain fixed assets can be *rented or leased*, e.g. plant, machinery and equipment, motor vehicles. This frees the organisation from having to find a lump sum and then having to pay interest on it. Another available option is to use *subcontractors*, for example, using them rather than providing every fixed asset and employing every single person to complete a construction contract.

What has happened to cash?

A *cash flow statement* can be drafted to answer the above question. The logic behind the calculation is quite easy to follow and understand, as illustrated by Figure 6.1. An alternative way of showing the same information is given in Figure 6.2.

Cash Flow
Sources of funds coming into the business during the period under review

less
Applications, i.e. the uses to which those funds were applied during that period

equals
The **increase or decrease in the cash and bank balances for the period**

Figure 6.1 – A cash flow for explaining what has happened to cash

---

Cash Flow
Opening balance of cash/bank

plus
Sources

equals
Applications plus (or minus) the closing balance of cash/bank

---

Figure 6.2 – An alternative cash flow for explaining what has happened to cash

87

In effect, Figure 6.2 is saying that what we start off with plus what we receive in the period should equal what we spend plus what we have left. If we spend more than we have, we end up with a negative amount, i.e. an overdraft. Figures 6.1 and 6.2 could also be described as funds flow statements, funds flows, or statements of sources and applications of funds.

The cash flow statement (FRS 1)

The cash flow statement should help you understand the reasons for the movement of cash during an accounting period. The formats adopted for reporting purposes (i.e. the published accounts) in the United Kingdom are prescribed by *FRS 1 (Financial Reporting Standard)* and cover the following major headings:

☐ net cash in or outflow from operating activities;

☐ returns on investments and the servicing of finance;

☐ taxation;

☐ investing activities;

☐ financing.

The final figure is the *increase or decrease in cash and cash equivalents*, e.g. an increase or decrease in the bank balance (Figure 6.3).

Cash flow statement for year ended 31 December 20X7

	£	£
Net cash flow from operating activities		
Returns on investments, and the servicing of finance:		
Dividends received		
Dividends paid		
Interest paid	___	___
Taxation:		
Tax paid	___	___
Investing activities:		
Purchase of tangible fixed assets		
Sale of tangible fixed assets		
Proceeds from sale of trade investments	___	___
Financing:		
Proceeds from new share capital		
Repayment of borrowings	___	___
Increase (or decrease) in cash and cash equivalents		___

Figure 6.3 – An FRS 1 cash flow statement

The net cash flow from operating activities may have to be computed by taking into account the increase/decrease in retained earnings, depreciation charged for the period, and the profits/losses on the sale of fixed assets, interest paid, tax appropriated, dividends appropriated and movements in stocks, debtors and creditors.

A much quicker way of computing it, provided the information is available, is to take the net profit before interest and tax (NPBIT) and add back depreciation and losses on sales of fixed assets (less any profits on the sale of fixed assets) and then adjust for the movements in stocks, debtors and creditors.

From your observations of Figure 6.3, you should be able to see how much cash went out during the period on dividends, taxation, new fixed assets and the repayment of borrowings and how these were financed, e.g. from ploughed-back profits (i.e. retained earnings), the sale of fixed assets and new borrowings.

You should be able to see how cash is moving through the organisation and the net impact on the cash balance at the year-end. It informs the user where the cash came from and where it went to. It should help investors, creditors and other users to determine the relationship between income and cash flows and provide an indication of the availability of each for dividends and long-term investment; it should also help users and managers to demonstrate the firm's ability to finance growth from internal sources.

We will now go through a step-by-step example to illustrate how we can prepare an FRS 1 cash flow statement.

Example   Preparation of an FRS 1 cash flow statement for Cheslett plc

Balance sheet as at 31 December 20X8

Authorised share capital:	£000			£000		
Ordinary shares	5,000			5,000		

Employment of capital:	This year 20X8 £000			Last year 20X7 £000		
Fixed assets	Cost £000	Depreciation to date £000	Net £000	Cost £000	Depreciation to date £000	Net £000
Land and buildings	3,820	Nil	3,820	2,800	Nil	2,800
Equipment, fixtures and fittings	489	100	389	201	50	151
	4,309	100	4,209	3,001	50	2,951

Working capital:
Current assets

Stock	190			150		
Debtors	750			635		
Cash at bank	120	1,060		114	899	

Less **Current liabilities**

Creditors	530			436		
Proposed dividend	100			60		
Taxation	270	900	160	140	636	263
			£4,369			**£3,214**

Capital employed:

Issued share capital

Ordinary shares of £1 each	2,500	2,000

Reserves

Share premium	500	—
Undistributed profits	869	414
(i.e. P&L balance)		
Capital plus reserves	3,869	2,414

Long-term debts

10% debentures	500	800
	£4,369	**£3,214**

Profit and loss appropriation account (extract) for the year ended 31 December 20X8 (this year)

	£000
Net profit before taxation*	900
Less Corporation tax based on this year's profits	270
	630
Less Dividend paid and proposed (includes an interim dividend paid of £75,000)	175
Undistributed profit for this year	**455**
Add Balance brought forward (from last year)	414
	869

*After depreciation £50,000 and interest on debentures £65,000.

There were no sales of fixed assets during the year to 31 December 20X8.

Step 1
Compute the net cash flow from the operating activities, as follows:

	£000
Retained profits (this is taken from the profit and loss account but could be calculated from the balance sheet (i.e. 869–414)	455
Plus depreciation (this is given, but could be calculated, see Working 1 (i.e. W1 below)	50
	505
Plus:	
Profit and loss on sale of fixed assets	—
Interest paid (given)	65
Tax appropriated (given in the P&L a/c)	270
Dividend appropriated (given in the P&L a/c)	175
	1,015

Movements in current assets and current liabilities:

Stocks (up), i.e. more cash tied up	40	
Debtors (up)	115	
Creditors (up)	(94)	
		61
		954

You should note that the £1,015,000 figure above is the net profit before interest and tax (NPBIT) plus the depreciation added back, which could be calculated as follows:

Net profit before tax (given)	900
Add Debenture interest (given)	65
	965
Net profit before interest and tax	50
Add Depreciation	**1,015**

Step 2
Calculate the amounts that were actually paid in cash during 20X8 for taxation and dividends. The way in which this may be done is shown in Working 2 (i.e. see W2 below).

Step 3
Next, compute the amount that has been spent on the purchase of new fixed assets, as follows:

	Cost of land and buildings £000	Cost of equipment, fixtures and fittings £000
This year, 20X8	3,820	489
Last year, 20X7	2,800	201
	1,020	288
Total	1,308	

Step 4

You then pick up the whole of the sale proceeds for any fixed assets or investments that have been sold during the period, if any. In this example there were none.

Step 5

Then you pick up any new finance coming in, such as share capital, loans or debentures, and borrowings repaid:

	This year 20X8 £000	Last year 20X7 £000	+ or – £000
Ordinary share capital	2,500	2,000	500
Share premium	500	nil	500
10% debentures	500	800	(300)

Step 6

Finally ensure that your calculations agree with the increase (or decrease) in the cash and bank balances:

	This year 20X8 £000	Last year 20X7 £000	+ or – £000
Cash at bank	120	114	6

Workings

W1   The calculation of the depreciation charge for the year

This was given as £50,000. However, if it is not given we compare the depreciation-to-date figures as follows:

	Depreciation of plant and machinery £000
This year, 20X8	100
Less Last year, 20X7	50
= Charged in this year's P&L account	50

However, this particular calculation will only suffice in cases where no sales of fixed assets have taken place. We will shortly look at how the sale of a fixed assets affects the figures that go into the cash flow.

W2   *The calculation of tax paid and dividends paid*

	Tax £000	Dividends £000
Brought forward from 20X7 balance sheet	140	60
Add Amount appropriated in 20X8 P&L a/c	270	175
	410	235
Less carried forward in	270	100
20X8 balance sheet (i.e. amounts that are still owing)		
Amount paid in cash in 20X8	**140**	**135**

Comment
The tax that was paid in 20X8 was the whole of last year's tax, £140,000, which was owing. The dividend that was paid must have been last year's £60,000, which was owing, plus an interim dividend of £75,000 for 20X8.

Step 7
You now have all the figures you need to complete the FRS 1 cash flow statement.

Cheslett plc
Cash flow statement for year ended 31 December 20X8

	£000	£000
Net cash flow from operating activities		954
Returns on investments, and the servicing of finance:		
Dividends received	—	
Dividends paid	(135)	
Interest paid	(65)	(200)
		754
Taxation:		
Tax paid		(140)
		614
Investing activities:		
Purchase of tangible fixed assets		(1,308)
Sale of tangible fixed assets		—
Proceeds from sale of trade investments		—
		(694)
Financing:		
Proceeds from new share capital including share premium	1,000	
Repayment of debentures	(300)	700
Increase (or decrease) in cash or cash equivalents		6

The sale of fixed assets

The sale of fixed assets makes the picture a little more complex and will be dealt with in the cash flow as follows:

☐ The profit or loss on sale will be adjusted for in the computation of the net cash flow from operating activities:

— a *profit on sale*, which could also be described as an over-provision for depreciation, must be deducted. This, in effect, takes the net profit before taxation back to what it was before the profit on sale was added;

— a *loss on sale*, i.e. an under-provision for depreciation, will be added back.

☐ The whole of the sale proceeds received must then be included in the investing activities section of the cash flow, as illustrated in Figure 6.3.

☐ Care must be exercised when computing the cost of new fixed assets purchased during the period under review and when computing the depreciation for the period, as illustrated below. The cost of new office equipment, furniture and fittings is £190,000.

Example   The sale of fixed assets

Office equipment, furniture and fittings	Cost	Depreciation to date	Net
	£000	£000	£000
20X3	800	500	300
20X4	950	580	370

During 20X4 equipment, which cost £40,000 and on which £24,000 depreciation had been charged, was sold for £14,000, thus:

Equipment	£000
Cost	40
Less depreciation	24
Book value	16
Sale proceeds	14
Loss on sale	2

The loss on sale of £2,000 would be added back in the computation of the net cash flow from operating activities and the £14,000 sale proceeds would be included as a source of funds in the investing activities section. The new fixed assets purchased and the depreciation for the period can be calculated, as follows:

Office equipment, furniture and fittings	Cost		Depreciation to date
	£000		£000
Brought forward from 20X3	800		500
Less Applicable to equipment sold	40		24
= Office equipment, furniture and fittings b/f but not disposed of	760		476
Carried forward 20X4	950		580
Cost of new office equipment, furniture and fittings =	190	Depreciation charged in 20X4 =	104

Summary: cash flow statements

A knowledge of cash flow statements will help answer questions such as:

What has happened to cash?
Why has profit gone up and cash gone down?
Where have the profits gone?
What has happened to the working capital?

In addition to showing the funds generated from operating activities during the period, a cash flow statement (funds flow) will also show the other funds that were received during the period and what has become of them, i.e. the uses to which they have been put.

The FRS 1 cash flow statement

The FRS 1 cash flow statement is the funds flow statement that is currently being used for external reporting purposes in the United Kingdom, i.e. it forms part of a company's published annual report and accounts.

As with other funds flows it is a reclassification and reordering of profit and loss account and balance sheet data. It shows:

☐ The *net cash flow from operating activities* – you should note that this is made up of the net profit before interest and tax, plus depreciation of fixed assets, plus losses on the sale of fixed assets (or less profit), and then adjusted for movements in stocks, debtors and creditors.

☐ *Returns on investments* (if any), and the *cost of servicing the financing*, for example, dividends paid to ordinary and preference shareholders, loan and debenture interest, etc. (see below for how we can calculate the amount paid out as dividends).

☐ *Taxation*; you should note the way in which we calculated the tax paid figure, as illustrated below:

	*Dividend £000	Taxation £000
Balance b/f 20X7, i.e. owing at the start of year	7	8
Add P&L account appropriation (for 20X8)	10	12
	17	20
Less Balance c/f (20X8), i.e. owing at year end	10	8
= Amount paid	£7	£8

* In any year, the amount paid out as dividends is last year's final dividend, plus the current year's interim dividend (if any).

☐ *Investing activities* – the purchase and sale of fixed assets, etc.

☐ *Financing* – details of new finance, e.g. more ordinary share capital and also details of repayments of loans and debentures, etc.

The final figure should then be equal to the increase or decrease in the cash and bank balances.

The sale of fixed assets

If a fixed asset (or an investment) is sold during the period under review, note the treatment for cash flow/funds flow purposes in computing the net cash flows from operating activities:

☐ a profit on sale is deducted, and

☐ a loss on sale is added back.

Concluding remarks

Please note that a cash flow forecast (cash budget) is a different kind of financial statement and is not another name for a cash flow statement or funds flow.

Thus, a cash flow statement is a historic statement prepared in addition to the profit and loss account and the balance sheet, and shows the manner in which a business has financed its operations over the last financial year or period.

Self-checks

Compare your attempts at each of the following self-checks with the appropriate part of this chapter.

1. What are the objectives of the cash flow statement?

2. List the key information that is shown in an FRS 1 cash flow statement.

3. Explain how the net cash flow from operating activities may be calculated.

4. How can we compute the tax paid and the dividends paid?

5. Describe and illustrate how the sale of a fixed asset affects the cash flow statement.

Self-assessments

You will find the suggested answers to all of the self-assessments in Appendix 1.

A6.1   From the information provided below see if you can prepare a cash flow statement by using the specimen blank FRS 1 layout, which follows the balance sheet and profit and loss appropriation account summary for Emmsock plc.

Emmsock plc
Balance sheet as at 31 December 20X8

Employment of capital

	Last year 20X7				This year 20X8	
Cost	Depreciation to date	Net		Cost	Depreciation to date	Net
£000	£000	£000	**Fixed assets**	£000	£000	£000
450	—	450	Land and buildings	500	—	500
104	34	70	Plant and machinery	114	50	64
40	8	32	Fixtures and fittings	45	15	30
594	42	552		659	65	594
			Working capital:			
			Current assets			
	27		Stock		33	
	31		Debtors		44	
	11		Bank		24	
	69				101	

97

	Last year 20X7				This year 20X8	
Cost	Depreciation to date	Net		Cost	Depreciation to date	Net
£000	£000	£000	Less **Current liabilities** £000		£000	£000
25			Creditors	14		
9			Taxation	13		
15	49	20	Proposed dividend	20	47	54
		572				648
			Authorised share capital:			
	600		£1 ordinary shares		600	
	200	800	10% preference shares		200	800
			Capital employed: issued share capital			
	200		Ordinary – issued/fully paid		400	
	—		10% preference shares		50	
		200				450
			Reserves			
	17		Share premium account		38	
	10		General reserve		15	
	20		Profit and loss account		45	
		47				98
		247	**Capital and reserves**			548
		165	8% debentures			100
		160	Loan			
		£572				**£648**

Profit and loss appropriation account summary for the year ended 31 December 20X8

	£000	£000
Net profit before tax*	65	
Less Corporation tax	15	50
Transfer to general reserve	5	
Proposed dividends	20	25
		25
Add Balance b/f from last year		20
Balance c/f (as per balance sheet)		45

*After depreciation
Interest on debentures and loans charged
in computing the profit amount to £22,000

Emmsock plc
Cash flow statement for year ended 31 December 20X8
(FRS 1 layout)

	£000	£000
Net cash flow from operating activities		
Returns on investments, and the servicing of finance:		
Dividends received		
Dividends paid		
Interest paid		
	——	——
Taxation:		
Tax paid		——
Investing activities:		
Purchase of tangible fixed assets		
Sale of tangible fixed assets		
Proceeds from sale of trade investments	——	——
Financing:		
Proceeds from new share capital		
Repayment of borrowings	——	——
Increase (or decrease) in cash or cash equivalents	——	——

Tutor-based assignment

Attempt this as directed by your instructor, tutor or lecturer.

T6.1 Now see if you can prepare a cash flow statement in the FRS 1 format from the information provided for Timvik plc.

	20X8 31 December	20X7 31 December
Capital employed:	£000	£000
Ordinary shares £1 each	500	400
Share premium	250	200
9% preference shares £1 each	200	100
P&L account	300	190
Bank loan	nil	80
Trade creditors	40	48
Dividend payable	30	25
Taxation	90	80
	1,410	1,123

	20X8 31 December	20X7 31 December
Represented by:		
Plant and machinery		
Cost	1,760	1,400
Aggregate depreciation	476	398
	1,284	1,002
Stock	56	68
Debtors	42	36
Bank	28	17
	1,410	1,123

You are also given the following summarised profit and loss appropriation account data for the year ended 31 December 20X8:

	£000
Profit before tax (after depreciation)	240
Less Corporation tax for the year	90
	150
Less Dividend paid and proposed (ordinary shares)	40
	110
Balance b/f	190
	300

You are also informed that during the year ended 31 December 20X8 machinery costing £80,000 on which £72,000 depreciation had been provided was sold for £12,000. The profit before tax was after charging bank loan interest of £4,000.

Further reading

Dyson, J., *Accounting for Non-accounting Students*, Financial Times Prentice Hall, 2001

Gillespie, I., Lewis, R. and Hamilton, K., *Principles of Financial Accounting*, Financial Times Prentice Hall, 2000

Mott, G., *Accounting for Non-accountants*, Kogan Page, 1999

Walton, P., *Financial Statement Analysis – An International Perspective*, Thomson Learning, 2000

Waterston, C. and Britton, A., *Financial Accounting*, Longman, 1999

Useful websites

www.bh.com/management
www.booksites.net/dyson
www.pearsoneduc.com/business
www.thomsonlearning.co.uk

7

Preparing a profit and loss account and a balance sheet from a trial balance

Learning objectives

It is not the intended aim of this chapter that you become an expert in this number-crunching and mechanical process. The idea of giving you the experience of preparing the *final accounts* (i.e. a profit and loss account and balance sheet) from a trial balance plus further information, is to:

☐ enable you to appreciate some of the problems involved with income measurement, i.e. the way in which we work out the profit or loss for a period, and the application of the accounting concepts which were discussed in Chapter 2;

☐ help you to understand more fully the terminology that is used;

☐ see how the value of certain assets, such as plant and machinery, equipment, motor vehicles and debtors, can be arrived at.

When you reach the end of this chapter you should be able to do the following:

☐ Sort out the debit and credit items listed in the trial balance into fixed assets, current assets, investments, expenses of the profit and loss account, sales and cost of sales data, issued share capital, reserves, long-term debt and current liabilities.

☐ Adopt and use a systematic approach to prepare the profit and loss account (including an appropriation account) and balance sheet of a limited company from a trial balance plus adjustments, for internal reporting purposes.

Example The preparation of a profit and loss account and a balance sheet from a trial balance, plus adjustments for internal reporting purposes

We will work through the example step-by-step. You are provided with the information relating to Scholes Manufacturing Ltd, as presented in Figure 7.1.

Scholes Manufacturing Ltd
Trial balance at 31 December 20X4

	Debit £000	Credit £000
Liabilities, income and capital:		
Sales		180
£1 ordinary shares		100
Creditors		17
Long-term loan		50
Bank overdraft		13
Balance on profit and loss account 31 December 20X3		46
Accumulated depreciation to 31 December 20X3 on fixtures and fittings		20
Accumulated depreciation on motor vans to 31 December 20X3		18
Assets and expenses:		
Trade debtors	40	
Purchases	87	
Opening stock 1 January 20X4	23	
Property at cost	120	
Fixtures and fittings (cost)	50	
Motor vans (cost)	36	
Directors' salaries	34	
Salaries	27	
Office expenditure	7	
Selling expenses	19	
Bank interest and charges	1	
	£444	£444

Figure 7.1 – The trial balance

Note the following adjustments:
1. Stock on hand at 31 December 20X4 is valued at cost, £21,000.

2. Depreciation on fixtures and fittings is calculated at 10% of cost per annum.

3. Accrued office expenditures (heat and light, telephone) are estimated at £2,000.

4. Selling expenses include prepaid advertising for 20X5 of £4,000.

5. Depreciation on motor vehicles is calculated at 25% of cost per annum.

Step 1: Knowing the destination of a balance on an account

The balances on all of the accounts are listed in a trial balance, to make sure that everything is in balance before the adjustments (listed as 1–5 above) are taken into account, and before the preparation of the final accounts. Figure 7.2, the trial balance and ALICE, should help you to remember where the items go without having to worry too much about debit and credit.

Trial balance as at 31 December 20X6		
ALICE	Debit	Credit
	£000	£000
Assets, e.g. equipment, fixtures, debtors	A	
Liabilities, e.g. creditors, loans, dividends owing		L
Income, e.g. sales, rent received		I
Capital and reserves, e.g. share capital, retained earnings (profit and loss account balance)		C
Expenditure, e.g. advertising, salaries	E	

Figure 7.2 – The trial balance and ALICE
Source: L. Chadwick, *Essential Financial Accounting*, Financial Times Prentice Hall, 2001

From your observation of Figure 7.2 you can see that debit balances are assets or expenses, and credit balances are liabilities, income, capital and reserves.

Where are they shown in the final accounts?
A (assets) will be shown in the balance sheet
L (liabilities) will also be shown in the balance sheet
I (income) will be shown in the profit and loss account
C (capital and reserves) will be shown in the balance sheet
E (expenses) will be shown in the trading account section if they are part of the cost of sales, and in the profit and loss account section if they are not.

Step 1 involves marking each item listed in the trial balance with its destination in the final accounts (destination column number 1) in Figure 7.3, as follows:

B/C = Balance sheet/Capital
B/Res = Balance sheet/Reserves
B/FA = Balance sheet/Fixed assets
B/CA = Balance sheet/Current assets
B/Inv = Balance sheet/Investments
B/CL = Balance sheet Current liability
B/LTD = Balance sheet/Long-term debt
T = Trading account section of the P&L account

P&L = Profit and loss account section of the P&L account

App = Profit and loss appropriation account

This simple procedure highlights the destination in the statement or account to which an item belongs, and the (group) section to which it belongs. The trial balance, Figure 7.3, is the same as the one that appeared as Figure 7.1 but with the 'destination' column completed.

Note that the opening stock at 1 January 20X4 goes to the trading account section of the P&L account only. The stock figure that will appear in the balance sheet will be the stock figure that is adjusted for after the trial balance. This is because it is the stock as at the balance sheet date, i.e. 31 December 20X4 in this particular case. The opening stock, shown as an asset in last year's balance sheet, in effect, becomes an expense of the current period, any that remains being included in the closing stock.

Trial balance at 31 December 20X4

(1)		Debit £000	Credit £000	(2) + or – Adjustment £000	(3) Balance sheet effect £000
Destination	**Liabilities, income and capital:**				
T	Sales		180		
B/C	£1 ordinary shares		100		
B/CL	Creditors		17		
B/LTD	Long-term loan		50		
B/CL	Bank overdraft		13		
App	Balance on profit and loss account 31 December 20X3		46		
–B/FA	Accumulated depreciation to 31 December 20X3 on fixtures and fittings		20		
–B/FA	Accumulated depreciation on motor vans to 31 December 20X3		18		
	Assets and expenses:				
B/CA	Trade debtors	40			
T	Purchases	87			
T	Opening stock 1 January 20X4	23			
B/FA	Property at cost	120			
B/FA	Fixtures and fittings (cost)	50			
B/FA	Motor vans (cost)	36			
P&L	Directors' salaries	34			
P&L	Salaries	27			
P&L	Office expenditure	7			
P&L	Selling expenses	19			
P&L	Bank interest and charges	1			
		£444	**£444**		

Figure 7.3 – The trial balance – the destination of the balances on the accounts

Step 2: Dealing with the adjustments

You must remember that the adjustments will have a dual effect. They will affect the profit and loss account or the profit and loss appropriation account, and the balance sheet.

For example, accruals and prepayments are taken into account in the profit and loss account so that the correct expense for the period is charged in computing the profit or loss for the period. The accruals and prepayments will then also appear in the balance sheet as follows:

☐ *accruals*, to indicate that the expenditure is still owing at the balance sheet date, are shown as a current liability.

☐ *prepayments*, which represent expenditure already paid out but which belong to the next (or a future) accounting period, are shown as a current asset.

Trial balance at 31 December 20X4

(1)		Debit £000	Credit £000	(2) + or − Adjustment £000	(3) Balance sheet effect £000
Destination	**Liabilities, income and capital:**				
T	Sales		180		
B/C	£1 ordinary shares		100		
B/CL	Creditors		17		
B/LTD	Long-term loan		50		
B/CL	Bank overdraft		13		
App	Balance on profit and loss account 31 December 20X3		46		(See also the appropriation account)
−B/FA	Accumulated depreciation to 31 December 20X3 on fixtures and fittings		20	Depreciation +5 P&L	FA − 25 to date
−B/FA	Accumulated depreciation on motor vans to 31 December 20X3		18	Depreciation +9 P&L	FA − 27 to date
	Assets and expenses:				
B/CA	Trade debtors	40		Closing	
T	Purchases	87		stock	
T	Opening stock 1 January 20X4	23		−21 T	21 (CA)
B/FA	Property at cost	120			
B/FA	Fixtures and fittings (cost)	50			
B/FA	Motor vans (cost)	36			
P&L	Directors' salaries	34			
P&L	Salaries	27			
P&L	Office expenditure	7		+2 Accrual	2 (CL)
P&L	Selling expenses	19		−4 Prepaid	4 (CA)
P&L	Bank interest and charges	1			
		£444	**£444**		

Figure 7.4 – The trial balance – the effect of the adjustments

The adjustments can be marked with regard to their destinations as follows (where: T = trading account section of P&L account; P&L = profit and loss account; and B = balance sheet):

T or P&L	B	Adjustments
T	CA	Stock on hand at 31 December 20X4 is valued at cost, £21,000
P&L	–FA	Depreciation on fixtures and fittings is calculated at 10% of cost per annum
P&L	CL	Accrued office expenditure (heat and light, telephone) is estimated at £2,000
P&L	CA	Selling expenses include prepaid advertising for 20X5 of £4,000
P&L	–FA	Depreciation on motor vehicles is calculated at 25% of cost per annum

Having marked the dual effect regarding the adjustments, as a means to promote greater accuracy, the effects of the adjustments are shown in columns (2) and (3) of the trial balance, Figure 7.4. Thus the effect of each adjustment on the profit and loss account and the balance sheet has been recorded and highlighted in columns (2) and (3) and illustrates the dual effect.

Scholes Manufacturing Ltd
Profit and loss account for the year ended 31 December 20X4

		£000	£000	£000
Sales				180
Less:	**Cost of sales**			
	Opening stock (at 1 January 20X4)		23	
	Add Purchases		87	
			110	
Less:	Closing stock (at 31 December 20X4)		21	89
	Gross profit			91
Less:	**Expenses:**			
	Directors' salaries		34	
	Salaries		27	
	Office expenditure	7		
	Add Accrual	2	9	
	Selling expenses	19		
	Less Prepayment	4	15	
	Bank interest and charges		1	
	Depreciation			
	Fixtures, fittings	5		
	Motor vans	9	14	100
	Net loss before tax			(£9)
P&L account brought forward (b/f) (from last year)				46
	Balance carried forward (c/f)			£ 37

Figure 7.5 – Profit and loss account

Step 3: Prepare the profit and loss account

This task is a matter of scanning the data and first picking up the information that is needed to compute the gross profit, and then picking up the other profit and loss information and computing the net profit (or loss).

As you transfer each item from the trial balance to the profit and loss account, it is a good idea to tick it off. This should help to ensure that all the items are dealt with. Thus the profit and loss account for the year ended 31 December 20X4 for Scholes Manufacturing Ltd will appear as Figure 7.5. The £37,000 P&L account balance at 31 December 20X4 is the figure that will go in this year's balance sheet, reserves section.

Scholes Manufacturing Ltd
Balance sheet as at 31 December 20X4

Employment of capital

	Cost	Depreciation to date	Net
	£000	£000	£000
Fixed assets:			
Property	120	Nil	120
Fixture and fittings	50	25	25
Motor vans	36	27	9
	206	52	154
Working capital:			
Current assets:			
Stock		21	
Debtors		40	
Prepayments		4	
Bank (overdraft)		(13)	
		52	
Less			
Current liabilities:			
Creditors	17		
Accruals	2	19	33
			£187

Capital employed

Authorised share capital not given

	£000	£000	£000
Issued share capital:			
Ordinary shares of £1			100
Reserves:			
Retained earnings (P&L account)			37
			137
Long-term debt:			
Debentures		Nil	
Loans		50	50
			£187

Figure 7.6 – The balance sheet

Step 4: Prepare the balance sheet

All the unticked items in the trial balance should be needed to complete the balance sheet. They should be picked up in the order in which they are required, as dictated by the format that is used, and adjusted to take account of the further information that was contained in the notes. As you transfer an item from the trial balance to the balance sheet, tick it off. Thus the balance sheet as at 31 December 20X4 for Scholes Manufacturing Ltd will appear as in Figure 7.6.

Summary: preparing final accounts from a trial balance

A systematic approach needs to be adopted. One suggested approach is as follows:

Step 1

Mark each item that appears in the trial balance with its destination or location in the final accounts, for example, the following:

B/CA = Balance sheet item, current asset;
T = Trading account section item;
P&L = Profit and loss account item;
App = Appropriation account item; and so on.

Step 2

Take into account the dual effect of adjustments and mark them in the adjustments section of the information supplied and/or combine it with the item to which it relates in the trial balance.

Step 3

Decide on the format you intend to use for the profit and loss account. Scan the trial balance to pick up the information as you need it. Having transferred it to the profit and loss account, tick the item off in the trial balance to signify that it has been dealt with.

Step 4

Decide on your balance sheet layout. Pick up the items from the trial balance as you need them. Having transferred each to the balance sheet, tick off the item concerned.

Finally

Remember Figure 7.2 – the trial balance and ALICE. This is a great help during the sorting process.

Self-checks

Having completed each of the self-checks that follow, compare your answer with the appropriate part of this chapter.

1. Why are the balances of the accounts listed in the trial balance?
2. How can 'ALICE' help you remember the component parts of the trial balance?
3. Which stock figure normally appears in the trial balance?
4. What effect does depreciation for the year have on the profit and loss account and balance sheet?
5. Where are directors' salaries dealt with?

Self-assessments

When you have completed each self-assessment compare it with the suggested answer provided in Appendix 1.

A7.1   **Port Peter plc**

(1)			(2)	(3)
			+ or −	
Destination details	Debit £000	Credit £000	Adjustment £000	Balance sheet effect £000
Authorised and issued £1 ordinary shares		400		
Sales		375		
Purchases	140			
Stock 1 January 20X4	29			
Share premium		25		
Bad debts written off	3			
Wages and salaries	48			
Motor vehicles (at cost)	40			
Depreciation to date on motor vehicles		16		
Motor expenses	9			
Overhead expenses*	30			
Freehold land and buildings	437			
Debtors	28			
Creditors		23		
Bank balance	32			
Profit and loss account		11		

(1) Destination details	(2) Debit £000	+ or − (2) Credit £000	(3) Adjustment £000	Balance sheet effect £000
10% debentures		50		
Directors' fees	56			
Taxation	—	—		
Fixtures, fittings and equipment (at cost)	80			
Depreciation to date on fixtures and fittings and equipment		30		
Provision for bad debts		2		
	£932	£932		

* Includes debenture interest of £5,000.

The following data are also available:

Note
1. Depreciation of fixed assets is to be provided as follows:
    ☐ fixtures, fittings and equipment at 10% of cost per annum;
    ☐ motor vehicles at 20% of cost per annum.
2. Rent prepaid included in the overhead expenses amounted to £4,000.
3. The directors propose to pay a dividend for the year of £30,000 to the ordinary shareholders.
4. The stock at 31 December 20X4 amounted to £20,000.
5. The estimated corporation tax for the year is £18,000.

Required:
See if you can use the method illustrated in the Scholes Manufacturing example to produce a profit and loss account and balance sheet for Port Peter plc for the year to 31 December 20X4.

Tutor-based assignment

This assignment can be attempted and brought along to a tutorial for feedback purposes or used as directed by the lecturer/tutor.

T7.1 Chua Lim Hi-tech Business Systems plc
       (a) From the following information provided see if you can prepare a profit and loss account for the year to 30 June 20X5 and a balance sheet as at that date.

Trial balance 30 June 20X5	Debit £000	Credit £000
Ordinary shares authorised and issued, fully paid in £1 shares		8,000
Share premium account		800
10% debentures		1,000
Profit and loss account balance		300
Freehold land and buildings at cost	8,500	
Computer hardware, office fixtures & equipment	1,600	
Vehicles at cost	400	
Provision for depreciation on computer hardware etc.		400
Provision for depreciation of vehicles		100
Sales and purchases	7,000	9,980
Stock at 1 July 20X4	940	
Debtors and creditors	850	980
General expenses	150	
Salaries	1,040	
Discount allowed and received	20	60
Directors' fees	720	
Provision for bad and doubtful debts		50
Debenture interest	100	
Telephone, stationery and printing	20	
Rates and insurance	50	
Audit fees	10	
Interim dividend paid to ordinary shareholders	160	
Cash and bank balances	110	
	£21,670	£21,670

The following information is also available:

Note
1. The closing stock at 30 June 20X5 amounted to £1,060,000.
2. The rates and insurance figure includes £10,000 paid in advance.
3. Depreciation on computer hardware, office fixtures and equipment is at the rate of 25% of cost per annum.
4. Depreciation of motor vehicles is at 25% of book value (i.e. 25% of cost less depreciation).
5. The provision for bad debts is to be increased by £30,000.
6. Corporation tax for the year is estimated at £250,000.
7. The proposed final dividend for the year is £200,000.

(b) Discuss and briefly comment on the accounting treatment of the freehold land and buildings and the depreciation of computer hardware, office fixtures and equipment.

Further reading

Black, G., *Introduction to Accounting*, Financial Times Prentice Hall, 2000
Hussey, J. and Hussey, R., *Business Accounting*, Macmillan, 1998
Pizzey, A., *Finance and Accounting for Non-specialist Students*, Financial Times Prentice Hall, 1998
Wood, F. and Sangster, A., *Business Accounting 1*, Financial Times Prentice Hall, 1999

Useful websites

www.booksites.net/black
www.macmillan-business.co.uk
www.booksites.net/wood

Performance measurement – the interpretation and analysis of financial statements

You should now be reasonably familiar with the principal accounting statements and have developed an understanding of the concepts on which they are based.

When you have completed this chapter you should be able to:

☐ analyse financial statements by using ratio analysis, and interpret the results;

☐ identify the requirements for effective ratio analysis and inter-firm comparisons;

☐ prepare a ratio analysis using the working notes system;

☐ appreciate the limitations of ratio analysis.

The analysis and interpretation of financial statements using accounting ratios

Ratio analysis is the tool by which we attempt to measure and compare financial performance. However, you must appreciate from the outset that the accounting ratios on their own are pretty meaningless. They should be looked at in conjunction with other data and not in isolation. The principal reasons for using *ratio analysis* are to:

☐ identify areas in which the company needs to carry out further investigations;

☐ pinpoint the areas in which the company may improve its performance or would appear to have a differential advantage over its competitors;

☐ provoke questions;

☐ enable comparisons to be made internally with earlier years, and externally with industry figures and the performance of competitors. However, you must remember that when it comes to inter-company (inter-firm) comparisons the ratios will be meaningless unless you compare like with like. The source data must have been arrived at using similar accounting policies and the ratios must be computed in the same way.

Which ratios should we use?

Ratio analysis is a minefield. There are numerous ratios, conflicting opinions and a vast amount of terminology.

The ratios that we advocate here are just a small selection of the ratios that can be used. However, they should provide you with a good framework with which to interpret and assess the financial performance of a company or companies.

Ratios may be classified in a number of ways; we will group them as follows:

☐ Profitability

This helps you to answer questions such as:
  —Am I getting a satisfactory return on my investment?
  —Are we getting a good return on all of the capital that has been invested in the business?
  —How does our return on capital compare with that of our competitors?

☐ Liquidity

This is all about the company's ability to pay its debts, the management of its working capital and, in particular, cash flow.

☐ Efficiency

This looks at the way in which the company uses and manages its assets.

☐ Capital structure

This is about the composition of and the relationship between the *equity* (i.e. the ordinary share capital or the ordinary share capital plus reserves) and *debt* (i.e. the other long-term sources of finance, such as preference shares, debentures, long-term loans).

☐ Employees

This is used to assess the efficiency with which the labour force is being used.

☐ Investment

This takes a look at the financial performance of the company's shares.

We will now take a more in-depth view of each group, and provide you with an indication as to why the ratios are used, who uses them, and how they are calculated. To illustrate the calculations in a practical way, we will use the data provided in Figure 8.1 relating to Bekiboo plc. Note that, throughout, all of the calculations are in £000s. Figure 8.1 shows an abridged version of the accounts of Bekiboo plc.

Bekiboo plc
Profit and loss account year ended 30 September

(£000s)		YEAR 4		YEAR 5
Sales		3,000		3,600
Less Cost of sales		1,800		2,400
Gross profit		1,200		1,200
Less Expenses (including debenture				
interest and depreciation)		800		900
Net profit before tax		400		300
Corporation tax		80		50
Net profit after tax		320		250
Less dividends (paid and proposed)		40		46
		280		204
Balance b/f	(year 3)	500	(year 4)	780
		780		984

Balance sheet as at 30 September

(£000s)			YEAR 4		YEAR 5
Fixed assets:					
Cost			1,260		2,534
Depreciation			200		400
Written-down value		**(A)**	1,060		£2,134
Current assets:	year 3				
Stock	240		300		290
Debtors	320		250		420
Bank			230		40
		(B)	780		750
Less **Current liabilities**	year 3				
Trade creditors	145	135		265	
Proposed dividend	25	25	160**(C)**	35	300**(C)**
Net worth (A) + (B) – (C)			**£1,680**		**£2,584**
Ordinary share capital (in £1 shares)			400		600
Reserves:					
Share premium account			—		200
Retained earnings (P&L account balance)			780		984
			1,180		1,784
Long-term debt:					
10% debentures			500		800
Capital employed			**£1,680**		**£2,584**
Other information:					
Market price per share			£1.75		£2.20
			£000		£000
Interest paid (included in the					
calculation of the net paid					
before tax)			40		65
Purchases			1,600		2,200

Figure 8.1 – Financial data of Bekiboo plc

Profitability ratios

Gross profit to sales

This is of great interest to the management of the company and also to the tax authorities. It indicates the average mark-up on the products or services that have been sold during the period. When you are dealing with millions or thousands of pounds, a small percentage increase or decrease in the gross margin (mark-up) can have a significant impact upon the profits.

Figure 8.2 gives a worked example of gross profit to sales which is calculated as follows:

$$\frac{\text{Gross profit}}{\text{Sales}} \times 100$$

Year 4	Year 5
$\frac{\text{£1,200}}{\text{£3,000}} \times 100 = 40\%$	$\frac{\text{£1,200}}{\text{£3,600}} \times 100 = 33.33\%$

Figure 8.2 – Gross profits to sales ratio

Possible reasons for the fall from 40% to 33.33% shown in Figure 8.2 could be:

☐ a reduction in selling prices;

☐ an increase in the cost of raw materials;

☐ an increase in carriage inwards, i.e. the carriage paid on materials purchased;

☐ stock losses due to pilferage, poor storage or obsolescence;

☐ stocktaking errors, e.g. pricing errors, or stock simply being omitted from the stock-taking sheets.

Net profit to sales (net margin)

In addition to the factors that affect the gross profit, the net profit/sales percentage is affected by what is happening to the overhead expenses and depreciation.

Figure 8.3 gives a worked example of the net profit to sales ratio which is calculated as follows:

$$\frac{\text{Net profit before tax}}{\text{Sales}} \times 100$$

Year 4	Year 5
$\dfrac{400}{£3,000} \times 100 = 13.33\%$	$\dfrac{300}{£3,600} \times 100 = 8.33\%$
i.e. £13.33 for every £100 of sales	i.e. £8.33 for every £100 of sales

Figure 8.3 – Net profits to sales ratio

Again, this will be useful for management because it helps them to keep a watchful eye on their overhead expenses.

The decrease in the net profit/sales percentage shown in Figure 8.3 could be caused by a variety of factors, which may have increased the overhead expenditure, such as the following:

☐ moving premises to an area where rents and/or business rates are higher;

☐ changes in the company's policy on the financing of fixed assets, e.g. renting or leasing;

☐ changes in the company's depreciation policy;

☐ an increase in bad debts and/or the provision for bad debts;

☐ more interest to pay on debentures. In Bekiboo plc some £300,000 more debentures were issued in year 5;

☐ the shedding of personnel, i.e. a reduction in the labour force and/or working less overtime;

☐ creative accounting, e.g. carrying forward significant stocks of stationery to the next accounting period, prepaid advertising.

Return on investment

Return on investment (ROI) can also be called *return on capital employed (ROCE)* or *return on assets*.

Financial management is particularly concerned with the productivity of all the capital employed. Thus, companies like to have an overall indication of the productivity of all their capital employed. The following ratio satisfies this need:

$$\frac{\text{Net profit before tax} + \text{Loan and debenture interest}}{\text{Capital employed (less Intangibles, if any)}} \times 100$$

or in other words:

$$\frac{\text{Net profit before interest and tax (NPBIT)}}{\text{Capital employed (less Intangibles, if any)}} \times 100$$

This ratio is demonstrated in Figure 8.4. The debenture interest was added back so that the ratio could show the return on all capital, irrespective of where it came from. Business is all about investing money in it, putting that money to work, and then being able to generate a satisfactory return for those who have provided it.

Year 4	Year 5
$\dfrac{£400 + £40}{£1,680} \times 100 = 26.19\%$	$\dfrac{£300 + £65}{£2,584} \times 100 = 14.13\%$

Figure 8.4 – Return on investment (ROI) ratio

The reasons for an improvement (or deterioration) in this ratio are those factors that explain the gross/sales percentage and net profit/sales percentage plus movements in share capital, reserves and long-term debt. In the case of Bekiboo plc there has been a significant increase in fixed assets. The benefit from this investment may take some time before it generates additional profits.

Operating profits to capital employed

This profitability measure focuses on the return generated from operating activities, and is computed as follows:

$$\frac{\text{Operating profit}}{\text{Capital employed}} \times 100$$

The **operating profit** is the trading profit from operating activities and does *not* therefore include profits from non-operating activities, such as rents received, investment income and extraordinary items, e.g. one-off currency gains.

Other authors may use net profit before tax or net profit after tax over capital employed. Also, note that capital employed equals ordinary share capital plus reserves, plus preference share capital (if any), plus long-term loans and debentures. Capital employed can also equal total assets less intangibles, less current liabilities, i.e. the net tangible assets (net worth less intangibles).

Liquidity ratios

Liquidity ratios are important to the management, shareholders, lenders and creditors because liquidity ratios provide a measure of the company's ability to pay its debts. A company can be quite profitable but still have liquidity problems. *Profitability and liquidity do not go hand in hand.* The ratios should provide an indication of whether or not the company has liquidity problems or excess liquidity.

The current ratio

The current ratio is given as follows:

$$\frac{\text{Current assets}}{\text{Current liabilities}}$$

A worked example of the current ratio is shown in Figure 8.5.

Year 4	Year 5
$\frac{£780}{£160} = 4.88$	$\frac{£750}{£300} = 2.50$
i.e. for every £1 owing to current liabilities they have £4.88 cover	i.e. for every £1 owing to current liabilities they have £2.50 cover

Figure 8.5 – The current ratio

It is difficult to comment on Figure 8.5 without a benchmark. If we assume that the industry average is 2 : 1, it would appear that for year 4 Bekiboo plc had excess liquidity. However, it is quite likely that this was used to invest in new fixed assets in year 5, because the bank balance appeared to be high at £230,000, and fell in year 5 to £40,000.

The acid test

The acid test (or quick) ratio is expressed as follows:

$$\frac{\text{Liquid assets (i.e. current assets less stocks)}}{\text{Current liabilities}}$$

As a rule of thumb, this ratio should be around 1.00 (i.e. one-to-one). However, many industries work on less than one to one. If, in the example shown in Figure 8.6, the industry average for the two years were 0.90 for year 4 and 0.85 for year 5, then clearly the picture portrayed by the ratios of 3.00 and 1.54, respectively, signifies excess liquidity.

Year 4	Year 5
$\dfrac{£780 - £300}{£160} = 3.00$	$\dfrac{£750 - £290}{£300} = 1.54$
i.e. for every £1 owing to current liabilities the company has £3 cover	i.e. for every £1 owing to current liabilities the company has £1.54 cover

Figure 8.6 – The acid test ratio

Efficiency ratios

The ratios that are grouped under this heading can also be referred to as *activity ratios* or *asset utilisation ratios*. They are of particular interest to management and analysts because they provide a measure of how efficiently the company is managing its assets and working capital.

The average collection period

This credit control ratio provides an indication of how long it is taking the company to collect its debts. It is, therefore, of particular importance to those who are involved in the company's financial management. The ratio is expressed as follows:

$$\frac{\text{Average debtors}}{\text{Sales}} \times 365 = \text{Average collection period in days}$$

The average debtors are: last year's balance sheet debtors plus this year's balance sheet debtors, divided by two.

From the example show in Figure 8.7 it can be seen that Bekiboo plc's debtors are taking around one day longer to pay the money owing from them for year 5 when compared with year 4. If the industry average is 60 days, which is not untypical, then the company's credit control function would appear to be doing a good job. However, this could have been achieved by offering generous discounts for prompt payment. A small percentage discount for early settlement does have a high APR (annual percentage rate of interest)!

The credit period taken

Creditors, from whom goods and services have been purchased on credit, are a source of short-term finance. Financial managers will be interested in this ratio to see if they are

121

Year 4	Year 5
(£000)	(£000)
Average debtors $= \dfrac{320 + 250}{2}$	Average debtors $= \dfrac{250 + 420}{2}$
$= 285$	$= 335$
$\dfrac{285}{3,000} \times 365 = 35$ days	$\dfrac{335}{3,600} \times 365 = 34$ days
(rounded up)	(rounded up)

Figure 8.7 – Debt collection (average collection period) ratio

paying off their debts too slowly or too quickly when compared with industry figures. The creditors will be interested in the figure so that they can compare it with the time it is taking the company to pay their amounts owing.

$$\frac{\text{Average creditors}}{\text{Sales}} \times 365 = \text{Credit period taken in days}$$

$$\frac{\text{Average creditors}}{\text{Purchases}} \times 365 = \text{Credit period taken in days}$$

The average creditors are last year's balance sheet creditors plus this year's balance sheet creditors, divided by two.

The second of the two calculations is the more realistic of the two (Figure 8.8). However, if the purchases figure is not available, then you have no choice but to use the

Year 4	Year 5
(£000)	(£000)
Average creditors $\dfrac{145 + 135}{2} = \underline{140}$	Average creditors $\dfrac{135 + 265}{2} = \underline{200}$
using the sales figure:	
$\dfrac{140}{3,000} \times 365 = 17$ days	$\dfrac{200}{3,600} \times 365 = 20$ days
using the purchases figure:	
$\dfrac{140}{1,600} \times 365 = \textbf{32 days}$	$\dfrac{200}{2,200} \times 365 = \textbf{33 days}$

Figure 8.8 – Finance from creditors (credit period taken) ratio

sales figure. It is assumed that the purchases were £1,600,000 for year 4 and £2,200,000 for year 5.

If the industry average is 45 days, it would appear from the data in Figure 8.8 that the company is paying off its debts too quickly. However, if this is to secure generous cash discounts for prompt payment it may not be such a bad idea. After all, as mentioned earlier, a small percentage discount allowed for prompt payment does have a high APR (annual percentage rate).

Stock turnover

Stock turnover is also known as *'stock turn'*, and it shows the number of times that the average stock held is sold in a given period. Stock represents capital tied up, so it is preferable to have a rapid rate of stock turnover to ensure that it is tied up for a minimum amount of time. The average stock is computed by dividing the opening stock plus the closing stock of the period by two. Two example calculations follow:

(a) $\dfrac{\text{Sales}}{\text{Average stocks}} = \text{The rate of stock turnover}$

(b) $\dfrac{\text{Cost of sales}}{\text{Average stocks}} = \text{The rate of stock turnover}$

The second of the calculations is the more realistic of the two because stocks (i.e. inventory) tend to be valued at cost price or lower. However, in cases where the cost of sales information is not available, the first calculation will have to be used.

If we divide the rate of stock turnover by 365, it tells us the average time for which the stock is held before being sold. For (b) of Figure 8.9, this would work out at:
For year 4 (365/6.66) = 55 days
For year 5 (365/8.14) = 45 days.

Year 4	Year 5
(£000)	(£000)
$\dfrac{240 + 300}{2}$ Average stock = 270	$\dfrac{300 + 290}{2}$ Average stock = 295
(a) $\dfrac{3,000}{270} = 11.11$ times	(a) $\dfrac{3,600}{295} = 12.20$ times
(b) $\dfrac{1,800}{270} = 6.66$ times	(b) $\dfrac{2,400}{295} = 8.14$ times

Figure 8.9 – The rate of stock turnover (stock turn) ratio

The higher the rate of turnover, the shorter the period of time for which stock is being carried. Thus, the above figures illustrate that the position has improved, i.e. stock is being tied up for 45 days compared with 55 days.

This means that there is also likely to be lower wastage caused by deterioration and obsolescence. A rapid rate of turnover equals fast-moving stock and less capital tied up.

Sales to fixed assets

This ratio provides a measure of asset utilisation. It should be treated with caution when attempting to carry out an inter-firm comparison. This is because companies may rent or lease a lot of their fixed assets. Fixed assets that are rented or leased (other than leasehold property) do not appear in the balance sheet, and are referred to as 'off-balance-sheet financing.'
A decision also has to be taken as to which fixed assets should be included in the ratio. Should we include all of the fixed assets or just the manufacturing fixed assets? Thus, we can calculate it in a number of ways, two of which are:

$$\frac{\text{Sales}}{\text{Fixed assets}}$$

$$\frac{\text{Sales}}{\text{Manufacturing fixed assets}}$$

Note that there is insufficient information provided in Figure 8.1 for Bekiboo plc from which to calculate the second of the two ratios.

According to the figures shown in Figure 8.10 the company became less efficient in year 5, generating a lower sales figure per £1 invested in fixed assets. However, the dramatic increase in fixed assets may not have taken place until towards the end of year 5 and, therefore, the benefit of the new investment should have an impact on the next year's and future years' performance. On the other hand, the company could have been caught out by a downturn in the economy.

Year 4	Year 5
$\frac{3,000}{1,060} = 2.83$	$\frac{3,600}{£2,584} = 1.39$
i.e. generating £2.83 of sales for every £1 invested in fixed assets	i.e. generating £1.39 of sales for every £1 invested in fixed assets.

Figure 8.10 – Sales to fixed assets ratio

Capital structure (gearing) ratios

Gearing (or leverage) is all about the relationship between the *equity*, i.e. ordinary share capital plus reserves, and *debt*, i.e. the other forms of long-term financing, including preference shares, long-term loans, debentures, and, if circumstances warrant it, the bank overdraft.

A company that has a high proportion of long-term debt financing is referred to as being *high-geared*. A company with a low proportion of long-term debt financing is said to be *low-geared*. In the event of adverse trading conditions it is the more highly geared companies that suffer, because of their obligations to make interest payments or repayments of capital and interest on long-term loans and debentures. The ratio is of particular importance to the company's financial management and the external providers of capital.

Gearing (leverage)

Examples of gearing ratios are as follows:

1. $\dfrac{\text{Debt (excluding the bank overdraft)}}{\text{Debt (excluding the bank overdraft)} + \text{Ordinary share capital} + \text{reserves}} \times 100$

2. As above, but including the bank overdraft.

3. $\dfrac{\text{Debt}}{\text{Equity (i.e. issued ordinary shares} + \text{reserves)}} \times 100$

which is also called the Debt/Equity ratio or the Borrowings/Ordinary Shareholders' Funds ratio.

For the example shown in Figure 8.11, it can be seen that the gearing has gone up slightly during year 5. To make a more informed comment you need to look at the industry figures. What is high- or low-geared will depend upon the industry in which the company operates, e.g. below the industry average could be classed as low, above could be classed as high. We will take a more in-depth look at gearing and capital structure in Chapter 10.

Year 4	Year 5
(£000)	(£000)
$\dfrac{500}{1,680} \times 100 = 29.76$	$\dfrac{800}{2,584} \times 100 = 30.96\%$

Figure 8.11 – Gearing ratio (using the example 1 calculation)

Interest cover

This is an income-based measure of gearing. It is of interest to the company's financial management and long-term lenders, such as debenture holders, bankers, etc. It shows how well the company can cover their interest payments, and is calculated as follows:

$$\frac{\text{Net profit before interest and tax (NPBIT)}}{\text{Loan and debenture interest}}$$

It can be observed from a review of Figure 8.12 that the slight increase in the gearing, coupled with the reduction in profits, has had an effect on the interest cover. Because of their higher gearing and increased investment in fixed assets (i.e. additional security), Bekibo plc are in a very good position to raise further debt capital, i.e. long-term loans and debentures secured on their assets should they need more finance.

Year 4		Year 5	
(£000)		(£000)	
Net before tax	400	Net profit before tax	300
Add back Debenture interest	40	*Add back* Debenture interest	65
NPBIT	440	NPBIT	365
$\dfrac{440}{40} = 11.00$ times		$\dfrac{365}{65} = 5.61$ times	

Figure 8.12 – Interest cover ratio

If we include the preference dividend in the calculation, the ratio then becomes known as the fixed charge cover, and the calculation is as follows:

$$\frac{\text{Net profit before interest and tax}}{\text{Loan interest plus debenture interest plus preference dividend}}$$

Employee ratios

Employee ratios tend to be used in an attempt to assess the productivity and efficiency of the labour force. Again, care has to be exercised when carrying out inter-firm comparisons to take account of the degree of mechanisation and the use of automation; and the location. For instance, wage rates for the same type of work could be higher or lower in other parts of the United Kingdom or Europe. Four types of employee ratios are detailed as follows:

☐ Average remuneration per employee:

$$\frac{\text{Total wages/salaries paid to employees for the year}}{\text{Average number of employees on the payroll}}$$

☐ Net profit per employee:

$$\frac{\text{Net profit before tax}}{\text{Average number of employees on the payroll}}$$

☐ Sales per employee

$$\frac{\text{Sales}}{\text{Average number of employees on the payroll}}$$

☐ Directors' efficiency

$$\frac{\text{Directors' remuneration (salaries, fees, etc.)}}{\text{Net profit before tax + Directors' remuneration}} \times 100$$

The fourth of these ratios shows the directors' earnings as a percentage of the profits generated after adding back their earnings, which is useful for interfirm comparisons and trade unions. Why a directors' efficiency ratio? Directors are responsible for the success of their company, especially when it comes to the *bottom line*, i.e. the profit or loss.

Investment ratios

This group of ratios looks at the financial performance of the company relating to the ordinary shares. The financial management, existing ordinary shareholders, would-be investors, analysts and competitors will all be very interested in these ratios.

Earnings/shareholders' equity (return on equity)

The *earnings/shareholders' equity* (or *return-on-equity ratio*) is a measure of the return on investment applicable to the ordinary shareholders. It is computed as follows:

$$\frac{\text{Net profit after tax less preference dividend (if any)}}{\text{Equity, i.e. issued ordinary share capital plus reserves}} \times 100$$

This ratio helps answer the question by ordinary shareholders of, what is in it for me? The ratio looks at what is left for the ordinary shareholders after paying or providing for the business expenses, including debenture and loan interest, directors' remuneration, taxation and preference dividends. Thus, it is in fact a ratio that reflects the self-interest of the ordinary shareholders, i.e. the equity shareholders.

The decrease in the figures shown in Figure 8.13 is probably due to the new and significant investment in fixed assets, which should benefit future accounting periods.

Year 4	Year 5
$\dfrac{320}{1180} \times 100 = 27.12\%$	$\dfrac{250}{1784} \times 100 = 14.01\%$

Figure 8.13 – Earnings/shareholders' equity ratio

Dividend yield (on ordinary shares)

The dividend yield ratio (Figure 8.14) simply relates the dividend to the market price of an ordinary share. However, it does give some idea to a potential investor of the expected rate of return on investment in terms of cash paid out. The ratio is expressed as follows:

$$\frac{\text{Dividend per share}}{\text{Market price per ordinary share}} \times 100$$

YEAR 4	YEAR 5
Dividend per share = £40,000 ÷ 400,000 shares = 0.10	Dividend per share = £46,000 ÷ 600,000 shares = 0.767
$\dfrac{£0.10}{£1.75} \times 100 = 5.71\%$	$\dfrac{£0.0767}{£2.20} 100 = 3.49\%$
i.e. generating £5.71 for every £100 invested at the share price concerned	i.e. generating £3.49 for every £100 invested at the share price concerned

Figure 8.14 – The dividend yield ratio

However, the question of which share price to use is debatable. Should it be the share price at the start or end of the period, or an average covering the whole of the period? Because share prices may fluctuate significantly, so it is perhaps fairer that an average be used. Thus the return calculated will then give the return on the average value of the shares for the period.

You should also remember that, in addition to dividends, the holders also receive capital gains (or losses) on their investment.

Earnings per ordinary share

The *earnings per ordinary share ratio* is also called the *earnings per share (EPS) ratio* and is expressed as follows:

$$\frac{\text{Net profit after tax less preference dividend (if any)}}{\text{Number of ordinary shares issued}}$$

The EPS is a measure of the earning power of each share and is closely linked to the share's market value. Thus, it shows the amount generated per share for the period (see Figure 8.15). Usually, a portion will be paid out as dividends and the balance ploughed back and retained in the company.

YEAR 4	YEAR 5
$\frac{\text{£320,000}}{400,000}$ = £0.80 per share	$\frac{\text{£250,000}}{600,000}$ = £0.417 per share

Figure 8.15 – Earnings per ordinary share ratio

Dividend cover

The dividend cover ratio shows the number of times that the current earnings cover the ordinary dividend that has been paid and/or proposed. It can be calculated as follows:

$$\frac{\text{Earnings per share}}{\text{Dividend per share}}$$

or, using the totals:

$$\frac{\text{Net profit after tax less preference dividend}}{\text{Total ordinary share dividend}}$$

Thus, it could be said that this ratio provides an indication of the likelihood that the company will be able to maintain its dividends while being able to enjoy a healthy plough-back of profits. A worked example of this ratio is shown in Figure 8.16.

YEAR 4	YEAR 5
$\dfrac{£0.80}{0.10} = 8$ times	$\dfrac{£0.417}{0.0767} = 5.44$ times
i.e. for every £1 needed to pay the dividend £8 has been generated	i.e. for every £1 needed to pay the dividend £5.44 has been generated

Figure 8.16 – Dividend cover ratio

The price/earnings ratio

A high **price/earnings (PE) ratio** means a high price in relation to earnings. This possibly reflects *market expectations* of greater things to come, i.e. a bright future is forecast.

A low PE implies a low price in relation to earnings. The reason for this could be low expectations on the part of the market. However, entrepreneurs have been known to take over companies with low PEs and over a period of two to five years perform a turnaround and then sell them, making millions of pounds in the process.

The price/earnings ratio is calculated as follows:

$$\frac{\text{Market price per ordinary share}}{\text{Earnings per ordinary share}}$$

This is the most commonly accepted relationship between a company's ability to generate profits and the market price of its ordinary shares.

The higher PE in year 5 shown in Figure 8.17 could be attributable to an increase in market expectations of anticipated good results in the future, possibly as the new investment in fixed assets begins to bear fruit.

YEAR 4	YEAR 5
$\dfrac{1.75}{£0.80} = 2.19$ times	$\dfrac{£2.20}{£0.417} = 5.28$ times

Figure 8.17 – The price/earnings (PE) ratio

The inversion of this ratio provides a ratio known as the *capitalisation rate* (or *earnings yield*), the rate at which the market is *capitalising* the value of current earnings, and is expressed as follows:

$$\frac{\text{Earnings per ordinary share}}{\text{Market price per ordinary share}} \times 100$$

As with the dividend yield, this ratio also gives an indication of the return on investment (ROI). These ratios can be compared to those of other similar-sized companies within the same industrial sector. A worked example of this ratio is shown in Figure 8.18.

YEAR 4	YEAR 5
$\frac{£0.80}{£1.75} \times 100 = 45.71\%$	$\frac{£0.417}{£2.20} \times 100 = 18.95\%$

Figure 8.18 – The capitalisation rate (or earnings yield) ratio

Using the information

The information that is generated can be presented using a comparative statement which could be drawn up along the lines of Figure 8.19.

Ratio	This year	Last year	Reasons for variances/comments
Turnover	£531 m	£452 m	
Profit before tax	£38 m	£24 m	
Earnings per share	24.4p	11.75p	
Dividend cover	3.0 times	1.4 times	

Figure 8.19 – Suggested layout for the comparative statement

The statement illustrated includes on the right-hand side a *working notes column* reserved for explanations of the reasons for variances and comments, e.g. strengths and weaknesses, and interrelationships between variances. The comparative statement could also include an assortment of data and ratios covering other areas such as liquidity, profitability, capital structure.

The format used in Figure 8.19 could also be used to compare two different companies, e.g. company A compared with company B, instead of this year/last year as shown.

Having made the working notes during the course of the analysis, the principal findings could then be summarised in a *conclusions section* together with any recommendations. Look at Figure 8.20 and see if you can spot the year in which Timvik experienced difficulties, i.e. a year that looks out of line when compared to the other years.

Timvik	Year	1	2	3	4	5	6
Liquidity:							
Current ratio		1.34	1.65	0.89	1.20	1.50	1.70
Acid test		0.70	0.90	0.48	0.60	0.65	0.95
Debtors' average collection period (days)		70	60	58	50	47	45

Figure 8.20 – Suggested layout for company financial analysis

You should have observed that year 3 was out of line and, yes, the company did encounter problems in that year. What were the problems? On the current ratio the company only had £89 of current assets to cover every £100 of current liabilities that it owed. The acid test position had also deteriorated significantly. For every £100 owing to its current liabilities, the company only had £48 worth of cover in terms of its liquid assets. However, its average collection period, i.e. the speed at which it collects its debts in from debtors, improved. This could be because of the adverse liquidity position in which it found itself. If you are short of cash you are encouraged to collect your outstanding debts more quickly. This trend continued and currently in year 6 the company is, on average, taking around 45 days to collect its debts. Also, you can see from the figures that since year 3, the problem year, the company has improved its liquidity position.

The important message of Figure 8.20 concerning financial analysis is that *you need at least five or six years' figures* to be in a position to make a more realistic appraisal, e.g. the identification of trends. It is difficult to make sound judgements simply on the basis of a two-year analysis.

A comparison of ratios, one year with another for the same company, does not indicate whether the performance was good, bad or indifferent. Hence, the quest for a bench-mark/yardstick, i.e. an objective standard against which performance can be measured. The benchmarks that can be used are *industry figures*, either by comparing with other companies in the same area that are of a similar nature or by looking at industry averages. A wealth of this type of information is available on computer databases, the World Wide Web (www)

	Motor component industry		
Company	N	O	P
Year-end	Dec 20X6	Jul 20X6	Dec 20X6
Ratio:			
Return on capital employed	17.0%	17.5%	19.1%
Profit margin	6.3%	8.5%	8.3%
Average collection period (months)	4.4	5.0	4.6
Gearing	47.7%	32.8%	39.1%
Interest cover (times)	6.1	7.1	6.4
Current ratio (times)	1.8	1.8	1.7
Acid test (times)	0.9	1.0	0.8

Figure 8.21 – Industry figures – motor components

and numerous publications. However, it is not always an easy task to carry out; for example, company 'O' in Figure 8.21 has a different year-end to the other companies! Thus, the comparison does not cover the same trading period.

The limitations of ratio analysis

One of the principal limitations of ratio analysis is the inadequacy of the source data (i.e. profit and loss accounts and balance sheets) which may be caused by the following:

☐ the way in which the *accounting concepts* are applied, for instance the use of subjective judgement, and the inconsistency with which certain figures are calculated;

☐ preparing accounts with the *tax authorities* in mind, e.g. the distinction between repairs and renewals and fixed assets is open to differing interpretations. Should we charge the expenditure (i.e. write it off) in the profit and loss account as an expense, or carry it forward in the balance sheet (i.e. capitalise it and treat it as an asset)?

☐ a change in the *accounting policies*;

☐ *'off-balance-sheet financing'*, e.g. the renting or leasing of machinery, plant, equipment and motor vehicles;

☐ *window-dressing (creative accounting)*, i.e. making the accounts look better or worse than they really are, e.g. having a special effort to collect cash in from debtors in the last few months of the accounting period. This means that the debtors' figure at the year-end could be totally unrepresentative of the position that existed throughout the year;

☐ The *revaluation of fixed assets*, e.g. freehold land and buildings.

Inter-firm comparisons can, therefore, be extremely difficult because the firms concerned could be using different accounting policies, applying the concepts in different ways and could be affected by off-balance-sheet financing, etc. This is why the most accurate and realistic comparisons are those that are done for internal reporting purposes and look at the company over a number of years. Even then, adjustments may have to be made to allow for changes in accounting policies, inflation, etc.

Another major limitation arises from the way in which some of the ratios are computed, for example the following:

☐ The treatment of *the bank overdraft*. Is it really a current liability? Nowadays, many companies do use it as a long-term source of funds. The way in which it is treated affects liquidity ratios and gearing ratios.

☐ Certain ratios use the sales figures when the cost of sales or the purchases figure would be more appropriate.

☐ Which *profit figure* should be used? Should it be:
  — Net profit before tax?
  — Net profit after tax?

— Net profit before interest and tax (NPBIT)?

☐ The *average creditors, debtors and stocks* are calculated using opening and closing balances. What happens throughout the period would thus appear to be irrelevant.

☐ Finally, the *terminology used* also acts as a limitation in that it does tend to confuse the user, for example capital employed, net assets and net worth can mean the same thing. Some gearing ratios include the bank overdraft, others exclude it. Return on investment can be called 'return on assets' or 'return on capital employed', and so on.

Summary: assessing financial performance – the interpretation and analysis of financial statements

Ratio analysis is a tool that is used in order to compare and evaluate financial performance. The source data from which the ratios are calculated may be internal, e.g. the company's own profit and loss account, appropriation account, balance sheet and data relating to debtors, creditors and stocks, etc., or external in the form of the published accounts of other companies and industry figures that are available from a variety of sources.

Ratios can help to:

☐ indicate areas in which further investigation is needed;

☐ highlight strengths and weaknesses

☐ provoke questions.

Ratios are of little value if they are used in isolation. To be useful, they need to be viewed in conjunction with other data, such as the following:

☐ information about the management;

☐ industry figures, which provide a benchmark with which more realistic comparisons and informed judgements can be made;

☐ the value of fixed assets and investments;

☐ opportunity costs, e.g. the returns available from alternative investments;

☐ government regulations and legislation already passed or pending;

☐ security, i.e. the degree to which the company has used its assets as security for loans and debentures.

The ratios

The following ratios should help you to make a reasonable assessment of the financial performance of a company.

Profitability

The *gross profit to sales ratio* is expressed as:

$$\frac{\text{Gross profit}}{\text{Sales}} \times 100$$

It indicates the average gross margin (mark-up) being made on the products or services that are being sold.

The *net profit to sales (net margin) ratio* is expressed as:

$$\frac{\text{Net profit before tax}}{\text{Sales}} \times 100$$

This shows how much profit is being generated by the sales and in addition to the effects of the gross profit it provides an indication as to what is happening to the overheads.

The *return on investment (ROI) ratio* (also called return on capital employed (ROCE) or return on assets) is expressed as:

$$\frac{\text{Net profit before interest and tax (NPBIT)}}{\text{Capital employed (less intangibles, if any)}} \times 100$$

This gives the overall return on all of the capital that has been invested in the business irrespective of the source from which it came, i.e. it is a measure of the productivity of all the capital invested in the business.

Operating profit to capital employed is:

$$\frac{\text{Operating profit}}{\text{Capital employed}} \times 100$$

It provides an indication of the return that is being earned by operating activities.

Liquidity

The *current ratio* (or the ratio of current assets to current liabilities) is expressed as:

$$\frac{\text{Current assets}}{\text{Current liabilities}}$$

This provides an indication of whether the company has excess liquidity, satisfactory liquidity or liquidity problems. It provides an indication of the company's ability to pay its short-term debts.

The *acid test* (or quick) *ratio* is expressed as:

$$\frac{\text{Liquid assets (i.e. current assets less stocks)}}{\text{Current liabilities}}$$

This is a key ratio used in the management of working capital, and looks at the ability to pay short-term debts with the liquid assets. As a general rule, this ratio is expected to be around one-to- one, i.e. £1 of liquid assets to every £1 owing to current liabilities. However, in practice the liquid assets tend to be less than £1 for every £1 owing to current liabilities.

Efficiency ratios

These ratios look at asset utilisation and provide an insight into the efficiency of inventory (stock) control and credit control.

The *average collection period ratio* is expressed as:

$$\frac{\text{Average debtors}}{\text{Sales}} \times 365$$

This provides us with an indication of how long it is taking to collect the amounts owing from our credit customers, i.e. our debtors.

The *credit period taken ratio* is expressed as:

$$\frac{\text{Average creditors}}{\text{Purchases (or sales if the purchases figure is not available)}} \times 365$$

This tells us the average time it takes us to pay our suppliers of goods on credit. Note that creditors represent a source of short-term financing to the company.

The *stock turnover ratio* is expressed as:

$$\frac{\text{Cost of sales (or sales)}}{\text{Average stock (i.e. opening plus closing stock divided by two)}} = \text{The rate of turnover}$$

This shows the number of times that the average stock held is sold in a given period of time.

The *sales to fixed assets ratio* is expressed as:

$$\frac{\text{Sales}}{\text{Fixed assets}} = \text{The overall efficiency with which the fixed assets are used}$$

or

$$\frac{\text{Sales}}{\text{Manufacturing fixed assets}} = \text{A measure of the utilisation of manufacturing fixed assets}$$

Capital structure ratios

The *gearing* (or leverage) *ratio* is expressed as:

$$\frac{\text{Debt, e.g. long-term loans and debentures}}{\text{Debt (with or without the bank overdraft) + ordinary share}} \times 100$$

This looks at the proportion of debt financing in relation to the total long-term financing and is of particular significance to financial management and the providers of finance.

The *debt to equity ratio* is expressed as follows:

$$\frac{\text{Debt}}{\text{Equity}}$$

Those companies with a high proportion of debt to equity, i.e. those that are highly geared, tend to be at greater risk in periods when trading conditions are poor. This is because they have to pay interest or repay capital and interest on debentures or loans irrespective of whether they are performing well, or performing badly.

Many companies nowadays use their bank overdraft as a long-term source of funds. Note that there are many more gearing ratios and that some authorities include the preference shares with the debt, whilst others include them as part of the equity! I suggest that, unless directed otherwise, you include preference shares with the debt, as they tend to be fixed interest, and usually do not have any voting rights.

The *interest cover ratio* is expressed as:

$$\frac{\text{Net profit before interest and tax}}{\text{Loan and debenture interest}}$$

This ratio shows how well the company can cover the interest it has to pay out. It is expressed as the number of times that it can cover the interest payments. If the preference dividend is added to the loan and debenture interest the ratio would then be described as the *fixed charge cover*.

Employee ratios

Employee ratios assess the productivity of labour in terms of sales and net profit. The ones that were covered in this chapter were:

☐ average remuneration per employee

☐ net profit per employee

☐ sales per employee

☐ directors' efficiency.

Investment ratios

Investment ratios are of particular significance to directors, shareholders, analysts, would-be investors and competitors.

The *earnings/shareholders' equity* (return on equity) *ratio* is expressed as:

$$\frac{\text{Net profit after tax, less preference dividends (if any)}}{\text{Equity (i.e. issued ordinary share capital + reserves)}} \times 100$$

This ratio provides the ordinary shareholders with an idea of what their return on investment is. The profit figure that is used in the calculation represents what is left for them after paying everything else including interest and tax, and dividends on preference shares.

The *dividend yield* can be expressed as:

$$\frac{\text{Dividend per ordinary share}}{\text{Market price per ordinary share}} \times 100$$

This ratio relates the profit distributed as dividend to the share price. It does not measure the return on investment for a shareholder because there are also the capital gains (*or capital losses*) on their shares to consider. However, it does provide a potential investor with an indication of the expected rate of return on investment in terms of cash paid out.

The *earnings per ordinary share* or earnings per share (EPS) *ratio* is expressed as:

$$\frac{\text{Net profit after tax less preference dividend}}{\text{Number of ordinary shares issued}}$$

This represents the earning power per share.

The *dividend cover* (on ordinary shares) *ratio* is expressed as:

$$\frac{\text{Earnings per share}}{\text{Dividend per share}}$$

This ratio shows how many times the company can cover its ordinary share dividends from its current earnings. It can also be calculated in the following way:

$$\frac{\text{Net profit after tax less preference dividend}}{\text{Total ordinary share dividend}}$$

The *price/earnings (PE) ratio* is expressed as:

$$\frac{\text{Market price per ordinary share}}{\text{Earnings per ordinary share}}$$

This ratio expresses the relationship between the company's ability to generate profits and the market price of its ordinary shares.

The *capitalisation rate* (or earnings yield ratio) is the PE ratio turned upside down, and is expressed as:

$$\frac{\text{Earnings per ordinary share}}{\text{Market price per ordinary share}} \times 100$$

It provides shareholders and investors with an indication of the current performance of the ordinary shares, i.e. it provides a measure of the cost of the equity share capital.

Self-checks

Attempt each of the self-checks, and compare your attempt with the relevant section of this chapter.

1. What are the principal reasons for using ratio analysis?
2. Describe briefly the possible reasons for a fall in the gross profit to sales ratio.
3. Which factors could cause a decrease in the net profit to sales ratio?
4. Which ratio provides an overall indication of the productivity of the capital employed?
5. What does the 'rule of thumb' suggest that the acid test ratio should be?
6. Why can a small percentage early settlement discount be expensive?
7. List two of the benefits that may result from having a rapid rate of stock turnover.
8. What is 'off-balance-sheet financing'?
9. When can a company be described as being 'highly geared'?
10. What could a low PE (price/earnings ratio) be a sign of?

Self-assessments

You will find the suggested answers to these self-assessments in Appendix 1.

A8.1   The following information relates to Intomarkt Consultants Ltd

Profit and loss account	£m
Sales	24
Less: Costs	12
	12
Less: Corporation tax	4
	8
Dividends payable (at 20p per share)	2
Retained profit for the year	6
Other information:	
Current market price of ordinary shares	£3.60
Number of ordinary shares in issue	10m

You are required to calculate:
Earnings per share
Price/earnings ratio
Dividend cover
Divided yield

A8.2   You have been provided with the following comparative information for Holme plc and Colne plc:

	Holme plc £000	Colne plc £000
Sales	5,000	10,000
Net profit before tax	1,000	1,600
Net profit after tax	800	1,200
Dividends proposed	200	Nil
Interest paid (deducted in computing net profit before tax)	60	400

Balance Sheet information

	£000	£000	£000	£000
Fixed assets		5,400		6,500
Current assets:				
Stock	1,000		2,400	
Debtors	800		1,200	
Cash and bank	200		—	
	2,000		3,600	
Current liabilities:				
Creditors	1,400		2,000	
Proposed dividends	200		—	
Bank overdraft	—		1,500	
	1,600	400	3,500	100
		£5,800		£6,600

Ordinary share capital	4,000	1,000
Reserves	800	1,600
Long-term loans	1,000	4,000
	£5,800	**£6,600**

Required

Calculate the following ratios for 20X8 for both Holme and Colne in order to compare the performances of the two companies (the industry average for each ratio is given below and indicated in brackets).

   Liquidity:
     Current ratio (2.00)
     Acid test (quick ratio) (0.90)
   Profitability:
     Net profit before tax to sales (20%)
     Return on investment (return on assets) (25%)
   Efficiency:
     Average collection period (60 days)
     Credit period taken (70 days)
     Stock turnover (7 times)
   Investment:
     Earnings/shareholders' equity (20%)
     Earnings per ordinary share (£0.30)

Having made your calculations and comparisons, prepare a brief report of your conclusions and recommendations.

A8.3

  (a) How should ratio analysis be used in practice?
  (b) What are the principal limitations of ratio analysis?
  (c) List the considerations that have to be taken into account when selecting another company with which to make a comparison of financial performance.

Tutor-based assignment

This assignment may be used for discussion, report writing and/or presentation purposes, as directed by your lecturer or tutor, and may involve you in some further research.

T8.1   'The figures that are used for financial analysis do have quite a number of drawbacks.' Discuss this statement.

Case studies incorporating a considerable amount of financial performance analysis are included in Chapter 11.

Further reading

Berry, A., *Financial Accounting: An Introduction*, International Thomson Business Press, 1999

Dodge, R., *Foundations of Business Accounting*, International Thomson Business Press, 1999

Harvey, D., Atrill, P. and McLaney, E., *Accounting for Business*, Butterworth-Heinemann, 2000

Holmes, G. and Sugden, A., *Interpreting Company Reports and Accounts*, Financial Times Prentice Hall, 2000

Hussey, J. and Hussey, R., *Business Accounting*, Macmillan Business, 1998

McKenzie, W., *FT Guide to Interpreting Company Reports and Accounts*, Financial Times Prentice Hall, 1998

Pendlebury, M. and Groves, R., *Company Accounts, Analysis, Interpretation and Understanding*, Thomson Learning, 2001

Pizzey, A., *Finance and Accounting for Non-specialist Students*, Financial Times Prentice Hall, 1998

Walton, P., *Financial Statement Analysis: An International Perspective*, Thomson Learning, 2000

Wood, F. and Sangster, A., *Business Accounting Vol. 2*, Financial Times Prentice Hall, 1999

Useful websites

www.bh.com/management
www.booksites.net
www.itbp.com
www.learn.co.uk/default.asp

Sources of industry data

UK Industrial Performance Analysis (published annually by ICC Business Publications Ltd)
Company annual reports and accounts
Company websites
Micro View by Extel and Micro Extat
WWW sources

9

The published financial statements of companies

The objective of this chapter is to provide you with some hands-on experience, via a series of projects, so that you will be able to add to and expand your existing knowledge. (For the remainder of this chapter we will, in the main, use the description 'published accounts' to mean the annual report and accounts of a company.)

Learning objectives

By looking at some real published accounts you should be able to do the following:

☐ understand the accounts;

☐ use the accounts;

☐ analyse the accounts by using some of the ratios described in Chapter 8;

☐ seek explanations about items that are new to you, such as extraordinary items, from business dictionaries, tutors, accountants, business contacts, etc;

☐ appreciate how certain of the figures have been calculated, such as fixed assets;

☐ know the kind of information that goes into the directors' report;

☐ identify and discuss the differences in accounting policies being followed by a number of companies;

☐ see how a profit and loss account or a balance sheet item is made up by a study of the notes to the accounts section of the published accounts;

☐ review the statistical data and/or ratio analysis which is included;

☐ see which of the statutory formats for the profit and loss account and the balance sheet have been adopted;

☐ understand the cash flow statement.

This chapter also provides you with a brief introduction to the role of the auditor.

The published accounts

For external reporting purposes, UK companies are bound by law to produce a set of accounts for publication, i.e. their annual report and accounts.

The *Companies Act 1985/89* prescribes the following:

- ☐ the format of the published accounts;
- ☐ the contents of the published accounts;
- ☐ the rules for computing figures that appear in those accounts;
- ☐ preparing the published *profit and loss accounts* according to one of the four statutory formats;
- ☐ publishing a *balance sheet* using one of the two statutory formats;
- ☐ adopting *historical accounting rules* which, with one or two exceptions, tend to follow existing practice. However, they may adopt any of the alternative accounting rules that are permitted by the Companies Act;
- ☐ providing information in the *directors' report*;
- ☐ including certain specific information in the *notes to the accounts*, such as the source of any increase or decrease in fixed assets;
- ☐ ignoring certain provisions contained in the Companies Act if doing so means that the accounts will show a true and fair view;
- ☐ publishing a section dealing with *accounting policies*.

Reporting exemptions for small and medium-sized companies

The Companies Act provides that small and medium-sized companies can be exempted from filing certain documents and information with the Registrar of Companies.

Filing exemptions for small companies

Small companies may file a modified balance sheet but need not file:

- ☐ a profit and loss account;
- ☐ the directors' report;
- ☐ details of higher-paid employees' and directors' emoluments;
- ☐ certain notes, e.g. accounting policies.

The Financial Reporting Standard for Smaller Entities was introduced in 1999 and updated in 2000 (effective from March 2000). Its coverage is vast.

Filing exemptions for medium-sized companies

Medium-sized companies may file a modified profit and loss account but do not have to disclose certain items by way of note.

Auditors and the modified accounts

A special auditors' report must verify that all the exemption criteria have been met. In addition the full text of the auditors' report contained in the full accounts must be filed with the modified accounts.

The statutory formats

The Companies Act 1985/89 provides formats that must be used in the published accounts of companies. However, there is a choice of four profit and loss formats, and of two balance sheet formats.

The statutory formats were introduced by the Companies Act 1981 and are as follows.

Profit and loss account formats

Format 1 (operational basis)

1. Turnover
2. Cost of sales
3. Gross profit or loss
4. Distribution costs
5. Administrative expenses
6. Other operating income
7. Income from shares in group companies
8. Income from shares in related companies
9. Income from other fixed-asset investments

10. Other interest receivable and similar income

11. Amounts written off investments

12. Interest payable and similar charges

13. Tax on profit or loss on ordinary activities

14. Profit or loss on ordinary activities after taxation

15. Extraordinary income

16. Extraordinary charges

17. Extraordinary profit or loss

18. Tax on ordinary profit or loss

19. Other taxes not shown under the above items

20. Profit or loss for the financial year

Format 2 (operational basis)

1. Turnover

2. Change in stocks of finished goods and work-in-progress

3. Own work capitalised

4. Other operating income

5. (a) Raw materials and consumables
   (b) Other external charges

6. Staff costs:
   (a) Wages and salaries
   (b) Social security costs
   (c) Other pension costs

7. Depreciation and other amounts written off tangible and intangible fixed assets

8. Other operating charges

9. Income from shares in group companies

10. Income from shares in related companies

11. Income from other fixed-asset investments

12. Other interest receivable and similar income

13. Amounts written off investments

14. Interest payable and similar charges

15. Tax on profit or loss on ordinary activities

16. Profit or loss on ordinary activities after taxation

17. Extraordinary income

18. Extraordinary charges

19. Extraordinary profit or loss
20. Tax on ordinary profit or loss
21. Other taxes not shown under the above items
22. Profit or loss for the financial year

Format 3 (type of expense basis)

A. Charges

1. Cost of sales
2. Distribution costs
3. Administrative expenses
4. Amounts written off investments
5. Interest payable and similar charges
6. Tax on profit or loss on ordinary activities
7. Profit or loss on ordinary activities after taxation
8. Extraordinary charges
9. Tax on extraordinary profit or loss
10. Other taxes not shown under the above items
11. Profit or loss for the financial year

B. Income

1. Turnover
2. Other operating income
3. Income from shares in group companies
4. Income from shares in related companies
5. Income from other fixed-asset investments
6. Other interest receivable and similar income
7. Profit or loss on ordinary activities after taxation
8. Extraordinary income
9. Profit or loss for the financial year

Format 4 (type of expense basis)

A. Charges

1. Reduction in stocks of finished goods and in work-in-progress
2. (a) Raw materials and consumables
   (b) Other external charges

3. Staff costs:
   (a) Wages and salaries
   (b) Social security costs
   (c) Other pension costs

4. (a) Depreciation and other amounts written off tangible and intangible fixed assets
   (b) Exceptional amounts written off current assets

5. Other operating charges

6. Amounts written off investments

7. Interest payable and similar charges

8. Tax on profit or loss on ordinary activities after taxation

9. Profit or loss on ordinary activities

10. Extraordinary charges

11. Tax on extraordinary profit or loss

12. Other taxes not shown under the above items

13. Profit or loss for the financial year

B. Income

1. Turnover

2. Increase in stocks of finished goods and in work-in-progress

3. Own work capitalised

4. Other operating income

5. Income from shares in group companies

6. Income from shares in related companies

7. Income from other fixed-asset investments

8. Other interest receivable and similar income

9. Profit or loss on ordinary activities after taxation

10. Extraordinary income

11. Profit or loss for the financial year

Balance sheet formats

Format 1

A. Called-up share capital not paid
B. Fixed assets

    I   Intangible assets
1. Development costs
2. Concessions, patents, licences, trade marks and similar rights and assets
3. Goodwill
4. Payments on account

    II Tangible assets
1. Land and buildings
2. Plant and machinery
3. Fixtures, fittings, tools and equipment
4. Payments on account and assets in course of construction

    III Investments
1. Shares in group companies
2. Loans to group companies
3. Shares in related companies
4. Loans to related companies
5. Other investments other than loans
6. Other loans
7. Own shares

C. Current assets

    I   Stocks
1. Raw materials and consumables
2. Work-in-progress
3. Finished goods and goods for resale
4. Payments on account

    II Debtors
1. Trade debtors
2. Amounts owed by group companies
3. Amounts owed by related companies
4. Other debtors
5. Called-up share capital not paid
6. Prepayments and accrued income

    III Investments
1. Shares in group companies
2. Own shares
3. Other investments

    IV Cash at bank and in hand

D. Prepayments and accrued income
E. Creditors: amounts falling due within one year

    1. Debenture loans

    2. Bank loans and overdrafts

    3. Payments received on account

    4. Trade creditors

    5. Bills of exchange payable

    6. Amounts owed to group companies

    7. Amounts owed to related companies

    8. Other creditors including taxation and social security

    9. Accruals and deferred income

F. Net current assets (liabilities)

G. Total assets less current liabilities

H. Creditors: amounts falling due after more than one year

    1. Debenture loans

    2. Bank loans and overdrafts

    3. Payments received on account

    4. Trade creditors

    5. Bills of exchange payable

    6. Amounts owed to group companies

    7. Amounts owed to related companies

    8. Other creditors including taxation and social security

    9. Accruals and deferred income

I. Provisions for liabilities and charges

    1. Pensions and similar obligations

    2. Taxation, including deferred taxation

    3. Other provisions

J. Accruals and deferred income

K. Capital and reserves

    I   Called-up share capital
    II   Share premium account
    III Revaluation reserve
    IV Other reserves
        1. Capital redemption reserve
        2. Reserve for own shares
        3. Reserves provided for by articles of association
        4. Other reserves

    V   Profit and loss account

Format 2

Assets

A. Called-up share capital not paid
B. Fixed assets

   I   Intangible assets
      1. Development costs
      2. Concessions, patents, licences, trade marks and similar rights and assets
      3. Goodwill
      4. Payments on account

   II   Tangible assets
      1. Land and buildings
      2. Plant and machinery
      3. Fixtures, fittings, tools and equipment
      4. Payments on account and assets in course of construction

   III Investments
      1. Shares in group companies
      2. Loans to group companies
      3. Shares in related companies
      4. Loans to related companies
      5. Other investments other than loans
      6. Other loans
      7. Own shares

C. Current assets

   I   Stocks
      1. Raw materials and consumables
      2. Work-in-progress
      3. Finished goods and goods for resale
      4. Payments on account

   II   Debtors
      1. Trade debtors
      2. Amounts owed by group companies
      3. Amounts owed by related companies
      4. Other debtors
      5. Called-up share capital not paid
      6. Prepayments and accrued income

   III Investments
      1. Shares in group companies
      2. Own shares
      3. Other investments

IV Cash at bank and in hand

D. Prepayments and accrued income

Liabilities

A. Capital and reserves

    I   Called-up share capital
    II Share premium
    III Revaluation reserve
    IV Other reserves
        1. Capital redemption reserve
        2. Reserve for own shares
        3. Reserves provided for by articles of association
        4. Other reserves

    V   Profit and loss account

B. Provisions for liabilities and charges

    1. Pensions and similar obligations
    2. Taxation including deferred taxation
    3. Other provisions

C. Creditors

    1. Debenture loans
    2. Bank loans and overdrafts
    3. Payments received on account
    4. Trade creditors
    5. Bills of exchange payable
    6. Amounts owed to group companies
    7. Amounts owed to related companies
    8. Other creditors including taxation and social security
    9. Accruals and deferred income

D. Accruals and deferred income

Group (consolidated) accounts

Where another company, i.e. a holding company, owns or controls a company or companies, i.e. subsidiary companies, group accounts are published. These will include a consolidated profit and loss account, and a consolidated balance sheet. A study of group accounts is outside the scope of this book. Suffice it to say that they do exist and you will, no doubt, come into contact with them during your review of real published accounts.

What kind of information must a company publish in its accounts or notes to the accounts?

The short answer to this question is 'enough to fill a book', i.e. a lot!

The following is a brief summary of some of the items you are likely to encounter:

☐ a breakdown of how the *operating profit and turnover* figures have been arrived at;

☐ details of *loans*, and an analysis of *interest payments*, e.g. on bank overdraft and loans;

☐ *taxation details*;

☐ *dividends* paid and proposed;

☐ Details of the *remuneration* paid or pension contributions relating to employees and directors;

☐ *retained earnings and movements in reserves*;

☐ if significant, charges for the *rent* or the *hire* of equipment, plant and machinery, and vehicles, etc.;

☐ *auditors' remuneration*;

☐ details of investments, investment income and rental income;

☐ details of *movements in fixed assets and the depreciation of fixed assets*, e.g. acquisitions, disposals, revaluations;

☐ *capital commitments*;

☐ how the individual *current asset or current liability figures* were arrived at, e.g. stocks, debtors, bank, cash, creditors;

☐ an analysis of *share capital, share premium, reserves and the profit and loss account* showing the source of any increase or decrease;

☐ information about *pensions*;

☐ details of any *contingent liability*, e.g. a debt the company may or may not be called upon to pay under a warranty or as a guarantor;

☐ *post-balance-sheet events*, e.g. the acquisition of a significant holding of ordinary shares in another company;

☐ *changes to accounting policies*;

☐ *corresponding figures for the previous accounting period*.

Corporate governance

The *Hampel Report and Combined Code* (1998) includes a significant number of recommendations from the earlier Cadbury and Greenbury reports. It seeks to protect investors and preserve and enhance the standing of companies listed on the UK stock exchange. It concerns itself with directors' duties and salaries, relationships with shareholders, institutional investors and auditors.

An introduction to the role of the auditor

The role of the auditor has been described as being that of a watchdog, rather than a bloodhound. The objectives of an audit are the following:

- [ ] to verify and report upon the financial state of an organisation, e.g. that the accounts give a true and fair view;
- [ ] to detect errors and fraud;
- [ ] to prevent errors and fraud.

Collapse was so avoidable (re Independent Insurance, June 2001)

Formally the board asked Price Waterhouse Coopers to be provisional liquidators.

The move was not triggered by a new 'black hole'. Rather, cash flow simply dried up since II stopped taking new business last week ...

There are plenty of questions for the watchdogs to answer. It is not just whether the II board should have been told earlier than February's profit warning that things had gone badly awry. For quite some time, insurance professionals were shaking their heads about the uniquely wide profit margins II was reporting. Did no one in authority detect even a whiff of a rodent?

Extracts from Brian O'Connor, 'Collapse was so avoidable', Daily Mail, *Tuesday, 19 June 2001*

O'Conner's article not only raises the question of what the regulators were doing, but also of what the auditors were doing. This case came close on the heels of the collapse of Equitable Life Insurance in the UK, and before the 2002 case of Enron in the US in which the same questions are being asked!

There are various classes of audit, as follows:

- [ ] *statutory*, for example for limited companies and building societies;
- [ ] *private firms*, by letters of appointment;

☐ *trust accounts*;

☐ *partnerships* (partnership agreement);

☐ *internal audit* by employees of the organisation.

A knowledge of basic documents is very important for conducting an audit – these basic documents include: invoices, statements, credit notes, goods received notes and contracts.

An outline of the work of an auditor can be summarised by the words verify, examine, report, enquire and check (VEREC). VEREC can be expanded upon as follows:

☐ *Verify* the existence, ownership and basis of valuation of the assets and ensure that the liabilities are fully and accurately disclosed.

☐ *Examine* (vouch) vouchers and any other evidence that may be required to prove that the entries in the books of account are complete and authentic.

☐ *Report* to the owners whether the balance sheet shows a true and fair view of the affairs, and the profit and loss account a true and fair view of the profit or loss for the financial period under review.

☐ *Enquire* as to the authority for transactions and see that all benefits that should have been accounted for have in fact been received.

☐ *Check* the arithmetic, i.e. the accuracy of the books of account.

Summary: the published financial statements of companies

The Companies Act 1985/89 requires companies to publish their accounts, i.e. their annual report and accounts. The published accounts and reports should do the following:

☐ contain a profit and loss account and balance sheet in one of the prescribed formats. A selection has to be made from four *profit and loss* formats and two *balance sheet* formats;

☐ contain figures that have been computed according to the rules laid down by the Companies Act, and contain the information required by the Companies Act.

The *published accounts* will tend to include the following items:

☐ information about directors

☐ the directors' report

☐ an auditors' report

☐ profit and loss account

☐ balance sheet

☐ a cash flow statement (i.e. a funds flow)

☐ a statement of accounting policies

☐ notes to the accounts

☐ statistical information, e.g. financial ratios.

The published profit and loss account and the balance sheet are in effect summaries of the detailed information that appears in the notes to the accounts.

Companies have to file a copy of their published accounts with the Registrar of Companies. Small and medium-sized companies are exempt from certain filing provisions.

Who needs the published accounts?

There are many parties interested in the published accounts of companies: for example, directors, shareholders, bankers, creditors, investors, employees, regulators, government, analysts.

What can we find out about a company from its published accounts?

The published accounts contain a wealth of information about the company, for example, information about the following:

☐ important events, future projects, and research and development activities;

☐ directors and employees;

☐ how the operating profit has been arrived at;

☐ taxation;

☐ extraordinary items;

☐ dividends;

☐ retained earnings, reserves and share capital;

☐ rent or hire of equipment, plant, machinery and vehicles;

☐ auditors' remuneration;

☐ investment and rental income;

☐ how the fixed assets, depreciation, current assets and current liabilities figures were computed;

☐ capital commitments;

☐ contingent liabilities;

☐ statistical information and corresponding figures.

Auditors

The role of the auditor can be summed up by the term VEREC, i.e. verify, examine, report, enquire and check. One of the auditor's major roles is the prevention and detection of errors and fraud.

Corporate governance

A combined code was issued following the Hampel Report (1998).

Concluding remarks

You can learn a lot about published accounts by reviewing a selection of them. This review, when combined with your knowledge gained from the earlier chapters of this text, should enable you to find out information about a wide variety of matters. You will, of course, have lots of questions that you would like answers to. You may find the answers to some of these questions from the published accounts themselves, e.g. in the notes to the accounts section, or from other books, tutors, friends or accountants. It is this investigative process, which needs an enquiring mind, that will help you to find out more and more about the published financial statements of companies.

'What I do, I know.'

Tutor-based assignments

As indicated in the objectives at the beginning of this chapter, you are expected to learn a lot about published reports and accounts through making use of some actual examples.

A lot of what you encounter will be familiar to you. You will come across many of the terms that have been used throughout this text. However, the format in which the information is presented is quite different. The profit and loss account and the balance sheet tend to include the totals of principal items or groups of items, and these are then explained and expanded upon through a series of quite detailed notes (notes to the accounts) which are designed to show the workings and any further information required by the Companies Act. The published reports and accounts will also include the following:

- ☐ an auditors' report
- ☐ a statement of accounting policies
- ☐ a directors' report
- ☐ a cash flow statement
- ☐ a statistical analysis.

Before you start the projects, you will need to acquire, through friends or a library or by writing to the companies concerned, copies of the published accounts of companies, as directed by your lecturer or tutor. These may include, for example, the last four years' published accounts for three companies from the same industrial sector. If you work for a public limited company, i.e. a plc, or a private-sector organisation, this could provide you with a useful source of data.

These projects may be used for group discussions, written reports and/or presentations, as directed by your lecturer or tutor.

T9.1   Select one set of published accounts. Then look through the profit and loss account, balance sheet and notes to the accounts and list all of the terms that you have not come across before. Find out what these terms mean by using other books, such as the *Collins Dictionary of Business*, or from tutors, friends, accountants, etc.

T9.2   Take the published accounts of three companies from the same industrial sector. Compare their accounting policies and highlight the principal differences between them.

T9.3   Prepare a report on what you have found interesting and unusual about the accounts of your selected company or companies.

T9.4   Make a critical review of the contents of the directors' reports for the company or companies that you have selected, and present your findings.

T9.5   Take your most recent set of published accounts for one of your selected companies and find the following items in the balance sheet:

>   Tangible fixed assets
>   Investments (securities, if any)
>   Stocks
>   Accounts receivable (debtors)
>   Shareholders' equity
>   Minority interests
>   Long-term debts
>   Current liabilities
>   Off-balance-sheet obligations (if any).

Then find the appropriate note that illustrates how these figures have been arrived at and see if you can understand the calculations.

T9.6   Take any two sets of published accounts and study the profit and loss account together with the appropriate notes to see how the following figures are arrived at:

>   Turnover
>   Interest
>   Profit on ordinary activities before taxation
>   Extraordinary items (if any)
>   Dividends.

T9.7   Having studied cash flow statements earlier in this text, look at any two of the companies' published cash flow statements and see if you can understand how the following have been arrived at:

>   Cash flow from operating activities
>   Cash flow from investing activities
>   Cash flow from financing activities.

T9.8 (a) Using the published accounts from the three companies from the same industrial sector, covering a period of five years, prepare a comparative financial performance analysis, including a SWOT analysis.

(b) Compare and contrast the quality of the three sets of published accounts as documents that seek to communicate financial and other information.

(c) Discuss whether or not they give a 'true and fair view' of their company's financial affairs.

T9.9 A management project/dissertation idea
Why not consider doing a long-term company financial history covering a twenty-year period?

Further reading

Gillespie, I., Lewis, R. and Hamilton, K., *Principles of Financial Accounting*, Financial Times Prentice Hall, 2000

Glautier, M.W.E. and Underdown, B., *Accounting Theory and Practice*, Financial Times Prentice Hall, 2001

Parker, R.H., *Understanding Company Financial Statements*, Penguin Business, 1999

Pendlebury, M. and Groves, R., *Company Accounts, Analysis Interpretation and Understanding*, Thomson Learning, 2001

PricewaterhouseCoopers Accounting Standards (latest edition)

Useful websites

www.booksites.net/glautierunderdown

Free FT Annual Reports Service: http://ft.ar.wilink.com

Company websites can prove to be very useful for research purposes, e.g.
AMEC plc: www.amec.co.uk
BP: www.bp.com
Deutsche Telekom: www.telekom.de/international
Heineken N.V.: www.heineken.nl
HSBC: www.ib.hsbc.com
The Royal Dutch Shell Group of Companies: www.shell.com
Siemens: www.siemens-knows.com
Syngenta: www.syngenta.com

For more on auditing and global accounting: www.wiley.co.uk/college

10

Performance measurement – other aspects

In Chapter 8 we said that we would take a more in-depth look at capital structure and gearing. In addition, we will also review working capital management, the concepts of value added, value-for-money audits (vfm) and the balanced scorecard, and the role of management accounting.

Learning objectives

On completion of this chapter you should be able to:

☐ appreciate what is meant by *capital structure* and how the current structure influences the raising of additional finance;

☐ know what management can do to manage the *working capital* more effectively;

☐ understand the concept of value added;

☐ explain how *value-for-money auditing* can be of benefit to both public- and private-sector organisations;

☐ acquire an insight into the way in which the *balanced scorecard* method of performance measurement operates.

Capital structure and gearing

Capital structure

You may recall that in a firm's balance sheet, the *capital employed* could consist of ordinary share capital, preference share capital, reserves and long-term debt (liabilities). Together, they make up the *capital structure*, i.e. the permanent and long-term financing that is being used by the organisation. If we add to this the current liabilities, i.e. the short-term sources of finance, we have a figure that may be described by certain authors as the *financial structure*. Thus, capital structure is concerned with the mixture of permanent and long-term financing and their relative proportions to each other. The mixture used or intended to be used in the future will determine the cost of capital figure for the organisation.

Gearing

As mentioned in Chapter 8, gearing is all about the relationship between the *equity*, i.e. ordinary share capital plus reserves, and *debt*, i.e. long-term loans, debentures and, in most cases, preference shares. If a company has a lot of debt in proportion to the total permanent and long-term financing, it is said to be *highly geared*, and if it has a small amount of debt, it is *low-geared*.

Gearing can significantly increase the wealth of the ordinary shareholders. In effect, it borrows money with one hand and puts it to work, and pays the interest on it with the other hand. Any additional amount that has been generated belongs to the ordinary shareholders. However, there is a downside: the higher the gearing, the greater the risk to the lender. In a bad year in which losses are sustained, the interest will have to be paid in the case of debentures, or paid or rescheduled in the case of long-term loans, or deferred in the case of preference shares. In a recession it is the more highly geared companies that are in danger of going out of business. The example, Figure 10.1, should help you to understand the link between capital structure, gearing and the return on equity.

You can observe from a review of Figure 10.1 how gearing can be used to increase the wealth of the ordinary shareholders in very good times, as portrayed by the return on equity. You can also see very clearly that where economic conditions are very poor the

Example **Capital structure:**	C	H	D
	£m	£m	£m
Equity (Ordinary shares + reserves)	800	400	200
Long-term loans and debentures @ 10%	nil	400	600
Gearing (debt as a % of the total)	nil	50%	75%
	£m	£m	£m
Net profit after interest and tax where the economic conditions are very poor	65	25	5
Return on equity	8.125%	6.25	2.5%
	£m	£m	£m
Net profit after interest and tax where the economic conditions are very good	140	100	80
Return on equity	17.5%	25%	40%

Figure 10.1 – Capital structure, gearing and the return on equity

performance of the more highly geared companies suffers, e.g. only a 2.5% return on equity for company D, compared with 40% in very good trading conditions.

The current level of gearing will affect a company's ability to raise more finance, and could well dictate what they can or cannot do. For example, if they are very highly geared, the market may be unwilling to lend them more via long-term loans and/or debentures. This means that they would have to consider other options, e.g. more ordinary shares or selling assets and/or investments, sale and lease-back, etc. However, issuing more ordinary shares could result in a loss of control, which helps explain the reluctance on the part of certain boards of directors to consider this option.

As you may recall, debentures in a company's capital structure increase their risk, and usually mean some loss of control and less freedom to manage assets. The actions of the trustees for the debenture holders are controlled by statute which means that they cannot delay in taking action against a defaulter. With a bank loan, on the other hand, it may be possible to arrange a compromise and reschedule the debt.

The bank overdraft

Certain companies do use their bank overdraft as a long-term source of funds. If this is the case, it could be included in the gearing calculation along with the other forms of long-term debt.

Preference shares

Some schools of thought include preference shares with the long-term debt, whilst others include them with the equity. One possible reason for this conflict of opinion is that preference shares carry an obligation to pay interest, as do long-term loans and debentures. Companies may, however, decide to defer paying the preference dividends.

The ratios

There are numerous gearing ratios and ratios that are concerned with the effects of capital structure, e.g. earnings per share, interest cover, dividend cover, price/earnings and the return on equity.

Working capital management

The working capital, i.e. current assets less current liabilities, has to be carefully managed. Stocks and debtors represent capital tied up. Cash flow problems can bring about the downfall of a company. Creditors are a source of short-term finance, as are other debts due to be paid within the next twelve months, i.e. the company has the use of those funds until the debt is eventually paid in full.

Stocks (inventory)

Efficient stock control systems should aim to keep the stock levels at an acceptable minimum without causing a 'stock-out'. In order to do this, maximum, minimum and reorder stock levels should be reviewed at frequent intervals. JIT (just-in-time) systems may be used, i.e. where the stock comes in for a very short period of time, say a day, before it is needed. In a manufacturing environment, there can be MRP (material requirements planning), where the stocks purchased and held (excluding a base level of stock) match up with the production requirements. All of these possibilities could *release space* for other purposes and also reduce the expensive *holding costs*, e.g. insurance of buildings and stocks, light and heat, administrative effort. The ratios of particular significance here are *stock/turnover and stock days*.

Debtors

Credit control is the system involved with the policy relating to *credit terms* and *ensuring that the debtors (receivables) pay* for the goods and/or services they have received on credit. This can involve: cutting down on the time it takes to send out invoices; targeting customers listed for not paying within the normal period of credit; considering granting a discount for prompt payment; persuading customers to pay via direct debit; obtaining information from credit rating agencies. The important ratio here is *debtor days*, i.e. how long it takes to collect the debts.

Investments held as current assets

Short-term investments could be realised very quickly, if and when they are required.

Cash and bank accounts

This, via the cash budget, could involve *treasury management*, i.e. investing surplus cash short-term. It could also include *delegation and authority*, e.g. who signs or counter-signs cheques; who keeps the keys or duplicate keys to the safe; who is responsible for paying cash or cheques received into the bank; who can authorise capital expenditure orders or payments.

Creditors and amounts due to be paid within the next twelve months

Whatever the expense owing, the organisation has the use of the funds, e.g. for creditors, tax owing and dividends owing, until the payment is due and paid. Some companies take far too long to pay their creditors, others may pay well within the period of credit granted by their suppliers of goods and services on credit.

Working capital ratios

The liquidity ratios reviewed in Chapter 8 look at the company's ability to pay its way. In addition we can also look at *the working capital/sales ratio*. This will provide a rough indication of how much working capital will be needed to support an increase in sales. When it comes to financing working capital, remember that a certain portion is always there, e.g. the base stock of raw materials and fuels etc. and a certain level of debtors, and should really be financed from long-term sources.

The concept of value added

The value added approach is an alternative way of looking at the information provided in the profit and loss account. **Value added** is the difference between the sales income and the materials and services bought from external suppliers. Value added therefore represents the additional wealth created by the company's own efforts through the application of its labour force and the use of its resources such as buildings, machinery and equipment. The *value added statement* illustrated in Figure 10.2 shows how the value added has been arrived at, and the way in which it has been shared between the value added stakeholders, who are as follows:

☐ the employees, including directors;

☐ the providers of the capital, e.g. dividends to ordinary and preference shareholders, interest to debenture holders and providers of long-term loans;

☐ the government for taxation;

☐ The company, as regards the depreciation of fixed assets and the retained earnings which are being ploughed back in the business.

```
Value added statement
                                                    £m
  Sales
Less Materials and/or services bought from
outside suppliers
      Value added                                  _____
Add Other income e.g. investment income            _____
      Value added available                        _____

Shared out between the stakeholders, as follows:
    Employees' remuneration
    Debenture and loan interest
    Preference share dividends
    Ordinary share dividends
    Taxation
    Depreciation
    Retained earnings                              _____
                                                   _____
```

Figure 10.2 – The format for a value added statement

Value added ratios

Value added can be divided by the number of employees, or the value of the external supplies of goods or services, or expressed as a percentage of the capital employed.

Value-for-money audit (vfm)

This has really taken off in the public sector and delivered savings running into millions of pounds. Its use, however, should not be restricted to the public sector, as it can be used to good effect in the private sector. It is used in evaluating services such as health-care and hospitals, and education.

The three Es

Vfm uses the three Es – *economy, efficiency and effectiveness* – to assess and monitor performance.

Economy

The aim is to reduce costs in all areas, e.g. marketing, research and development, purchasing, administration, distribution and in-company services. The productivity of the capital employed should be improved by cutting down on or preventing wasteful, unrewarding and extravagant expenditure.

Efficiency

This attempts to ensure that resources, such as finance, fixed assets, materials, labour and overheads, are managed efficiently. For example, the disposal of fixed assets and/or materials that are no longer required brings in some cash flow, and could release space for other purposes, and reduce the overhead expenses such as light and heat, insurance and indirect labour.

Effectiveness

This refers to the realisation of objectives in quantitative and qualitative terms, for example, sales targets, market share, profitability, health and safety. It also involves the sensitive area concerned with reviewing policy decisions and their implementation.

Management has a duty to ensure that the scarce resources placed at their disposal are used wisely; vfm can help them with this task.

Balanced scorecard

The *balanced scorecard* approach of performance measurement was developed several years ago by Robert Kaplan and David Norton in the USA. Possible reasons suggested for its introduction were: the need to provide managers with performance drivers to enable their company to survive and prosper in the long term; the over-reliance on financial performance measures; and short-term thinking which could run counter to long-term goals.

The four perspectives

As its principal focus, the method reviews a portfolio of four areas, which we will describe briefly:

☐ The *financial perspective* includes key financial ratios such as return on capital employed (ROCE) and cash flow. It also involves budgeting and forecasting. It does, therefore, suffer from all of the problems and limitations associated with financial accounting statements and ratio analysis, and the problems associated with the estimates used for budgets and forecasts.

☐ The *customer perspective* involves marketing techniques: For example, the assessment of customer needs and customer satisfaction; reviewing pricing, distribution and promotion of products and/or services; the identification of target markets or segments, e.g. to attract new customers; customer retention, e.g. via relationship marketing.

☐ *Internal business processes* such as the efficiency of the operations process, for production purposes, for internal services and functional areas of the business, and for the provision of external services; processes that promote innovation; searching for new products or services; monitoring sales, competitors and the environment; after-sales service.

☐ *Innovation and learning* provides the support and organisational structure in which the objectives of the other three perspectives may be achieved. It involves the realisation that employees are a principal asset and need to be rewarded, motivated, developed, satisfied and retained. It also involves information systems and innovation.

For those who would like to delve a little deeper into this area, the following concise and very well-written article should prove to be very useful.

Do you know the score?

Why bother to measure performance? Wouldn't it be better to channel effort directly into improving performance rather than just measuring it?

The answer of course is that by measuring performance in a constructive way you can actually make some profound improvements to the overall performance of your organisation.

On the face of it measurement may seem a dry and analytical activity but in reality this needn't be the case. Of course it does involve some number crunching but that is only part of the job.

It is possible to gain the enthusiasm and commitment of your managers and staff and thus use your performance measures as a way of aligning effort and activity to business goals.

A good measurement system will help you to:

☐ Establish your current position – how you are currently performing
☐ Communicate direction – show your people where you want to go
☐ Stimulate action – help identify when things need to be done
☐ Facilitate learning – help you understand how your business works
☐ Influence behaviour – encourage the right activity.

On the down side, a badly constructed performance measurement system will destroy performance by encouraging emphasis on the wrong activities.

Right ingredients

A good performance measurement system should include:

☐ A balance of financial and non financial measures
☐ A balance of past achievement measure and those that help to predict the future
☐ Measures that communicate strategic direction and goals
☐ A mechanism for raising awareness and stimulating action
☐ A mechanism for learning, from the information the measures provide.

The system itself is important – but even the most carefully constructed system will fail if there is no commitment to keep it up to date and use the information it provides.

So, the system you implement should be as 'user friendly' as possible and should be capable of delivering the most appropriate information with the least amount of effort.

Measurement framework

The balanced scorecard, popularised by Robert Kaplan and David Norton, is increasingly being used as a framework for performance measurement. Kaplan and Norton identified four perspectives, each representing an important facet of the organisation:

☐ Financial
☐ External customers
☐ Internal process
☐ Innovation and learning

In business it is accepted that financial needs have to be met. At the most basic level there must be cash flow to sustain the enterprise. Beyond this, the business must provide the cash to cover any interest on its debts. Finally, the shareholders or owners are looking for a return on their investment.

However, focusing purely on financial aspects is not enough. Firstly, the focus often results in people taking the easiest options to improve performance, reducing costs rather than encouraging growth. This may be beneficial in the short term but in the longer term cuts in investment, research and development will harm the business.

Secondly, financial measures are 'result measures'. They provide a measure of how well all the other activities have been done. They do not tell you how to improve performance and this is why financial measures alone are insufficient to manage the business.

Customers are the lifeblood of the business; their orders and payments are the reason for the business to exist. It is therefore very important to understand the needs of current and prospective customers so you know why they buy from you now and what will determine whether they will buy from you in the future.

This is why you need the customer perspective. However, satisfying customers is not enough in itself. For example, you could give your product or service away to the delight of your customers but (to) the ruin of your business! Other business objectives have to be brought in to create a balance.

To satisfy customers and make a financial return, the business must be efficient and effective, hence the third perspective, internal process. The objective here is not to be good at everything but to be brilliant at producing the products or services that match the exact needs of your customers.

If the world stood still, we would only need three perspectives but, as we know, it changes constantly. To keep up with the ever increasing demands of your customers and the ever improving performance of your competitors, you need to innovate and learn.

The fourth perspective is all about developing the capabilities and processes you will need for the future. This perspective often contains most of the measures for people development.

The great advantage of such a framework is that it represents on one page the key objectives of the business. When these are quantified as performance measures, everyone can see where the business is and what it is trying to achieve.

What to measure

The balanced scorecard emphasises four key perspectives for business success but it doesn't tell you what to measure. If you want to build your own scorecard you need to go through the following steps:

1 Decide what are the key objectives your business needs to achieve
2 Design a set of key performance measures which quantify these objectives
3 Implement the measures and incorporate them into a regular reporting system
4 Review the results, take action on the measures and publicise progress
5 Review the whole system so that it stays up to date.

Organisational benefits

Measures can be used in a variety of different ways. At the macro level, they can help to bring about culture change – instilling a culture of achievement for example. They can also be used to provide early indicators of trends – favourable and unfavourable – which can affect the business. At a more detailed level they can reveal connections – between performance in one area and results in another – and factors affecting your business, which you may not have considered. As one senior manager put it: 'This is the single biggest improvement tool we have used. We moved further, faster with this than with anything else.'

M. Bourne and P. Bourne, *Professional Manager*, November 2000, pp. 42–3.

SWOT analysis

SWOT, stands for *strengths, weaknesses, opportunities and threats*. To survive and prosper in the long term, organisations have to monitor both their internal and their external environment. They need to identify their strengths and try to build on them, e.g. so that they can develop them into a *competitive advantage*. They need to be self-critical in order to identify weaknesses, so that they can consider the most appropriate form of action. Their aim should be to turn weaknesses into strengths. For example, they could be either strong or weak in the following activities: credit control, inventory (stock) control, treasury management, marketing, distribution, operations management, human resource management, international trade. They also need to *monitor the environment* for opportunities and threats, so that they can decide at an early stage how they will respond to the challenge: for example, new markets, new products or services, exchange rates, interest rates, anticipated changes in the rate of inflation.

The role of management accounting

One of the major problems of financial performance analysis, e.g. using ratios, is that it uses *historic data*, i.e. it looks backwards at performance after the event. This is on top of the problems associated with the accuracy and reliability of the financial statements. *Management accounting*, on the other hand, tends to use predetermined figures which focus on the future, e.g. budgetary control and standard costing. The two systems set targets for future performance, and then compare the targets with actual performance at frequent intervals. The difference between target and the actual is called the **variance**. Variances are reported to management so that consideration can be given to the kind of action that needs to be taken. However, you must remember that the target figures that are used are only estimates. We will look at management accounting shortly within this text and, in particular, its role in planning, control and decision making.

Summary: performance measurement – other aspects

Capital structure and gearing

Capital structure refers to the permanent and long-term financing that is shown in a company's balance sheet, e.g. ordinary share capital, reserves, long-term loans and debentures. Of particular interest is the relationship between the debt (i.e. long-term loans and debentures) and the equity (i.e. ordinary share capital plus reserves). This relationship is expressed in the *gearing ratio*. If a company has a high proportion of debt, it can, depending on the industry average, be described as being *highly geared*. The additional earnings generated by the investment of debt financing increases the wealth of the ordinary shareholders. Once the service cost on the debt, i.e. the *interest*, has been paid, the remainder of the amount generated belongs to the ordinary shareholders, and increases their stake in the company.

In times of poor trading conditions, the highly geared companies are most at risk, as they still have to make their repayments on long-term loans, and pay interest on their debentures.

One of the principal starting points, when considering which type of new finance to go for, is to look at the current level of gearing in relation to the industry average. For example, if it is too high, lenders may be unwilling to provide more debt finance.

Working capital management

Working capital management includes the management and control of cash and bank balances, short-term investments, credit control (e.g. collecting amounts owing from debtors and credit screening), and stock (inventory) control. It is also concerned with the short-term financing from creditors who have supplied goods and services on credit.

Value added

Value added is calculated by subtracting the cost of materials and services bought from external suppliers from the sales figure. It represents the wealth created by the company's own labour force.

Value-for-money audits (vfm)

Vfm has been used to good effect in public organisations, e.g. in the UK via the National Audit Office. Vfm audits assess and monitor the three Es: *economy, efficiency and effectiveness*.

The balanced scorecard

The *balanced scorecard* approach to performance appraisal was developed to provide managers with performance drivers, and also in response to the need to include both financial and non-financial performance indicators. The balance scorecard looks at four perspectives:

☐ the financial perspective
☐ the customer perspective
☐ internal business processes
☐ innovation and learning.

SWOT analysis

SWOT reviews an organisation in terms of its strengths, weaknesses, opportunities and threats. It helps to identify where the company has a differential advantage over its competitors, and also where it needs to use its resources and focus its efforts, e.g. to turn a threat into an opportunity.

The role of management accounting

Management accounting provides a vast amount of information for costing products, services, decision making and control, e.g. in budgetary control and standard costing, by providing targets, standards and benchmarks against which to monitor, measure, report and control performance.

Self-checks

Attempt each of the self-checks that follow, and then compare your solution with the appropriate part of this chapter.

1. Define in your own words:
   (a) Capital structure
   (b) Financial structure
   (c) Gearing

2. 'Using gearing to increase the wealth of the ordinary shareholders.' Discuss this statement.

3. Explain why 'high gearing' can be very risky.

4. Describe briefly what management can do to:
   (a) improve stock control
   (b) improve credit control
   (c) safeguard cash and bank balances

5. How is value added calculated?

6. Who are the value added stakeholders?

7. What do value-for-money audits (vfm) focus on?

8. Define, in your own words, what is meant by 'the balanced scorecard approach'.

9. Describe briefly the ingredients needed to produce a good performance measurement system.

10. What should the balanced scorecard system measure?

Self-assessments

On completion, compare your attempt for each individual self-assessment with the suggested answer provided in Appendix 1.

A10.1 (a) From the information provided below, compute the return on total capital employed,

	B Ltd	P Ltd
	£m	£m
Equity	172	100
12% Loan stock	48	120
	220	220

if the net profit before interest for each of the companies was £24m in year 1, £36m in year 2 and £10m in year 3, comment briefly on the results.

(b) For each of the years in question, compute the EPS (earnings per share), if B Ltd had issued £100m ordinary shares of £1 each, and P Ltd had issued £50m ordinary shares of £1 each, and comment briefly on your findings.

A10.2 'If all the holders of convertible loan stock convert into ordinary shares, there will be a dilution of earnings.' Discuss this statement.

Tutor-based assignments

The answers to these tutor-based assignments can be via reports, group discussions, or presentations, as directed by the tutor.

T10.1 You have been provided with the following information relating to Standedge Gate plc:

Year	20x6	20x5	20x4
	£m	£m	£m
Current assets:			
Stock	50	40	36
Debtors	42	38	32
Cash and bank	6	12	8
Current liabilities:			
Creditors	36	32	28
Ordinary share capital	20	10	10
Reserves	28	23	20
Long-term loan 10%	12	12	6

	20X6	20X5	20X4
	£m	£m	£m
Sales (turnover)	380	220	190
Operating profit	13,200	8,200	7,600
Interest paid	1,200	1,200	600
Tax	4,000	3,000	2,000
Dividend paid and proposed	3,000	2,400	2,000
Retained earnings	5,000	3,000	3,000

The ordinary shares have a face (par) value of £1 each. The company's average share price for the last two years has been: 20X6, £4.80; 20X5, £4.20.

(a) From the limited information available, discuss the company's working capital management.

(b) For each of the years in question compute:
   (i)   The gearing
   (ii) The earnings per share
   (iii) The price/earnings ratio
   and comment briefly on your findings.

(c) The company is considering obtaining more funding to finance its ambitious expansion plans of £20m and has asked you to review the three proposed alternatives:
   ☐ A new issue of ordinary shares at £4.75 per share
   ☐ An issue of 8% convertible loan stock
   ☐ An issue of 10% debentures.

T10.2 Prepare a report and/or presentation illustrating how vfm has been used to good effect in the public sector, and indicate how it can be applied to the private sector.

T10.3 **Case study: E-Pub plc**

Ruud van Rom and Tamara Singh set up E-Pub plc in the Netherlands in the mid-1990s in the fast growing electronic publishing business. Since its incorporation it has grown at a rapid rate but is by no means a key player in the market. The market continues to grow and so does the competition. To keep pace with the technological advances that have been and are now taking place the company always seems to be short of cash. Cash flow is a major problem. They have consistently ploughed most of their earnings back into the business and paid out a very modest dividend to their shareholders. Their share price has fallen from a high of 16 euros two years ago to its current level of 7.50 euros. To improve performance they are considering employing all or some of the following courses of action:
☐ reduce the number of full-time staff and use more subcontractors;
☐ sell off their obsolete equipment;
☐ refocus their target marketing to the most profitable areas;
☐ improve their credit control system;
☐ secure more long-term financing via a long-term loan or another share issue;
☐ merge with another electronic publishing company.
The company's profit and loss account and balance sheet for the last two years are provided for your inspection and review:

Profit and loss account data:

	20X4 Euro 000s	20X3 Euro 000s
Net sales	25,600	22,100
Cost of sales	2,950	2,700
Gross profit	**22,650**	**19,400**
Operating expenses	20,700	15,200
Operating profit	**1,950**	**4,200**
Interest paid	442	390
Profit before tax	**1,508**	**3,810**
Taxation provision	450	1,070
Profit after tax	**1,058**	**2,740**
Dividend paid	375	350
Retained profit	**683**	**2,390**

Share data:		
Earnings per share in euros	0.071	0.274

Balance sheet data:

	20X4 Euro 000s	20X3 Euro 000s
ASSETS		
Fixed assets	19,500	12,200
Current assets:		
Stock/inventories	2,150	1,050
Debtors/receivables	21,900	15,800
Cash and bank balances (overdraft)	−1,350	−640
Total current assets	**22,700**	**16,210**
Total assets	**42,200**	**28,410**
LIABILITIES		
Creditors falling due after more than one year:		
Current liabilities:		
Creditors/accounts payable	11,200	8,300
Long-term debt (long-term loans and debentures)	6,800	6,000
Shareholders equity (share capital and reserves)	24,200	14,110
Total liabilities and equity	**42,200**	**28,410**

Required:

1. Using the data provided assess the company's financial performance for 20X4 and 20X3.
2. Discuss in detail each of the proposed alternative courses of action.
3. State, with reasons, which course or courses of action proposed, or otherwise, you consider the company should follow.

Further reading

Bourne, M. and Bourne, P., *Understanding the Balanced Score Card in a Week*, Hodder & Stoughton, 2000

Greenwood, R.P., *Handbook of Financial Planning and Control*, Gower, 2001

Kaplan, R.S. and Norton, D.P., *The Balanced Scorecard*, Harvard Business School, Boston, 1996

Knott, G., *Financial Management*, Macmillan Business, 1998

Millichamp, A., *Auditing*, Continuum, 2000

Pike, R. and Neale, B., *Corporate Finance and Investment*, Financial Times Prentice Hall, 1999

Useful websites

www.bh.com/management
www.continuumbooks.com
www.gowerpub.com
www.macmillan-business.co.uk

11

Case studies

The 'open-ended' case studies used in this chapter are based on real UK and European companies. To answer them you will need to carry out additional research, e.g. via looking at the published reports and accounts of similar companies, relevant journal articles, textbooks and appropriate WWW sources. You will also need to integrate with and apply knowledge gained in other areas, e.g. marketing, strategic management. The case studies have been designed to help you revise and consolidate important aspects of your learning to date, and to expand your knowledge by providing integration with other business-related study areas.

The financial information provided in any case study or real-life business situation is just one component part of the big picture, and the analytical and decision-making processes. Thus, when you do prepare your solutions to a case, you have to look at the whole case, and review financial and non-financial matters.

Learning objectives

When you have attempted all or some of the case studies, you should:

☐ have improved your analytical skills, e.g. in financial performance appraisal;

☐ have developed your comprehensional skills, e.g. report writing, reflective learning;

☐ be able to integrate with other relevant areas of knowledge, so as to be more aware of the big picture;

☐ via hands-on experience be able to research appropriate literature, e.g. journals, WWW sources;

☐ have become more competent and confident by being involved in such things as group discussions and presentations.

An outline answer is provided in Appendix 1 for the self-assessment case study. For tutor-based case studies, outline answers and comments will be provided in the tutor's manual.

Self-assessment

A11.1 Case study: Worlden Insurance AG
This case study is based on a real company and its real competitor.

Worlden Insurance AG came into being as a result of a merger between Worlwid Insurance AG of Bonn, Germany, and Denu Alliance Insurance of Linz, Austria, in 1995. The company established its head office in Berlin in 1997. In addition to having a strong market presence in Europe, it also has a strong presence in Asia, the USA and Canada. In fact, it is fast becoming one of the top ten global players within the industry. However, the consolidation process within the industry continues with a number of possible mergers on the horizon. If certain key competitors do merge the directors fear that this would disrupt their progress towards becoming one of the leading players.

The market continues to grow. Possible disasters, e.g. floods, fires and terrorism, need to be insured against for vast amounts, and premiums tend to increase by a significant amount each year. Natural and other disasters do appear to be on the increase. Currently 70% of the company's turnover comes from the reinsurance market, with the remainder coming from its direct insurance business.

You have been provided with a summary of the key ratios for the company and one of its competitors, Davikamp Insurance of Utrecht in the Netherlands, and also with industry averages for 20X5.

KEY RATIOS FOR 20X5

Profitability	Worlden	Davikamp	Industry average
Return on equity (%)	15.2	10.8	19.6
Return on capital employed (%)	18.6	16.0	24.3
Gross profit/sales (%)	13.4	5.8	16.4
Assets utilisation ratio (times)	25.3	32.0	36.0
Liquidity			
Quick ratio	0.94	1.10	0.96
Debtor's turnover (days)	75	64	58
Gearing			
Long term debt/capital employed (%)	30	20	40
Stock market ratios			
Price/earnings ratio (times)	15.6	22.7	20.3
Dividend cover (times)	4.2	8.5	7.4

Required:

1. Compare the financial performance of Worlden and Davikamp for 20X5 using the information that has been provided.
2. What financial benefits would have been derived from the merger which took place in 1995?
3. How can Worlden become one of the industry's future leading players?

Tutor-based case studies

The mode of presentation of the case studies which follow will be as directed by the lecturer or tutor.

T11.1 **Case study: The financial performance of the top teams in UK soccer**

Soccer (football) in the UK has become 'big business'. The top teams in the industry, because of their need for significant injections of finance, have become public companies and are now quoted on the London Stock Exchange. There does appear to be a strong link between financial success and success on the football field. Premiership football clubs now receive vast sums of money from gate receipts, television rights, sponsorship, advertising, merchandising, corporate entertaining, other activities concerned with the use of their facilities, and the trading of players.

The current climate is one of large signing-on fees and high salaries. All the top players now tend to employ agents to look after their financial arrangements and negotiations with their existing clubs and with new clubs. As a result, all football clubs of any significant size have been considering strategies to assure them of a continuous and reliable supply of short-term and long-term financing. In addition, they have become much more marketing-oriented and have developed their brand names and merchandising activities.

You have been provided with the following information for three UK premier league football clubs: Hotspur City, Wanderers United and Forest Rangers.

Profit and loss account and balance sheet data for 20X7/8:

Amounts in £000

20X7/8	City	United	Rangers
Turnover	37,741	53,316	8,990
Cost of Sales	3,667	17,396	6,170
Capital Employed	40,711	54,462	1,367
Shareholders' Funds	37,436	40,762	1,310
Long-term Loans	3,275	13,700	57
Tangible Fixed Assets	35,093	61,295	633
Intangible Fixed Assets	10,215	0	19
Current Assets	17,668	32,397	5,027

Current Liabilities	17,705	22,060	4,312
Stock	289	2,072	720
Average Trade Debtors	2,560	6,560	3,612
Average Stock	2,385	2,038	720
Operating Profit (Loss)	12,374	14,167	162
Profit (Loss) before Interest and Tax	12,309	15,925	172

Turnover growth

Five-year Financial Summary:

	20X7/8	20X6/7	20X5/6	20X4/5	20X3/4
City	37,341	25,083	22,326	25,265	19,308
United	53,316	60,622	43,815	25,177	20,145
Rangers	8,990	5,196	5,333	770	550

Required:

1. From the information provided, compare the financial performance of the three football clubs for 20X7/8, and comment on their growth in turnover.
2. Discuss the reasons for and problems associated with raising additional funds via:
   - ☐ a new issue of ordinary shares;
   - ☐ a 'rights issue';
   - ☐ convertible debentures.
3. What other ways of increasing revenue are being used, or could be investigated?
4. Is premiership soccer a sport or a business?
5. Which post-balance-sheet events can significantly affect the picture that has been portrayed by the annual report and accounts?

T11.2 Case study: The valuation of soccer clubs

How do you value a soccer (football) club?

This is more than a sporting matter, given the number of flotations in recent years, e.g. Newcastle, AC Milan. In the old days, goals and injuries determined value. But even since the milestone of British Sky Broadcasting's massive Premier League television rights contract in 1992, valuation methods have become much more scientific. Manchester United's upgraded stadium, aggressive marketing and global brand make it the premium benchmark for valuations. It tends to trade at a seemingly high prospective price/earnings ratio 50% above the market average. But if you apply leisure-sector multiples to gate receipts and merchandising income, and media-sector multiples to television and sponsorship profits, you get close to the current share price. Soccer clubs are like film studios, providing a steady supply of programming for the proliferation of TV channels around the globe. But, unlike studios, they do not produce box-office flops – so long as they stay in the top league! Nike is allegedly paying $400m (£244m) for a 10-year sponsorship deal with Brazil's national team. That is not far below United's stock market value and a lot more than its competitors', which include some globally recognised brands.

Source: Extracts from the Lex Column: Football clubs, *Financial Times*, 14 December 1996

Required:

1. How should you value a soccer club?
2. How should players' valuations be dealt with in the balance sheet?
3. Explain and illustrate why it can make good financial sense for soccer clubs to have their own soccer schools of excellence.

T11.3 **Case study: Gulpit NV**

Gulpit NV is a medium-sized international brewery based in the Netherlands. It was established in 1781 by Jan van Gulpnar and his son Eric and daughter Winifried. It now employs over one thousand people and exports its beers and non-beer products worldwide. Its main markets are Europe, Asia and the USA.

The company's current strategy is to produce quality beers and not to diversify into more non-beer products. It is independent and does not intend to merge with a larger brewery. However, it would consider taking over suitable small brewers of speciality beers in the Netherlands, Belgium, Germany and the UK.

Their current share of the home market is 15%, and this is not expected to grow significantly over the foreseeable future. Thus, they have to export in order to survive and prosper. They are currently looking internationally for large distribution partners who have well-established distribution networks.

During 20X7 they sold their shares in Hulet NV, a company involved in non-brewing activities. They currently face increasing competition in their Asian markets and this has not been helped by currency fluctuations and political and economic problems.

The company's capital expenditure for the past five years, including trade loans to hotels, cafés and bars, has been as follows:

(All amounts in millions of euros)	20X3	20X4	20X5	20X6	20X7
Capital expenditure	98	75	36	62	82

Gulpit NV's performance for 20X5 was as follows:

KEY FIGURES: (all in millions of euros)	20X5
Total sales	554.1
Total cost	473.9
Operating profit	80.2
Net profit	52.4
Ratios:	
Return on capital employed	13.8%
Sales to capital employed	0.74
Fixed asset utilisation	2.63
Current ratio	2.28
Acid test ratio	1.24
Gearing	45%

For the year 20X7, key performance indicators of two of their major competitors were as follows:

	Hulmanns	Wessdamer
TURNOVER Euro (millions)	12,190	4,695
PROFITABILITY		
Operating Margin	8%	6%
Return on Capital Employed (ROCE)	14%	17%
EFFICIENCY		
Sales to Capital Employed	1.63	3.10
Fixed Assets Utilisation	2.21	3.02
LIQUIDITY		
Current Ratio	1.30	1.30
Acid Test (Quick) Ratio	1.00	0.80
STABILITY		
Solvability	42%	46%
Gearing	59%	64%
Interest Cover	8.7	7.4

See Appendix A of this case study to find the formulae that were used.

A summary of Gulpit NV'S financial data for the years 20X6 and 20X7 is provided below:

	20X6	20X7
Profit and loss account (Euro millions)		
Total sales	630	677
Other operating income	8	20
Total operating income	638	697
Materials	148	183
Overhead expenses	195	203
Salaries	68	74
Depreciation	40	41
Marketing expenses	98	100
Total cost	549	601
Operating profit	89	96
Less taxation	30	35
Net profit after tax	59	61
Balance sheet		
Fixed assets	209	284
Investments	28	34
Stocks	33	43
Debtors	88	85
Cash	152	58
Total assets	510	504
Equity	250	300
Long- term debt 5%	200	134
Creditors	60	70
Total liabilities	510	504

Required:
1. From the information provided, assess the company's financial performance for 20X6 and 20X7.
2. Discuss the company's strategy regarding the specialisation in quality beers.
3. Why can teaming up with large distribution partners prove to be a financially viable option for Gulpit NV?
4. Comment on the problems faced by Gulpit NV in its Asian markets and suggest what it can do to face up to the competition.
5. In addition to any financial strengths and weaknesses that were identified in question 1 above, a SWOT analysis (strengths, weaknesses, opportunities, threats) prepared at the end of 20X7 revealed:

Strengths
- ☐ Position in home market
- ☐ Market leader in Poland
- ☐ Strong brand image

Weaknesses
- ☐ Relatively small company
- ☐ No economies of scale
- ☐ Funding future capital expenditure

Opportunities
- ☐ Increasing exports
- ☐ Distribution partners
- ☐ Expanding operations and activities in selected countries
- ☐ Diversification in the leisure market

Threats
- ☐ Facing competition and economic challenges in Asia
- ☐ Being taken over
- ☐ Home market saturated

Based on the financial analysis already carried out and the above SWOT analysis, discuss and critically evaluate what the company should do in order to survive and prosper in the future.

Appendix A: The formulae that were used

PROFITABILITY

Operating margin
$$\frac{\text{Operating profit}}{\text{Total sales}}$$

Return on capital employed (ROCE)
$$\frac{\text{Operating profit}}{\text{Ordinary share capital plus long-term debt}}$$

EFFICIENCY

Sale to capital employed
$$\frac{\text{Total sales}}{\text{Ordinary share capital plus long-term debt}}$$

Fixed assets utilisation (sweating the assets)
$$\frac{\text{Total sales}}{\text{Fixed assets}}$$

LIQUIDITY

Current ratio
$$\frac{\text{Current assets}}{\text{Current liabilites}}$$

Quick ratio
$$\frac{\text{Current assets} - \text{Stock}}{\text{Current liabilities}}$$

STABILITY

Solvability (shows the percentage of total assets funded by the equity)
$$\frac{\text{Equity}}{\text{Total assets}}$$

Gearing (this is just another way of expressing the gearing)
$$\frac{\text{Long-term debt}}{\text{Equity} + \text{Long-term debt}}$$

Interest cover
$$\frac{\text{Net profit before interest and tax}}{\text{Interest paid}}$$

12

An introduction to cost and management accounting

You were introduced to the role of the management accountant and the management accounting function in Chapter 1. The impression portrayed in that chapter was that the management accountant could be described as an *information manager*. The role includes: providing information to management to assist them with their decision making and control; advising management; forecasting, planning and control; communications; flexibility; links with other functional areas; 'gate-keeping'; and costs for decision making.

Learning objectives

When you have completed this chapter, you should be able to:

☐ appreciate why predetermined cost and management accounting systems are needed;

☐ understand and illustrate what is meant by 'elements of costs';

☐ describe the different types of cost.

The management accounting information provided to the management should help enable them to achieve their corporate objectives, e.g. information to assist management with their decision making, monitoring and control.

Cost and management accounting systems

One of the ways of describing cost and management accounting systems, as shown in Figure 12.1, is splitting them into *historic systems*, and *predetermined systems*.

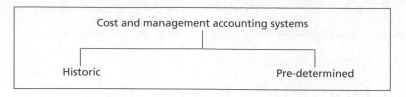

Figure 12.1 – The two types of cost and management accounting systems

Historic cost and management accounting systems

These systems cost the product or service provided, after the event. They look backwards at past performance. Although they can provide reflective learning via hindsight, they do not provide a sound basis for comparing and controlling performance. The past results, if used as a benchmark, could represent a performance that is good, bad or indifferent!

Predetermined cost and management accounting systems

Predetermined systems, such as *budgetary control and standard costing*, provide targets against which to measure actual performance, e.g. sales targets, expenditure targets. The targets set can then be compared with the actual results at frequent intervals, e.g. monthly. The differences, known as the *variances*, can then be reported to management, so that management may consider an appropriate course of action. They do, in fact, provide management with an early warning system which identifies where things are not going according to plan. The reported variances, e.g. significant adverse variances, provide management with a focus for their time, skills and talents. The targets set should be realistic and attainable. If not, this could bring about behavioural problems, e.g. a decline in motivation, staff leaving to work elsewhere.

The predetermined, figures, i.e. the *forecasts*, will make use of data relating to past performance, but this is one of many factors that will need to be taken into account. Account will also have to be taken of, for example, the anticipated rate of inflation, the forecast of demand, the level of pay settlements, the economic environment. If the assumptions on which the targets were based change significantly, the targets should be revised and recomputed. If not, they will be worthless for monitoring and control purposes, as any variances computed will be meaningless.

These systems use *estimated figures*, based on past performance updated by the best available information about the future. If the information is not very good, the whole system could suffer from *GIGO* (*garbage in, garbage out*)!

The elements of cost

How do you cost a product?
How do you cost a service?
How do you cost research and development?
How do you cost a feasibility study?

The answer to every one of the above questions is, 'In exactly the same way as you try to cost anything else!' It does not matter whether you are a manufacturer, a road passenger transport company, an insurance company, a bank, an educational establishment, the health service, the BBC, a firm of accountants or consultants, because the cost of anything is made up of the *elements of cost*, as illustrated in Figure 12.2, and is made up of the prime cost plus overheads.

The prime cost (or direct cost)	=	Direct materials, plus direct labour, plus direct expenses
The prime cost + the OVERHEAD EXPENSES = the COST (i.e. indirect expenses)		

Figure 12.2 – The elements of cost

The prime cost

This consists of the direct labour, direct materials and direct expenses.

Direct labour

The labour is used to transform raw materials into finished goods, to set the machines and equipment, or to deliver a service, e.g. a management consultant working for a client, a lecturer in a college, the director or the scriptwriters or tape editors of a television programme, the small business advisers in a bank, security staff for a security service.

Direct material

The material which forms part of the product, including packing material, or which is used to provide the service, e.g. fuel oil for road transport, cleaning fluids for a cleaning company, dressings in a hospital, presentation packs used by consultants for a specific client, materials used to build a theatre or film set.

Direct expenses

These are the expenses that can be charged to a specific job, product, service or client, e.g.

travelling and hotel expenses chargeable to a particular client, carriage inwards, advertising specific to a product or service, fees paid to subcontractors.

Overheads

The *indirect expenses* tend to be described as the *overheads*. Examples of overhead expenses are: the remuneration of cleaners and cleaning materials for factory and office cleaning, the salaries of canteen and welfare staff, insurance of buildings, light and heat, office stationery, printing and telephones, etc.

Overheads are one of management accounting's most problematic areas.

The pricing of labour uses forecast labour rates for direct and indirect labour, but problems can and do arise in relation to overtime and incentive bonus payments. The quantity side of labour can be estimated in terms of hours.

Material prices and quantities used can be estimated with reasonable accuracy for direct and indirect materials. The problem with the materials component of the elements of cost is valuation. Should we use FIFO (first in, first out) or LIFO (last in, first out) or AVECO (average cost) or some other basis for valuing stocks of raw materials and work-in-progress?

Overheads have to be estimated from past experience, plus what is known about their movements in the future. The big problem with overheads is, how much should we incorporate in the cost of the product or service to recover the overheads? For example, in large construction contracts or a university, each contract or university department may be charged with a certain proportion of central administration overheads. These are costs over which managers involved with the contracts or departments have no control. The charging out of such costs can be highly political and in many cases demotivating.

Another question that has to be resolved is, which types of overheads should we include in the cost of the product or service? For example, manufacturing concerns may only include the production overheads. Other types of business may include all or some of the administration, selling and distribution overheads.

In this text we look at three alternative systems for accounting for and dealing with overheads in the cost of products or services:

☐ total absorption costing
☐ marginal costing
☐ activity-based costing.

Cost has many meanings

Both private- and public-sector organisations are forever trying to find ways of reducing their costs of labour, materials and overheads and to improve their operating efficiency. Cost reduction can bring about improvements to the 'bottom line', improve cash flow, and enhance long-term success and survival. Look no further than any issue of the *Financial Times* to appreciate the importance and high-profile nature of cost, as illustrated in the display box.

Financial Times headlines

Guinness to be merged with UDV – Diageo set to link drinks divisions in cost-saving move *A. Edgecliffe-Johnson, 17 July 2000.*

ING buys Aetna units in $7.7bn deal *A. Michaels, 21 July 2000.*

Both of these reported cases illustrate the quest for synergy, which is illustrated as 1 + 1 = 3. The joining together should hopefully increase efficiency and reduce costs.

Dome gets £43m advance to remain open *S. Daneshkhu and C. Adams, 4 August 2000.*
One possible problem with this project was that it could have cost much more to close it down early than to keep it open! The actual income received was well below the budget and insufficient to cover the costs.

Toyota aims to cut costs by 30% *T. Burt, 27 September 2000.*
Their aim was to cut the cost of the development, production and marketing of future models, and to increase the cost reductions brought about by reforming their global procurement systems and increased use of IT in R&D.

Ford to axe more jobs in Europe *T. Burt, 18 December 2000.*
'We are not making money, and headcount is one aspect of it'. As part of their cost-cutting exercise, they also announced that they were seeking a 20% saving in their European logistics and transportation budget.

When we talk about cost, we need to know which cost we are talking about, as there are many different types of cost, including those we have referred to already: *historic costs*, *pre-determined costs*, and *prime* (or direct) *costs*. We shall now consider other costs that you may come across from time to time.

Fixed costs

These have to be paid out irrespective of the level of activity (output), but within a relevant range. However, when certain levels of activity are reached, there may be an increase in the fixed costs (a '*step fixed cost*'), e.g. more rent of buildings, more fixed equipment cost.

Variable cost

These vary with the level of activity, within a relevant range, e.g. an equipment rental based on output.

There can also be a mix of the above, known as *semi-variable* or *semi-fixed*.

Sunk costs

Once spent, these may be gone for ever, e.g. certain fixed costs such as insurance of buildings, fixed rentals paid for equipment. For the short term, most fixed costs do tend to be sunk costs, e.g. those that have to be paid out whether or not a project goes ahead.

Relevant or incremental costs (and revenue)

These costs (and revenues) only happen if the project goes ahead.

Replacement cost

This is the cost of replacing fixed assets and stocks of raw materials, fuels, etc.

Opportunity cost

The opportunity forgone is the cost of the opportunity sacrificed in order to go ahead with a project, such as a lost future residual value of some old equipment which had to be traded in at the commencement of the project. If you trade in now, you gain the trade-in value, but you lose the residual value for the year in which you would have disposed of the asset in question.

There are also other costs, e.g. standard costs and budgeted costs.

How much will it cost?

A question frequently asked by directors, managers, executives and others is, how much will it cost to do this? To be more specific, here are some typical questions that may be posed:

☐ A question from an insurance company:
How much will it cost to set up our own in-company staff training centre?

☐ A question from a large provider of computer systems:
How much will it cost to put on a series of twelve road shows around the country, where top management can report progress to regional and senior managers?

☐ A question from a medium-sized printing company:
How much will it cost us to put on an induction training programme for new employees?

☐ A question from an inventor of some high-tech equipment:
How much will it cost to set up, produce and market the product?

☐ A question from a company moving into the business of making TV programmes:
How much will it cost to make a series of six half-hour programmes about the history of the Green Movement?

☐ A question from a manufacturer of gardening equipment:
How much would it cost to set up our own transport department?

Other organisations, such as service-providing companies, government departments, charities, local government, all tend to ask similar questions.

The answers to all such questions can be approached by asking a series of questions, as follows:

☐ What would their balance sheet look like?
This provides a detailed appraisal of the fixed assets and working capital needed, which in turn provides an indication of the additional finance required. It will also give rise to many other questions, such as whether we need lots of new fixed assets or a few, and how we will raise the finance.

☐ What will their profit and loss account or income statement look like?
This forces them to consider both costs and revenue. Looking at the costs, particularly in terms of the elements of cost, i.e. direct materials, direct labour, direct expenses and overheads, should ensure that they consider all of the costs involved, including the overheads.

In addition to the above, they should also review the impact on cash flow, and attempt to answer the question, what happens if things go wrong? If things do go wrong it could be very costly!

Summary: an introduction to cost and management accounting

Cost and management accounting uses both *historic costing* and *predetermined costing*. Historic costing looks backwards at the figures after the event. Predetermined systems such as budgeting and standard costing look to the future, e.g. setting targets.

The elements of cost

The *elements of cost* are: direct materials, direct labour, direct expenses and overheads. The cost of any product or service for private- or public-sector organisations will be made up of a combination of the above costs.

The meaning of cost

There are lots of different types of cost, e.g. fixed costs, variable costs, direct costs and indirect costs (indirect costs are also described as 'overhead costs' or 'overheads').

How much?

When trying to assess how much a product or service will cost, it is useful to visualise what the organisation's balance sheet and profit and loss account will look like. This should provide a good indication of the expenditure needed for financing the assets, the finance charges, and the direct and indirect (overhead) costs.

The big problem, however, is in answering the big question, which is, how much should we include in the cost of the product or service to cover the overheads?

Self-checks

Following your attempt at each self-check, compare your answer with the appropriate section of this chapter, and also Chapter 1.

1. Describe the role of the cost and management accounting function (*Chapter 1*).

2. Explain briefly what is meant by the term 'prime cost'.

3. What are the elements of cost?

4. Explain the differences between:
   (a) fixed and variable costs
   (b) direct and indirect costs
   (c) net realisable costs and replacement cost
   (d) sunk costs and relevant costs.

Self-assessments

You will find the suggested answers to these self-assessment questions in Appendix 1.

A12.1 'The elements of cost can be found in the cost of any product or service.' Discuss this statement.

A12.2 Describe the costs that would be involved in setting up the following new business ventures:
   (a) Dani and Lim to form a small company to trade as insurance brokers.
   (b) An existing engineering company to start up a travel agency business.

Tutor-based assignments

The following series of questions could be used for individual assignments and/or group reports and presentations.

T12.1 Explain and illustrate the costs involved in setting up the following activities or projects, and suggest appropriate ways of financing them:
   (a) A dot.com mail order company to be set up by an existing mail order company.
   (b) The building and running of a chain of small hotels by a construction company.
   (c) The setting up of a central distribution depot, including the acquisition of a fleet of delivery vehicles, by a manufacturer of soft drinks.
   (d) A major marketing campaign by a leading college or university.
   (e) A new television one-off two-hour documentary about life after being a top professional sportsperson.
   (f) Setting up a specialist section by a medium-sized accounting firm to deal with personal tax matters.

Further reading

Chadwick, L., *Essential Management Accounting for Managers*, Financial Times Prentice, Hall, 2001
Drury, C., *Costing: An Introduction*, International Thomson Business Press, 1998
Dyson, J.R., *Accounting for Non-accounting Students*, Financial Times Prentice Hall, 2001
Lucey, T., *Management Accounting*, Continuum, 2000

Useful websites

www.continuumbooks.com
www.drury-online.com
www.booksites.net/dyson
www.thomsonlearning.co.uk

13

Materials and labour

Learning objectives

When you have worked your way through this chapter you should be able to:

☐ appreciate that both price and quantity affect the costing of materials and labour;

☐ describe briefly how *FIFO* (first in, first out), *LIFO* (last in, first out) and *AVECO* (average cost) work, and that their use can affect stock valuations. *Note*: it is not the objective of this text that you become expert in the 'number-crunching' side of stock valuations;

☐ understand why the *materials usage analysis* can be useful to management;

☐ know how management can reduce their stock levels to an acceptable minimum;

☐ appreciate the importance of the *payroll analysis*;

☐ describe briefly the role of management accounting relating to incentive schemes;

☐ know what is meant by '*labour turnover*', and discuss what management can do to reduce it.

How to cost a product or service

The cost of materials and labour that are included in the cost of a product or service are made up of two parts, *quantity* and *price*.

Quantity

The quantity side of the calculation tends to be quite straightforward. We can work out the quantity of materials to be used, from parts lists, specifications, chemical mixes, etc. We know from data relating to past performance how much will be wasted or scrapped. With labour, we know from experience, or can estimate, how long it will take to manufacture a product or deliver a service.

Price

The pricing side is not always an easy task and will require a certain degree of judgement. For example, there are a number of methods that can be used to value materials, and when valuing labour consideration must be given to the problems of differential rates of pay, bonus and overtime payments, etc.

Materials

The valuation of materials

There are a number of valuation methods that can be used for the pricing of materials issued to production and for stock valuation purposes:

☐ FIFO (first in, first out)
This method prices material issued to products by following the sequence in which the stock arrived. This means that the material element of the product cost is at an earlier price, lower or higher than the price at which the material is currently being purchased. The stock valuation, however, reflects the more recent prices.

☐ LIFO (last in, first out)
The effect on product costs and stock valuations is the opposite of that produced by the FIFO method.

☐ AVECO (average cost)
There are a number of variations of this method which may be used. For example, one method recomputes the average cost every time a new delivery of stock is received, as follows:

$$\text{Average cost} = \frac{\text{Value of balance of stock b/f} + \text{Value of new stock received}}{\text{Total number of units}}$$

Only the FIFO (first in, first out) method is in line with the recommended way in which the materials should be physically issued. All other methods are, therefore, purely methods of pricing. Thus, the method used will affect the stock valuations for raw materials, work-in-progress and finished goods.

From a management point of view, you must appreciate that:

☐ With the exception of FIFO these are not methods by which materials are to be physically issued, but merely methods for the pricing of materials issued to production and for ascertaining the valuation of stocks on hand. For example, although we may use LIFO or AVECO for evaluation purposes, the materials involved should still be physically issued on a FIFO basis to avoid losses caused by obsolescence, deterioration, etc.

☐ They could produce significantly differing results in terms of product costs and stock valuations.

☐ The figures will be affected by price fluctuations, the quantities received and issued, and the frequency of those receipts and issues.

☐ There are other methods that could be used, e.g. standard cost or replacement cost.

The materials usage analysis

It is possible to keep a record of the usage of direct and indirect materials. The information can help when it comes to budget preparation time. It can show how much was used, where it was used, how much was scrapped, wasted and so on.

Materials management

The cost of stocks of raw materials and fuels, and the material content of work-in-progress and finished goods consists of:

☐ the capital used to purchase the materials

☐ plus the cost of the capital used

☐ plus the holding costs, e.g. overheads, acquisition costs, handling costs.

Thus, for many organisations vast sums of money are used to finance the holding of stocks. Stock held represents *capital tied up*. Management should aim to keep its stocks at an acceptable minimum level. For example, it was reported in the *FT* on 8 November 2000 by T. Foremski ('Cisco inventory cut hits chips') that Cisco Systems, the world's largest network equipment company, was reducing its high component inventory levels. However, this kind of policy is likely to increase the risk of a 'stock-out' which could mean failing to honour delivery promises and lost orders. In Cisco's case, the raw materials inventory level of $631m (more than four times higher than in the previous quarter) was their insurance against chip shortages.

A lot of management accounting information relating to materials can assist management with *stock (inventory) control* and decision making, for example:

☐ reviews of maximum, minimum and reorder stock levels, at frequent intervals;

☐ identifying surplus, slow-moving and obsolete stocks and disposing of them;

☐ 'Pareto analysis' – there are various applications of Pareto's 80%/20% rule, e.g. 20% of your stock could account for 80% of the value of all of the stock that is being held;

☐ the use of subcontractors in the make-or-buy decision;

☐ standard costing – variance analysis and reports;

☐ with budgeting, e.g. the analysis of material consumption using budget and actual comparative statements.

In addition, management should be prepared to play an active part in the following:

☐ matching material requirements to production requirements, for example making use of JIT (just-in-time) systems;

☐ variety reduction programmes, and product design regarding the material content, so as to reduce inventory levels;

☐ random stock checks, to help detect errors and fraud;

☐ coding and classification systems;

☐ monitoring the environment to identify threats, opportunities, strengths and weaknesses in the materials area.

Labour

The payroll analysis

One of the principal means of providing cost and management accounting information is the *payroll analysis*. Both direct and indirect workers can record how they spend their time via time sheets, clock cards, computer keyboards, etc.

Direct workers will record how much time they spend producing products or working on jobs or the provision of a service, and how much of their time is non-productive (i.e. idle). Thus, payroll analysis will be able to provide labour costs per product, job, department or section, or service. This will enable comparisons to be made with budgets and/or standards and the reporting of variances. It will also provide valuable information which should assist with the task of preparing and producing budgets for future financial periods.

Another aspect of payroll analysis is *idle (non-productive) time analysis*. This analysis will show how many hours are lost for each cause.

Some of the causes of idle time are:

☐ waiting for materials

☐ waiting for work

☐ waiting for the setter

☐ machine breakdown

☐ training a new operative

☐ committee meetings, etc.

☐ travelling time.

To become more efficient management must strive to reduce idle (non-productive, lost) time. The attendance time of direct workers can be reconciled:

Attendance time recorded = Productive time recorded + Idle time recorded

As mentioned earlier, indirect workers, e.g. cleaners and welfare and maintenance staff, can keep a record of how and where they spend their time. The payroll analysis will therefore include an analysis of indirect labour per department or section. This analysis should prove useful in the estimation of the predetermined indirect labour budget figure which is needed for computing departmental overhead absorption rates (see Chapter 14). The analysis of indirect labour can also be used to compare with budgeted figures for control purposes, e.g. to see if any overspending has occurred.

Incentive schemes

The management accounting section can provide useful information relating to incentive schemes, for example:

☐ monitoring existing schemes

☐ the effects of amendments to existing schemes

☐ a comparison between proposed schemes

☐ productivity records.

The cost of labour turnover

Management needs to become more aware of the real cost of employing people, i.e. the *cost of labour turnover*.

What is labour turnover?

It is the rate at which people leave an employer, and may be calculated as follows:

$$\frac{\text{Number of persons leaving}}{\text{Average number of persons on the payroll}} \times 100 \text{ (for, say, per month, quarter or half-year)}$$

See for example, Figure 13.1.

Quarter 2 Department	No. of persons who left	Average no. on payroll	Rate of labour turnover %
S	78	352	22.16
T	32	240	13.33

Figure 13.1 – The rate of labour turnover

News about labour turnover and the cost of labour turnover does not make the headlines much at all. However, from time to time it does appear and, when it does, it usually comes with some surprising facts and figures, as illustrated by a story in the *FT* (R. Taylor, 16 May 2001, see also www.cbi.org.uk).

Workplace absence unchanged but labour turnover increases

In addition to pointing out that absenteeism had lost British business around £10.7bn, it also reported a slight increase in the level of labour turnover. As many as one in five of those employed in the private sector had changed their job in 2000 (the biggest rates being in retailing 30%, followed by construction 25%),compared with 14% in the public sector. Employee morale and commitment is a very important factor.

Source: R. Taylor was commenting on *Pulling Together: 2001 Absence and Labour Turnover Survey*, Confederation of British Industry, 2001

Which costs should be included?

The short answer to this question is 'a lot more than you would expect to see'. Labour turnover could include the following costs:

☐ *Advertising* vacancies.

☐ *Recruitment* – including the cost of drawing up job specifications and the employment of specialist recruitment agencies, 'headhunters', etc.

☐ *Selection* – interviews in terms of the personnel involved and the facilities provided, the hire of accommodation, meals, refreshments, travelling expenses, etc. Where special selection tests are used there are costs associated with their design, development, testing, monitoring, marking, administration and review.

☐ *Engagement* – records, medicals, special clothing and equipment needs.

☐ The *human resource management* (personnel) function – in terms of salaries, offices, fixtures, fittings and equipment, and associated overheads such as light and heat, printing, stationery, telephone costs.

☐ *Training costs*, e.g. induction training (courses for new employees) to inform them about the organisation and its products or services), pre-job training in the organisation's own training school, courses, textbooks, travelling expenses.

☐ *Production costs*, such as lost production of those who are supervising the work of new operatives. There is also the likelihood of a reduced level of output and a higher level of defective output (or errors in the case of a service) from new employees.

☐ *Morale and motivation* – these are both difficult to quantify but can have a dramatic impact on the organisation and its products or services.

What can be done to reduce the cost of labour turnover?

Management needs to know the rate of labour turnover and the reasons why people leave. Managers may, for example, compute the rate of labour turnover:

☐ per department, service, or section;

☐ for males and females according to age groups.

They need to find out why people are leaving and analyse whether the reasons are controllable or uncontrollable. This kind of information can be collected via interviews or questionnaires conducted by the personnel department. Employees could leave for one or more of the following reasons:

☐ pay

☐ the nature of the work

☐ promotion

☐ the hours

☐ working conditions

☐ discrimination and/or harassment

☐ relationships with superiors and/or subordinates

☐ hot desking

☐ housing and/or transport problems

☐ welfare and social considerations

☐ health

☐ moving away from the area, etc.

It can be seen that the process of employing people entails a great deal more than simply engaging them and paying them a wage or salary. There are many costs involved in the employment of labour. In fact, it can be said in conclusion that the cost of employing people represents a significant investment and that the cost of labour turnover is far greater than a lot of people would imagine. Much is said nowadays about customer retention – employee retention is also very important.

Other matters

Quite recent developments in the labour area will continue to make demands upon the management accounting section. The implications of the following will all need to be costed, analysed, compared with appropriate data and monitored:

☐ productivity deals
☐ the introduction of flexitime
☐ the provision of a nursery places for the children of employees
☐ profit-sharing schemes
☐ employees' share schemes
☐ executives, designers, etc. working from home via computer links
☐ corporate rewards and incentives, e.g. holidays for sales staff.

From a review of the above it can be seen why we described the role of the management accounting function in Chapter 12 as being that of 'an information manager'.

Summary: materials and labour

The costs of materials and labour are made up of two elements, namely quantity and price.

Materials

The valuation of materials

There are numerous methods that may be applied for cost and management accounting purposes; three of them are as follows:

☐ *FIFO*: first in, first out
☐ *LIFO*: last in, first out
☐ *AVECO*: average cost.

FIFO

In times of rising prices this method has the effect of including the older, lower prices in the product costs and the higher, more recent prices in the stock-in-hand valuations. However, it does follow the order in which the stock should be physically issued, i.e. the stock should be issued in the order in which it arrived so as to avoid losses caused by obsolescence, deterioration, etc.

LIFO

The LIFO method is not in line with the method by which the stock should be physically issued (i.e. FIFO). However, in times of rising prices, it does charge the higher, more recent prices to product costs, leaving the older, lower prices in the closing stock valuation. Thus, the product costs are more realistic and reflect current prices; however, where prices are rising, the closing stock valuation will be understated.

AVECO

The advantage claimed for this method is that all products, for a time, are charged for the same material at a uniform rate.

The method adopted will affect the valuation of stocks of raw materials, work-in-progress, finished goods or the cost of materials used to provide a service.

Materials management

Stocks of materials, work-in-progress and finished goods represent *capital tied up* and also generate expensive *holding costs*, e.g. heating, lighting, insurance, staff time. In attempting to keep stock (inventory) levels to an acceptable minimum management can take various actions, e.g. reviewing stock levels at frequent intervals, selling off stock that is surplus to requirements, 'Pareto analysis', variety reduction programmes.

Labour

Payroll analysis

The payroll can be divided into two categories:

☐ Direct labour
  The labour used to transform the raw material into finished goods or for the provision of a service. The direct labour content of a product or service can be ascertained via the time recording system, by e.g. time sheets, time cards and computer systems as a by-product of the payroll recording system.

☐ Indirect labour

Non-manufacturing workers and those not directly involved in providing a service, such as cleaners, welfare workers, canteen staff and maintenance personnel, can also record how they spend their time via time sheets or time cards, etc. It should therefore be possible to produce a payroll analysis for the indirect workers, per department, section, or service, etc.

Another important part of payroll analysis is the idle (non-productive) time analysis. This should direct the attention of management to the areas in which hours are being lost so that, where possible, corrective action may be taken to help remedy the situation. The payroll analysis can be a considerable help during the budget preparation period and with the setting of standards.

Incentive schemes

Management needs to be provided with information such as updates of existing schemes, comparative figures for new schemes and productivity records.

The cost of labour turnover

This is a cost that tends to be overlooked or ignored by management; but it is a cost that can and does involve huge sums of money.

$$\text{The rate of labour turnover} = \frac{\text{Number of persons leaving}}{\text{Average number of persons on the payroll}} \times 100$$

on, say, a monthly, quarterly or half-yearly basis. It represents the rate at which employees leave a particular employer.

The costs associated with the employment of the labour force are:

☐ *administrative*, e.g. advertising, recruitment, selection, engagement and the personnel function;

☐ *training*, e.g. induction training, training courses, own training schools;

☐ *production*, e.g. losses caused by new employees, defective production;

☐ damage to *morale and motivation*.

Management needs to ensure that records are kept of why employees leave and that controllable causes are noted and investigated so that appropriate corrective action may be taken.

Further thoughts

Management accounting information will be needed for both current and future developments in the labour area, e.g. to assess the impact on the cost of providing nursery places for employees' children or allowing certain executives, designers, etc. to work at home via computer links.

Self-checks

On completion of each self-check, compare your answer with the appropriate section of the chapter.
1. Why is the pricing side of materials and labour not always an easy task?
2. In a period of rising prices how would the stock of raw materials and the stock of finished goods be affected by:
   (a) using FIFO and
   (b) using LIFO?
3. Explain the way in which the payroll analysis is built up, and the kind of information it may generate.

Self-assessment

When you have completed the question, compare your attempt with the suggested answer which you will find in Appendix 1.

A13.1 Explain what management can do to improve their materials management.

Tutor-based assignments

Discuss the questions and be prepared to present your answers, as directed by the lecturer or tutor.

T13.1 (a) What is the cost of labour turnover, and how is it calculated?
      (b) Why do people leave their employment?
      (c) What can management do to reduce the cost of labour turnover?

T13.2 What costs would be involved in setting up a training school for the employees of a world-class airline?

Further reading

Drury, C., *Costing: An Introduction*, International Thomson Business Press, 1998

Hussey, J. and Hussey, E., *Cost and Management Accounting*, Macmillan, 1998

Storey, R., *Introduction to Cost and Management Accounting*, Macmillan, 1995

Weetman, P., *Management Accounting: An Introduction*, Financial Times Prentice Hall, 1999

Useful websites

www.drury-online.com
www.booksites.net/weetman

14

Total absorption costing

Learning objectives

By the time you have finished studying this chapter, you should be able to do the following:

☐ understand how overheads are incorporated into the cost of a job, product or service;
☐ prepare an overhead distribution summary and calculate:

—a machine hour rate
—a direct labour hour rate
—the cost of a job or product;

☐ explain how and why the *under- or over-absorption* (recovery) of overhead occurs, and its accounting treatment;
☐ appreciate the *limitations* of total absorption costing.

The principal aim of *total absorption costing* (also called absorption costing or total costing or the full cost method) is to attempt to ensure that all the overhead costs are covered by the revenues received. It should be mentioned here that *it does not attempt to produce accurate costs*. It is, however, an attempt to answer the question of how much should be included for overheads in costing jobs, products or services.

An introduction to overheads and cost centres

Overheads

Overheads comprise the indirect expenditure of a business, i.e. that expenditure that does not form part of the product, job or service and includes such costs as:

- [ ] *indirect labour*: cleaners, canteen staff, security staff, supervisory staff, etc;
- [ ] *indirect materials*: cleaning materials, maintenance materials, etc;
- [ ] *indirect expenses*: rent, insurance of buildings, heating, lighting, etc.

The overheads can be subdivided into fixed overheads and variable overheads. They can also be classified as production overheads, selling overheads, distribution overheads, administration overheads, etc.

Cost centres

Cost centre is the name given to a location to which costs are allocated and apportioned. It could be a department, a process, a function, a service, a group of machines or a person. The aim is to arrive at a total overhead cost for each cost centre.

All organisations including those that provide a service, e.g. the BBC, banking, insurance, education, may have numerous cost centres.

You may also come across the term **profit centre**. This is much the same as a cost centre, but is also revenue-earning. Thus, a profit or loss for the centre can be computed.

The absorption of overheads

Overhead absorption (also called overhead recovery) is the process of sharing out the overheads between jobs, products or services by means of *absorption rates* (recovery rates), e.g. a rate per direct labour hour or a rate per machine hour.

Absorption costing differs from marginal costing (which we will look at in Chapter 16) in that it attempts to include most of the overheads in product/job/services costs. Marginal costing, on the other hand, includes only the variable overheads in product costs.

We will now describe how a typical absorption costing system in a manufacturing environment works by reference to the absorption of overheads diagram (see Figure 14.1). Because the overheads have to be charged to jobs, products or services throughout the period or year, the recovery rates must be calculated before that accounting period begins, i.e. they have to be predetermined.

Stage 1

The production overheads, i.e. the indirect materials, labour and expenses associated with the production process, have to be *estimated* for the forthcoming accounting period.

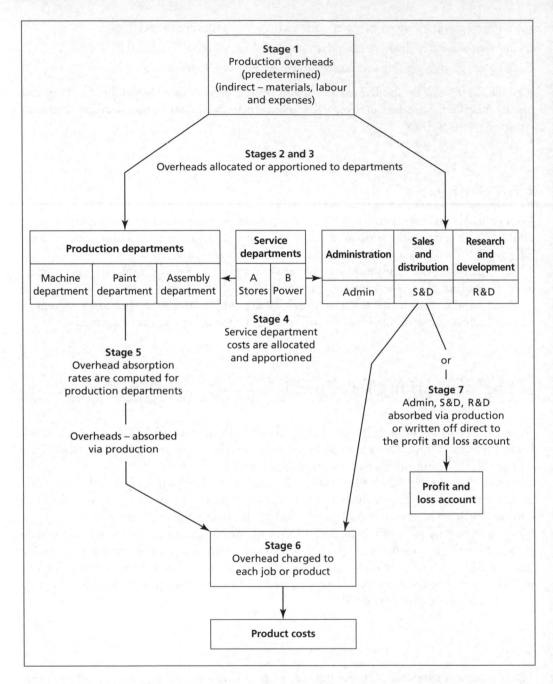

Figure 14.1 – Total absorption costing in a manufacturing environment
Source: L. Chadwick, *Essential Management Accounting for Managers*, Financial Times Prentice Hall, 2001.

Stage 2

Those overheads that can be *identified with and traced* to a department or cost centre are charged to the department or cost centre concerned, i.e. they are *allocated* to it.

Stage 3

Overheads that *cannot be allocated* to the cost centres, i.e. those that cannot be identified and traced to departments/cost centres will have to be apportioned to departments/cost centres using some arbitrary basis. A number of overheads tend to *vary more with time than with output* and will have to be shared out between the cost centres using some method of apportionment (see Figure 14.2).

Item of overhead expenditure	Basis of apportionment
Rent/heating	Floor area or cubic capacity
Supervision/canteen	Number of employees

Figure 14.2 – The apportionment of overheads

Stage 4

Having collected all the overheads applicable to the service departments, the *total overhead cost of each service department can be shared out* between the user departments/costs centres according to the technical estimates or by using some arbitrary basis of apportionment, e.g. in proportion to the number of issue notes for the stores department.

Stage 5

The *overhead absorption* (overhead recovery) rates are calculated. The total overhead for each production department, inclusive of its share of service department costs, is divided by the estimated machine hours or direct labour hours, as appropriate:

$$\frac{\text{Machine department overheads}}{\text{Estimated no. of machine hours}} = \text{Rate per machine hour}$$

$$\frac{\text{Paint department overheads}}{\text{Estimated no. of direct labour hours}} = \text{Rate per direct labour hour}$$

Stage 6

☐ If a job/product spends 6 machine hours in the machine department, it will be charged with 6 machine hours' worth of overheads at the rate per machine hour.

☐ If a job/product spends 2 direct labour hours in the paint department, it will be charged with 2 direct labour hours' worth of overheads at the rate per direct labour hour.

As the products move from department to department they *accumulate* a portion of each department's overheads. The overheads are being recovered hour by hour.

Stage 7

The administration, selling and distribution expenses are charged either to the profit and loss account or to jobs/products. The way in which they are treated is at the discretion of the management.

The following simplified but comprehensive example should help you to understand the process more fully.

Example   Marcel Van Wong plc

We have been provided with the information shown in Figures 14.3 and 14.4 relating to Marcel Van Wong plc for the forthcoming period. The estimated number of machine hours in department G was 144,000 and the estimated number of direct labour hours in department N was 80,000.

Estimated overhead expenses:	£000	Allocation or apportionment
Indirect materials and labour:		
Production department G	115	Allocation
Production department N	93	Allocation
Service department I	151	Allocation
Service department II	72	Allocation
Rent of buildings	210	Floor area
Insurance of buildings	30	Floor area
Supervision	64	Number of employees
Repairs and renewals	60	Technical estimate
		G N I II
		60% 20% 10% 10%
Depreciation of machinery:		
Production department G	180	Allocation
Production department N	20	Allocation
Service department I	35	Allocation
Service department II	10	Allocation

Figure 14.3 – Marcel Van Wong plc: estimated overhead expenditure

There are quite a number of other overhead absorption (overhead recovery) rates that could have been used. A study of them is outside the scope of this book.

	G	N	I	II
Area (in square metres)	1,200	500	200	100
Number of employees	12	16	2	2
Technical estimates for service departments:				
The use of service I	50%	30%	—	20%
The use of service II	75%	25%	—	—

Figure 14.4 – Marcel Van Wong plc: apportionment data

We will now work through how to:
1. prepare a departmental overhead summary and calculate a direct labour hour rate for department N and a machine hour rate for department G; and

2. prepare a quotation for a job, number XL90, to which the following data are applicable:
   (a) direct material: £3,452
   (b) direct labour:
       department G 8 hours at £10 per hour;
       department N 14 hours at £8 per hour;
       machine hours in department G were 20.
   The company uses a mark-up of 40% on cost.

Answer
Having been provided with the predetermined overheads, we can prepare the departmental overhead summary in which we allocate and apportion the overheads to departments or cost centres. When this has been completed, we then share out the service department costs between user departments according to the technical estimates supplied. This will take us up to the point of having total overhead figures for departments G and N. See Figure 14.5 for the overhead distribution summary.

We now know the total overhead that has been allocated and apportioned to production departments G and N, and the overhead absorption (recovery) rates for the two departments can now be calculated. The rate for production department G is:

$$\frac{\text{Overheads}}{\text{Machine hours}} = \frac{72,000}{144,000} = \text{£5 per machine hour}$$

For production department N it is:

$$\frac{\text{Overheads}}{\text{Direct labour}} = \frac{32,000}{80,000} = \text{£4 per direct labour hour}$$

The quotation for the job XL90 can now be prepared, and it is as shown in Figure 14.6.

Overhead	Allocation or apportionment	Total £000	Production departments G £000	N £000	Service departments I £000	II £000
Indirect materials and labour	Allocated	431	115	93	151	72
Rent and insurance	Floor area	240	144	60	24	12
Supervision	No. of employees	64	24	32	4	4
Repairs and renewals	Technical estimates	60	36	12	6	6
Depreciation	Allocated	245	180	20	35	10
		£1040	499	217	220	104
Service I	Technical estimates		110	66	-220	44
					Nil	148
Service II	Technical estimates		111	37		-148
		1040	720	320		Nil

Figure 14.5 – Marcel Van Wong plc: overhead distribution summary

	£
Direct materials	3,452
Direct labour	£
(8 hrs × £10) Department G	80
(14 hrs × £8) Department N	112	192
Overheads	
Department G (20 hrs × £5)	100
Department N (14 hrs × £4)	56	156
Cost	3,800
add mark-up @ 40% (profit)	1,520
	£5,320

Figure 14.6 – Quotation for job XL90

Comments

You should note that the quotation for the job XL90 is made up of four elements:

☐ direct materials

☐ direct labour

☐ overheads

☐ mark-up.

The direct materials and direct labour were given, but you should remember that they also will have to be predetermined or estimated in practice.

Finally, note that for department G the hours used to arrive at the overhead cost of £100 were the 20 machine hours, not the direct labour hours. Why? Because the overheads for that department are being recovered using a machine hour rate.

The under- and over-absorption of overheads

In total absorption costing, products, jobs or services are charged with fixed overheads at so much per unit, or per machine hour or per direct labour hour, i.e. using a predetermined overhead absorption (recovery) rate, such as:

$$\frac{\text{Budgeted fixed overheads}}{\text{Budgeted units produced}} = \text{Fixed overhead rate per unit of output}$$

If the total amount of fixed overheads absorbed is greater than the actual fixed overhead expenditure there is **over-absorption**. An over-absorption of fixed overheads should be *added back* to the profits (or used to reduce the loss) in the profit and loss account. This is because the product costs have included too much for the overheads, which in turn reduces the profit which has been calculated.

If the total amount of fixed overheads absorbed is less than the actual fixed overheads incurred, there is an **under-absorption**. An under-absorption of fixed overheads should be *deducted* from profits (or go to increase the loss) in the profit and loss account, since product costs have been understated. However, note that we do not, and cannot, go back and amend the product/service costs – they are history. A single under- or over-absorption adjustment will be made to the profit and loss account at the end of the accounting period. This is because the products/jobs/services accumulate a share of the overheads via the predetermined fixed overhead absorption rate throughout the whole of the period.

Problems and limitations

Finally, remember that total absorption costing does have its problems and limitations, e.g. the accuracy of the forecast overheads, the accuracy of the estimated machine hours and direct labour hours, the selection of methods of apportionment, and the under- or over-recovery of overheads.

An introduction to ABC (activity-based costing), a more sophisticated version of the total absorption costing method, will be covered in Chapter 15.

Summary: total absorption costing

To my mind the diagram illustrated in Figure 14.1 sums up the essence of total absorption costing. The overheads, i.e. indirect expenditure, both fixed and variable, have to be estimated, i.e. predetermined, before the period to which they relate commences. *Total absorption costing* is also called absorption costing, full or total costing.

It is just an attempt to ensure that all the costs are covered. It does not profess to produce accurate costs for jobs or products or services.

Overheads

Overhead or indirect cost is defined by CIMA (the Chartered Institute of Management Accountants) in the UK as 'Expenditure, labour, materials or services which cannot be economically identified with a specific saleable cost unit'. A cost unit could be a job, a product or a service.

Those overheads that can be identified and traced to a department or cost centre can be charged direct to the department or cost centre, i.e. *allocated*. Those that cannot be identified or traced to a department or cost centre will have to be *apportioned* according to some arbitrary basis, e.g. floor area, number of employees.

The costs of running the various service departments, such as stores and power, have to be accumulated to arrive at a cost for running each service. The service department cost is then shared out between user departments via technical estimates or on some arbitrary basis.

Overheads can be analysed into groups, e.g. production, administration, selling and distribution, research and development. They can also be subdivided into fixed overheads and variable overheads.

Services

Although the illustrations in this chapter relate mainly to a manufacturing type of environment and internal services, those organisations that provide services, e.g. health, auditing, education, radio and television, do face similar problems. In costing their services they also have to account for overheads.

Problems and limitations

If you wish to know how the system works and what the problems and limitations are, a critical review of the diagram, Figure 14.1, should help improve your understanding.

Self-checks

Check your attempt with the relevant section of this chapter.

1. What is the principal aim of total absorption costing?

2. Describe briefly what overheads are.

3. Explain and illustrate what cost centres are.

4. Describe how the absorption (recovery) rate in a manufacturing environment should be arrived at.

5. Explain how an under- (or over-) absorption of overheads can arise, and how it would be dealt with in the profit and loss account.

Self-assessments

A14.1 (a) Explain how the selector goes about choosing a basis, e.g. cubic capacity, for apportioning overheads.

(b) Why is a 'time-based' method of absorption considered a more appropriate way of including overheads in the cost of a product or service.

(c) What is meant by the description 'overhead accumulation'?

(d) How is the cost-plus method of pricing sometimes used in an absorption costing environment.

A14.2 Bonnopia plc operates three production departments (machining, painting and assembly) and two service departments (stores and power). Their budgeted overheads for the period are:

	£000
Rent	200
Repairs to machinery (excluding power plant)	144
Depreciation of machinery (excluding power plant)	192
Depreciation of power plant	12
Power	108
Employers liability insurance	20
Supervision	80

Indirect materials and labour:	£000	
Machining	48	
Painting	36	
Assembly	12	
Stores	20	
Power	24	140

The following information is available for the five departments:

	Machining	Painting	Assembly	Stores	Power
Area (m²)	800	1,400	1,200	400	200
Employees	20	16	42	4	2
Plant and machinery value	£800,000	£100,000	£50,000	—	£250,000

Services departments are shared up on a percentage basis as follows:

Power	50	20	20	10	—
Stores	40	30	30	—	—

Machine hours for the machining department were estimated at 40,000.
Direct labour hours for the painting department were estimated at 30,000.
Direct labour hours for the assembly department were estimated at 12,000.

Required:

(a) Prepare a departmental overhead distribution summary.

(b) Calculate the overhead absorption rates for the three production departments.

(c) Calculate the cost of Job No. 007XL5 from the following data:

Direct material   £68,200
Direct labour:
Machining – 40 hours @ £10 per hour (machine hours 80)
Painting – 20 hours @ £9 per hour
Assembly – 48 hours @ £8 per hour

(d) Comment on the validity of the methods of apportionment that have been used.

Tutor-based assignments

The following assignments can be used for discussions, projects and/or presentations, as directed by the lecturer or tutor.

T14.1   Describe and illustrate the problems and limitations that are associated with total absorption costing.

T14.2   The Westway Hotel in North Yorkshire has three service departments:

  ☐ maintenance
  ☐ administration
  ☐ laundry.

The costs of these departments are shared between three departments through which customers are charged:

  ☐ conference
  ☐ restaurant (which includes kitchen), and
  ☐ accommodation

The methods of apportionment to be used are:

  ☐ Maintenance – area occupied
  ☐ Administration – a fixed percentage thus:

Laundry	10%
Conference	20%
Restaurant	30%
Accommodation	40%

  ☐ Laundry variable costs – items processed
  ☐ Laundry fixed costs – maximum processing capacity.

The apportionment is carried out on a step basis, i.e. once a department's cost has been apportioned the department does not receive any other apportionment. A detailed budget has been prepared and this has been summarised into appropriate fixed and variable costs which are shown on the following page:

	1 M't'ce £000	2 Admin. £000	3 Laundry £000	4 Conf'ce £000	5 Rest'nt £000	6 Accom. £000
Variable costs			60		180	144
Fixed costs	70	50	75	120	240	180
Other information:						
Area (sq metres)		5,000	7,500	30,000	12,500	195,000
Laundry:						
Items processed				2,000	10,000	50,000
Maximum processing capacity				30,000	13,000	80,000

You are required to:

(a) Complete the process of service department cost allocation and apportionment so that the total cost of each department can be established. The variable and fixed costs should be dealt with separately.

(b) For what purpose(s) might the above information be used?

Further reading

Chadwick, L., *Management Accounting*, International Thomson Business Press, 1998

Drury, C., *Costing: An Introduction*, International Thomson Business Press, 1998

Hussey, J. and Hussey, R., *Cost and Management Accounting*, Macmillan, 1998

Upchurch, A., *Management Accounting: Principles and Practice*, Financial Times Prentice Hall, 1998

Useful websites

www.booksites/upchurch
www.booksites/weetman

15

Activity-based costing

From your review of Chapter 14, you will appreciate that total absorption costing does have quite a number of problems and limitations. There will always be a quest for something more sophisticated. Activity-based costing was developed in the USA by R. Cooper and R. S. Kaplan during the late 1980s to fulfil this need, and also to respond to the ever-changing diverse and complex business environment. Nowadays, significant sums are spent on support activities, such as setting machines and equipment, quality control and inspection. The direct labour cost for many products and services tends to represent a much smaller proportion of the total cost. Thus, management has become more aware of the need to take more notice and focus on their organisation's support activities and overheads (indirect expenses).

Learning objectives

When you have completed your study of this chapter, including the self-checks, self-assessments and tutor-based assignments, you should be able to:

☐ appreciate the need for *activity-based costing (ABC)*;

☐ define in your own words what is meant by:
— cost objects
— resource costs
— resource cost drivers
— activity cost pools
— activity cost drivers;

☐ prepare activity-based product cost computations and profit statements using the activity-based costing approach;

☐ appreciate the limitations associated with activity-based costing.

The principal objective of total absorption costing is to ensure that all the costs are recovered. Marginal costing (see Chapter 16) is considered more appropriate for decision-making purposes, but does not always lead to all of the costs being recovered via the cost of the product or service. ABC provides a more common-sense approach for assigning overheads to products, services, jobs, distribution channels, sales areas, etc.

The business environment

The business environment in which organisations operate has over recent years become more complex and diverse with the advent of advances in technology, World Wide Web (WWW) threats and opportunities, e-business, e-marketing, shorter product life-cycles, higher quality expectations, greater portfolios of products and services, and increased competition. In the past, materials and labour costs tended to be the dominant costs. Not so nowadays – for many companies, the consumption of support costs and overheads can amount to a considerable sum. Hence the need for ABC.

What is activity-based costing (ABC)?

A review of the definitions of **activity-based costing** and the diagram, Figure 15.1, should provide you with a good insight into what activity-based costing is, and how it works.

The CIMA (Chartered Institute of Management Accountants) in their 1991 publication, *Official Terminology*, define ABC as:

> cost attribution to cost units on the basis of benefit received from indirect activities e.g. ordering, setting-up, assuring quality.

It has also been defined as:

> a process of using multiple cost drivers to predict and allocate costs to products and services; an accounting system collecting financial and operational data on the basis of the underlying nature and extent of business activities; an accounting information and costing system that identifies the various activities performed in an organisation, collects costs on the basis of the underlying nature and extent of those activities, and assigns costs to products and services based on consumption of those activities by products and services.

> J.T. Barfield, C.A. Raiborn and M.R. Kinney, *Cost Accounting Traditions and Innovations*, West Publishing, 1993.

Another definition describes it as:

the collection of financial and non-financial data about an enterprise's activities for two primary purposes:

☐ Costing the enterprise's cost objects*
☐ Providing information for effective cost management through activity-based management

J.G. Burch, *Cost and Management Accounting: A Modern Approach*, West Publishing, 1994.

---

* Cost objects are the products, services, batches, jobs, sales areas, etc.

Speaking at the European Accounting Conference at Maastricht in April 1991, R.S. Kaplan said that he considered ABC to be much more than a product costing system and that in his view it could be better described as a *resource consumption system*.

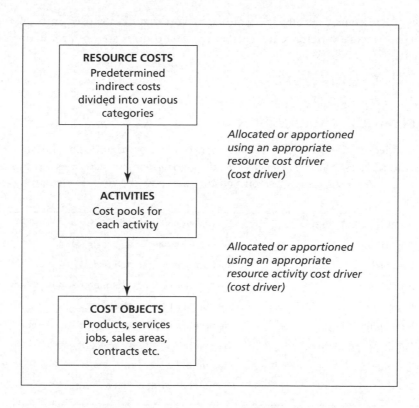

Figure 15.1 – Activity-based costing
Source: L. Chadwick, *Essential Management Accounting*, Financial Times Prentice Hall, 2001.

The resource costs

You need to appreciate at the outset that the costs we are dealing with are the *indirect costs*, i.e. the *overheads*, as direct costs are charged direct to the cost object, e.g. the product or service. You should also note that the resource costs have still got to be *estimated* prior to the commencement of the budget period.

The resource costs (indirect costs) could include costs such as: insurance of buildings, wages and salaries, rent of premises, maintenance of equipment, depreciation of various fixed assets.

The resource costs that are specific to one cost pool can be *allocated* to the cost pool concerned and do not present a problem. Those that are incurred on behalf of a number of cost pools will have to be apportioned using appropriate *resource cost drivers* (cost drivers). The resource cost driver is linked to the usage of the resource by the activity, for example in terms of:

☐ the number of employees

☐ the area or cubic capacity

☐ hours.

This type of cause-and-effect relationship is, as you may recall, used in total absorption costing. The principal difference here is that the cost centres are not production or service departments, but activities.

The activities

ABC is founded on the belief that the *activities cause the costs* and that the *cost objects*, e.g. products and services, *create the demand for those activities*. The activities have to be identified and a *cost pool* (cost centre) established for each cost activity. There can be numerous

ACTIVITY COST POOL	ACTIVITY COST DRIVER
Advertising	the value of sales in each sales area
Despatch	the number of despatch notes
Handling	the number of times the material is handled
Inspection	the number of inspections
Purchasing	the number of purchase orders
Receiving (goods inwards)	the number of goods-received notes
Setting-up	the number of set-ups
Stores	the number of stores-issue notes

Figure 15.2 – Assigning activity pool costs via activity (cost) drivers to cost objects
Source: L. Chadwick, *Essential Management Accounting*, Financial Times Prentice Hall, 2001.

activities. They can be allocated to a product or service where they are specific to that product/service. In cases where they serve a number of products/services they will have to be apportioned using *activity cost drivers* (cost drivers), as illustrated in Figure 15.2.

Thus, the amount assigned to each product or service will depend on the use made of the activity cost pool via an appropriate activity cost driver.

The ABC focus

ABC causes management to focus on what creates the demand for the resources and the redeployment or elimination of excess resources. ABC attempts to estimate the resources consumed by products.

You should therefore note that:

☐ *resource cost drivers* attempt to measure the resources consumed by the activity cost pools;

☐ *activity cost drivers* attempt to measure the activities consumed by the cost object, e.g. product or service. The aim is to charge the cost object with the overheads that it actually uses.

The following step-by-step example should help you to understand the mechanics of an activity-based costing system.

Example: Wikwok Lui plc

The following indirect predetermined resource cost categories have been identified, together with the resource cost driver by which they will be assigned to activity cost pools, for the forthcoming period:

Resource cost	£000	Resource cost driver
Wages and salaries	900	Number of employees
Computing	600	Computer hours
Office space	1,000	Cubic capacity

The activity cost pools and data relating to the consumption of the resource costs are:

Activity cost pool	Number of employees	Computer hours	Cubic capacity
Purchasing	10	46,000	4,000
Receiving	5	10,000	16,000
Despatch	15	4,000	30,000

The activity cost pools will therefore be:

	Purchasing £000	Receiving £000	Despatch £000	Total £000
Wages and salaries	300	150	450	900
Computing	460	100	40	600
Office space	80	320	600	1,000
	840	570	1,090	2,500

The resources have now been shared out between the 'activity cost pools' according to their estimated usage of the resource costs by each of the activities, by means of the resource cost drivers.

The company sells three products – W, O and K – and then assigns the costs of activities to them using the following activity cost drivers:

Activity cost pool	Activity cost driver
	The number of:
Purchasing	purchase orders
Receiving	goods-received notes
Despatch	despatch notes

The following estimates have been prepared for the period:

	Products			
Number of:	W	O	K	Total
Purchase orders	50,000	26,000	8,000	84,000
Goods-received notes	64,000	36,000	14,000	114,000
Despatch notes	20,000	30,000	4,500	54,500

From the above information we can now work out the cost per order or note for each of the activity cost drivers

	Purchasing	Receiving	Despatch
Cost	£840,000	£570,000	£1,090,000
Activity cost driver	84,000 orders	114,000 notes	54,500 notes
Cost per order/note	£10 per order	£5 per note	£20 per note

We can now assign the activity pool costs to the three products, as follows:

(£000)	Products			
	W	O	K	Total
Purchasing @ £10 per order	500	260	80	840
Receiving @ £5 per note	320	180	70	570
Despatch @ £20 per note	400	600	90	1,090
Cost of overheads assigned to products	1,220	1,040	240	2,500

In this simplified example we only had three lots of resource costs, three activity cost pools and three products. In practice you will find that there are many more categories of resource costs, many more activity cost pools to deal with, and many more products or services to contend with. Compared with products W and O, product K consumed a much lower amount of the activity cost pool costs.

You should note that *resource cost drivers* and *activity cost drivers* can be:

☐ time-based

☐ value-based (e.g. in £ sterling)

☐ transaction-based

☐ percentage-based.

The one that should be used is the one that has a direct cause-and-effect relationship. Thus, with activity-based costing, a choice has to be made as to which cost driver is the most appropriate for the assignment of resource costs and activity costs to cost objects.

Problems and limitations

When ABC was first introduced, consultancy firms were quick to adopt it and promote its use amongst their corporate and other clients. However, although it is a step in the right direction, it does have a number of problems and limitations. Many of the problems and limitations associated with total absorption costing still remain.

First and foremost, the expenditure figures that are used, i.e. the resource costs and the activity cost drivers etc., have to be *estimated*. Yes, the figures that are used have to be pre-determined, and could be way out!

ABC seeks to find out what causes the indirect expenditure (i.e. the overheads). This is not an easy task as many of the overheads vary more with time than with output and several of the suggested cost drivers are those that are already recommended for use in total absorption costing, e.g. the machine hours and the direct labour hours.

You also have to select which cost driver you consider to be the most appropriate. This is not always clear-cut. In addition you have to estimate the number of machine hours, direct labour hours, set-ups, purchase orders, etc. before commencement of the period to which they relate.

Remember, when you deal with *setting-up costs*, that the actual setting-up labour cost is a direct cost and should not be included in the overhead costs. For example, where a setter spends one hour setting up a machine for a production run for a batch of similar products, the setter's time can be charged to the specific batch concerned.

One recommended way of sharing out the stores cost is to share it out using the *number of stores-issue notes* (stores requisitions) as the cost driver. This method does not take account of size, weight, value, handling problems, special storage problems, etc. However, from this you should be able to conclude that it would be impossible to find a way of sharing out this cost which could be described as being both fair and accurate.

However, it is recognised that ABC is a step in the right direction, but not the end of the story, as the quest for something better continues to provoke thought, debate and research.

Summary: activity-based costing (ABC)

Activity-based costing attempts to identify which of the activities cause the overhead costs and then link them up via the use of *'cost drivers'* (i.e. resource cost drivers and activity cost drivers) to *cost objects* such as products, services, sales areas. The cost objects in effect create the demand for the activities. (See Figure 15.1 for a further review of how activity-based costing systems work.)

For examples of activity cost pools and activity cost drivers see Figure 15.2.

For activity-based costing to have a chance of working, it is necessary to:

□ identify the *activities*;

□ create *cost pools* for each resource centre and each activity;

□ identify the *'cost drivers'* for resource cost drivers and activity cost drivers;

□ assign costs to *cost objects*, e.g. products, services, etc.

It is accepted that ABC is a more accurate method for dealing with overheads and support activities than traditional total absorption costing, and is a step in the right direction. However, quite a number of the recommended 'cost drivers' are just the same as those used for total absorption costing, e.g. using the number of direct labour hours or the number of stores-issue notes, and therefore they suffer from the same limitations, problems and drawbacks.

Costs do not cause activities – activities cause costs.

Self-checks

Attempt each of the self-checks provided below, and then compare your answer with the relevant part of this chapter.

1. Define activity-based costing in your own words.
2. Explain how an activity-based costing system works.
3. Describe what resource costs are.
4. Provide four examples of activity cost drivers which are used to share out the activity cost pools.
5. Why is the business environment so complex and diverse?
6. What are the principal drawbacks and limitations of ABC?

Self-assessments

On completion of each self-assessment compare your solution with the suggested solution provided in Appendix 1.

A15.1   Prepare a flow chart accompanied by brief notes which explains how activity-based costing works, from estimating the resource costs onwards.

A15.2   The following self-assessment assumes that you would have no problem in assigning costs to resource cost pools. The mechanics for this are very similar to those you came across in total absorption costing, when you allocated and apportioned overheads to cost centres.

The Chadus company manufactures two products, R and T. The following budgeted information relating to the company for the forthcoming period has been made available to you:

| | Products | |
	R	T
Sales and production (000 units)	400	400
	£	£
Selling price (per unit)	36	56
Prime cost (per unit)	16	36
	Hours	Hours
Department 1 (machine hours per unit)	2	4
Department 2 (direct labour hours per unit)	1	6

Details of the amounts assigned to activity cost pools and their cost drivers are:

	Activity cost pool £000	Activity cost driver
Department 1	1,020	Machine hours
Department 2	820	Direct labour hours
Setting-up costs	80	No of set-ups
Computing	300	No of hours
Purchasing	100	No of orders
	2,320	

You have also been provided with the following estimates for the period under review:

	Products		
	R (000)	T (000)	Total (000)
Machine hours	100	240	340
Direct labour hours	50	360	410
No of set-ups	32	48	80
Computer (hours)	40	20	60
Purchasing (no of orders)	40	10	50

Required:

Using an activity-based costing approach prepare a profit statement that shows the profit or loss for each product and the total profit or loss.

Tutor-based assignments

The assignments that follow are to be completed as directed by your lecturer or tutor.

T15.1 Timple Ltd

The company produces three products: T, I and M. The following budgeted overhead resource costs, together with their resource cost drivers, relate to the forthcoming period:

Resource cost	£000	Resource cost driver
Indirect labour	120	Number of employees
Lighting & heating, etc.	150	Square metres
Computing	600	Computer hours

Details of the activity cost pools and resource cost drivers are as follows:

| | ACTIVITY COST POOLS | | | |
	Purchasing	Receiving	Despatch	Total
Number of employees	6	3	3	12
Square metres	5,000	8,000	12,000	25,000
Computing hours	20,000	6,000	4,000	30,000

The data relating to the activity cost drivers are as follows:

| Activity cost pool | Activity cost driver | PRODUCTS | | | |
		T	I	M	Total
Purchasing	No. of orders	7,000	3,000	2,000	12,000
Receiving	No. of received notes	3,200	1,000	800	5,000
Despatch	No. of despatch notes	6,000	1,000	1,000	8,000

Required:

Using an ABC approach, calculate the overheads that will be assigned to each of the products.

T15.2 **Whitley Beaumont plc**
The company manufactures three products, details of which are as follows:

Product	Volume Units	Material cost per unit (£)	Direct labour per unit (hours)	Labour cost per unit (£)	Selling price price per unit (£)
L	1,200	20	4	8	84.00
F	6,000	12	10	20	250.00
D	1,000	10	5	12	160.00

The overheads for the period under review are as follows:

	£000
Material handling	100
Set-up costs	80
Maintenance costs	60
Despatch costs	72
Storage costs	180
	492

Details for the cost drivers that are to be used for activity-based costing purposes are:

Activity	Cost drivers	L	F	D	Total
Material handling	No. of requisitions	4,000	2,000	2,000	8,000
Set-up costs	No. of set-ups	100	80	60	240
Maintenance costs	No. of call outs	80	50	20	150
Despatch costs	No. of despatch notes	800	400	600	1,800
Storage costs	Floor area (sq. m)	1,000	7,000	2,000	10,000

Required:

(a) Calculate the overhead that would be assigned to each product:
   (i) using total absorption costing, based on direct labour hours, and
   (ii) using activity-based costing.
   Produce brief profit statements for each of the above methods.
(b) Discuss the implications of the picture that is revealed from your review.

Further-reading

Chadwick, L., *Management Accounting*, International Thomson Business Press, 1998
Drury, C., *Management Accounting for Business Decisions*, Thomson Learning, 2001
Horngren, C.T., Foster, G. and Datar, S. M., *Cost Accounting*, Financial Times Prentice Hall, 2000
Weetman, P., *Management Accounting: An Introduction*, Financial Times Prentice Hall, 1999

Useful websites

www.drury-online.com
www.thomsonlearning.co.uk
www.prenhall.com/horngren5/
www.booksites.net/weetman

16

Marginal costing and break-even analysis

When you have completed your study of this chapter, you should be able to:

☐ appreciate how costs behave, and the way in which fixed costs are treated in marginal costing;

☐ understand the relationship between *selling price*, *variable cost* and the *contribution*;

☐ use the *marginal cost equation* to solve a variety of problems, e.g. profit targets, make-or-buy decisions, closing down a product line or department, pricing and limiting factors;

☐ calculate the *profit/volume (PV) ratio*, and use it to work out the *break-even point*;

☐ describe what management can do to reduce the effect of or eliminate *limiting factors*;

☐ understand and be able to prepare *break-even charts*;

☐ prepare and reconcile profit statements using marginal costing and total absorption costing;

☐ explain how *under- or over-absorptions* of overheads occur and their accounting treatment;

☐ discuss the principal differences between marginal costing and total absorption costing.

An introduction to marginal costing

Marginal costing (which is also known as variable costing or direct costing or differential costing) is concerned with the treatment of fixed costs and the relationship that exists between three figures: sales, variable costs and the contribution.

What is the contribution? Answer: **contribution** is the name given to the difference between sales and variable cost in the marginal cost equation.

What does the contribution contribute towards? Answer: the contribution contributes towards the recovery of the *fixed costs* (fixed overheads) and then *profit*. If the contribution is less than the fixed costs, the result will be a loss.

Marginal costing differs from total absorption costing in the way in which it deals with the fixed overheads. In marginal costing the fixed overheads are treated as *'period costs'*, i.e. they are written off in total in computing the profit or loss for the period to which they belong. The exception to this rule occurs in a multi-product or multi-service environment in which the individual products or services have certain fixed costs which are *specific* to them. In such cases the general fixed costs would be deducted in total in computing the profit or loss.

The marginal cost equation

One of the corner-stones of marginal costing is the **marginal cost equation** which is sales revenue less the variable = the contribution (or $S - VC = C$), or contribution less fixed cost (or $C - FC = P$) = the profit or loss.

Figure 16.1 provides an illustration of the marginal cost equation in action. Its use can help us to resolve a wide variety of problems.

	Per unit £	4000 units £000	% of sales
Sales	200	800	100
Less Variable costs	150	600	75
Contribution	50	200	25
	Less fixed costs	140	
Profit		60	

Figure 16.1 – The marginal cost equation

The profit/volume ratio (PV ratio)

This is an extremely useful ratio, and is simply *the contribution as a percentage of sales*. Using the figures in Figure 16.1 it works out as follows:

$$\frac{\text{Contribution}}{\text{Sales}} \times 100, \quad \text{e.g.} \quad \frac{200}{800} \times 100 = 25\%$$

You may have already noticed that we showed the 25% figure in Figure 16.1.

As you will discover shortly, the profit/volume ratio can also be used to calculate the break-even point.

Contribution tables

A good way of dealing with problems involving changes in selling prices and/or variable costs is to construct a contribution table (see Figures 16.2, 16.3, 16.4). The tables show the contributions made by each product or service and, where appropriate, the effect of the change or changes to the contribution

£000		A	products/services B	C	D	Total
	Contribution	50	40	120	70	280
less	Fixed costs					160
	Profit					120

Figure 16.2 – A multi-product/multi-service environment
Note that the fixed costs are just deducted in total as 'period costs'.

Question: what would happen if product A was discontinued? Answer: the contribution of £50,000 would be lost, the fixed costs of £160,000 would still have to be paid. The profit would, therefore, fall to £70,000, i.e. assuming that contributions from products B, C and D remain unchanged at £230,000 less the fixed costs of £160,000,

Specific fixed costs

You should note that in a multi-product/multi-service environment each product line or service could have fixed costs that are specific to itself. This means that we can have two levels of contribution, as illustrated in Figure 16.3.

£000	E	F	Products/services G	H	I	Total
Contribution	150	720	4,200	90	420	5,580
Less specific fixed costs	20	40	1,060	40	60	1,220
Contribution after specific fixed costs	130	680	3,140	50	360	4,360
Less other fixed costs (general fixed costs)						510
Profit						3,850

Figure 16.3 – A multi-roduct/multi-service environment with specific fixed costs

The specific fixed costs have been paid out on behalf of a specific product or service. If any one of these is discontinued there would be a saving of its specific fixed costs. Question: what would happen to profits if product/service H were discontinued? Answer: the contribution (after deducting specific fixed costs) of £50,000 would be lost. The profit would go down by £50,000 to £3,530,000.

Why use marginal costing?

Marginal costing is preferred to total absorption costing for *decision-making purposes*. The principal reason for this is that it produces more realistic costs because it only calculates and uses the marginal (variable) cost of the product or service. It does not include any of the fixed costs in the cost of a product or service, and therefore does not have to deal with the process that allocates and apportions the fixed overheads to cost centres or departments.

Marginal costing can be used for:

☐ *decision making*: e.g. pricing, profit targets, special contracts, make-or-buy decisions, whether or not to discontinue a product or service, break-even analysis, future projects;

☐ *changes in the business environment*, e.g. the effect of changes in: demand, variable costs and selling prices on the contribution/profits.

However, beware: its use could lead to a price war, and *it is not always easy to separate and analyse costs as fixed or variable costs*. For example, if the labour force receives fixed salaries it is a fixed cost, if their remuneration varies with output it is a variable cost.

Problem solving using marginal costing

We will now illustrate how to use the marginal costing arithmetic to enable you to solve problems.

Example   The effect of a change in the selling price and/ or the variable cost

Using the strategic choice figures from Figure 16.4 as our starting point, we can work out the effects of different strategies for the forthcoming period (see Figure 16.5).

	Selling price per unit £	Variable cost per unit £	Demand (units)	Fixed costs £
Current period	200	120	1,500	40,000
Strategy 1	Increase by £20	No change	1,300	40,000
Strategy 2	No change	Reduce by £10	1,500	50,000

Figure 16.4 – Strategic alternatives

	Current period	Strategy 1	Strategy 2
	£	£	£
Selling price (per unit)	200	220	200
less Variable cost (per unit)	120	120	110
Contribution (per unit)	**80**	**100**	**90**
Units sold demand	1,500	1,300	1,500
Total contribution	**120,000**	**130,000**	**135,000**
less Fixed costs	40,000	40,000	50,000
Profit	**80,000**	**90,000**	**85,000**

Figure 16.5 – Contribution table

It can be seen that strategy 1 will generate the higher profit in the forthcoming period, provided that the forecast demand is correct. It should also be noted that a movement in either the selling price or the variable cost will be reflected by a movement in the contribution, as follows:

☐ An increase in the selling price or a decrease in the variable cost will result in an increase in the contribution.

☐ A decrease in the selling price or an increase in the variable cost will bring about a decrease in the contribution.

Note also that the fixed costs may vary, e.g. in strategy 2 in order to reduce variable costs fixed machine costs would have to be increased to provide a more efficient production system.

Profit targets

If management sets a profit target, all you have to do is remember that the *contribution is equal to fixed costs plus profit* ($C = FC + P$). Adding the fixed costs that have to be covered to the profit target will give you the total contribution that has to be generated. The total contribution required must then be divided by the contribution per unit. This tells you how many units will need to be sold in order to generate the required contribution:

$$\frac{\text{Contribution required}}{\text{Contribution per unit}} = \text{Number of units that must be sold in order to generate the contribution required}$$

Remember:

Fixed costs *plus* Profits or *less* Loss = Contribution required

Example   Generating the required contribution

Using the current period information in Figure 16.5, and assuming management has set a target profit of £100,000, we can work out how many units we would have to sell to achieve this, plus the workings:

		£
	Fixed costs	40,000
add	profit target	100,000
	Contribution required	140,000

The workings would be:

$$\text{Must sell} = \frac{\text{Contribution required}}{\text{Contribution per unit}} = \frac{£140,000}{£80} = 1,750 \text{ units}$$

In terms of value this would be:

1,750 units @ £200 unit selling price = £350,000

Example   The pricing decision

The Betidut Mitlander Hotel has, after many years in business, decided to offer special weekend rates to make use of idle capacity. A trainee manager has produced the following figures:

Number of rooms:	£	*Normal rates per room £	Variable cost
Doubles	70	120	40
Family	30	160	50
Single	20	100	30

* including continental breakfast

Question: what is the lowest price at which each type of room could be offered?

Answer: each room could be offered at an amount equal to the variable cost, i.e. it would break-even in terms of not making any profit or loss from offering those rates.

Comment: it is most likely that the price would be the price that covers the variable cost plus a margin.

Question: how much additional profit would be made at 100% capacity if the room rates were:

	£
Doubles	60
Family	80
Singles	50

Answer: this would result in an additional total contribution of:

	£		£
Doubles	70 × 20	=	1,400
Family	30 × 30	=	900
Single	20 × 50	=	1,000
			£3,300

Other scenarios using different room rates and different room occupancy rates can be worked out in a similar way. However, the rates that are offered by competitors will also have to be taken into account. Increasing the number of visitors could also help to increase revenue from car parking fees, bar receipts, additional meals taken in the restaurant or via room service, the gift shop (if any), leisure facilities, etc.

Limiting factors

The **limiting factor** (also called the *key factor* or *principal budget factor*) is the factor that constrains the activities of a business. Thus, when budgets are being prepared, the limiting factor is the starting point of the budgeting process and has to be taken into account first. For example, if sales demand is the limiting factor, i.e. if the company could only sell a limited number of products during a period, this would limit the production needed, the amount of labour, the material requirements, and so on.

Other examples of limiting factors are as follows:

☐ the supply of materials, e.g. Figure 16.6

☐ the availability of labour

☐ production capacity

☐ finance

☐ legislation.

Example   Limiting factors

	Product R	Product J
	£	£
Selling price (per unit)	1,200	1,000
Variable cost (per unit)	600	500
Material required to produce one unit	4 litres	2 litres

Figure 16.6 – Product data

The supply of a particular material is limited to 5,000 litres per period. It can be used to produce either product R or product J, details of which are given in Figure 16.6.

The contribution per unit of limiting factor, i.e. the contribution per litre, would be calculated as:

		Product R	Product J
		£	£
	Selling price (per unit)	1,200	1,000
Less	Variable cost (per unit)	600	500
	Contribution	600	500

$$\frac{\text{Contribution}}{\text{Quantity needed}} \text{ is } \frac{£600}{4} = £150 \text{ per litre;} \qquad \frac{£500}{2} = £250 \text{ per litre}$$

The maximum contribution possible is therefore:

Quantity of material available × contribution per litre

5,000 litres × £150 = £750,000

5,000 litres × £250 = £1,250,000

Product J is therefore the one that should be produced. By producing it, a contribution of £1,250,000 is generated, which is £500,000 greater than the contribution that could be generated by producing product R.

What can management do to reduce or eliminate the impact of a limiting factor?

Limiting factors are not static. Management can, by their actions, eliminate them altogether, or reduce their effect.

In *the case of materials*, management can search for new supplies; investigate the use of a substitute; have the product redesigned to use none or less of the material concerned; improve production and inspection techniques to reduce waste and the number of defectives.

What can be done if there is a shortage of labour? Answer: quite a lot. Where labour is the limiting factor management can transport workers in from the home labour market; attract labour from other countries; introduce overtime and shift work; undertake to train or organise the training of new operatives; lease or buy labour-saving equipment or machines; use subcontractors.

If the limiting factor is insufficient production capacity, managers can: introduce more overtime and shift work; lease or buy more equipment or machinery; use subcontractors; reorganise the production flow to reduce idle (i.e. non-productive) time; review the design of the product, e.g. the degree of the precision needed, so as to reduce the time spent making the product.

Management has several options available *where finance poses the problem*. Finance is always available from a multitude of sources, but usually at a cost that reflects the risk to the lender! In addition to the issue of share capital, and loans from various sources, there are also government schemes and grants; EU schemes and grants; sale and lease-back; the sale of the company's own surplus fixed assets, e.g. buildings, machines, equipment and current assets such as stocks of raw materials, fuels and finished goods.

What can be done *if the limiting factor is legislation?* Answer: not a lot. However, management can approach local council representatives, MPs, trade associations, chambers of trade and various pressure groups.

When a business's activities are constrained because of a limiting factor, it has to attempt to maximise its contribution. This can be done by means of a simple technique. The technique calculates the *contribution per unit of the limiting factor*. The alternative that gives the highest contribution per unit of the limiting factor, e.g. per hour or per kilo, is the one that will maximise the contribution.

The limitations and drawbacks of marginal costing

It will always be difficult to assess how both fixed costs and variable costs will be affected by changes in output. Direct labour, direct materials and direct expenses can be affected in a multitude of ways. It must be pointed out here that one of the drawbacks, which is not always appreciated, is that it is often not such an easy task to segregate costs into their fixed and variable elements. Some items of expenditure that are very similar can be treated differently, e.g. the rent of machinery paid on a fixed rental would be treated as a fixed cost, but if the rental paid were based on output it would be treated as a variable cost!

Oversimplified marginal costing can lead to the under-pricing of products and a loss-making situation. The incorrect assumption made by certain users that fixed costs tend to remain constant, irrespective of the level of activity, may account for the under-pricing of certain products and loss-making situations.

Before we move on and take a look at break-even analysis, it is perhaps useful to carry out an interim consolidation via some self-checks and self-assessments. This should help ensure that what has been learned is firmly fixed in your mind and understood.

Self-checks

Please compare your attempt to each with the appropriate earlier part of this chapter.

1. What are the uses to which marginal costing may be put, and what are its advantages?

2. In relation to marginal costing, explain:
   (a) what 'period costs' are;
   (b) how to compute the profit/volume ratio;
   (c) what 'limiting factors' are;
   (d) how we go about calculating the sales necessary to achieve a particular profit target.

Self-assessments

You will find the answers to the self-assessments in Appendix 1.

A16.1 Should we close one of our services?

You have been provided with Figure 16.7 which relates to the Mainzbonn Leisure Centre for the six-month period that has just ended:

(£000)	Steam room, sauna and solarium	Fitness gym	Swimming pool	Climbing wall	Restaurant	Total
Income	40	60	120	24	36	280
Variable costs	10	30	70	8	12	130
Specific fixed costs	4	6	25	2	2	39
Apportioned general fixed costs	11	14	40	10	10	85
Profit (loss)	15	10	(15)	4	12	26

Figure 16.7 – Mainzbonn Leisure Centre

The board of directors are holding a meeting soon to discuss the proposed closure of the swimming pool, which, as indicated in the table, has been running at a loss of £15,000 for the last half-year.

Required

(a) Using a marginal costing approach, produce figures to illustrate why the swimming pool should be closed or kept open.

(b) Comment on the effect that closing the swimming pool may have on the other leisure services that are provided.

A16.2 Jonbec Ltd

The company manufactures three products, details of which are as follows:

	Product		
	J	O	N
	£	£	£
Variable cost	30	30	40
Selling price	50	40	64
Maximum output per day (units)	100	60	50

Management wishes to know the optimum level of production and upon investigation you find that:

☐ if sales of product J exceed 60 units per day the selling price for the sale of any further units will have to be reduced to £40;

☐ if sales of O exceed 20 units per day, the remaining output will have to be sold for £36 per unit;

☐ if sales of product N exceed 24 units per day the selling price for any additional units will have to be sold at £60 per unit.

The company works a total of 600 productive minutes per day.

Required:

The limiting factor is the productive time available. (No further overtime or shift working is possible.) Prepare a statement that shows which combination of products will generate the optimum contribution per day.

Break-even analysis

Earlier in this chapter you were introduced to cost behaviour. However, a quick recap may prove helpful.

☐ Fixed costs

These costs, in the short term, remain unchanged within a relevant range of activity or output.

☐ Variable costs
These costs, in the short term, vary with the level of activity/output within a relevant range.

A combination of the two is known as a *semi-variable* or a *semi-fixed cost*, e.g. a cost that is made up of a fixed rental plus an amount that is paid per unit of output produced.

How to calculate the break-even point

The **profit/volume ratio (PV ratio)**, i.e. the contribution as a percentage of sales, can be used to calculate the break-even point, as follows.

Fixed costs divided by the PV ratio

For example, using a profit/volume ratio of 25%, and fixed costs of £140,00 (as in Figure 16.1) would be:

$$£140,000 \times \frac{100}{25} = £560,000$$

To compute the break-even point in terms of units, we can make use of the contribution per unit. All we have to do is:

Divide the fixed costs by the contribution per unit

If the contribution per unit were £50 and the fixed costs £140,000. For the Figure 16.1 information this would work out as:

$$\frac{£140,000}{£50} = 2,800 \text{ units}$$

To convert this to the break-even point in terms of value, we just have to multiply the break-even number of units by the selling price per unit. It can be observed from the calculations, that the break-even point is *the point at which the contribution generated is equal to the fixed costs*.

Self-assessment

A16.3 Now see if you can calculate the break-even point from the information contained in Figure 16.8.

	Per unit £	40,000 units £000
Sales	40	1,600
less Variable cost	24	960
Contribution	16	640
less Fixed costs		336
Profit		304

Figure 16.8 – Break-even data

On completion, check your answer with that provided in the suggested answers section in Appendix 1.

Break-even charts

Break-even charts are a *short-term planning device*. They should not be used in isolation, but in conjunction with other data.

We will now illustrate three different types of break-even chart:

☐ the conventional break-even chart (Figure 16.9);

☐ the contribution break-even chart (Figure 16.10);

☐ the profit graph (profit/volume diagram) (Figure 16.11);

using the following data:

		£000	
	Sales	2,000	
less	Variable costs	1,200	
	Contribution	800	(PV ratio 40%)
less	Fixed costs	200	
	Profit	£600	

From a review of all of the break-even charts you can observe that the break-even point is £500,000. We can calculate and prove this by using the profit/volume ratio, as illustrated earlier, as follows: (£000)

$$\text{Profit/volume ratio} = \frac{\text{Contribution}}{\text{Sales}} \times 100 = \frac{£800}{2,000} \times 100 = 40\%$$

$$\text{Fixed costs divided by PV ratio} = £200 \times \frac{100}{40} = £500$$

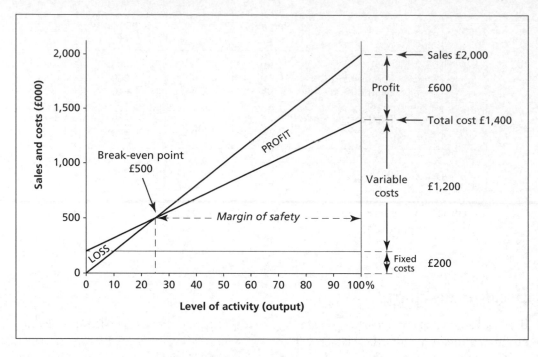

Figure 16.9 – A conventional break-even chart

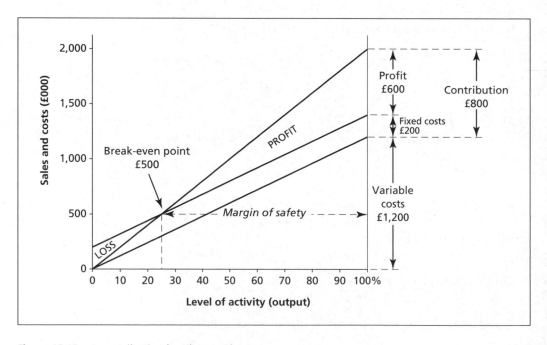

Figure 16.10 – A contribution break-even chart

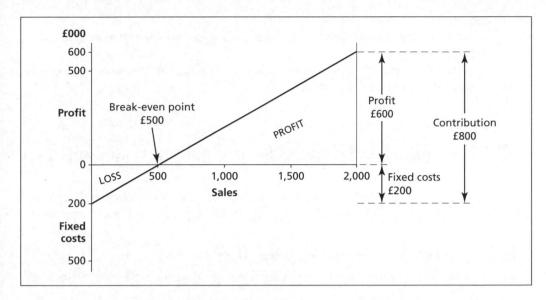

Figure 16.11 – A profit graph (profit volume diagram)

In this particular case the break-even point occurs at a 25% level of activity (output). There is therefore a 75% *margin of safety* between the break-even point and the maximum level of activity. The earlier the break-even point, the greater is the margin of safety.

Note in Figure 16.10 the way in which we plot the fixed costs, i.e. parallel to the variable costs. This enables us to see more clearly the contribution that is being generated at the various levels of activity (output). It shows that below the break-even point it is the fixed costs that are not being covered.

Another alternative form of break-even chart, Figure 16.11 the profit graph (profit/volume diagram), also shows that the contribution is equal to the fixed costs plus the profit. It clearly shows that once the fixed costs have been covered and the break-even point reached, we are then in profit.

Self-assessment

Now it is your turn. May I suggest that you find some graph paper and then attempt the following problem. When you have completed your answer, compare it with the suggested answer in Appendix 1.

A16.4 The firm's forecast figures for the forthcoming period are:

Output units	80,000
	per unit
Sales	£500
Variable cost	£100
Fixed costs	£18,000,000

Required:
1. Prepare a break-even chart and show the break-even point and margin of safety.
2. Show what the position would be if the output achieved were only 64,000 units (i.e. 80% of the level of activity).

The limitations and drawbacks of break-even analysis

The assumptions on which break-even analysis is based, e.g. how costs behave, a constant product mix, constant selling prices, do not always hold true in the real world, even in the short term.

☐ Fixed and variable costs will not always behave as expected.

☐ Sales of a product may have to be made to different customers or market segments at different prices.

☐ The decisions made by management can affect variable and fixed costs.

☐ Efficiency levels within a manufacturing concern are not always constant.

☐ The product mix will have to respond to changes in demand and cannot therefore be forecast with accuracy.

Marginal costing and total absorption costing – a comparison

You do need to remember that:

☐ total absorption costing includes fixed costs

☐ marginal costing excludes fixed costs.

Total absorption costing stock valuation includes overheads via an appropriate absorption rate, e.g. per unit, per machine or per direct labour hour. Administration, selling and distribution costs may be treated as *period costs* in both methods, i.e. written off as an expense in the profit statement for the period to which they relate.

The difference between those profits (losses) computed using total absorption costing with those computed using marginal costing is caused by the way in which the fixed costs are treated.

You should also remember that the stock figures produced in the operating statements can be affected by the method of stock valuation used, e.g. average cost, first-in first-out (FIFO) or last-in first-out (LIFO), which we mentioned briefly in Chapter 13. Also, note that variations in selling prices and costs will no doubt take place and that the actual selling prices and costs are likely to differ quite significantly from those that were budgeted.

We will now contrast and compare marginal costing and total absorption costing by constructing and reviewing profit statements. Kop, the example that follows, should help you to appreciate:

☐ how the two systems affect stock valuations and,

☐ the treatment of under- and over-absorption (recovery) of overheads.

Example   Kop Ltd Total absorption costing v. marginal costing

Kop Ltd's budget is as follows:

	10,000 units £	per unit £
Direct materials	20,000	2.00
Direct wages	10,000	1.00
Prime cost	30,000	3.00
Variable overheads	20,000	2.00
Variable cost	**50,000**	**5.00**
Fixed cost	30,000	3.00
Total cost	**80,000**	**8.00**
Sales	100,000	10.00
Profit	**20,000**	**2.00**

Using the above figures, we will prepare the budgeted profit statements for the next two periods using:

☐ total absorption costing, and

☐ marginal costing;

and taking into account the assumptions of Figure 16.12.

Opening stock	Nil
Period 1: Production units Sales units	12,000 8,000
Period 2: Production units Sales units	10,000 10,000

Figure 16.12 – Assumptions for Kop Ltd

Solution

The solution is shown in Figure 16.13.

Total absorption costing Period 1	£	£	Marginal costing Period 1	£	£
Sales (8,000 @ £10)		80,000	Sales (8,000 @ £10)		80,000
Opening stock	Nil		Opening stock	Nil	
Manufacturing stock:			Manufacturing cost:		
Variable cost	60,000		Variable cost	60,000	
(12,000 × £5 per unit)					
Fixed overheads	36,000		*Less*		
(12,000 × £3 per unit)			Closing stock		
	96,000		(4,000 × £5)	20,000	40,000
Less			**Contribution (8,000 × £5)**		**40,000**
Closing stock					
4,000 × 8	32,000	64,000	*Less*		
Gross Profit (8,000 × £2)		**16,000**	Fixed Cost		30,000
			Net profit		**£ 10,000**
Add					
Over-absorption of					
Fixed overhead		6,000			
Net profit		**£ 22,000**			

NB Over-absorption of fixed overheads = £30,000 (from budget) – £36,000 absorbed, therefore £6,000 over-absorbed must be added back.

Total absorption costing Period 2	£	£	Marginal costing Period 2	£	£
Sales (10,000 @ £10)		100,000	Sales (10,000 @ £10)		100,000
Opening stock	32,000		Opening stock	20,000	
Manufacturing cost:			Manufacturing cost:		
Variable cost			Variable cost		
(10,000 × £5)	50,000		(10,000 × £5)	50,000	
Fixed overheads				70,000	
(10,000 × £3 per unit)	30,000				
	112,000		*Less*		
			Closing stock		
Less			(4,000 × £5)	20,000	50,000
Closing stock			**Contribution (10,000 × £5)**		**50,000**
(4,000 × £8)	32,000	80,000			
Gross profit (10,000 × £2)		**20,000**	*Less*		
			Fixed cost		30,000
Add					
Under- or over-			**Net profit**		**20,000**
absorption of fixed					
overhead		nil			
Net profit		**20,000**			

Figure 16.13 – Kop Ltd: total absorbtion and marginal costing profit statements

The difference between the two net profit figures in period 1 is due to the use of different totals for the manufactured cost used in the calculation of the value of the closing stock (i.e. £36,000 higher in the case of absorption costing, as fixed overheads are 'absorbed' at the rate of £3 per unit). Marginal costing makes no use of fixed costs in the stock value calculation, hence its valuation is relatively lower.

Also note that:

☐ Profits are the same for both methods when production equals sales (no changes in stock level).

☐ Where production exceeds sales (increasing stock levels) the absorption costing system produces higher profits.

☐ Where sales exceed production (declining stock levels) the marginal costing system produces higher profits.

☐ Profits or losses for both systems will be the same over time, because we are using the same costs and revenues.

This only holds true where the actual fixed overheads are equal to the budgeted fixed overheads. At the end of the day, the fixed overheads absorbed have to be compared with the fixed overheads that were actually incurred. In practice, it is unlikely that the actual fixed overheads will be the same as the budgeted fixed overheads.

Marginal costing is considered to provide more useful information for decision making, and removes the effect of changes in stock valuations from the profit. It also avoids fixed overheads being capitalised in unsaleable stock.

Total absorption costing, however, does attempt to ensure that all costs are covered.

The choice depends on the circumstances, for example:

☐ Volatile sales and changing stock levels favour marginal costing for internal monthly or quarterly profit measurement.

☐ Seasonal sales where stocks build up in advance favours absorption costing.

Summary: marginal costing and break-even analysis

Marginal costing

Marginal costing differs from total absorption costing because of the way in which it deals with fixed costs (overheads):

☐ Fixed costs, in marginal costing, are treated as *period costs*, i.e. they are written off in the period to which they belong.

☐ Fixed costs are not included in stock valuations and are not therefore carried forward to future accounting periods.

Sales *less* Variable cost = Contribution

The *marginal cost equation* (above) expresses what marginal costing is all about. It is about the relationship between sales, variable cost and the contribution. Movements in the selling price and/or variable cost will be reflected by a corresponding movement in the contribution. If the selling price goes up (down) or the variable cost goes down (up), the contribution will go up (down) by the same amount. The contribution generated contributes towards the recovery of fixed costs, the remainder being the profit. The contribution per unit can be very useful when it comes to solving problems such as the following.

How many units must be sold in order to break even?

$$\frac{\text{Fixed costs}}{\text{Contribution per unit}} = \text{Break-even point in units}$$

How many units must be sold to produce a specified profit target?

$$\frac{\text{Fixed costs + Profit target}}{\text{Contribution per unit}} = \text{Number of units that must be sold to achieve the profit target}$$

Note that when we are dealing with profit target problems, the key is to calculate the total contribution that must be generated:

Total contribution required = Fixed cost + Profit target

The *profit/volume ratio* explains the relationship between the contribution and sales:

$$\text{PV ratio} = \frac{\text{Contribution}}{\text{Sales}} \times 100 \quad \text{or} \quad \frac{\text{Contribution per unit}}{\text{Selling price per unit}} \times 100$$

This can also be used to help solve problems, e.g. to compute the break-even point in terms of value:

Break-even point = Fixed costs divided by the profit/volume ratio

If a constraint, e.g. the supply of materials or productive hours available, limits the activities of a business, there is a *limiting factor* (also called a key factor or principal budget factor) at work and a simple technique can be applied in order to solve the problems that emerge. The technique expresses the *contribution per unit of the limiting factor*, e.g. contribution per kilo, contribution per litre, contribution per hour. Where a choice has to be made between alternative products, the products that give the highest contribution per unit of the limiting factor should be produced, as this will maximise the contribution. The impact of a limiting factor can be eliminated or reduced by the actions of management.

Marginal costing, which is also called direct costing or variable costing or differential costing, is certainly a very useful *decision-making technique*. However, it must be appreciated that its use can lead to underpricing and that it is not always as easy as might be imagined to separate the fixed from the variable costs.

Break-even analysis

The construction of a break-even chart is a relatively straightforward activity. The break-even point can be computed mathematically, so why do we need to produce a chart? The answer lies in the fact that with the chart you can read off the estimated position at various levels of output or activity and highlight the margin of safety. The limitations of break-even analysis stem from the fact that in practice costs do not always behave as might be expected: sales of a product may have to be made using a variety of prices and the product mix is difficult to forecast.

Total absorption costing compared with marginal costing

Organisations that use total absorption costing do so because they are attempting to ensure that they cover all of their production overheads (or the overheads incurred in providing a service) and also generate enough income to cover other expenses, e.g. administration, selling and distribution expenses.

However, those organisations that opt for marginal costing tend to do so because it is more realistic and aids the decision-making process. Marginal costing is particularly useful for illustrating what the position will be if there is change in selling prices, volume, variable costs and fixed costs. It can be used for decisions involving taking on special contracts and make-or-buy. The costs are more accurate than those computed using total absorption costing because only those costs that can be identified with or traced to the product or service are included, e.g. direct labour, direct materials and variable overheads. Marginal costing does not include fixed costs (costs that tend to vary more with time than with output) in product costs and thus does not depend upon subjective judgement about methods of apportionment and the selection of absorption rates applicable to total absorption costing.

Managers who use a marginal costing treat the fixed overheads (costs) as *period costs* and charge them in the profit and loss account for the period to which they relate. This means that fixed overheads are not included in the product costs and are not, therefore, carried forward to future accounting periods in stock valuations. Thus, judgements about the selection of bases of apportionment, absorption rates and the estimation of machine hours or direct labour hours are simply not required. The costs are accurate since they include only those costs, i.e. variable costs, that can be identified with and traced to the product or service.

However, there are difficulties and dangers in marginal costing:

☐ the difficulty of classifying costs as fixed or variable;

☐ the assumption by some managers that if they increase volume, profits will rise because their fixed costs will remain unchanged;

☐ limitations to the use of break-even analysis, e.g. constant product mix, step fixed costs, etc.

However, the contribution per unit can be used to provide a lot of very useful decision-making information about changes in volume, changes in prices, changes in variable costs, profit targets, make-or-buy information, limiting factors, and break-even calculations or charts.

In conclusion,

☐ total absorption costing is an attempt to ensure that, as far as possible, all costs are covered;

☐ marginal costing is an attempt to have more realistic costs which can be used for decision-making purposes.

One or the other or a combination of both can be used.

Self-checks

3. Explain and illustrate how fixed costs that are specific to a particular product, service or activity are treated in marginal costing.

4. What can management do to eliminate or reduce the effect of the following limiting factors:
   (a) the supply of materials
   (b) the availability of labour
   (c) production capacity?

Self-assessments

A16.5 Emmrom plc

The company manufactures CD-ROM players and has provided you with the following information on variable costs per unit for the current year 20X8:

	£
Direct labour:	24
Direct materials	74
Variable overheads	22
Total variable costs	120

Fixed costs   £240,000
Selling price per unit   £320
Expected sales   40,000 units

The sales target for next year, 20X9, has been set at 60,000 units, and fixed costs are expected to rise to £260,000. The selling price would fall to £300 per unit and the variable costs would increase by £4 per unit.

Required:
(a) The total contribution and net profit for 20X8 and 20X9.
(b) The break-even point for 20X8 and 20X9.
(c) The sales level which would have to be attained in 20X9 in order to generate a profit equal to what was earned in 20X8.
(d) The maximum amount that could be spent on additional fixed costs at a sales level of 56,000 units to produce a profit of £8,500,000.

A16.6 Wic Products Ltd

Now see if you can solve the following limiting factor problem; the figures do change and are more complex, but the principles and techniques remain unchanged.

Wic Products Ltd make three products – W, I and C. Details are given in Figure 16.14.

	Product		
	W	I	C
	£	£	£
Selling price (per unit)	80	120	60
Cost per unit:			
Direct material	30	84	20
Direct labour	16	10	9
Variable overhead	14	14	15
	60	108	44
Time taken to produce one unit	40 mins	20 mins	30 mins

Figure 16.14 – Wic's three products

The constraint under which the company is currently working is that, until management can take appropriate action, its total productive hours are limited to 60 hours per day. However, all sales of W in excess of 30 units will have to be sold at £75 per unit; all sales of I in excess of 30 units will have to be sold at £110 per unit; and all sales of C in excess of 50 units will have to be sold at £45 per unit.

Work out the maximum contribution that could be earned per day (see Appendix 1 for the suggested answer).

A16.7 Vandi and Chungi

	Vandi	Chungi
Fixed costs	£200,000	£160,000
Profit volume ratio	60%	40%
Capital invested	£800,000	£500,000

Foundations plc operates two stores, Vandi and Chungi. From the data given above attempt to calculate:

(i) each store's breakeven point, and
(ii) the sales required in each case to achieve a net profit of 20% on the capital invested.

Tutor-based assignments

T16.1 Describe the major differences between marginal costing and total absorption costing.

T16.2 Indigo Care
Indigo Care have asked you to help them with their business plan. They are considering two ventures.
Venture 1   To provide flats plus a community centre for elderly people. The estimated costs of doing this are as follows:

The variable cost per resident	£5,000
Fixed costs	£75,000
Rents etc. receivable per resident	£8,000
Maximum number of residents	32

Required
(a) What would the profit (or loss) be at full capacity?
(b) How many residents are needed to break even?
(c) If the number of residents could be increased to 40 at an additional fixed cost of £10,000 what effect would this have on the profit or loss?
(d) If the management were to set a profit target of £51,000 if the capacity was increased to 40, what amount would have to be charged per resident for rent etc.?

Venture 2   To open a motel called 'Driver Inn'. The estimated income and expenditure for the first year is as follows:

	£000
Income	480
Variable costs	120
Fixed costs	200
Administrative costs (all fixed)	50

The average spend per room per night is £80 including meals. The motel has 24 rooms.

Required

(i)   What is the estimated profit?

(ii)   Calculate the break-even point.

(iii) Compute the occupancy rate assuming that the motel is open for 365 days.

(iv) At what occupancy rate could we make a profit of £160,000?

T16.3   Kim plc

Kim plc have provided you with the following information.

The opening stock for the quarter of 3,000 units would be valued at £60,000 for absorption costing purposes and £45,000 for marginal costing purposes, i.e. 3,000 units at £20 and 3,000 units at £15 respectively. At the end of the period the actual results were as shown below. The actual selling prices and costs were the same as those that were budgeted. For budget and results see Figure 16.15.

Kim plc: budget		
	Per unit £	20,000 units
Direct materials and labour	12	240,000
Variable overheads	3	60,000
Marginal cost	15	300,000
Fixed cost	5	100,000
Total cost	20	400,000
Sales	24	480,000
		80,000
less Selling price and distribution expenditure		29,000
Profit		51,000

Kim plc: actual results (units)		
Production	Sales	closing stock
21,000	19,500	4,500

Figure 16.15 – Kim: budget and results

1. Prepare operating statements for the period, using:

(a) absorption costing

(b) marginal costing.

2. Explain the difference that arises between the profits reported in the two operating statements.

Further reading

Atrill, P. and McLaney, E., *Management Accounting for Non-specialists*, Prentice Hall Europe, 1998
Drury, C., *Management Accounting for Business Decisions*, Thomson Learning, 2001
Upchurch, A., *Management Accounting: Principles and Practice*, Prentice Hall Europe, 1998

Useful websites

wwwbooksites.net/atrillmclaney
www.drury-online.com
www.booksites.net/upchurch

17

Budgetary control

We now move on to budgetary control, a topic area that affects all of us, both at home and at work. Budgetary control is of prime importance to both public- and private-sector organisations. It is perhaps management accounting's most important topic area. You need to note the benefits, and the rules for effective budgeting, and ascertain whether or not they apply to your organisation or an organisation with which you are familiar.

Learning objectives

When you have completed this chapter, you should be able to:

☐ appreciate the benefits of budgeting;

☐ describe, discuss and illustrate the principles of *effective budgeting*, and contrast these with what happens in practice;

☐ explain the following:
  — attainable goals
  — control by responsibility
  — frequent comparison
  — management by exception
  — participation;

☐ prepare a *cash budget* (cash flow forecast), and appreciate its purpose and importance;

☐ produce a budgeted profit and loss account and a budgeted balance sheet;

☐ contrast the cash budget and the budgeted profit and loss account, i.e. why an increase or decrease in profits is not matched by a corresponding increase or decrease in the cash and bank balances;

☐ appreciate that budgets are interrelated;

☐ construct a flexible budget, and appreciate why it is necessary;

☐ describe how the capital expenditure budget is arrived at;

☐ know how zero-base budgeting (ZBB) works;

☐ discuss the behavioural aspects of budgeting;

☐ understand what a standard is, and some of the considerations involved in its formulation and composition;

☐ appreciate that a cost variance can be subdivided into a price variance and a quantity variance;

☐ understand why a variance is either adverse or favourable;

☐ appreciate the kind of information that should be given in variance analysis reports and statements.

CIMA (Chartered Institute of Management Accountants) provides clear definitions of some of the terms associated with budgeting and budgetary control. Here are three of the most important ones:

☐ **Budget** – a plan expressed in money. It is prepared and approved prior to the budget period and may show income, expenditure and the capital to be employed. It may be drawn up showing incremental effects on former budgeted or actual figures, or be compiled by zero-based budgeting.

☐ **Budget centre** – a section of an entity for which control may be exercised and budgets prepared.

☐ **Budgetary control** – the establishment of budgets relating the responsibilities of executives to the requirements of a policy, and the continuous comparison of actual with budgeted results, either to secure by individual action the objectives of that policy, or to provide a basis for its revision.

Budgeting is mainly about the *allocation of scarce resources between competing influences*. This is true from small businesses to large multinational companies, public services and government departments. Resources are not infinite and therefore have to be managed with care.

It is a form of *predetermined costing*, i.e. the costs and revenues have to be estimated before the commencement of the budget period, e.g. six months, twelve months or longer. You must appreciate, at the outset, that the budgets produced can only be as accurate as the original data, and there could be GIGO (garbage in, garbage out)! The estimates rely heavily on a set of *assumptions about the environment*, e.g. the rate of inflation, the rate of pay settlements, the cost of capital, the level of activity in terms of sales. If these assumptions change significantly, budgets are of little or no use for control purposes, and should be recomputed.

The benefits of budgeting

A budget provides and sets targets to aim at, and by frequent comparisons with actual performance it provides a means of control for both costs and revenues. The principal benefits of budgeting and budgetary control provide an indication of why its value to business is of paramount importance.

Planning, co-ordination and co-operation

Success in both public- and private-sector organisations is closely linked to success in planning for the future. Planning involves the formulation of policies designed to ensure that corporate objectives are realised. It provides a *formal planning framework* and does in fact force management into action by getting them to meet and discuss, and to think about the future. It requires *co-operation* from all business functions and departments to produce all of the functional budgets, e.g. sales, purchasing, research and development, culminating in a master budget. The **master budget** consists of a *budgeted profit and loss account*, a *budgeted balance sheet* and a *cash budget*. Budgeting dictates that clearly defined objectives are set which provide a focus for managers, and to a great extent prevents them from following their own personal objectives. Meetings will have to be scheduled and held to discuss the setting of *objectives*, and the formulation of the *policy*, which they must follow in order to achieve the objectives. Many organisations do in fact have a *budget committee* which consists of representatives from all the functional areas, e.g. marketing, finance, research and development, administration, selling and distribution, and a *budget controller*, i.e. a person who oversees and co-ordinates their activities. The budget controller will seek to ensure that relevant data are collected, analysed, collated and distributed, to assist those who need them for budget preparation purposes. He or she must also attempt to secure the *co-operation* of others to see that committee decisions are *communicated clearly and effectively*. The meetings will have to be held well before the new budget period commences. Time will have to be devoted to the discussion of plans, the review of data, and the revision of plans, etc. Hence the need for a *timetable for the budget preparation period*, so that by the time the new budget period commences, the budget is ready to be implemented. This preparation of budgets in advance is a prerequisite for effective budgeting.

The budget preparation process and meetings held to discuss the budget direct the attention of management to:

☐ appreciate the fact that *budgets are interrelated*, e.g. there is a link between the income budget and the expenditure budget. If income is to be used for one particular type of expenditure then it is not available to finance other expenditure. The budgeting process is rather like a large jigsaw, i.e. all the pieces must fit together, because together they should form a coherent picture. Something affecting one budget will tend to have a ripple effect in that it will also affect some of the other budgets. Thus, during the budget preparation period the budget committee has to meet regularly to ensure that the individual functional budgets, e.g. sales, production, plant utilisation, all fit together;

☐ identify their *principal budget factor*, i.e. limiting factor such as demand, as this will constrain their activities. They will also have to decide whether or not to take action designed to eliminate or reduce the effects of the principal budget factor;

☐ decide upon how they are going to *share out the scarce resources* which they have at their disposal between the competing factions, e.g. alternative projects, production needs v. research and development needs v. marketing needs, and so on. This will involve discussions, negotiations, relationship skills and trade-offs.

Authorising and delegating

The adoption of the budget by management explicitly *authorises and delegates* responsibility to individual managers for a section or subsection of the budget, without having to refer back to higher levels of management. This frees top- and higher-level managers to concentrate, for example, on more strategic matters. Delegating a specific part of the budget to a particular person may be described as 'control by responsibility'. The person concerned will have to attempt, for example, to keep spending in line with the targets set, and provide explanations for periods in which targets are not met.

Evaluating performance

Budgets provide a *scorecard*, enabling us to see, for example, how well a salesperson has done. By setting targets, the budget provides a '*benchmark*' against which performance can be evaluated and assessed. Before a budget can be successfully used, it must be accepted as being fair and reasonable by all those who are responsible for carrying it out.

Identification of trends

It is important that management should be made aware as soon as possible of any new trends, whether in relation to production or marketing. The budget, by providing specific expectations against which actual performance can be *continuously* measured, provides a mechanism for the early detection of unexpected trends.

Communication and motivation

The budget communicates first during its preparation stage which involves the two-way communication process between top management and line managers about objectives and the methods of achieving them. Second, after it is prepared, it communicates the objectives of the firm from top management downwards, so that all are aware of what the targets are, and what is expected of them.

Control

This is the most often cited advantage of budgeting. Having set its goals, management uses the budget to control the running of the business. To formulate plans, and then take no action to see that they are achieved, would be a pointless exercise. The budgeting system provides a mechanism for achieving control. By continuously comparing actual with planned results, deviations are readily noted and reported, and appropriate corrective action is considered and taken.

There is, however, a danger in adhering to the budget too rigidly. As mentioned earlier, circumstances may change and the budget, if it is going to be of any use, should change accordingly.

The principles of effective budgeting

If budgeting and budgetary control are going to be really effective in promoting the attainment of corporate objectives, and the long-term success and survival of an organisation, they need to incorporate the following principles:

A team effort

It should be a *team effort* – all of those involved should work together in harmony and adopt a *common-sense approach* throughout the budgeting process. This will involve the realistic appraisal of income, expenditure and the employment of capital.

Attainable targets

A budget that includes unattainable targets is likely to be rejected by the people involved. From a management point of view, it is most important that budgets are accepted as being *fair and reasonable*. If targets are too difficult people may just give up trying to achieve them, and become de-motivated and/or leave.

Participation

Ensure that all those who would be involved get a chance to *participate* in the budget preparation process. Participation and involvement by, e.g., certain worker representatives and/or supervisors can result in the setting of more realistic budgets and improved morale and motivation. The people involved may even bring to the attention of management information that is vital to the success of the budgeting process, and stop them from going ahead with a development that could have disastrous consequences.

Management by exception

In reporting the variances, those that are considered to be significant, and the reasons why they have occurred, should be highlighted on the comparative statement, Figure 17.1. This will enable management to focus on them, and give high priority to sorting out the appropriate corrective action. This system of highlighting significant variances can be described as '*management by exception*'.

Plan for changes in basic assumptions

Watch out for *changes in the basic assumptions* upon which the budgets were based. This is why budgets should, where possible, be flexible, i.e. designed to change as levels of activity or output change, and be revised to take account of environmental change.

Control by responsibility

Budgets need to be built up by *areas of responsibility*. For example, the sales and marketing director would be responsible for the overall sales target and this could be subdivided between sales area managers, and subdivided again between sales staff. This could be imposed from above, i.e. the *top-down approach*, or built up from the lowest level of accountability and responsibility, i.e. the *bottom-up approach*.

Monitoring

Budgets must be co-ordinated, monitored and reviewed, e.g. watched for changes in basic assumptions. Monitor progress at frequent intervals, e.g. monthly, by looking at budget and actual comparative statements, drafted along the lines of Figure 17.1.

Simple Budget and Actual Comparative Statement (Details of purpose, etc.) Date				
Item	Actual £000	Budget £000	Variance £000	Reasons for variance*

Figure 17.1 – Simple budget and actual comparative statement
Details for the previous year could also be included for comparison.
* The variance is the difference between the actual and the budget. For example, if the actual expenditure exceeds the budgeted expenditure it is adverse, i.e. an overspend; the converse would be a favourable variance.

Management will be particularly interested in significant adverse variances. These would be highlighted on the budget and actual comparative statements together with the reasons why they have occurred. Managers can then devote their time and energy into putting right whatever is going wrong. This should ensure the early detection of items that are not going according to plan.

Early detection means early action!

Communications

There must be good clear communications to avoid misunderstandings regarding objectives, targets and deadlines, etc. Approval of budgets must be specifically communicated down the line to indicate management acceptance, as a basis for control, i.e. management in action.

Flexible budgets

Control must be by flexible budgets, so that *'like can be compared with like'*. We will look further into this aspect in due course. Reported actuals must match the budgeted content before comparison is valid, e.g. it has been known for budgets and actuals to be worked out using different ways of calculating them.

Education

All those involved should be educated about the benefits of budgeting. If they know and understand more about the process and the aims, they are more likely to participate more whole-heartedly and more fully.

Behavioural factors

You need to appreciate that budgets do affect people's behaviour and that behavioural factors cannot and should not be ignored, e.g. the gate-keepers' personal objectives, political access, etc. (A 'gate-keeper' is a person who has control of an important information junction, e.g. the management accountant.)

Control should be directed towards actions rather than recriminatory post-mortems. If this becomes the norm, the budget may become the 'scapegoat', i.e. blamed for everything that is going wrong – after all, it could have been caused by GIGO (garbage in, garbage out)! In any case, budgets are only estimates. We will go into a little more depth about this area shortly.

Cost–benefit analysis

The cost of the system must not exceed the value obtained.

Cash budget (cash flow forecasts)

What is a cash budget?

It is important to remember that income and expenditure, as recorded for profit measurement purposes, are frequently not the same as the cash receipts and payments. This is particularly obvious in the case of expenditure on fixed assets where large sums of cash can be paid in one period, which are then written off for profit and loss measurement purposes over future periods by way of depreciation. Another example is the time lag between buying or selling goods on credit and paying or receiving the cash. Note that the *cash flow forecast* (an alternative name for the cash budget) is *not* the same as the cash flow statement that is published in the reports and accounts of companies.

The purpose of a cash budget

The principal purposes of a cash budget (cash flow forecast) are to:

☐ make sure that cash is *available when needed*, e.g. to purchase fixed assets and/or pay dividends;

☐ *highlight cash shortages*, so that early action can be taken, e.g. to increase the overdraft limit, or internal action for collecting debts in more quickly, or a slow-down in paying creditors;

☐ *highlight cash surpluses*, so that it can be considered for investment short-term, e.g. overnight, one-week, one-month.

There are a number of other uses to which the cash budget (cash-flow forecast) can be put, including:

☐ an aid to management in controlling its cash resources, e.g. the treasury function which is involved with the investment of surplus cash. The prediction of cash peaks and troughs allows management time to devise and implement appropriate action;

☐ an aid to monitoring performance in areas where cash control is an important performance indicator, e.g. credit control. As with all budgets, the comparison of the actual with the budget, together with the relevant variance analysis, should be carried out;

☐ a control device to enable changes in plans or remedial action to be taken to correct an outcome that initially looks as if it will be unsatisfactory or unacceptable. This can happen both at the outset of an activity or during the course of the activity;

☐ a discussion document in obtaining third-party co-operation in project implementation, e.g. with banks and other lending institutions where financing facilities are being sought, or supervisory boards and the like when project approval is being sought.

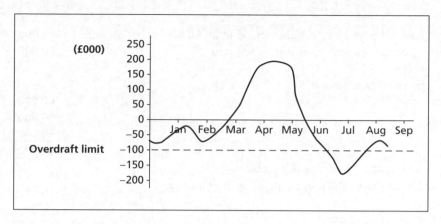

Figure 17.2 – A cash graph

Profit does not always equal cash over any given period. The criteria for success in business are to make profits and generate cash. Problems can arise because the two are not necessarily concurrent. A profitable business can be problematic because of the time lag in collecting the associated cash, which as a result puts severe strain on *cash flow*. It is important, therefore, to know if and when these cash demands may be made on the business – hence the need to forecast.

Cash budgets (cash flow forecasts) may also be needed in support of new business activities or projects, particularly when there is competition for the limited resources, in order to demonstrate to the appropriate person that:

☐ the project is viable in terms of the ultimate cash returns, and

☐ the intervening cash demands will not be excessive or impossible to find, or as burdensome as competing projects! Figure 17.2 shows a cash graph; the critical point is when the cash flow falls below the overdraft limit.

Producing a cash budget

We will now work through the example of Charlotte Ltd to illustrate how to produce a cash budget, a budgeted profit and loss account, and a balance sheet.

Example   Charlotte Ltd

Charlotte is starting up a new business on 1 January 20X6 and has provided you with the following information:

	£
Quarterly rent of premises (first payment due on 25 March 20X6)	6,000
Cash outlay on equipment – payable in January	180,000

Monthly planned purchases of stock for resale:

	£
January	40,000
February	60,000
March	84,000
	184,000

All stock is bought on one month's credit
For example, January's purchase is paid for in February

Monthly planned sales are:

	£
January	30,000
February	90,000
March	120,000
	240,000

All sales are on two months' credit.
Planned gross profit each month is, on average, 33.333% of sales.
The monthly cash outlay on general expenses is expected to be £12,000.
Salaries are expected to be £5,000 per month.
Depreciation of equipment on the first quarter-year is expected to be 5% of the initial cost.
Charlotte Ltd will commence trading with an ordinary share capital, paid into the business bank account on 1 January 20X6, of £250,000.

Required
Form the data in the example, prepare a monthly cash budget for the quarter-year to 31 March 20X6, a budgeted profit and loss account for the quarter-year, and a closing balance sheet, as at 31 March 20X6.

The method of going about this task is described and illustrated below:

To complete the cash budget we first pick up the opening balance, in this case the £250,000 ordinary share capital, which will be used to start the business. Note that the cash budget includes all of the cash and bank balances.

Next you pick up the sales, then the purchases, taking into account the periods of credit given or taken. You then pick all the other expenses, plotting them in the month in which they are paid out.

Having inserted all the data, the next step is to balance each month, starting with January. The closing balance for January becomes the opening balance for February, and so on.

Charlotte Ltd solution

Cash budget to 31 March 20X6

		Jan	Feb	March
Receipts:		£000	£000	£000
Balance b/f		250	53	(4)
Sales (2 months' credit)		—	—	30
	(A)	**250**	**53**	**26**
Less **Payments:**				
Purchases (1 month's credit)		—	40	60
Rent		—	—	6
Salaries		5	5	5
General expenses		12	12	12
Fixed assets		180	—	—
	(B)	**197**	**57**	**83**
Balance c/f (A)–(B)		**53**	**(4)**	**(57)**

Calculation of the closing stock:

		£000
	Total sales	240
Less	Gross profit @ 33.333%	80
	Cost of sales	160
	Total purchases	184
	Difference = Closing stock	24

We can now prepare a budgeted profit and loss account, which includes all the sales and purchases for the period and also accounts for depreciation of fixed assets. We can then prepare a budgeted balance sheet, which lists all the assets, capital and liabilities.

Comment

The cash budget is drawn up using predetermined figures. It records them during the month in which they are expected to come in or go out. In doing this it has to take periods of credit allowed by suppliers of goods and services, or to customers, into account. For example, it does not really matter about the month in which a sale is made or the period covered by a dividend received. What does matter is when the cash from the sale or dividend is actually received. Non-cash items, e.g. depreciation, are not included in the cash budget. The cash moves when the asset is paid for, not when it is depreciated.

Using the same data we will now prepare the budgeted profit and loss account, and budgeted balance sheet.

Charlotte Ltd

Budgeted profit and loss account for the three months to 31 March 20X6

	£000	£000
Sales		240
Cost of Sales:		
Purchases	184	
Less Closing stock	24	
		160
Gross profit		**80**
Less **Expenses:**		
Rent	6	
Salaries	15	
General expenses	36	
Depreciation (5% × £180,000)	9	
		66
Net profit		**14**

Charlotte Ltd

Budgeted balance sheet as at 31 March 20X6

	£000	£000
Fixed assets:	180	
Less Depreciation	9	171
Working capital:		
Current assets:		
Stock	24	
Debtors (90 + 120)	210	
Cash and bank	(57)	
	177	
Current liabilities:		
Creditors	84	93
		264
Capital employed		
Ordinary share capital		250
Reserves (profit for period)		14
		264

The budgeted profit and loss account illustrated above is made up of the total sales and total expenses for the three months.

Capital budgets for financing and expenditure

The **capital budget** (Figure 17.3) spells out the organisation's future requirements in terms of:

☐ *fixed assets*, e.g. buildings, machinery, equipment;

☐ *working capital*, e.g. an increase in stock holdings and/or more sales on credit;

☐ *investment in securities*, e.g. shares in UK companies;

☐ *redemption of preference shares and debentures*;

☐ *repayment of loans*;

☐ the *types of finance* to be used, and their timing.

The capital expenditure budget will be subdivided into short-term and long-term plans. These plans will need to be carefully monitored and action taken to combat the effects of changes in the perceived environment. (Note that capital investment appraisal is covered in Chapter 18.) It must also be noted that all budgets, e.g. sales, production, capital expenditure, research and development, are interrelated.

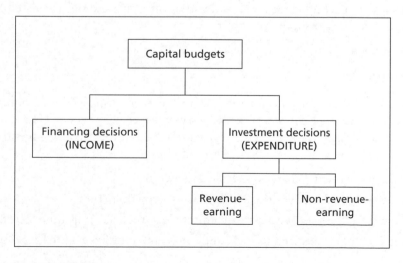

Figure 17.3 – Capital budgets

Budgeting the finance needed

The planned requirements in terms of expenditure must be financed from internal or external sources. Although the financing decision is closely related to the investment decision, it is in fact a quite independent decision. The capital budget relating to the financing requirements will be drawn up to cover:

☐ the amount required to cover the budgeted expenditure;

☐ the timing of the expenditure. In this respect, the cash budget is a very important tool as it indicates when the cash is needed;

☐ the type of finance to be used, e.g. debt, equity, internal financing.

It is most important to keep a watchful eye upon what is happening in the capital markets. The possibility of the refinancing of existing borrowings should not be ignored. Refinancing could well save an undertaking (be it in the public or the private sector) a lot of money. It is imperative that alternative courses of providing fixed assets be considered, such as hiring, renting, leasing, and sale and lease-back.

Capital expenditure budgets

The preparation of the capital expenditure budgets could be organised along the following lines.

Timetable

A timetable will need to be drawn up and circulated in good time, giving dates for submission of proposals, meeting dates for consideration of proposals, and the date of the final meeting when the budget should be approved.

Co-ordination

The person responsible for co-ordinating all the budgets, usually the accountant, must ensure that all personnel concerned know what is expected of them. The co-ordinator should also make available, to all those who are involved in the capital budgeting preparation process:

☐ details of environmental change (internal and external);

☐ industry figures, such as performance indicators, growth in sales;

☐ the revenue implications of capital expenditure, e.g. the recurring annual costs;

☐ the company's policy on credit, stock, and replacement of fixed assets, tax implications, etc.

In order to obtain the *co-operation and participation* of those involved, it is essential that there is clear and effective *communication*.

Assessing the needs

To a large extent, the needs in terms of machinery, equipment, computer systems, fixtures and fittings, etc. will be determined by the other, interrelated budgets. The usual starting point in the budgeting process for a manufacturing company is sales, because sales determines how much needs to be produced; the production budget then determines the purchasing budget, and so on. However, the effects of the principal budget factor, i.e. the limiting factor, cannot and must not be ignored.

Submitting proposals

Departmental managers or executives will need to formulate and submit their proposals.

It is important for management to formulate a replacement policy for revenue-earning and non-revenue-earning capital expenditure, for instance, executive cars could be replaced every three years, while certain machines could be replaced every five years. A replacement schedule may be drawn up containing details of the fixed assets that are to be replaced (e.g. estimated residual values) and their proposed replacements.

For non-revenue-earning capital expenditure the managers concerned should provide those who have the final say with satisfactory *justification* for the expenditure. Organisations spend a great deal of money on items that are non-revenue-earning, such as fixtures, fittings and office equipment.

Search

When submissions have been received, a search should take place to reveal other alternatives that were not pointed out on the original submission. Ignore the search process at your peril! It could cost you a lot of money.

Preliminary vetting

The management concerned will look carefully at all the proposals and obtain further information if necessary. They will then decide which proposals will go through to the next stage of the exercise. Rejecting some proposals at this stage will avoid wasting valuable time and effort later on.

Evaluation

The evaluation of the revenue-earning capital budgets will take place using, for example, capital investment appraisal. Various factors such as price, quality and reliability will have to be taken into account when assessing alternative non-revenue-earning capital expenditures.

Presentation

The results of the evaluation will be presented to management in an appropriate form. Meetings may be arranged to discuss the proposals with the staff concerned.

Selection

After careful consideration of the information contained in the evaluation, plus any further information, management will meet to decide whether or not to approve the capital expenditure budget. Several revisions may be necessary before the final approval is given.

Communications

The process does not end with the approval. It is also important to inform the appropriate personnel of the decisions that have been reached, and to thank them for playing their part in the budgeting exercise.

Capital allocations

When faced with the task of allocating capital expenditure between the various departments and cost centres, the following points should be taken into account:

☐ Is capital expenditure over the last few years a good guide as to what will be expected to happen next year? This approach tends to look backwards and not forwards, and goes against the principles of sound budgeting. The information relating to past allocations is just one very small component part of the mass of information required. If historic capital expenditures were acceptable as a basis for fixing future allocations, this would encourage spending on unnecessary projects. *Justification* of projects is therefore of paramount importance.

☐ *Across-the-board cuts* in capital expenditure do not make any sense. This kind of compromise has the effect of cutting essential as well as non-essential projects.

☐ It is important that needs are assessed, expenditure justified and projects and alternatives considered and carefully appraised. A *zero-based budgeting (ZBB) approach* may be worth considering, particularly for non-revenue-earning projects.

Capital expenditure – the role of the audit

It is the duty of the external auditor to verify:

☐ the existence, and

☐ the ownership, and

☐ the basis of valuation

of fixed assets and investments.

The external and (if there are any) internal auditors are particularly concerned with *internal control systems* governing the purchase of fixed assets. They will look most carefully to see that the purchase has been correctly *authorised* by the appropriate personnel. Their role also extends to preventing and/or detecting errors and fraud in this area, and thereby eliminating losses.

Flexible budgets

An organisation can use either a fixed budget or a flexible budget. A **fixed budget** is a budget that is designed to remain unchanged irrespective of the level of activity (i.e. level of output) actually attained, whereas a **flexible budget** is a budget that, by recognising the differences between fixed, semi-fixed and variable costs, is designed to *change in relation to the level of activity attained*. An example of a flexible budget is shown in Figure 17.4.

A fixed budget is not really suitable for comparing performance because you could be comparing two completely different levels of activity. The idea behind flexible budgeting is to overcome that problem, so that the actual level of activity attained can be compared with a budget appertaining to the same level of activity.

We shall consider this example of a flexible budget. In order to prepare it, we need to separate the costs into their fixed and variable components. Also, observe how the fixed costs remain the same at £30,000 up to a sales level of £200,000 and that there is then an increase of £6,000, in other words, a step in the fixed costs.

Monthly departmental flexible budget					
	£000	£000	£000	£000	£000
Sales	**160**	**180**	**200**	**220**	**240**
Direct costs	72	81	90	99	108
Variable overheads	24	27	30	33	36
Fixed overheads	30	30	30	36	36
Total cost	**126**	**138**	**150**	**168**	**180**
Profit	**34**	**42**	**50**	**52**	**60**

Figure 17.4 – A flexible budget

Example

We have been provided with the following information:
Operating statement

	Budget	Actual
Output (units)	100,000	120,000
	£000	£000
Sales	1,200	1,410
Cost of sales (see note 1 below)	800	1,104
	400	306
Fixed costs	280	294
Net profit	120	12

Note 1
The cost of sales is made up of the
following variable costs:

	£000	£000
Direct materials	400	504
Direct labour	240	360
Variable overheads	160	240
	800	1,104

Solution
First, if we look at the budget, we can compute the following unit selling prices and costs:

Selling price	$\dfrac{£1,200,000}{100,000 \text{ units}} =$	**£12 per unit**

Cost of sales:

		Per unit
		£
Direct materials	$\dfrac{£400,000}{100,000 \text{ units}} =$	4.00
Direct labour	$\dfrac{£240,000}{100,000 \text{ units}} =$	2.40
Variable overheads	$\dfrac{£160,000}{100,000 \text{ units}} =$	1.60
		£8.00

Secondly, with this knowledge we can now flex the budget, i.e. recalculate it to reflect the actual output of 120,000 units, as follows:

Flexible budgets
Comparative statement

Units		120,000	120,000		
(000s)		**Budget** £000	**Actual** £000	**Variance** £000	
Sales (120 × 12)	**(A)**	**1,440**	**1,410**	**(30)**	**Adverse**
Costs of sales:					
Direct materials (120 × £4)		480	504	(24)	Adverse
Direct labour (120 × £2.40)		288	360	(72)	Adverse
Variable overheads (120 × £1.60)		192	240	(48)	Adverse
	(B)	**960**	**1104**	**(144)**	**Adverse**
Less Fixed overheads	**(C)**	280	294	(14)	Adverse
Net profit **(A) less (B) + (C)**		**200**	**12**	**(188)**	

Observations

The initial comparison was not really a valid comparison as it was comparing a budget based on 100,000 units with an actual performance of 120,000 units.

The target profit went up by a considerable amount.

Now that the budget has been flexed it can be observed that the selling price expected was not realised and, for various reasons, an average lower selling price per unit had to be accepted.

On the cost side, all the direct costs and variable costs increased, and this will have to be investigated to find out why.

The fixed overheads went up, perhaps as a result of a step in the fixed costs because of moving up to a higher level of activity.

The adverse position revealed does pose quite a number of questions, was it just caused by e.g. changes in the environment or poor estimating?

The behavioural aspects of budgeting

Budgeting takes place within a human environment, and behavioural factors cannot be pushed aside and ignored. Budgets are in fact designed to affect people's behaviour. However, people do not always respond as expected. Their response could be affected by the way in which the budget was drawn up; the way in which it was communicated; people's education and training; the way in which the budget is to be implemented; and so on. Some of the causes of the behavioural problems relating to budgeting that are frequently encountered in an organisation are listed below.

Perceptions

Perceptions about the objectives of an organisation and the interpretation of policy may be caused by poor communications and a lack of participation.

Personal goals

Those who have to abide by the budget, and achieve the targets set, also have *their own personal objectives*. These personal objectives may conflict with and run counter to the objectives laid down by management. For example, '*empire builders*' within an organisation can involve it in unnecessary expenditure. Actions by such individuals and/or groups may fulfil their own personal objectives, but these may run contrary to the organisation's corporate objectives. The organisation in such cases could well find itself with a high proportion of surplus assets such as equipment and buildings.

Participation

A principle of budgeting, which is sometimes overlooked, results in those who should be involved and consulted deciding to withdraw their full-hearted co-operation and support. They may even fail to point out to management something that could well have saved a lot of money and a vast amount of time dealing with unnecessary problems. For example, managers have been known to buy expensive equipment but fail to realise that the equipment concerned could only work if certain additional equipment was also purchased. Had they involved their subordinates, they may have avoided making such a disastrous and expensive decision. In one case, subordinates were not consulted, they all knew of the decision by their 'know-all manager', and all remained silent, and were not prepared to point out the mistake!

Figure 17.5 – Why haven't you achieved your sales target?

Aspiration levels

The achievement of the budget is perceived and treated as success, and non-achievement is perceived and treated as failure. This can affect *motivation* and *morale*.

Targets

If the targets are set too high employees may opt out of trying to achieve them. However, if they are set too easy, e.g. in an incentive scheme, employees may agree between themselves what the level of production should be! This is because they are afraid that the targets will be revised if managers realise they have made the targets too easy.

Obsessions

Some managers are obsessed by the idea that the budget must be achieved at all costs. This is due partly to their aspirations and an uncalled-for perception of accuracy. Some managers tend to forget that the budgeted figures are only estimates.

Excuses

If things go wrong, e.g. where there are organisational problems, it is not uncommon for the budget to get the blame. And if some managers or supervisors wish to justify something that has to be done, they say, 'Oh well, we have to do this to keep within our budget'. This then leads their subordinates to treat the budget as a *scapegoat*, i.e. the cause of everything that is going wrong!

Resource allocation

This is always an area in which conflict can arise, possibly as a result of departmental goals or empire building.

Seats of power

Certain individuals and/or groups within an organisation may be able to exert considerable influence over the outcome of, for example, proposed capital expenditure. This could lead the organisation in a direction that conflicts with its corporate objectives. Eventually it could destroy itself by, for example, going overboard with the introduction of a new product, or research and development. The power referred to may be by *political access*, i.e. access to top management, or by voting rights on committees.

Gate-keepers

Gate-keepers, i.e. personnel who sit on important information flow junctions, are in a position to regulate the flow of information and therefore in a position to determine what the various levels of management may or may not see.

Beating the system

Individuals or groups may be able to beat the system. They may even take pride in doing so. For example, a company places a limit of £100,000 on the ordering of capital equipment. Above this limit, additional authority is required. The person beating the system simply buys a machine for, say, £120,000 by making out two orders, one for say £90,000 and the other for £30,000.

Imposition

If management imposes budgets 'from above', the personnel who 'work below' may reject them and fail to pledge their support or generally just demonstrate a lack of enthusiasm.

Sub-optimal decisions

If budgets have to be cut, an across-the-board cut will weaken both the strong and the weak! Again, this will undoubtedly result in conflict.

No thanks, not even a 'well done'!

Many systems point out poor performance, but fail to recognise and reward good performance (with the exception of sales, which may be rewarded by bonus payments and/or executive perks). This imbalance may cause problems and de-motivation in areas other than sales.

Management therefore needs to tread very carefully when preparing and introducing budgets. To some extent, success will depend upon the way in which managers deal with the education and training of their employees The success of the system will also depend on the extent of employee participation, good clear communications, and the regular review and monitoring of behavioural factors.

Zero-base budgeting

It has been found that zero-base budgeting is particularly useful when applied to service and support areas such as research and development and executive training. However, it is possible for the zero-base concept to be used in the manufacturing area by making up decision packages to identify alternatives and discretionary activities, allowing management to rank these packages in relation to packages identified for other areas.

ZBB seeks to achieve a more effective allocation of resources in the service and support areas by carefully *describing, classifying, sorting* and *ranking* the individual activities concerned.

The basic steps for effective zero-base budgeting are to:

☐ describe each discreet company activity in a *decision package*;

☐ *evaluate and rank* all these packages by cost–benefit analysis;

☐ *allocate resources* accordingly.

When a company applies ZBB it must explain to all levels of management the decision package concept and then present guidelines for them to break their area's activities into workable packages. Next, it must set in motion a ranking and consolidation process, whereby important packages are identified and given a top-rank classification, and less important packages are ranked lower.

Decision packages are usually formulated at the ground level. This promotes *detailed specification of activities and alternatives* and generates interest and participation by the manager who will be operationally responsible for the approved budget.

Each manager takes his or her area's forecast expenditure level for the current year, identifies the activities creating this expense, and calculates the cost for each activity. Managers should not try to identify alternatives or increments at this stage. After the managers have broken their current operations into preliminary decision packages, they look at their requirements for the coming year. To aid them, management should issue a formalised set of assumptions on: activity levels, wage and salary increases and so on for the coming year. Finally, the managers should identify all new activities in their area for the coming year, and develop decision packages to handle them.

Having completed the set of packages the managers' next task is to commence the *ranking process*. The ranking process provides management with a technique with which to allocate its limited resources, by ensuring that they concentrate on important questions such as: how much they should spend, and where should they spend it.

Management may use quantitative or qualitative evaluation techniques in ranking each package, giving a higher rank to packages that satisfy minimum operating and legal requirements, and a lower rank to the more discretionary packages. All the packages identified need to be listed in order of decreasing benefit to the company. Management identifies the benefits to be gained at each level of expenditure and studies the consequences of not approving additional decision packages.

It is helpful to have a review session after detailed ranking has been carried out, in which the votes of the members are displayed, misunderstandings of package content and differences of opinion are discussed, and a final ranking is established. The ranked list gives management the means to evaluate the desirability of various expenditure levels throughout the budgeting process. It also provides a reference point in the coming year to identify activities that are to be reduced or expanded if allowed expenditure levels change.

A number of variations of the zero-based budgeting approach have developed in practice. One variation places a limit on the number of proposals that may be made by each cost centre or department or service. Another requires a full review of some or all cost centres spread over a longer period of, say, two or three years.

Standard costing

A **standard cost** is a *predetermined target cost* designed to provide a benchmark against which to measure actual performance. The setting of a standard may involve consideration of: quantities, prices, rates of pay, qualities and a detailed review of all the relevant factors. Standards can be set for selling prices, and the elements of cost, i.e. materials, labour and overheads.

Variance analysis

Control in standard costing is achieved by *variance analysis*. Figure 17.6 should help you to

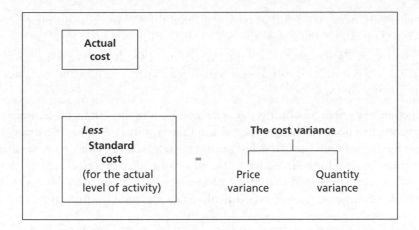

Figure 17.6 – Variance analysis

understand how variance analysis works. At the end of the period under review the actual cost is compared with the predetermined standard cost for the actual level of activity that was attained. This difference is known as the **variance**.

All variances are the result of two factors, *price* and *quantity*. Thus, the *total cost variance* can be subdivided into that part of the variance that arises from price differences, and that part that arises from the differences in quantities, see Figures 17.6 and 17.7. The names of these sub-variances may cause confusion, but the principles remain unchanged.

The cost (total) variance is the difference between the standard cost (for the actual level of activity) and the actual cost. This can be subdivided into two sub-variances, as shown in Figures 17.6, 17.7 and 17.9:

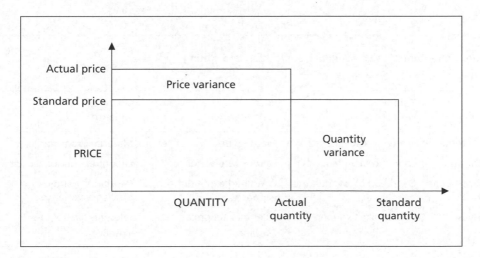

Figure 17.7 – The sub-variances

☐ The **price variance** is the result of paying different actual prices from the prices or rates that were planned, i.e. the standard.

☐ The **quantity variance**, over which the management tends to have more control, is the difference between what the organisation planned to use, i.e. the standard usage, and the actual quantity that was used.

Taken together, the price and quantity variances add back to the cost variance, which provides a quick arithmetic check on the accuracy of the figures. Finally, it must be recognised that, after all, standards are only estimates! They must, therefore, be carefully computed and monitored – hence the need for constant feedback, and consequent revision (see Figure 17.8).

Standard costing developed as a result of the quest for a benchmark against which to measure actual performance. A standard is therefore a predetermined target cost or target revenue.

You should note that Figure 17.8 applies to both budgeting and standard costing. The comparison of standard with actual results should take place at frequent intervals, e.g. monthly. The variance can be adverse (or negative), e.g. where the actual expenditure exceeds the standard expenditure, or *favourable* (or positive), e.g. where the actual expenditure is less than the standard expenditure. These will be reversed for sales variances.

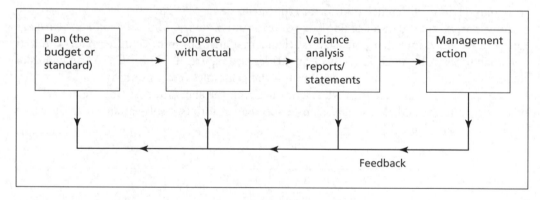

Figure 17.8 – Control using budgeting and/or standard costing

	Total/cost variance		Price variance		Quantity variance
Materials	Material cost variance	=	Material price variance	+	Material usage variance
Labour	Labour cost variance	=	Labour rate variance	+	Labour efficiency variance
Overheads	Overhead cost variance	=	Overhead expenditure variance	+	Overhead volume or efficiency variance
Sales	Sales margin variance	=	Sales margin price variance	+	sales margin volume variance

Figure 17.9 – Variances: materials, labour, overheads and sales

Variance	Responsible person
Sales margin variance	Sales manager or regional manager
Material price variance	Chief buyer

Figure 17.10 – Control by responsibility: variance analysis

The variance analysis in the form of reports and statements supplied should: highlight controllable adverse variances, identify the causes of the variances, and advise *those responsible* (see Figures 17.9 and 17.10). This follows the principle of *management by exception*. Managers can then focus their time and talents towards solving problems, which can have a dramatic impact upon performance. This should mean that any necessary corrective action is taken at the earliest available opportunity. It also means that managers are using their valuable time more productively.

Summary: budgetary control

The master budget

You should note that the cash budget, budgeted profit and loss account, and the budgeted balance sheet are frequently referred to as the *master budget*. If management approves it, it will be implemented. If it is not approved, then they go back to the drawing board to review and revise targets, policies, etc. The master budget, once approved, is the culmination of the budget preparation process. It is the coming together of all the component parts of the budgeting jigsaw. It communicates in advance of the start of the budget period (e.g. a six- or twelve-month period), the outcome in terms of cash flow, profits, assets and liabilities, capital expenditure, etc.

Preparation

It is essential that the budget preparation process commences well before the budget period to which it relates, and that the *principal budget factor* (i.e. a constraint) is identified. The preparation process will be co-ordinated by the budget controller. The *authority and responsibility* for a particular budget or section of a budget will be *delegated* to a named individual. The *budget controller* will supply that person with appropriate information to help with their budget preparation. From the outset all those involved will have to be issued with instructions and a *timetable*. The timetable will state when schedules and other information will be required and the dates and times of meetings. Meetings are needed to plan, discuss, review and revise the budgets, to ensure that everything fits together. This is because budgets are *interrelated*. One budget cannot be prepared in isolation and without reference to the other budgets. When the process is complete, managers must ensure that the information on objectives, policy, targets, etc. is communicated to the appropriate personnel, which indicates top management's acceptance of the budget.

Control

Control in budgeting is exercised by regular comparisons (e.g. monthly) between budgeted and actual results. The statements produced inform management of where in their organisation things are not going according to plan. Management can then decide on the form of any corrective action that needs to be taken (see Figure 17.8). It is, in fact, an *early warning system*.

Effective budgeting

Budgeting is a management technique that uses predetermined estimates and figures. Management needs to set objectives and *formulate policy*. The budgets provide targets that reflect the *objectives*, and the policy is the means by which those targets should be achieved. Management must see that the targets that are set are *fair, reasonable and attainable*.

Effective budgeting improves efficiency, in that it demands the following:

☐ working in harmony and a *common-sense approach*;

☐ careful planning and the provision of information for management, e.g. *timetables* for budget preparations, meetings, etc;

☐ identification of the limiting factors, i.e. the *principal budget factor*;

☐ the *participation* of both management and workers;

☐ *co-ordination and co-operation, negotiation and relationship skills*;

☐ a *sound accounting system*;

☐ making *assumptions about the future*, and revising budgets to take account of environmental change, e.g. where the original assumption no longer holds true;

☐ that new trends and inefficiencies be detected at an early stage of the planning or control process, via *monitoring at frequent intervals*, e.g. monthly, and reporting the findings to management;

☐ the *delegation of duties and authority*. This will mean that job specifications will have to be clear and unambiguous;

☐ *control by responsibility*;

☐ *management by exception*;

☐ a sound evaluation system for *comparing and reporting* on budgeted and actual results, and consideration of alternative courses of action, trade-offs and interrelationships with other budgets;

☐ the *motivation* of the workforce;

☐ good clear *communications*;

☐ *corrective action* by management to remedy adverse situations;

☐ the allocation of *scarce resources*;

☐ ensuring that *behavioural factors* are taken into account.

This can happen only if all those who are involved understand what budgeting is trying to do and are able to express their views during the budget preparation process, and if the budget is flexible enough to take account of changes in assumptions and circumstances.

Cash budgets

A common cause of business failure has been identified as *poor cash flow management*. The cash budget is a very important and integral part of good cash flow management. Cash budgeting aims to do the following:

☐ make sure that *cash is available when it is needed*;

☐ *identify shortages* in good time, so that appropriate remedial action can be taken;

☐ identify surpluses of cash so that, where possible, they can be transferred or invested where they can earn a satisfactory return. Nowadays, the *treasury function* of an organisation deals with the investments of surplus cash in the short term, e.g. overnight or for, say, a week or a month.

Flexible budgets

Flexible budgets are designed to change with the level of activity (output) to ensure that *like is compared with like*.

The behavioural aspects of budgeting

Budgets do affect the way in which people behave. Behavioural factors should not be ignored, particularly when they affect motivation. Some of the *keywords* relating to behavioural factors that we encountered were:

☐ perceptions

☐ personal goals

☐ participation

☐ aspiration levels

☐ targets

☐ obsessions

☐ an excuse (scapegoat)

☐ resource allocation

☐ seats of power

☐ gate-keepers

☐ beating the system

☐ imposition

☐ sub-optimal decisions

☐ no thanks!

Human beings are very complex variables and will react in a variety of ways to situations involving budget preparation, implementation, control, etc.

Zero-base budgeting

Another approach to budgeting is that of *zero-base budgeting* (*ZBB*). This has been found to be particularly useful in service or support areas, e.g. canteen, welfare, research and development. It forces the managers who are responsible for budgets to *justify* them and to *rank* them according to their importance, and also to evaluate more or less costly alternatives as appropriate. Top management can then screen and discuss the proposals, and decide which ones will go ahead. This, it is claimed, promotes a much more efficient allocation of resources. This is because managers have to *justify* how much they want and why they want it, and set out their *priorities*.

Standard costing

Standard costing involves setting standard quantities and standard prices for each element of cost. For materials, the standard quantity of materials that goes into the product, e.g. parts to make motor components, or the mix of chemicals needed to produce the product, has to be predetermined, and so does the standard price of the materials. With labour, standard times for performing various production operations have to be established e.g. by using work study techniques, and standard labour rates of pay have also to be estimated. Standard rates have also to be calculated for the overheads.

Control is carried out by *comparing* actual performance with the predetermined standard, and then reporting the *variances* to management. They can then consider what form of corrective action will be the most effective response.

Control – budgets and standards

Management will be particularly interested in the significant adverse variances, which will be highlighted in statements and reports. This system, which singles out those variances that management should look at very carefully, is known as *management by exception*. Managers spend their time and energy putting right things that are going wrong, and keeping the organisation on course to achieve its objectives. Frequent comparisons do provide systems for the *early detection and warning* of inefficiencies, and the emergence of new trends and environmental changes.

Control is also exercised by delegating to an individual the responsibility for a particular budget or subsection of a budget, i.e. *control by responsibility*. That person alone has to justify and explain to management why targets have not been achieved.

However, if the reported variances are to be of any use, it is essential that the budgeted and actual figures have been computed in the same way and relate to the same level of activity. This is why, if at all possible, a flexible budget should be used, i.e. a budget that is designed to change as the level of activity changes.

If budgeting is to become really effective it must be remembered that it is only a *forecast*. The budget itself, once implemented, must be *monitored* at frequent intervals and, if necessary, amended to take account of changes in basic assumptions.

Management will also have to monitor *behavioural factors* on a regular basis. 'People problems', if allowed to fester and multiply, can become the principal reason for the non-attainment of budget targets.

Staff development and education can be a most worthwhile investment. If staff know more about budgeting and what it is trying to do then, provided that they are able to participate and express their opinions, more reasonable, accurate and realistic budgets should be produced.

Finally, remember that control should be directed towards problem solving and not the creation of conflict!

Budgets – why ignore good practice?

To conclude this chapter we will look at an edited version of Chapter 12 of L. Chadwick, *Myths and Realities of Accounting and Finance*, Financial Times Prentice Hall, 1998. This will help you to appreciate the fact that what happens in practice can be quite different from the theory and what is considered to be good practice.

CIMA (Chartered Institute of Management Accountants) defines budgetary control as: 'The establishment of budgets relating the responsibilities of executives to the requirements of a policy, and the continuous comparison of actual with budgeted results, either to secure by individual action the objectives of that policy or to provide a basis for its revision'.

The four phases of control in the budgeting were illustrated in Figure 17.8 and were:

☐ *Plan*. Budgets have to be prepared using a combination of the previous year's/period's figures updated by what is known or expected about the future. Thus, it is essential that the budget is prepared well before the start of the period to which it relates.

☐ *Compare* with the actual figures. These have to be computed in the same way as the budgeted figures. The comparison between the budget and actual figures should be carried out at frequent intervals, e.g. monthly.

☐ *Report*. The variances that are adverse and significant should be highlighted on the variance reports submitted to management. The report should also contain explanations why specific significant variances have occurred.

☐ *Action*. Management can then concentrate on the adverse significant variances and decide what kind of action would be appropriate. In doing this they must ensure that the cost of the proposed action does not exceed the benefits.

The benefits of budgeting were outlined earlier in this chapter and were as follows: planning and co-ordination and co-operation; authorising and delegating; evaluating performance; the identification of trends; communication and motivation; and control.

The principles of effective budgetary control

The variances between the principles of sound budgeting and what happens in practice can cost an organisation a lot of money and have an adverse effect on morale and motivation. Over many years of lecturing to managers and executives in the UK and overseas, the author has found out first hand that what actually happens in the real world does not necessarily accord with what could be regarded as good practice. We will now review some of the comments made about budgeting and try to set the record straight as to what is considered to be good practice.

Comments:

Not much planning takes place.
No one consults us!
We just look at last year's figures and add 6%.

It needs to be appreciated from the outset that budgeting and budgetary control is a management planning technique. To do this involves the collection and analysis of data, timetables for meetings and good clear communications of objectives, policies, etc.

Comments:

No one is responsible for seeing that we achieve our targets.
If we overspend, so what!

It is essential that someone somewhere in the organisation be responsible for a particular budget or a subsection of a budget. For example, for a production budget, the overall responsibility would be with the production director; then the sub-budgets would be the responsibility of departmental managers, and within the departments their budgets could be delegated to heads of sections, supervisors, etc. Thus, if the targets are achieved at the lower levels, the targets will be achieved by those responsible at the higher levels. This is a very important principle, and is known as 'control by responsibility'.

Comments:

We don't do it that way.
It is simply imposed from above.
No one asks for our opinions.
That wouldn't happen at our firm.

A fundamental principle, and one that can save a lot of money, is participation. If targets are to be fair and realistic, it is important that lower levels of management and worker representatives are involved in the budget preparation process. They could be able to put their points of view forward, and because of their specific knowledge they may be able to explain why what is being proposed may not be feasible. It is accepted that to introduce more participation in the budget preparation process is not an easy task. However, if it is introduced successfully, it can pay dividends. However, note that not everybody is capable of participation, or wants to participate.

Comments:

Our targets are set so high no-one can achieve them.
Why can't we have our say on what we consider to be a realistic target?

If a target is set too high employees may give up trying to achieve it and their morale and motivation is likely to be low. Thus, target setting should be very carefully thought out. Consultation with lower-level management and worker representatives could lead to the setting of targets that are considered to be fair, reasonable and attainable.

Comments:

It never seems to hang together.
We hand it in and that's the last we see of it.

Budgets are interrelated, e.g. sale levels affect production levels, production affects stocks of raw materials, and so on. Thus there is a need to ensure that the budgets fit together as a coherent whole. This dictates that representatives of the various functions must meet on a regular basis during the budget preparation period and that someone co-ordinates the process. The co-ordinator, usually an accountant, would be responsible for the budget preparation timetable, arranging and chairing meetings and supplying information to those responsible for preparing the budgets that would assist them with that task.

Comments:

No one tells us.
We don't know what is expected of us.
Usually we have to guess what management wants.

The approved budgets, objectives and policies should be *clearly communicated* to appropriate personnel so that they know what they have to achieve. If they have to perceive what the objectives are and what is expected of them, their perceptions could be totally out-of-line.

Comment:

Once our budget is set, it will not change, whatever happens, and we are still expected to achieve it.

Control should really be exercised via flexible budgets, i.e. a budget that is designed to change in line with the actual level of activity (actual level of output). To compare an actual level of activity with a budget computed for a completely different level of activity is a meaningless exercise and will not aid the control process.

Comments:

Our print-outs just show the actual, budget and variance for each item of expenditure, and we are not told why the variances have occurred.
The information we receive isn't like that.

It is important that the variance reports highlight significant adverse variances, and also give reasons describing why they have happened. This is known as the principle of '*management by exception*'. The exceptional items are reported so that management can devote their time and talents towards taking appropriate action to 'right the wrong'.

Comments:

If we don't achieve our targets we could be for the chop!
The manager gets very angry if we don't keep within budget.

As mentioned earlier, budgeting is a management technique, and control should be directed and focused on action rather than recriminatory post-mortems. After all, budgets are only estimates, and estimates can be wrong.

Comments:

They never explain why we do it.
We don't know how we fit into the system.
Budgeting just wastes a lot of time and money.

It is important that personnel receive 'budget education' which explains how it works, what the benefits are, what their role is, etc. An efficient and effective budgeting system can help an organisation to survive and prosper. This would benefit both stakeholders and employees. However, the cost of such a system should not exceed the value obtained, i.e. cost must be weighted against benefit.

Comments:

*It's not our fault it's that **** budget!*
If we had a fair and realistic budget we would achieve our targets.

The budget is sometimes used as a scapegoat. Rightly or wrongly, it can be blamed for a variety of things that go wrong or as an excuse for not achieving targets.

Comments:

Why should we bother?
The illness was caused by stress.
The stress was caused because I just couldn't achieve the target set.

Budgets can and do affect behaviour in terms of performance, morale and motivation. The budget education referred to above is very important for all managers and supervisors. They need to appreciate the behavioural aspects, and that their management style relating to how they achieve their budget can lead to personnel problems and conflict. They need to realise that it is not a case of 'achieving the budget at all costs'. They must also receive instruction about how to use the information generated in a constructive manner.

Comments:

The information from outside sources never reaches us.
Had we known that, we would not have produced such a budget.
When we find out, it's too late anyway.

There could be a 'gate-keeper' at work. A gate-keeper is someone within the organisation who is located at an important information junction. They are therefore able to control information flows upwards and downwards within their organisation, and block information coming in from or going out to the external environment. Their motives could include *'empire building'* or the pursuit of their own *'personal goals'*.

Conclusion

What we described earlier as good practice and principles, in many cases, tends to be much better than what actually happens in reality!

Self-checks

Having attempted each self-check, compare your answer with the appropriate part of this chapter.

1. Describe, briefly, the principal benefits of employing a budgetary control system.

2. Explain why the budget preparation process may be described as 'attention directing'.

3. In relation to effective budgeting, explain the importance of:
   (a) having attainable targets
   (b) making use of participation in the preparation process
   (c) management by exception
   (d) control by responsibility
   (e) employing a good communication system.

4. What is the purpose of having a cash budget (cash flow forecast)?

5. What does a capital budget spell out?

6. Describe, briefly, the way in which a capital expenditure budget would be arrived at.

7. In relation to the behavioural aspects of budgeting, comment briefly on each of the following:
   (a) perceptions and personal goals
   (b) participation
   (c) seats of power
   (d) gate-keepers
   (e) sub-optimal decisions.

8. Define, in your own words, what is meant by zero-base budgeting (ZBB).

9. What does zero-base budgeting seek to achieve?

10. Explain how variance analysis works in standard costing and budgetary control.

Self-assessments

A17.1 Describe briefly the principal differences between:
(a) a cash budget (cash flow forecast) and a cash flow statement, and
(b) a cash budget and the budgeted profit and loss account.

A17.2 'A cash budget forces management into action.' Discuss this statement.

A17.3 Mythical Ltd
The company intends to start up in business on 1 January 20X7. They have the following information:

	£000
Ordinary share capital	2,000
Quarterly rent of premises, due on 25 March and 25 June	100
Cash outlay on equipment payable 1 Jan	200

	£000
payable 1 Mar	120

Monthly planned purchases of stock for re-sale

	£000
January	44
February	48
March–June	36

All stock is bought on one month's credit, i.e. January purchases are paid for in February, and so on.

Monthly planned sales are:

	£000
January	20
February	36
March	54
April – June (per month)	48

All sales are made on two months' credit.

The monthly cash expenditure on general expenses and salaries is estimated to be £16,000 per month.

The closing stock at 30 June 20X7 is expected to be £20,000.

Depreciation of the equipment for the first half-year is estimated at £32,000.

Required:

(a) Prepare a cash budget for the half-year to 30 June 20X7.

(b) Prepare a budgeted profit and loss account for the half-year, and budgeted balance sheet, as at 30 June 20X7.

(c) Explain briefly the importance to an organisation of preparing a cash budget.

A17.4 **Bonbon Ltd**

The company manufactures one uniform product only, and activity levels in the assembly department vary widely from month to month. The following statement shows the departmental overhead budget based on an average level of activity of 40,000 units production for June 20X5, and the actual results for June 20X5.

	Budget for June 20X5	Actual for June 20X5
Production (units)	40,000	35,000
	£	£
Indirect labour – variable	50,000	47,600
Consumables – variable	2,000	2,500
Other variable overheads	10,800	9,000
Deprecation – fixed	25,000	25,000
Other fixed overheads	15,000	18,000
	102,800	102,100

Required:

Prepare a performance report based on a budgeted production of 35,000 units by the company for June 20X5 and compare with the actual production costs for June 20X5.

Tutor-based assignments

These assignments can be used for discussions, reports or presentations as directed by your lecturer or tutor, and they may involve further research.

T17.1 Explain and illustrate the interrelationships between budgets.

T17.2 Describe the factors and considerations that will have to be taken into account when estimating the budgets for:
(a) office staff salaries
(b) overhead expenses
(c) motor vehicle expenses.

T17.3 Busford Grammar School
You are provided with the following information relating to the Busford Grammar School for the forthcoming budget period, 1 September 20X1 to 31 December 20X1.

		£000
Estimated cash and bank balances at 1 September 20X1		120
Wages and	September	84
salaries	October	80
	November	96
	December	64

(payable on the last Friday of each month)

Food	September	16
purchases	October	20
	November	24
	December	8

(payable 25% in current month and the remainder during the following month)

Coach hire	September	4
	October	4
	November	4
	December	2

(payable after one month's credit)

Overheads	August	60
	September	75
	October	70
	November	90
	December	50

(payable 20% in the current month and 80% in the following month)

Fixed assets (all bought on two months' credit):

	Month of purchase	£000
Fixtures and fittings	July	80
Equipment	October	84
Minibus	December	26

The fees for the term due in September should amount to £586,000. However, it is anticipated that £36,000 will not be received until October. Other income will be received as follows:

		Actual month £000
Travel money	September	14
Autumn fair (net)	November	2
School play (net)	December	1
Bank interest	December	8
Sale of old minibus	December	5

Required:
(a) Prepare a cash budget for the period ending 31 December 20X1.
(b) Explain briefly how the cash budget may assist in improving cash flow management of the school.
(c) Why could the school end up with a situation in which they have a net profit, but the cash and bank balances decrease by a significant amount?

T17.4 Orgundia Design plc
The company produced the information that follows. They were told that to compare the information in its current state would be a pretty meaningless exercise.

	Budget	Actual
Output (unit)	200,000	240,000
	£000	£000
Sales	500,000	660,000
Cost of sales (see note 1 below)	360,000	420,000
	140,000	240,000
Selling and administration (see note 2 below)	84,000	100,000
Net profit	£ 56,000	£120,000

Note 1
The cost of sales is made up of the following variable costs:

	£000	£000
Direct materials	120,000	132,000
Direct labour	150,000	192,000
Direct expenses	90,000	96,000
	£360,000	£420,000

Note 2
The selling and administration is made up of:

	£000	£000
Selling expenses	50,000	60,000
Administration expenses	34,000	40,000
	84,000	100,000

Material and labour costs vary in direct proportion to output.
Selling expenses are treated 20% fixed and 80% variable.
Administration expenses are all fixed.

'Why will the comparison be meaningless?' enquired one of the directors. The reply received was, 'To compare a budget based on 200,000 units with an actual level of 240,000 units is just unrealistic and unrepresentative. You have to compare like with like. All you have to do is flex the budget, which means recomputing the budget for the actual level of 240,000 units.' All the costs and revenues included in the revised budget will then reflect an output of 240,000 units.

Required:
Prepare the flexible budget for an output of 240,000 units and compare it with an actual performance based on 240,000, and comment on the results.

T17.5 Explain how the behavioural aspects of the budgeting can affect motivation and the attainment of a company's corporate objectives.

Further reading

Chadwick, L., *Management Accounting*, International Thomson Business Press, 1998

Drury, C., *Costing: An Introduction*, International Thomson Business Press, 1998

Drury, J.C., *Management Accounting for Business Decisions*, Thomson Learning, 2001

Dyson, J.R., *Accounting for Non-accounting Students*, Financial Times Prentice Hall, 2001

Horngren, C.T., Bhimani, A., Foster, G. and Datar, S.M., *Cost and Management Accounting*, Financial Times Prentice Hall, 2001

Horngren, C.T., Foster, G. and Datar, S.M., *Cost Accounting*, Financial Times Prentice Hall, 2000
Hussey, J. and Hussey, R., *Cost and Management Accounting*, Macmillan, 1998
Weetman, P., *Management Accounting: An Introduction*, Financial Times Prentice Hall, 1999

Useful websites

www.accounting.itbp.com
www.itbp.com
www.drury-online.com
www.ftmanagement.com
www.booksites.net/dyson
www.prehall.com/horngren5/ or 2/
www.macmillan-business.co.uk
www.booksites.net/weetman

18

Capital investment appraisal

Capital expenditure decisions are crucial to the long-term viability, success and survival of a company. Capital investment appraisal provides a framework in which capital projects can be considered, screened and evaluated. Because of the inflexible nature of capital projects, risk and uncertainty, and environmental change, e.g. the tax factor, changes in government policy and technological change, it is essential that they are carefully selected and evaluated, to ensure that they will help the organisation to achieve its objectives. Whilst all evaluation procedures make assumptions, such decision rules must be as objective as possible.

Learning objectives

On completion of your study of this chapter, you should be able to:

☐ understand the concept of relevant (incremental) cash flows;

☐ understand how the payback and average rate of return methods of capital investment appraisal work;

☐ know how to use the discount tables, and in particular the *sum of an annuity of £1 table*, *the present value of £1 table*, and *the present value of an annuity of £1 table*, and use them to solve some introductory problems;

☐ carry out an elementary sensitivity analysis;

☐ describe and discuss the limitations to all of the methods demonstrated.

The principal aim of this chapter is to show you how to use the present value tables to produce information that will help management with capital investment decision making. Please note that other authors may refer to *capital investment appraisal* as capital budgeting or project appraisal or discounted cash flow.

The concept of relevant (incremental) cash flows

The costs and revenues that need to be used for decision-making purposes should be relevant costs/revenues (some authors refer to these as 'incremental costs and revenues').

Which costs and revenues are relevant to a decision? The short answer is 'Only those costs and revenues that arise as a direct result of going ahead with the project under review'.

Sunk costs

Sunk costs are those costs that have already been paid out before the specific project under review was ever considered. For example, the cost of a machine purchased some time before the project was first thought of, but which is to be used for the project, is irrelevant. The machine will be there whether or not the project goes ahead, i.e. the money used to buy it was *sunk* at the time of its purchase. You should, therefore, remember that sunk costs are irrelevant when estimating cash flows or assessing projects.

However, it is not always quite so simple!

Fixed costs

Fixed costs may also be described as 'sunk costs' and as such tend to be irrelevant. Most fixed costs will have to be paid whether or not the project goes ahead. They can be described as 'water under the bridge', i.e. they are history, they have been paid out, and are gone forever. However, this is not always the case. If as a result of a project's going ahead additional fixed costs have to be paid out, i.e. fixed costs *specific to the project*, the additional amount is a relevant cost. Conversely, if as a direct result of the project going ahead, there is a saving in fixed costs, the amount saved will be treated as a relevant cash inflow.

Labour costs

Those wages and salaries that continue to be paid whether or not a project goes ahead are irrelevant, e.g. in cases where the employee concerned works on the project for part or all of their time. The reason for this is that the incremental effect on the company is nil. It costs them no more and no less. Those wages and salaries that have to be paid as a result of taking on the project are relevant, e.g. having to pay overtime, or taking on new employees.

Materials

Those materials that have to be purchased specially for the project are relevant. The cost of those materials that are already in stock and for which no other use is possible, apart from using them on the project, is not a relevant cost. However, any lost residual or scrap value would be a relevant cost.

Depreciation

Depreciation is not a relevant cash flow. The cash moves when the fixed asset concerned is paid for. Depreciation is a non-cash item. However, the *trade-in* of equipment that is being replaced is a relevant inflow, but its *future disposal value is lost* and has to be treated as a relevant cost (cash outflow). If the project goes ahead, on the one hand you gain the trade-in, but on the other hand, you lose its future disposal value.

Lost sales

If, as a result of taking on a new project, sales of other products are lost, the relevant costs and revenues will be: the sales revenue lost less the cost of those lost sales, which equals the gross profit lost. Although sales revenue is lost, the cost of producing those goods does not have to be paid out. The net effect is a *loss of gross profit*.

Feasibility studies

Finally, one of the best examples of the concept of relevant cash flows is a feasibility study. A feasibility study is commissioned to decide whether or not to go ahead with a project. If the project goes ahead, it has to be paid for. If the project does not go ahead, it still has to be paid for. It is therefore not a relevant cost.

The guiding principle

You need to note that cash flows are only relevant if they happen as a direct result of the project's going ahead.

Methods of evaluating capital investments and projects

We will now review some of the methods of capital investment appraisal by keeping the numbers simple so that you can focus on the way the techniques are used.

Payback method

This simple approach looks at how long it takes an investment to repay its initial cost (see Figure 18.1 for an example). At the outset, you need to remember that the relevant cash flows that are used in most of the methods illustrated are only *estimates*.

It can be observed that project J has a payback of two years and project R has a payback of three years. Management tends to favour those projects that pay back more quickly, because the longer a project takes to repay, the greater is the uncertainty, the greater the risk. However, this method does not take account of the *time value of money*, i.e. that over a period of time the value of money tends to go down, e.g. £1 now will be worth less in, say, three years' time.

Average rate of return method

Also called the *unadjusted rate of return method*, this is a somewhat oversimplified method which expresses the average annual net cash flow as a percentage of the original investment (see Figure 18.2). This return-on-investment type of method assumes that the net cash flows generated are the same from year to year. The cash flows from projects J and R (see Figure 18.1) could fluctuate significantly from year to year and also vary significantly between each other, i.e. it does not take into account the *timing of the cash flows* generated.

The initial investment for each project, after deducting a trade-in, is £500,000		
Relevant cash flows:	Project J	Project R
Year	£000	£000
1	250	100
2	250	200
3	100	200
4	100	200
5	100	100
Total	800	800

Figure 18.1 – The payback method

Here also, the time value of money (the fact that £1 tomorrow will be worth less than £1 today) is ignored.

Taking the figures in Figure 18.1	Projects	J £000	R £000
Initial investment		500	500
Total cash flows over the five years		800	800

The average annual cash flow for each project will be the same at £160,000. Expressed as a percentage of the initial investment this gives a return of 32%.

This could also be expressed as a percentage of the average investment (£500,000 divided by 2) and would double the return, i.e. £160,000 as a percentage of £250,000 = 64%. The reason for this is that over the project's life it has an initial value of £500,000, and an assumed residual value at the end of five years of nil.

Figure 18.2 – The average rate of return method

Accounting rate of return

This method uses the estimated financial accounting profits.

Each of the above methods suffers in that they ignore the *time value of money*. Also, the timing of the cash flows, i.e. the year in which the money comes in or goes out, can have a dramatic impact upon a project.

How to use discounted cash flow tables

When confronted with a number of discounted cash flow tables for the first time, managers and executives on short courses, and students on long courses, soon begin to ask questions, such as:

☐ What are all these for?

☐ How do we use them?

☐ Why use this table, and not that one?

☐ Which of these should we use to discount the cash flows?

☐ What do they tell us?

☐ Which of these do we use for capital investment appraisal?

Year	10%	12%	14%	16%	18%	20%
1	1.100	1.120	1.140	1.160	1.180	1.200
2	1.210	1.254	1.300	1.346	1.392	1.440
3	1.331	1.405	1.482	1.561	1.643	1.728
4	1.464	1.574	1.689	1.811	1.939	2.074
5	1.611	**1.762**	1.925	2.100	2.288	2.488
6	**1.772**	1.974	2.195	2.436	2.700	2.986

Figure 18.3 – Compound sum of £1 (extract from tables)

☐ They look far too complex – can you explain, simply, what they are?

Let us now have a look at the tables and see if we can provide the answers to the above questions.

The compound interest table (compound sum of £1)

Figure 18.3 shows how much an investment of £1 will amount to, at a certain fixed rate of interest, in a certain number of years' time.

It tells us how much £1 invested now at, say, 12% will amount to in, say, five years' time, i.e. rate column 12%, year 5 £1.76p to the nearest 1p, as indicated by the 1.762 which was highlighted. Each year the interest is reinvested, and also generates interest as illustrated in Figure 18.4.

If you invest a sum of money at a fixed rate of interest for a specific period of time, all you have to do is multiply the sum invested by the appropriate figure given in Figure 18.3.

For example, to invest £1,500 today at 10% for six years would accumulate to £2,658 at the end of the sixth year. This is computed as follows:

Rate 10% for 6 years. Amount invested now:
1.772 × £1,500 = £2,658

	Investment	£
Example	Invest £1 today	1.00
End of year 1	Interest @ 10% × £1	0.10
Cumulative		**1.10**
End of year 2	Interest @ 10% × £1.10	0.11
Cumulative		**1.21**
End of year 3	Interest @ 10% × £1.21	0.12
Cumulative		**1.33p and so on**

Figure 18.4 – Compound interest on £1

Year	10%	12%	14%	16%	18%	20%
1	1.000	1.000	1.000	1.000	1.000	1.000
2	2.100	2.120	2.140	2.160	2.180	2.200
3	3.310	3.374	3.440	3.506	3.572	3.640
4	4.641	4.779	4.921	5.066	5.215	5.368
5	6.105	6.353	6.610	**6.877**	7.154	7.442
6	7.716	8.115	**8.536**	8.977	9.442	9.939

Figure 18.5 – The sum of an annuity of £1 for *N* years (extract from tables)

In addition to working out the amount accumulated, this table can be used to produce an *opportunity cost*, i.e. the value of the benefit forgone. For example, an amount invested in a business project could alternatively have been invested in a bank high-interest account.

Investing an annual sum (sum of an annuity of £1 for *N* years)

From a review of Figure 18.5 it can be observed that it shows what happens if £1 is invested at the end of each year, at a fixed rate of interest, and for a certain number of years. Notice that the table is drawn up on the assumption that the investment is made at the end of each year.

An investment of £1, at the end of *each* year for six years (i.e. an annual investment of £1) at 14% would produce £8.54p to the nearest 1p (see Figure 18.5). How this builds up is shown in Figure 18.6.

If a fixed amount of money is to be invested at the end of each year, the annual amount is multiplied by the appropriate figure given in Figure 18.5, according to the rate at which the amount is invested and the length of time involved. To invest an annual amount of £2,000 at the end of each year for five years at 16% would compound (i.e. accumulate) to £13,754. This is computed as follows:

Rate 16% for 5 years. Annual investment:
6.877 × £2,000 = £13,754

End of year	Annual investment	1.00
End of year 2	Interest @ 14% × £1	0.14
	Annual investment	1.00
		2.14
End of year 3	Interest @ 14% × £2.14	0.30
	Annual investment	1.00
		3.44 and so on

Figure 18.6 – Compound interest for an annual investment of £1

Thus, although the amount invested is only £10,000 (i.e. £2,000 per year × 5 years), it generates an additional £3,754 because of the accumulation of the compound interest.

The present value table (present value of £1)

From a capital investment appraisal point of view, this is the most important and most frequently used table (see Figure 18.7).

This table is all about the *time value of money*, i.e. the fact that over a period of time the value of money will tend to decrease. The table can be looked at in two ways:

1. It *shows us how much we need to invest at a specific fixed rate of interest, and for a particular period of time, to produce £1*, e.g. if we want to produce £1 at the end of year 1 at a 10% rate of interest we have to invest 90.9p at the beginning of year 1, as follows:

Investment (to nearest 1p) at the start of the year	= 91p
At the end of year (to nearest 1p) interest @ 10% × 91p	= 9p
∴ investment + interest	= £1

    Or, if we want to produce £1 in six years at a 12% rate of interest we would have to invest 50.7p now (51p to the nearest 1p). This, together with the compound interest, would produce £1 at the end of year 6 (as indicated by the 0.507 figure which is highlighted in Figure 18.7).

2. The other way of looking at the table is that it tells us *what the value of £1 receivable in a certain number of years' time, taking into account a specific rate of interest, will be*, i.e. the present value of receiving £1 in the future.

    In capital investment appraisal, this philosophy is the one that is followed, as it tends to explain the time value of money. For example, the present value of £1 receivable in five years' time, and taking into account a rate of interest of 18%, is 43.7p (or 44p to the nearest 1p); or the present value £1 receivable in three years' time, at a rate of interest of 10% is 75.1p (or 75p to the nearest 1p). (See Figure 18.7.)

Year	10%	12%	14%	16%	18%	20%
1	**0.909**	0.893	0.877	0.862	0.847	0.833
2	0.826	0.797	0.769	0.743	0.718	0.694
3	**0.751**	0.712	0.675	0.641	0.609	0.579
4	0.683	0.636	0.592	0.552	0.516	0.482
5	0.621	0.567	0.519	0.476	**0.437**	0.402
6	0.564	**0.507**	0.456	0.410	0.370	0.335

Figure 18.7 – Present value of £1 (extract from tables)

Year	10%	12%	14%	16%	18%	20%
1	0.909	0.893	0.877	0.862	0.847	0.833
2	1.736	1.690	1.647	1.605	1.566	1.528
3	2.487	2.402	2.322	2.246	2.174	2.106
4	3.170	3.037	2.914	**2.798**	2.690	2.589
5	3.791	3.605	3.433	3.274	3.127	2.991
6	4.355	4.111	3.889	3.685	3.498	3.326

Figure 18.8 – Present value of an annuity of £1 (extract)

The value of £1 received today is £1, but if you receive it in the future its value will tend to be less than a pound. *The rate of interest* could be in line with the organisation's *cost of capital, or the required rate of return* for the *risk category* of the project that is being reviewed.

The present value of an annuity table

This table can also be used in capital investment appraisal for certain situations (see Figure 18.8).

It can also be viewed in two ways:

1. It tells us how much we need to invest now, at a specific fixed rate of interest, to generate £1 at the end of each year for a specified number of years. For example, if we wish to receive £1 at the end of each of the next four years, and taking interest into account at 16%, we would have to invest £2.798 (£2.80), i.e. £2.80 invested now at 16% will generate £1 per year, at the end of each of the next four years.

2. It *represents the present value of receiving the same amount at the end of each year, for a certain number of years*, and taking interest into account at a specific rate. It can be used to find out the time value of cash flows, but only in cases where the same amount is received each year, for a number of years, and is therefore of limited application.

The present value method

In capital investment appraisal, the time value of money is taken into account by revaluing the cash flows at their *present values*.

The appraisal process will involve the following:

☐ *The estimation of the cash flows* over the life of the project. The cash flows to be estimated should be the relevant/incremental cash flows, i.e. they take account only of

Risk category	Required rate of return
Low	12%
Medium	16%
High	20%

Figure 18.9 – Capital investment appraisal: risk categories

those items of income or expenditure that come in, or go out, if the project goes ahead; e.g. if a new employee has to be taken on if a particular project goes ahead, the remuneration paid to the new employee is a relevant/incremental cost, even though the new employee may not be working on the new project. The incremental effect that is being considered is the incremental effect over the whole enterprise.

☐ Taking taxation into account, e.g. when the payments or repayments will occur.

☐ *Selecting the rate of interest* that is to be used as *the discount rate*. A company could opt for: the cost of capital; or a rate that takes into account the *risk category* of the project (see Figure 18.9); or a *cut-off rate*. If the net present value of a project's cash flows, as discounted using the cut-off rate, is negative, the project will not go ahead.

We will now proceed to work through a series of illustrations to demonstrate how the present value tables are used. More detailed present value tables can be found in Appendix 2. However, for the examples that follow, we will use the table extracts that have been included so far.

Example   Working out an equivalent cash price

Machinery can be purchased on payment of the following amounts:

£2,000 immediately, and
£10,000 at the end of each of the next four years, and
£5,000 at the end of the fifth year.

Using the appropriate tables, we will calculate the present value or equivalent cash price that could be offered if payment were to be made in full now. Interest needs to be taken into account at 10% per annum.

Answer

	£
Amount payable immediately	2,000
Present value of an annuity of £2,000 for 4 years @ 10%	
= £10,000 × 3.170	30,170
Present value of £4,000 at the end of 5 years @ 10%	
= £5,000 × 0.621	3,305
Present value (equivalent cash price)	35,475
This is the cost of producing	2,000 now
plus £10,000 × 4 =	40,000
and £5,000 × 1 =	5,000
	£47,000

Figure 18.10 – Calculating the equivalent cash price using present value tables

It will cost £35,475 at 10% per annum compound interest to pay £2,000 now, and to produce the four annual instalments of £10,000 each, and one instalment of £5,000 at the end of year five.

Example   Identical cash flows, after adjusting for depreciation

The forecast incremental receipts and payments applicable to the purchase of a new machine are as shown in Figure 18.11.

The new equipment will cost £40,000 and will be depreciated at 20% on cost per annum, i.e. the straight line method. The reason why you have been given the information about depreciation is that if the income and expenditure is after deduction of depreciation, you have to add it back. The company's cost of capital is 10%.

Answer
First of all we adjust the net income figures for each year by adding back the depreciation.

Year	1 £000	2 £000	3 £000	4 £000
Receipts	28	28	28	28
less Payments*	16	16	16	16
Net income	12	12	12	12

*The payments include depreciation at £8,000 per year. When added back the figure of £20,000 represents the relevant cash flow.

Figure 18.11 – Identical cash flows

Because the cash flows are the same each year, we can use Figure 18.8, the present value of an annuity of £1 table, to discount the cash flows, as follows:

annual net cash flows × discount rate = present value

£20,000 × 3.17 = £63,400

We can deduct the initial cost of the project:

less Initial investment (£40,000) = Net present value (NPV) = £23,400

The NPV is positive and the project is therefore wealth-creating, and worthy of acceptance or further consideration.

In the real world of business it is more likely that the estimated cash flows that result from taking on a new project will vary from year to year. This means that each individual amount will have to be discounted using the present value of £1 table, as illustrated in Figure 18.7.

Example   Fluctuating cash flows

Tecwik plc is considering purchasing some new high-tech equipment for a small offshore gas industry project. The anticipated receipts and payments resulting from its purchase are as shown in Figure 18.12.

An immediate cash outlay of £400,000 is needed to finance the purchase. The company's cut-off rate for this particular category of project is 16%.

You can observe from Figure 18.13 that the NPV is negative, −£144,030, which means that the project is not wealth-creating and, according to the company's decision rules, not worthy of further consideration. Note that the cash flows had to be adjusted because depreciation had been included in the payments figures. Discounting the cash flows in this way may also be described as discounted cash flow (DCF).

Year	£000 1	£000 2	£000 3	£000 4
Incremental receipts	80	240	200	120
Incremental payments*	140	190	180	160
	(60)	50	20	(40)
*Includes depreciation of £100,000 per annum. Thus, we need to exclude the depreciation from the payments, or add it back, to arrive at the net relevant cash flows, as indicated in Figure 18.13.				

Figure 18.12 – Fluctuating cash flows

Year	Receipts £000	Payments £000	Cash flow £000	Discount factor £000 (16%)	Net present value £000
1	80	40	40	0.862	34.480
2	240	90	150	0.743	111.450
3	200	80	120	0.641	76.920
4	120	60	60	0.552	33.120
		Present value of the cash flows			255.970
		less **initial outlay**			400.000
		Net present value			(£144.030)

Figure 18.13 – The net present value of fluctuating cash flows

If in the above example the net present value had been positive, the decision rule would be *worthy of further consideration*, before coming to a final decision. The reason for this caution is that the financial data are just one part of the capital-investment, decision-making jigsaw. There are many non-financial factors that have to be taken into account, e.g. reliability, the efficiency of the supplier's after-sales service, standardisation.

Residual values

If the machinery or equipment under review has a residual value at the end of the project, this should be included as an additional cash flow for the period in which it is to be received.

However, beware! Many examples in numerous texts assume that the residual value will be received at the end of the year in which the project comes to an end. In reality, when the project does come to an end, it may be some time before the machinery or equipment is disposed of. The cash from such a disposal should therefore be included as a cash flow of the year in which it is anticipated that it will be received.

Taxation

In producing the cash flows the tax factor should be taken into account assuming that the company will be paying tax as follows:

☐ The *tax benefit* (i.e. the tax allowance at the tax-paying business's rate of tax) should be deducted from the cash flows of the period in which that the benefit is received as a repayment or used to reduce the amount of tax that has to be paid over.

☐ The *tax payable on income*, e.g. taxable cash flows received and taxable profits on the disposal of machinery and equipment, should be deducted from the cash flows received (if any) of the period in which the tax will actually be paid over.

In both of the above cases there is usually *a time lag* between the period to which the benefit or tax payable relates, and the period that derives the benefit or in which the tax is paid.

Discounted payback

The payback method referred to earlier in this chapter can also be computed using the present value of the cash flows. **The discounted payback period** is the time that it takes for the cumulative present value of the cash flows to equal the initial investment.

Internal rate of return (IRR)

This is also called the *yield method*: the internal rate of return is the discount rate that will discount the cash flows to a *net present value of nil* (i.e. the present value of the cash flows less the initial investment is equal to a nil NPV). It is, therefore, a return-on-investment approach, the IRR being an indication of what a particular project is likely to earn. The following example, using 'the trial and error method', illustrates how we can compute the IRR, and for simplicity uses a project that generates the same annual cash flow.

Example   How to calculate the internal rate of return

Proposed new equipment costs £200,000
Relevant cash flows for 5 years: £60,000

This means that we can use the present value of an annuity of £1 table.
All we have to do is to find a rate that will give us a positive NPV, and a rate that will give us a negative NPV. Having done this, we then know that the IRR, i.e. the NPV of nil, is somewhere between the two, and can work it out.

Using 10% gives £60,000 × 3.791   = £227,460 less £200,000   = NPV £27,460
Using 20% gives £60,000 × 2.991   = £179,460 less £200,000   = NPV (£20,540)
        10% difference in rates used = a gap between the two of   £48,000

The IRR is therefore:

$$10\% + \frac{£27,460}{£48,000} \times 10 = 15.721\%$$

The above scenario can also be illustrated, as shown in Figure 18.14.

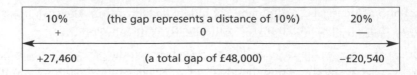

10%	(the gap represents a distance of 10%)	20%
+	0	−
+27,460	(a total gap of £48,000)	−£20,540

Figure 18.14 – The internal rate of return (IRR)

The profitability index

The **profitability index** is the present value of the cash flows, divided by the initial investment. For example, if the present value of the cash flows for a project costing £200,000 is £250,000, the profitability index will be 1.25, i.e. every £1 invested in the project generates £1.25 of present-value cash flows.

Non-financial factors

In addition to reviewing a capital investment project by using one or more of the methods of capital investment appraisal described and illustrated in this chapter, there are also a number of non-financial factors that need to be considered. For example:

☐ the need for state-of-the art technical superiority;

☐ flexibility, adaptability and durability, e.g. can it be upgraded?

☐ capacity;

☐ the quality and reliability of servicing and back-up support, e.g. availability of spare parts, service contracts, and the after-sales service;

☐ installation factors, e.g. problems of size and weight, the removal of walls, the strengthening of floors, how long it takes to install;

☐ the ease of maintenance and the clarity of service manuals;

☐ operational factors, e.g. staff may need special protective clothing, and/or may need special training and/or recruiting externally;

☐ other peripherals needed for efficient operation, e.g. high-tech equipment purchased may need one or more additional items of equipment if it is going to be used to good effect;

☐ standardisation, e.g. compatibility with existing equipment and processes, from an operating perspective, and cutting down on the variety, volume and value of stocks of spare parts;

☐ loyalty towards tried and trusted suppliers;

☐ equipment purchased from overseas, e.g. possible delivery hold-ups, documentation, exchange rates, availability of service and spare parts in your country.

Sometimes what starts off as a practical, or non-financial implication, may have financial consequences, e.g. necessary structural alterations that have to be made to a building, or having to pay for expensive training courses for staff.

Sensitivity analysis

This is a method of assessing the extent to which a change in one or more of the assumptions on which a capital investment project (or a budget) was based would affect the outcome. For example, higher- or lower-than-expected pay settlements, machine running costs, and residual values of plant disposed of could significantly affect the possible outcome. This enables managers to review a number of possible outcomes, particularly in situations where the exact outcome is difficult to predict, and thereby assists them with their decision making.

In conclusion

The methods that use the net present value tables are to be preferred because they all take into account the *time value of money*. However, *it must be stressed that the selection of a discount rate* is not always an easy task, e.g. there are a number of ways of calculating a company's cost of capital. With all methods, it must be remembered that the cash flows and residual values of machinery and equipment are only *estimates*.

Summary: capital investment appraisal

Relevant (incremental) cash flows

The methods described in this chapter all depend upon the predetermination of the cash flows. Thus, you should always be aware that the cash flows used in *capital investment appraisal* (also called project appraisal and capital budgeting) are only *estimates*. Their accuracy will depend upon the data and the validity of the assumptions used in their preparation. The cash flows that are to be used should be *relevant cash flows*.

Relevant cash flows are those that occur as a result of taking on a new project, for example:

☐ a new worker has to be employed and paid £50,000 per year;

☐ a special maintenance contract has to be purchased at a cost of £64,000 per year;

☐ certain materials have to be purchased;

☐ the residual value or scrap value is received at the end of the project's life;

☐ additional fixed costs have to be paid out, i.e. those that are specific to the project.

Examples of *irrelevant costs* are:

☐ A *feasibility study* would have to be paid even if the project does not go ahead.

☐ If a supervisor is paid a salary of £38,000 per annum whether or not the project is undertaken, it has no incremental effect on the organisation as a whole.

☐ Factory rent has to be paid whether or not the project under review goes ahead.

Note that, when estimating the cash flows, *depreciation* should be ignored, or adjusted for if it has been deducted in computing the cash flows. The cash moves when the fixed asset concerned is paid for. **Depreciation is a non-cash item**.

The time value of money

This means that £1 tomorrow will be worth less than £1 today. Thus, cash flows that are to be received in the future will not be worth as much as they are now.

The tables

If you are to master capital investment appraisal, you need to be able to use the following: the *present value of £1 table*, an extract of which is shown as Figure 18.7, and the *present value of an annuity of £1 table*, an extract of which appears as Figure 18.8.

Methods of capital investment appraisal

We can classify the methods of capital investment appraisal in a number of ways. For this introductory study, I suggest that we simply divide the methods into those that do not take into account the time value of money, and those that do take into account the time value of money.

Methods that do not take the time value of money into account

Payback
This method calculates how long it takes the cash flows generated by a specific project to recover the initial cost of the investment. Those who use this method of evaluation prefer

those projects that repay the cost of the initial investment in the shortest time. In estimating the cash flows the earlier cash flows are likely to be more accurate than later cash flows.

The average rate of return (unadjusted rate of return)

This return-on-investment method expresses the average cash flow per year as a percentage of the initial investment, or the average initial investment. Although it is simple to calculate it must be pointed out that it does ignore the *timing of the cash flows*, i.e. it averages the cash flows over the life of the project when in fact they could fluctuate quite significantly from year to year.

Methods that take account of the time value of money

The net present value method

To find the *net present value* (NPV), each of the cash flows is multiplied by the appropriate discount factor, using Figure 18.7 (the *present value of £1 table*). These are then added up and the initial investment deducted, at the outset or at the end. If the resulting figure, the NPV, is positive, the project is worthy of further consideration; if the NPV is negative, the project should be rejected because it is not a *wealth-creating* opportunity. Note that when using this method, if all the cash flows are identical, Figure 18.8, the *present value of an annuity of £1 table*, could be used, and this would save calculation time. This discounting process may also be called *DCF (discounted cash flow)*.

The internal rate of return (IRR) or yield method

The internal rate of return is the discount rate that will produce *an NPV of nil*, i.e. the cash flows discounted less the initial cost of the machine/equipment/project = nil.

   Therefore projects with an IRR greater than the company's normal discount rate appropriate to the particular project under review are well worth further investigation.

Discounted payback

This method simply calculates the payback using the discounted cash flows.

Of the above methods, those that take into account the *time value of money* are preferable to those that do not.

The impact of risk

Risk and uncertainty can be taken into account via probability approaches, and/or the use of discount rates that take account of the *risk profile* of the project.

Taxation

Taxation allowances must be included in the cash flows for the period that benefits from those allowances. Tax payments must be included in the cash flows for the period in which they are to be paid over. Thus care needs to be exercised in taking the tax factor into account by taking the various *time lags* into account, e.g. the tax on the income of year 1 could be paid in year 2.

Non-financial factors

From the outset it should be noted that the financial information provided to management forms just one of the many component parts needed to effectively vet a capital investment proposal. Indeed, there are numerous non-financial factors which have to be taken into account, e.g. efficiency of servicing, reliability, problems associated with buying from overseas suppliers, standardisation, operational considerations.

Sensitivity analysis

Sensitivity analysis can provide management with a range of possible outcomes resulting from one or more changes in the basic assumptions on which the data used is based.

Self-checks

When you complete answering each of the self-checks, compare your answer with the appropriate part of this chapter.

1. Explain briefly, the meaning of the following:
   □ A sunk cost
   □ Relevant (incremental) cash flows
   □ The 'time value of money'
   □ The payback method
   □ The net present value method
   □ The internal rate of return method.

2. How are the following items dealt with in the computation of the relevant cash flows?
   □ Fixed costs
   □ Depreciation
   □ Future disposal values of equipment in the case of:
      – that which is traded in, and set off against the price paid for new equipment;
      – the new equipment/machinery
   □ A feasibility study.

3. Which discount table should be used when all the cash flows are the same each year?

4. List and describe briefly five non-financial factors that may have a significant impact on a capital investment project.

Self-assessments

You will find the suggested answers in Appendix 1.

A18.1 Using the appropriate discount tables (see Appendix 2), calculate the following:
   (a) The present value of £50,000 receivable in 10 years' time at a cost of capital rate of 10%.
   (b) The present value of £20,000 receivable in 5 years' time, plus £20,000 receivable in 10 years time, at a cost of capital rate of 15%.
   (c) The present value of being able to receive £4,000 at the end of each of the next 5 years, using an interest rate of 10%.
   (d) The present value of receiving £8,000 at the end of each of the next 4 years, plus £12,000 at the end of year 5, using an interest rate of 12%.

A18.2 The directors of Homedale.com plc are considering the acquisition of new equipment which could generate incremental cash inflows and outflows as shown in Figure 18.15. The immediate initial outlay to acquire the machine and set it up for operations is estimated at £100,000, and it will have a residual value at the end of year 5 of £20,000. (For financial accounting purposes new machinery is depreciated on a straight-line basis.) The company's corporate planning team has categorised all projects, and these are as shown in Figure 18.16. The risk category of this project is considered to be average.

You are required to evaluate the project, using:

   (a) the payback method, and
   (b) the net present value method, and
   (c) comment briefly on your findings.

Year	1 £000	2 £000	3 £000	4 £000	5 £000
Income	60	80	80	50	30
Expenditure before depreciation	40	40	30	30	20

Figure 18.15 – Homedale.com plc incremental cash flows

Risk	Required rate of return
A Low	10%
B Average	16%
C High	20%

Figure 18.16 – Homedale.com plc risk categories

A18.3 Just over four years ago your company purchased some equipment for £160,000. As a result of advances in technology the company is falling behind its competitors. It is currently faced with two options. It can either upgrade the equipment, or replace it with a more up-to-date model. Details of these options are provided below for you to review and consider.

Option 1 Upgrade the existing equipment

This would cost £100,000 and the payment of £5,000 per year for a maintenance contract. At the end of year 5 the equipment could be disposed of for £8,000.

Option 2 Trade the equipment in now and replace it

The trade-in, only available against the new equipment, would be £40,000 (at the end of its life in five years' time it would be worth nil, but would cost the company £4,000 to dispose of). The total cost of the new equipment would be £220,000, and its residual value at the end of year 5 would be £20,000. Maintenance costs would be £3,000 per annum.
The company's cost of capital is 12%.

Required

Using a net present value approach, advise the company on which of the two options is to be preferred, and comment briefly on the situation in which it finds itself.

A18.4 Explain the relevance of each of the following to the capital investment decision:
(a) Look before you buy
(b) Human, social and environmental factors
(c) The importation of equipment from another country.

Tutor-based assignments

These should be attempted as directed by the lecturer or tutor, and could involve a certain amount of additional research.

T18.1 Prepare a report that explains to non-financial managers:
(a) The concept of relevant cash flows
(b) What is meant by 'the time value of money'
(c) Why discounted cash flow techniques tend to give a false perception of accuracy
(d) How to estimate and forecast the relevant/incremental cash flows.

T18.2 In relation to capital investment appraisal, provide answers to the following frequently asked questions:
(a) What does the present value table show us?
(b) What does the net present value of a project tell us?

(c) Why do we ignore depreciation?

(d) Which discount rate should we use?

(e) What are the principal problems and limitations associated with the NPV method?

T18.3 **A computer system**

One of your suppliers of computer equipment has offered to provide you with a system on the following terms:

£20,000 payable immediately
£16,000 payable at the end of each of the next 4 years
£5,000 payable at the end of year 5

If the company sold the equipment at the end of year 5, after making the final payment, it is estimated that they could sell it for £8,000.
The company's cost of capital is 10%.

Required

Using appropriate discount tables, calculate the equivalent cash price that could be offered, if payment were to be made in full at the time of delivery.

T18.4 **Case study   Oil and gas projects**

Abermouth Explorations plc is a company that contracts to the oil and gas industry mainly in the UK and Norway. Management is now insisting that all projects within the company, and contracts outside the company, are evaluated using the net present value method. In order to evaluate and screen projects and proposed contracts, the management have directed that a discount rate that takes the risk profile of the proposed venture into account be adopted. Two proposed projects have just been handed to you for preliminary vetting, to see if they are wealth-creating taking into account their risk profiles. You are required to prepare a brief report on each proposal using the NPV approach, and pointing out any practical considerations and drawbacks.

On examination of the information, you find that there is one internal project and one external contract proposal, details of which are as follows:

Project 007 6688431 The purchase of new high-tech equipment

Two tried and trusted suppliers have been identified.
The discount rate for this kind of project is 15%.

Details: (all £m)	Drillit plc	Hidl AG
Cost of new equipment	10	12
Trade-in on old equipment	1	2
Residual value at the end of year 4	1	2

Estimated incremental savings:

YEAR			
1		4	3
2		4	3
3		3	4
4		2	4

Contract XL5 992288X Subcontract work for North Sea exploration

If the contract is to go ahead, existing equipment will need to be replaced. The equipment concerned is due to be disposed of in three years' time for £200,000.

It can be disposed of now for £2m. The new replacement equipment, costing £16m, would have a life of five years, and would be disposed of at the end of year 5 for £500,000.

The estimated incremental net cash flows for the five-year contract would be:

Year 1 £6m   Year 2 £8m   Year 3 £6m   Year 4 £4m   Year 5 £2m

However, if the contract goes ahead the impact on other parts of the business would be:

Employees currently earning £160,000 would be moved on to the contract and paid an extra 10% per annum for each of the years 1 to 5.
Certain employees earning a total of £100,000 per year would have to be made redundant, and redundancy pay paid out in year 1 amounting to £120,000.

Net revenue would be lost by one of their departments, and also on another contract, amounting to £500,000 for years 2, 3 and 4.

From the start of the contract a new on-shore administrator would have to be employed at a salary of £60,000 per year, and additional clerical and IT staff with salaries amounting to £80,000.

Certain old equipment with a scrap value of nil will have to be disposed of at a cost of £10,000 in year 1.

The discount rate for this type of contract is 20%.

Further reading

Atrill, P. and McLaney, E., *Financial Management Accounting for Non-specialists*, Financial Times Prentice Hall, 2000

Cullen, J., *Managing Financial Resources*, Institute of Management, 1997

Knott, G., *Financial Management*, Macmillan, 1998

Lumby, S. and Jones, C., *Investment Appraisal and Financial Decisions*, International Thomson Business Press, 1999

Pike, R. and Neale, B., *Corporate Finance and Investment*, Financial Times Prentice Hall, 1999

Useful websites

www.booksites.net
www.bh.com/management
www.gowerpub.com
www.macmillan-business.co.uk
www.pearsoneduc.com
www.thomsonlearning.co.uk

19

Case studies

This, the penultimate chapter of the text, provides you with a selection of case studies which have been designed to provide valuable recapitulation and consolidation of some of the areas studied during your journey through this text. As mentioned earlier in the text, the case study scenarios are based on real-world organisations and situations, and incorporate much more than pure accounting and finance. When you attempt any of the case studies, review the whole case including non-financial factors and practical considerations.

The overall aim of the case studies

The overall aim of these 'open-ended' case studies is to provide you with a comprehensive coverage of issues that involve a knowledge of financial accounting, management accounting, financial management and other areas of business and management, so that you can:

☐ apply and develop further your knowledge of these areas;

☐ use and improve your comprehensional skills, analytical skills, communication skills, presentation skills, powers of critical evaluation and reflective learning skills, and team-playing skills, e.g. by being involved in group projects and presentations.

All of the cases supplied in this chapter are tutor-based and involve a significant amount of further research. The mode of completion, e.g. written reports, group discussions and presentations, should be as directed by your lecturer or tutor.

T19.1 **Case study – Part 1**

Easter Gate Scientific Supplies Inc.

Easter Gate Scientific Supplies Inc. is one of the leading global suppliers of instruments, equipment and services to the scientific community. Nowadays, just over 50% of their products and services are sold via the Internet. They currently employ over 6,000 people world-wide. However, because of the advances in technology they do not foresee any dramatic increase in this number in the future. Their customer focus tends to be directed at research organisations, educational establishments, government departments and health-care. The company offers a very wide range of scientific goods and acts as a distributor for the products of over 4,000 different companies. Its aim is to meet all the needs of its customers in terms of the supply of scientific goods and services.

The business operates on a high volume of turnover and low profit margin. This policy is currently being followed in order to increase market share. At the end of 20X4, the company's market share amounted to 17.5%. Growth over the next five years is forecast to run at around 5% per annum, but several leading analysts have remarked that they regard this as being on the conservative side.

One of their principal competitors which currently has a 5% market share is Axel Scientific AG, a company based in northern Germany.

You are provided with profit and loss accounts and balance sheet information for the three years up to and including 20X4 for both companies.

Required:

Critically evaluate and compare the financial performance over the three-year period of the two companies.

Easter Gate Scientific Supplies Inc. Profit and loss account data:

	20X4 $million	20X3 $million	20X2 $million
Net sales	3,218	1,867	1,436
Cost of sales	2,350	1,364	1,049
Gross profit	868	503	387
Selling, distribution and administration	706	410	305
Research and development	20	24	30
Operating profit	142	69	52
Interest paid	41	20	15
Profit before tax	101	49	37
Taxation provision	47	23	19
Profit after tax	54	26	18
Dividend paid	2	2	1
Retained profit	52	24	17
Share data:			
Earnings per share ($)	2.08	1.48	1.05
Number of shares	25,000,000	16,250,000	16,250,000

Easter Gate Scientific Supplies Inc. Balance sheet data:

	20X4 $million	20X3 $million	20X2 $million
ASSETS			
Fixed assets	**630**	**542**	**417**
Current assets:			
Cash	12	19	24
Marketable securities	32	40	26
Debtors/receivables	236	142	102
Stock/inventories	150	65	53
Total current assets	**430**	**266**	**205**
Total assets	**1,060**	**808**	**622**
LIABILITIES			
Current liabilities:			
Creditors/accounts payable	155	98	75
Accrued expenses	57	54	41
Total current liabilities	**212**	**152**	**116**
Long-term debt (long-term, loans & debentures)	572	448	346
Shareholders equity (share capital & reserves)	276	208	160
Total liabilities and equity	**1,060**	**808**	**622**

Axel Scientific AG. Profit and loss account data:

	20X4 $million	20X3 $million	20X2 $million
Net sales	1,118	720	536
Cost of sales	871	560	422
Gross profit	**247**	**160**	**114**
Selling, distribution and administration	174	125	94
Research and development	26	17	10
Operating profit	**47**	**18**	**10**
Interest paid	36	15	6
Profit before tax	**11**	**3**	**4**
Taxation provision	4	1	1
Profit after tax	**7**	**2**	**3**
Dividend paid	1	1	1
Retained profit	**6**	**1**	**2**
Share data:			
Earnings per share ($)	0.90	0.15	0.30
Number of shares	6,666,667	6,666,667	6,666,667

Axel Scientific AG. Balance sheet data:

	20X4 $million	20X3 $million	20X2 $million
ASSETS			
Fixed assets	**421**	**417**	**54**
Current assets:			
Cash	4	3	2
Marketable securities	9	11	7
Debtors/receivables	164	138	70
Stock/inventories	108	53	41
Total current assets	**285**	**205**	**120**
Total assets	**706**	**622**	**174**
LIABILITIES			
Current liabilities:			
Creditors/accounts payable	103	75	37
Accrued expenses	38	41	9
Total current liabilities	**141**	**116**	**46**
Long-term debt (long-term, loans & debentures)	381	345	88
Shareholders equity (share capital & reserves)	184	161	40
Total liabilities and equity	**706**	**622**	**174**

Part 2

The market shares for all the companies in the scientific equipment and services world-wide are currently as follows:

	%
Easter Gate	17.5
Axel Scientific	5
Norsweda	5
Osterswiser	5
Local dealers	22.5
Direct suppliers (via the Internet and/or catalogues)	45
	100

Required:

1. Comment on Easter Gate's growth strategy (i.e. regarding the pricing policy and market share).
2. Why could their aim of meeting 'all needs' prove to be an expensive policy?
3. What are the financial advantages of having goods sent direct from the manufacturers to Easter Gate's customers?
4. How can they increase their market share further?

5. How can they improve their profitability?
6. If they wanted to raise a further $100 million, how do you suggest that they should raise it?

T19.2 Case study: The Lee Chew Cheng Wong Chemical Company

The company is based in Malaysia and produces high-quality speciality chemicals. It currently exports around 85% of its output to the USA, Europe and other countries in south-east Asia. Since its incorporation in the mid-1980s its focus has been on shareholder value. It has just recently appointed a new chief executive, Lee Sah Loke Teo. To continue the focus, she has proposed to:

☐ improve the productivity of the capital employed by disposing of fixed assets (plant, equipment and fixtures, etc.) that are surplus to requirements, and;
☐ rationalise by concentrating production on a single site rather than on the two existing sites, which would involve closing one site and expanding the remaining site;
☐ conduct a major review of their pricing strategy;
☐ lower their cost of capital;
☐ speed up the time taken to bring new products to the market.

You have been provided with the profit and loss account and balance sheet data for the last three years, plus other information relating to Sun See Chemical Ind. (a major competitor), and some of the current industry averages.

The Lee Chew Cheng Wong Chemical Company: Profit and loss account data:

	20X8 $million	20X7 $million	20X6 $million
Net sales	4.200	4.800	5.600
Cost of sales	2.700	3.200	3.800
Gross profit	**1.500**	**1.600**	**1.800**
Operating expenses	0.480	0.820	0.840
Research and development	0.120	0.140	0.150
Operating profit	**0.900**	**0.640**	**0.810**
Interest paid	0.070	0.056	0.056
Profit before tax	**0.830**	**0.584**	**0.754**
Taxation provision	0.320	0.380	0.420
Profit after tax	**0.510**	**0.204**	**0.334**
Dividend paid	0.110	0.104	0.100
Retained profit	**0.400**	**0.100**	**0.234**
Share data:			
Earnings per share ($)	1.02	0.408	0.668

The Lee Chew Cheng Wong Chemical Company: Balance sheet data:

	20X8 $million	20X7 $million	20X6 $million
ASSETS			
Fixed assets	**3.390**	**2.634**	**2.092**
Current assets:			
Cash	0.060	0.140	0.224
Debtors/receivables	0.790	0.850	1.180
Stock/inventories	0.560	0.616	0.724
Total current assets	**1.410**	**1.606**	**2.128**
Total assets	**4.800**	**4.240**	**4.220**
LIABILITIES			
Current liabilities:			
Creditors/accounts payable	0.280	0.225	0.290
Accrued expenses	0.020	0.015	0.030
Total current liabilities	**0.300**	**0.240**	**0.320**
Long-term debt (long-term loans & debentures)	0.700	0.600	0.600
Shareholders equity (share capital & reserves)	3.800	3.400	3.300
Total liabilities and equity	**4.800**	**4.240**	**4.220**

Sun See Chemical Ind. Performance ratios:

	20X8	20X7	20X6	20X8 Industry averages
Gross profit to sales (%)	40	42	45	44
Operating profit to sales (%)	25	20	24	30
Return on capital employed (%) (operating profit/total assets)	24	20	45	25
Earnings per share ($)	2.25	2.12	3.06	–
Current ratio	1.34	1.27	1.36	1.25
Acid test	0.95	0.99	0.98	0.89
Average debtors (days)	60	64	66	56
Average creditors (days)	40	38	44	48
Stock turnover (times)	11.0	10.5	8.5	14
Gearing (long-term debt over long-term debt plus equity)	25	30	32	40
Interest cover (times)	18	15	20	12

Required:

(Attempt all or some of the questions, as directed by your lecturer or tutor.)

1. Critically evaluate the financial performance of the Lee Chew Cheng Wong Chemical Company over the three-year period and compare its performance with Sun See Chemical Ind. and the industry figures that have been provided.
2. How can the disposal of unwanted fixed assets help improve the company's finances and the productivity of the capital employed?
3. Comment on the benefits and problems associated with the proposed rationalisation.
4. How can the company reduce its cost of capital?
5. The company is going to write down the value of their stocks and certain fixed assets by significant amounts in 20X9. What impact will this have on profits and the return on capital employed?
6. The company is considering paying a lower dividend per share in 20X9. Will this reduce its share price?
7. The company currently uses a total absorption costing approach and is considering introducing activity-based costing. Prepare a report for the management advising them of the benefits of such a system.
8. Prepare a report for management describing a procedure for the budgeting and control of capital expenditure.

T19.3 **Case study: Uniwik**

The company was formed to take over Tiktok Electro Ltd, a UK company engaged in the production of electronic control units, but in recent months had been constrained in its activities through a shortage of finance.

Tiktok was purchased for £25,000 in year 0 by Sue Chua and Les Wik, who together made all the financing and financial control decisions. In year 4, Sue's brother Tom joined the company, and soon became involved in the raising of finance (with a special responsibility for negotiating bank loans and overdrafts). The control of cash was given a high priority, since it was felt that it was in this area that problems could be recognised and early solutions arrived at.

Products and distribution

Year 0
Production of electronic control units: 'The Uniunit Range'.

Year 1
Electronic sub-units, 'The Unisub Range'. In fact, the real reason for acquiring Tiktok was in order to develop this range, which was the result of an idea by Les Wik some $2\frac{1}{2}$ years earlier. The prototype 'Unisub' had been developed and tested during the period up to year 0 with great success, and its commercial viability had been investigated. Numerous applications for the range had been recognised in a number of markets which included: the chemical industry; computers; electronic multi-systems.

Year 4
Became sole UK distributor for two large US electronic components companies. This involved taking over a number of carefully selected warehouses in the UK. All the warehouses were old industrial properties, and were all given extensive refurbishments.

Year 5
Uniwik began to distribute electronic components for various other US companies and also for certain UK companies.

During years 1 to 4 the company had also ventured into the production of computer peripherals, and plastic mouldings for the electronics industry and motor industry.

Years 6 to 8
Saw a period of consolidation of existing products with quite a large amount spent on R&D, focused on product improvement and new product development.

Only a small number of new franchises were accepted during this period, as it was decided to concentrate on the promotion and distribution of products of existing suppliers. You have been provided with the following accounting information:

UNIWIK LTD Profit and loss accounts (£000s)

YEAR	1	2	3	4	5	6	7	8	9
Total sales	43	135	451	820	1,223	1,940	2,747	4,200	6,750
Directors' fees	8	16	25	35	55	65	75	80	120
Rent of properties	12	15	26	29	31	42	45	54	61
Rent of plant & machinery	—	—	3	6	12	16	23	36	29
Loan interest paid	—	—	—	3	5	6	9	11	32
Depreciation	3	6	9	11	20	40	58	70	102
Net profit before tax	(−9)	(−11)	(−13)	24	49	62	55	154	403
Net profit after tax	(−9)	(−11)	(−13)	7	27	35	19	91	278
Dividends: [ord & pref] (paid/proposed)	—	—	—	—	5.5	8	14	18	90

Uniwik Ltd Balance sheet (£000s)

YEAR	1	2	3	4	5	6	7	8	9
Capital employed:									
Ordinary shares	30	70	100	120	180	250	250	280	400
Reserves	(−5)	(−5)	(−8)	22	141	173	540	618	1,316
Preference shares (6%)	—	—	—	—	92	102	224	224	520
HP outstanding	—	—	10	25	40	33	18	5	—
Long-term loans	—	—	—	50	50	80	100	100	300
	25	65	102	217	503	638	1,132	1,227	2,536
Represented by:									
Fixed assets	**13**	**28**	**43**	**85**	**260**	**430**	**663**	**669**	**1,372**
Current assets									
Stock & WIP	14	44	91.5	184	401	621	839	1,102	1,201
Debtors	16	46.5	95.5	184	315	453	693	1,108	1,715
Cash	—	0.5	4	1	3	3	9	18	14
A Total current assets	**30**	**91**	**191**	**369**	**719**	**1,077**	**1,541**	**2,228**	**2,930**
Current liabilities									
Bank overdraft	—	—	48	62	106	277	219	367	368
Current taxation	—	—	—	—	16	28	14	20	42
Creditors	18	54	84	134	264	360	604	1,000	1,016
Others	—	—	—	41	90	204	235	283	340
B Total current liabilities	**18**	**54**	**132**	**237**	**476**	**869**	**1,072**	**1,670**	**1,766**
Working capital (A − B)	**12**	**37**	**59**	**132**	**243**	**208**	**469**	**558**	**1,164**
Net assets	**25**	**65**	**102**	**217**	**503**	**638**	**1,132**	**1,227**	**2,536**

Required:

(Answer all or a selection of the questions, as directed by your lecturer or tutor.)

1. Discuss Uniwik's capital structure.
2. Comment on the way in which it financed its assets in years 1 to 9 inclusive.
3. What are the financial and practical advantages of acquiring old existing warehouses?

4. Review years 1–9 and illustrate and indicate when (and why) significant changes took place in their financing policy.
5. Illustrate how the situation portrayed can link up with the 'product life-cycle'.
6. What is the relationship between the figures for years 1 to 9 and the financial life-cycle theory (i.e. using the amended Boston Matrix, as described in Chapter 4)?
7. Why was there such a low 'plough-back' in year 7?
8. Explain the possible reasons for the large increases in the reserves in year 7.
9. From the information supplied comment on Uniwik's working capital management for years 1–9 inclusive.
10. Comment upon the way in which they appear to be using their bank overdraft.
11. If Uniwik decided it needed to raise £2,500,000 in year 10, how do you suggest they raise it, and why?
12. Prepare a report that explains to the directors how they should go about vetting and appraising capital investments or new projects, e.g. e-business, international expansion.

Beware of accountants!

Having almost completed your journey through this book, it is perhaps fitting that we conclude with a review of some of the principal problems and limitations of accounting and accounting information, and also look towards the future.

When you have reviewed this, our final chapter, you should be able to:

☐ understand why we need to beware of accountants;

☐ appreciate the problems associated with the annual reports and accounts;

☐ know how an accountant is able to paint different pictures, via creative accounting;

☐ illustrate why the terminology used is so complex;

☐ describe the impact of 'off-balance-sheet financing' and the revaluation of fixed assets on the profit and loss account, the balance sheet and the assessment of financial performance;

☐ appreciate that there are problems and limitations associated with management accounting and financial management;

☐ know why it is dangerous to ignore the advice offered by an accountant;

☐ be aware of other managerial and accounting issues.

For consolidation purposes a number of self-checks and discussion or presentation projects are included at the end of the chapter.

The management, investors, bankers, employees, government, creditors and society at large are all interested in the financial performance of companies. They tend to be extremely interested in whether or not the company has made a profit or loss, how much the company is worth, and in the company's ability to pay its debts as they become due for payment.

Why should we beware of accountants?

The answer to this question is quite simple. Accounting *is not an exact science*, and to a great extent the output that is produced depends upon the judgement of those who are involved in its production. The text and illustrations that follow should enable you to appreciate why this is so.

The annual report and accounts

The annual report and accounts produced and distributed by a company tend to promote a *perception of accuracy*.

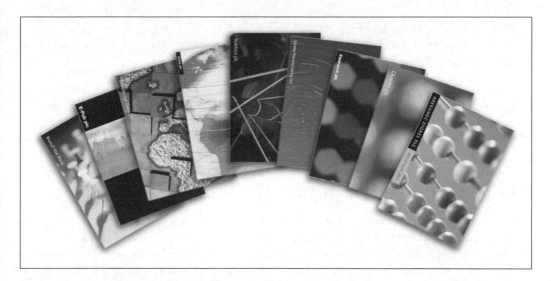

The way in which certain figures contained in the report and accounts are arrived at are shown in greater detail in the *notes to the accounts*. This does enable those who want to know more about the figures to go into greater depth. There is, however, one big problem: lots of those who are interested in the accounts find them extremely difficult to read and understand!

The auditors, if they are satisfied with the accounts, do state in their auditors' report that the profit and loss account and balance sheet give a '*true and fair view*'. The truth of the matter is that because accounting is not an exact science, the profit and loss account and balance sheet can never ever give a 'true and fair view'. As mentioned earlier, those who prepare the information have to use their judgement. Also, what is true and fair is a matter of opinion! An important part of the auditor's role is to detect and prevent fraud. This is not always the case, as evidenced from time to time by reports in the financial press, and as illustrated by the *FT* headlines given here.

Resort Hotels director censured *(M. Peel, 22 March 2001)*
Coopers fined over failings at Resort Hotels *(M. Peel, 20 April 2001)*

The former finance director was censured for failing to correct a false impression given to investors. The company's managing director had used his control of the company to forge documents relating to profitability, which led shareholders to subscribe £20.6m for a rights issue in 1992! The MD was sentenced to 8 years for fraud in 1997 (reduced to 6 years on appeal). Coopers, the auditors, were fined on 19 April, 2001, £100,000 for failings in their work, but did have a charge of dishonesty rejected.

Dutch bourse launches probe into Buhrmann *(G. Cramb, 20 April 2001)*
The Amsterdam bourse authorities called for an inquiry into whether or not Buhrmann, the office products group, had withheld information from shareholders, before issuing a profit warning.

Enron accountant may be key witness *(P. Spiegel, 13 February 2002)*
At the centre of all questionable transactions between Enron and the controversial off balance sheet partnerships.

C&W used swap deals to boost its accounts *(D. Roberts and R. Budden, 13 February 2002)*
Cable and Wireless, one of Europe's biggest telecoms, admitted to using controversial accounting techniques

The accountant – the artist!

The accountant is rather like an artist and can, by manipulating the data in different ways, paint completely different pictures! Someone once said to an accountant, 'Could you work out my financial results for me?' to which the accountant replied, 'Yes, but do you want a high profit, a low profit, or no profit?' Accountants can, working within the law and following established concepts and conventions, still paint quite different pictures if they so wish. Why is it, when there is a conflict between employers and trade unions, that the financial claims made by both sides, e.g. the cost of the disputes to the company, are so different? The short answer is that their accountants are serving different parties. In the case of the trade union's accountants, they will not have access to most of the data that is available to the company's accountants.

The language of accounts

Accountants can and on many occasions do 'blind people with science'. The language of accounts is like a 'minefield', quite complex and in a number of cases quite misleading. A review of the following examples should help you to understand just why this is the case:

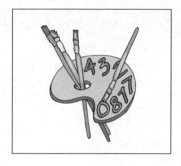

☐ The following descriptions can all be used to mean the same thing:
  — profit and loss account balance
  — retained earnings
  — ploughed-back profits
  — undistributed profits
  — unappropriated profits.
☐ The *return on capital employed* (*ROCE*), can also be called:
  — return on capital, and
  — return on investment.
☐ *Marginal costing* can also be described as direct costing or variable costing.
☐ The *limiting factor* can be referred to as the key factor, governing factor or principal budget factor.
☐ *Ordinary share capital* can also be called equity share capital or the equity.
☐ The *profit and loss account* can be described as the trading and profit and loss account or the income statement.
☐ *Gearing* can be described as leverage.
☐ There are different ways of calculating certain figures, e.g. the cost of sales figure could include direct material and labour costs plus certain overhead costs.
☐ Confusion exists because there are many different types of profits, many different types of shares and different types of reserves.
☐ The *cash flow statement* (published in a company's annual report and accounts) looks back over the accounting period. The *cash flow forecast* (cash budget) is completely different: it estimates future cash flows and does not appear in the published report and accounts.
☐ Capital investment appraisal uses the relevant (also called the incremental) cash flows.
☐ *Cost drivers*, which are used in activity-based costing, are not always easy to identify and define.
☐ Beware of *group accounts*, prepared for a holding company and its subsidiaries. They are complex, frightening and really quite unintelligible to many of those parties who are interested in them.

Currently, there is no standard terminology for financial accounting purposes in the UK. CIMA (Chartered Institute of Management Accountants), one of the UK's major accountancy bodies, does publish a terminology of cost accounting.

Creative accounting and 'window-dressing'

The way in which the accounting concepts and conventions are applied can have a dramatic effect upon the picture painted by the accountant. Decisions will have to be made on matters such as:

☐ Which accounting policies should we adopt?

☐ Do our existing accounting policies need to be changed?

☐ Should certain items of expenditure be written off (i.e. charged as an expense for the period in computing the profit or loss), or should the items be capitalised (i.e. carried forward in whole or part into the next accounting period, as an asset in the balance sheet)?

☐ Whether to write off or capitalise an expense, and judging whether or not its value is significant.

☐ Which accounting ratios will we use to give an overview of our financial performance in our published annual report and accounts?

☐ How is the particular item dealt with in the industry sector to which we belong? For example, in the hotel and catering industry, cutlery, crockery and glassware may be charged as an expense in the profit and loss account, and not capitalised.

The way in which accounting concepts, policies and conventions affect the profit and loss account and the balance sheet was dealt with in Chapter 2.

'Off-balance-sheet financing'

Many companies have some fixed assets (those assets bought for use in the business over a period of years and not for resale, e.g. land and buildings, machinery, office equipment and motor vehicles, etc.) which do not appear in their balance sheet! This is not uncommon.

The way in which the fixed assets are financed will help to determine their accounting treatment. Those that are of significant value and bought outright, plus leasehold land and buildings will be shown in the balance sheet. (The reason for this can be deduced from looking at the definitions of short and long leases. A short lease is a lease for up to fifty years, and a long lease is a lease of over fifty years.) Those fixed assets that are rented, hired (but not on hire purchase) or leased will not be shown in the balance sheet. These alternative ways of acquiring and using fixed assets is what we mean by '**off-balance-sheet financing**'. The rents, hire charges, etc. paid for the use of such fixed assets will be charged as an expense in the profit and loss account.

How can you carry out a satisfactory comparative financial performance analysis between one company which owns all or most of its fixed assets with another company which rents, hires or leases most of its fixed assets? The short answer is, with extreme difficulty! The company that purchases all or most of its fixed assets will need to have a lot more long-term capital, e.g. in the form of ordinary shares and long-term loans. There will also be a need to '*plough back*' more of the profits. As a result, it will tend to have a much *higher capital employed figure*. This can have an alarming effect on certain of the accounting ratios that are computed to help assess financial performance, for example, the return on capital invested.

For example, if we work out the profitability for Company L which owns all or most of the fixed assets, and Company W which makes extensive use of 'off-balance-sheet financing', the following illustration could be quite typical of companies that finance their assets in a similar way.

	Company L (Buy most of their fixed assets) £m	Company W (A lot of 'off-balance-sheet financing') £m
Capital invested by shareholders, long-term loan providers, etc.	120	40
Profit	8	8
Return on capital invested (also called return on capital employed)	6.67%	20.00%

It can be observed from the above illustration that the company with more 'off-balance-sheet financing' is making a better return on the capital employed.

In the somewhat over-simplified example the profit figures have been assumed to be the same, as Company L will be charging depreciation for the use of its fixed assets and Company W will be charging the rent, hire and leasing charges for the use of its fixed assets.

The revaluation of fixed assets

If a fixed asset is revalued, the fixed asset in question goes up and a capital (or revaluation) reserve goes up by the same amount (see Figure 20.1). The revaluation does **not** affect the

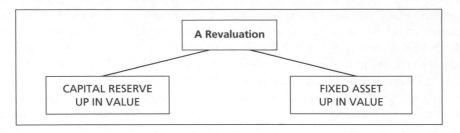

Figure 20.1 – The effect of a revaluation of fixed assets

profit or loss in the profit and loss account. Why? you may ask. The answer is: it is not a realised profit; cash has not moved. Cash only moves when you buy or sell a fixed asset.

If certain fixed assets, such as land and buildings or machines and equipment, are revalued upwards, the capital employed figure will grow by the same amount. The profit computed in the profit and loss account for the period in question would be unaffected by the revaluation, apart from, maybe, an increase in the amount of depreciation charged, depending on the type of fixed asset. Thus, the effect the revaluation will have on the return on capital employed will tend to be similar to what was described for Company L in the 'off-balance-sheet financing' example. Expressing the same or almost the same profit over a higher capital employed figure *causes the return on capital employed to go down*, usually by a significant amount. This is one of the principal reasons why directors of companies are not always willing to revalue their company's fixed assets.

The following example should help you to appreciate the possible effects of a revaluation:

	Without a revaluation £000	With a revaluation £000
Capital employed	2,000	3,600 (after a revaluation of 1,600)
Profit	400	280 (after charging more for depreciation)
Return on capital employed	20.00%	7.78%

All of a sudden, the same company's financial results do not look quite so good!

Daewoo executives charged with £23bn accounting fraud

South Korean prosecutors indicted 34 Daewoo executives and accountants over inflation of the bankrupt group's assets by £23bn in one of the world's biggest accounting frauds. False accounting was used to hide losses and persuade banks to make new loans of 10,000bn won, as Daewoo teetered on the brink of insolvency in 1997 and 1998. Daewoo inflated its books through asset swaps within the group and the double counting of sales. The scandal has provoked calls for improved accounting standards in Korea.

J. Burton, Financial Times, *20 February 2001*

The balance sheet

Another description of the balance sheet is as a position statement, i.e. it only shows the position at a particular point in time. However, UK companies are required to disclose in their published accounts those details of post-balance-sheet events that have a significant impact on the reported figures. What is significant is debatable!

Management accounting

Many of the figures that are used in management accounting are predetermined, i.e. they are just estimates. They are based on forecasts of the level of activity, rates of inflation and pay settlements, and whatever else is known or assumed about the future.

Costs that are not really designed to be used in decision making, e.g. those computed in accordance with total absorption costing principles, have in fact been used by certain companies for decision-making purposes. For example, sharing up the research and development expenditure between the products or services could lead to the profits for certain products being understated and profits for certain other products being overstated. This situation happens as a direct result of the way in which the product or service was costed.

Financial management

This area of accounting and finance which is concerned with investment decisions and financing decisions also involves lots of assumptions and subjective judgement. You only have to look at some of its areas of activity to understand why this is so, for example:

☐ The *cost of capital* can be calculated in a number of ways, e.g. weighted average cost or anticipated future cost.

☐ There are many methods that can be used to estimate *how much a company is worth*. It is only when you sell a company that you find out what it is really worth.

☐ When using the *net present value method* of capital investment appraisal, the selection of the discount rate that is to be used is open to a number of different interpretations.

☐ In capital investment appraisal, there are a number of ways of taking the *risk factor* into account.

Ignore accountants at your peril!

However, at the end of the day those groups or individuals who ignore the advice of their accountants do so at their peril. For example, where the balance of power at boardroom level is held by those intent on promoting their company's research and development activities, the cash flow implications pointed out by the accountant may simply just be ignored. Cash flow is very important if the company wishes to survive and prosper in the long term. Without adequate cash flow, the company could go out of business.

Constructive advice from accountants, based on the best available information, should always be considered. The accountant is just another team member, and does have a vital role to play.

Summary

The published reports and accounts of companies are affected by the way in which the accepted accounting concepts, conventions and policies are implemented. Because accounting is not an exact science, such published accounts will never ever be able to give a true and fair view.

Accountants can, using the same data, paint a number of quite different pictures of profits, losses, assets and liabilities.

The *language of accounts* is confusing and in many cases quite misleading, e.g. a number of descriptions may all mean the same thing!

The way in which the concepts and conventions are applied can be quite *creative*, and enable the accountant to portray many different pictures of the organisation in terms of the profit and loss accounts and balance sheets. For example, whether to charge expenditure in the profit and loss or carry it forward into the future as an asset.

'*Off-balance-sheet financing*', where fixed assets such as machinery, equipment or motor vehicles are rented, leased or hired makes comparability of financial performance between companies difficult. For example, when comparing a company that buys all or most of its fixed assets with a company that uses a lot of 'off-balance-sheet financing'. Companies that purchase their own fixed assets compared with those that rent, lease or hire them will tend to have a much higher amount of capital employed. This will then affect all of the financial performance accounting ratios that use capital employed in their calculation. This is also the case where a company *revalues its fixed assets*. For example, where a revaluation has taken place the return on capital employed will tend to be less than it would have been without the revaluation!

The *balance sheet* shows the position at a particular moment in time. Prepare another a week or month or so later, and there could be major differences!

Management accounting uses predetermined figures. It needs to be remembered, however, that such figures are still just estimates. The way in which products are costed can affect whether or not they will continue.

Financial management involves numerous problems involving the exercise of personal judgement on the part of the accountant or manager concerned. For example, which cost of capital to use, how to value a private company, or which discount rate to use.

The future

Finance and accounting will continue to play an important role in the quest for long-term success and survival, and be closely associated with strategic management. In addition to the material covered in this text there are many other areas of finance and accounting that you may come across in the future, e.g. transfer pricing, the valuation of companies, goodwill, take-overs and mergers, group accounts, activity-based management, strategic management accounting, green accounting, investment strategy, ethical investments.

A tribute to accountants

Having said all this, accountants do strive to be objective and eliminate personal bias, and to work within the law. They do try to ensure that accounts are prepared on a consistent basis and that the treatment of the various component parts is reasonable. They also, given the fact that accounting is not an exact science, and given the various interpretations of the concepts and conventions, report in the annual report and accounts on their opinion as to whether or not the accounts give a true and fair view. Ignore them at your peril!

Self-checks

When you have attempted the following self-checks, compare your attempt with the appropriate part of this chapter.
1. Explain briefly why the accountant is considered to be rather like an artist.
2. What is meant by 'creative accounting'?
3. Describe what 'off-balance-sheet financing' means, and explain the likely impact of it on the return on capital employed.
4. How does a revaluation of fixed assets affect the balance sheet?
5. Why is it dangerous to ignore the advice that is received from the accountants?

Suggested ideas for projects and presentations

These may be done on an individual or group basis and should include a review of other suitable literature.

(a) Do the profit and loss account and the balance sheet that are published in a company's annual report and accounts give a true and fair view?

(b) Prepare a report entitled 'Confusing Accounting Terminology'.

(c) Investigate, describe and illustrate three of the ways in which creative accounting may take place.

(d) Illustrate and explain how 'off-balance-sheet financing' may make inter-firm comparisons of financial performance difficult to perform.

(e) Describe what happened in a case (or cases) of accounting fraud, and what lessons can be learned to help prevent such happening/s in the future.

(f) How can the management accounting function help to ensure that a company will survive and prosper in the long term?

Further reading

Chadwick, L., *Essential Financial Accounting for Managers*, Financial Times Prentice Hall, 2001

Chadwick, L., *Essential Management Accounting*, Financial Times Prentice Hall, 2001

Chadwick, L., *Myths and Realities of Management Accounting and Finance*, Financial Times Pitman Publishing, 1998

Dyson, J.R., *Accounting for Non-accounting Students*, Financial Times Prentice Hall, 2001

Myddelton, D.R., *Managing Business Finance*, Financial Times Prentice Hall, 2000

Useful websites

The International Encyclopaedia of Business and Management: www.iebm.com

www.booksites.net/dyson

www.bh.com/management

www.ftmanagement.com

www.gowerpub.com

www.macmillan-business.co.uk

www.osbornebooks.co.uk

www.pearsoneduc.com

www.thomsonlearning.co.uk

www.wiley.co.uk/college

Appendix 1

Suggested answers to self-assessment questions

This section of the text provides you with suggested answers to the self-assessment questions (i.e. the 'A' questions), together, where appropriate, with helpful hints and comments.

Answers to numerical questions are given in full, with particular attention being paid to layout and presentation.

The answers to written questions and case studies, many of which are quite 'open-ended' are given in full, or as an outline answer. Attention here is focused on structure, answer planning and the need to provide clearly illustrated explanations.

A1.1 Food for thought

How should we have gone about answering this question?

First, we need to read and re-read the question carefully, so that we can focus on the question set, and not the question we would have liked to answer!

Second, do a quick brainstorm plus additional research. As thoughts come into your head, write them down, under appropriate headings, as follows:

SME (small or medium-sized enterprise)	Large multinational company
Cannot afford any/many accountants	Specialisation – big picture
Concerned with recording system	Highly qualified accountants
Costing products/services	Complex issues, e.g. transfer pricing
Day-to-day operating decisions	Foreign exchange
Make use of other services	management
From external auditor/accountants	Corporate report
e.g. preparation of final accounts and	Corporate strategy
taxation	Internal audit
Does not always keep pace with growth	

Third, plan out the structure of the answer. For example:

Answer plan

☐ Introduction and purpose – work similar up to a point

☐ Contrast effects of number of accountants

☐ What they do that is different

☐ Audit

☐ Conclusions.

Fourth, write the answer, but if you think of anything else that is relevant, write it down as an additional point. The answer to the question set could be along the following lines:

Whatever the size of an enterprise, certain finance and accounting matters have to be completed. For example, the enterprise needs to have an efficient and reliable financial recording system in order to produce its final accounts. It needs to work out its costs so it can cost the products or services it provides. The difference in size between SMEs (small and medium-sized enterprises) and large multinational companies will affect the role of accounting and finance.

SMEs may be unable to afford to employ a qualified accountant. Their accounting and finance function could be restricted to dealing with the recording system, the acquisition of new finance and the costing of the products or services, plus some involvement in budgeting. As SMEs grow, certain functions do not always keep pace with the growth, e.g. the accounting and finance function. This could result in a shortage of up-to-date relevant information for decision-making and control purposes. The multinational company, on the other hand, may be able to employ several qualified accountants and recruit them to specialise in certain areas, e.g. financial accounting, credit control, management accounting, treasury management and internal audit.

The SME will tend to rely on external accountancy firms for the preparation of its annual report and accounts, internal financial accounts, taxation matters and audit. For the multinational, with the exception of external audit, the bulk of these could be done in-house. The multinational would also have more management accounting information to assist it with its planning, control and decision-making activities, for example, detailed capital expenditure budgets. In addition the accounts in the multinational would also have to deal with other complex issues such as foreign exchange management, corporate reporting, performance appraisal and strategic planning.

The multinational could have its own internal audit department which could contribute towards, for example: inventory control, credit control, testing systems of internal control, and support for the work carried out by the external auditor.

Conclusions

Size enables the multinational to employ specialists in all or most of the areas of accounting and finance, e.g. treasury management. The role of accounting and finance in such a company is much more geared towards providing information for planning decision making and control, and involved with corporate and strategic issues. SMEs just cannot afford to employ many accountants; thus their accounting and finance role is more involved with operating activities and record keeping, and may have to rely heavily on external auditors or accountants to plug the gaps.

A1.2

Your answer to (a) would depend on how you decide to value the cost of sales figures, e.g. you could use FIFO (first in, first out) or LIFO (last in, first out) or some other method of valuation.

(a)

		Profit statements			
			FIFO £000		LIFO £000
Sales:	100 @ £50		5		5
	200 @ £60		12		12
	200 @ £75		15		15
	500	(A)	32		32
Cost of sales:					
	100 @ £20				
	200 @ £20				
	300 @ £20		6		6
	100 @ £20		2	200 @ £30	6
	100 @ £30		3		
	(B)	(B)	11		12
Profit (A) – (B)			21		20

(b)

Calculation of the closing stock:		£000	£000
Total bought	400 @ £20	8	8
	500 @ £30	15	15
	900	23	23
Less cost of Sales	500 (as above)	11	12
Closing stock	**400**	**12**	**11**

Comment

As you can see, calculating a profit is not an easy task and someone has to decide on which method of stock valuation is going to be adopted, e.g. FIFO, LIFO, or some other method such as average cost (AVECO).

A2.1 Some advice

This question asked you to describe and illustrate. 'Illustrate' means provide an example in either numerical or narrative form, as appropriate. When you are asked to explain something, in most cases an illustration helps to clarify the explanation.

The plan for the answer could be as follows:

☐ explain what 'off-balance-sheet financing' is, and provide examples;

☐ describe why it is difficult to make comparisons;

☐ provide an example/illustration and comment on it;

☐ brief conclusion.

Off-balance-sheet financing and the problems of comparability

'Off-balance-sheet financing' describes the situation where fixed assets such as machinery, equipment and motor vehicles are rented, hired or leased. The fixed assets concerned will not be shown on the balance sheet. However, where the amount is significant it will be disclosed in a company's published report and accounts.

It is difficult to compare the financial performance of companies that purchase all or most of their fixed assets with companies that have a significant amount of 'off-balance-sheet financing'. The reason is that their profit figures could be quite similar. This would bring about considerable differences in the ROCE (return on capital employed) and other ratios such as assets/turnover.

The following illustration assumes that the profits are similar. The one without 'off-balance-sheet financing' has charged much more depreciation. The company that does use a lot of 'off-balance-sheet financing' charges the hire and rent of fixed assets in computing their profit.

Example

Company K: balance sheet extract for a company which buys most of its fixed assets:

	£000
Fixed Assets	3,600
Working Capital	
(i.e. Current Assets less Current Liabilities	1,400
= Capital Employed	£5,000

Company L: balance sheet extract for a company that has a lot of 'off-balance-sheet financing':

	£000
Fixed Assets	600
Working Capital	1,400
= Capital Employed	£2,000

The net profit before interest and tax earned by each company is £840,000.

For Company K the ROCE will be:

$$\frac{840}{5,000} \times 100 = \underline{\textbf{16.8\%}}$$

For Company L the ROCE will be:

$$\frac{840}{2,000} \times 100 = \underline{\textbf{42\%}}$$

If both companies had similar sales levels there would also be wide variations in the ratio of fixed assets to turnover. Thus, as indicated above, it is extremely difficult to compare a company that uses a lot of 'off-balance-sheet financing' with a company that purchases all or most of its fixed assets.

Comment

The above scenario was designed to illustrate the point being made. It was simple and concise, and its message was made very clear.

A2.2

You needed to note that two questions were asked here, and therefore both need to be answered. Sometimes there is a tendency to focus on the first part of the question and then ignore or forget about the second part.

The original source data from which accounts are prepared are:

☐ Sales – when preparing the invoices. For example, when preparing the sales invoices, the figures can be posted to each individual customer's account and listed in a sales day book (or whatever it is called); it is then posted to the sales account.

☐ A similar system will be used for credit notes. The preparation stage can also involve writing up the individual customer's account and the sales account.

☐ Purchases and expenses – the source data here consists of invoices received and credit notes from suppliers. These will be listed and analysed, and then posted to the individual suppliers' accounts, and the various totals posted to the purchases account and the appropriate expense accounts.

☐ Cash and bank – the key information for the bank consists of paying-in slips and details of cheques paid. The analysis of cash received will be used to update the customer accounts and accounts such as the rent received account and the dividends received account. The analysis of amounts paid out will be used to update the accounts of the suppliers of goods and services on credit and various expense accounts such as bank interest and charges, rent of equipment paid for by direct debit, and amounts transferred to petty cash.

☐ Other original data that could be used include contracts, bills of exchange, receipts, petty cash vouchers.

Why is it necessary to prepare a trial balance?

A trial balance lists all the balances on the accounts. It is taken out simply to ensure that everything is in balance before going ahead with the preparation of the final accounts. It will not reveal compensating errors, i.e. errors that cancel out each other, or errors where a transaction has been posted to the wrong account.

A2.3

The 'cut-off procedure' is the system designed to dictate the date after which any further sales or purchases will not be included in the accounts for the year (period) just about to end.

For example, a company has a year-end of 31 December 20X5. Its cut-off date for that year could have been fixed at 23 December 20X5. Thus any sales or purchases after that date will not be included in the sales or purchases for the year to 31 December 20X5, and no adjustment will be made to stocks, debtors or creditors. It is important to note that where goods are not included in sales, they should still be treated as being in stock; and that where goods are not included in purchases, they should not be treated as being in stock.

If a company has a significant amount of sales during the 'cut-off period', any profit earned on those sales will be included in the following year's profits. The amount of profit not taken can vary depending on the date, e.g. bringing it forward just one day could exclude a significant amount of sales.

Comment

Note that by not including the sales, the stock as at the year-end will tend to be higher, and the debtors lower. The effect of excluding purchases is purchases lower and also stocks lower, and also creditors lower. Thus the cut-off will affect ratios such as debtor days, the credit period taken, stock/turnover etc. in addition to affecting reported profits, and the tax payable!

A3.1 The straight line method of depreciation

1. £8,200 annual depreciation for fixtures and fittings.
2. £3,125 annual depreciation for office equipment.
3. £24,000 annual depreciation for plant and machinery.

A3.2 The reducing balance method of depreciation

Year 1 £4,000
Year 2 £3,000
Year 3 £2,250

A3.3 The revaluation method of depreciation

Year 1 £7,000
Year 2 £16,000

A4.1

Obtaining finance has been described as 'a system of costs and risks'. If a company is considered to be a high risk it has to pay more for its financing. For example, a 'problem child' company, i.e. a company with high growth but a shortage of cash, will be considered a higher risk than say a 'star' company which has lots of growth and lots of cash. This is because it may not yet have established a sound financial performance record, and also may not yet have a significant amount of asset cover, i.e. fixed assets to pledge as security for loans. Figure A4.1 provides a good indication of the link between risk and return.

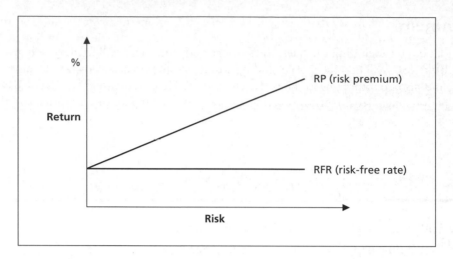

Figure A4.1 – Risk and return

The RFR (risk-free rate), e.g. government stocks, remains the same as risk increases, and the return will tend to be quite low. Those who want a higher return and to benefit from RP (the risk premium), e.g. ordinary shareholders, expect a higher return, but take on more risk, and are paid out last on a winding-up. The share price may go up or down and company earnings may go up or down.

Thus the system of costs and risks applies to the financial instruments. For example, secured loans and debentures pose lower risk to the lender, therefore the rate of interest will be lower than that which would be charged for unsecured loans.

A 'dog' company, i.e. low on growth and low on cash, and possibly with a poor financial performance record and fixed assets already pledged as security, will, because of its higher risk, have to pay much more for its finance.

Comment

Notice that we were able to include some examples from the amended Boston Matrix to help illustrate the answer.

A4.2

The principal factor to take into account where a family company is contemplating issuing more ordinary shares is *control*. If the members of the family wish to retain control, they need to take up enough of the shares to ensure that they have a controlling interest, i.e. over

50% of the issued ordinary share capital. However, the family members would have to have sufficient cash available to purchase the shares. If they have insufficient cash, but still wish to retain control, they could consider a rights issue.

Another consideration would be the gearing situation. If the company is 'low-geared', i.e. having a small proportion of debt financing, e.g. long-term loans and debentures, it may be worth thinking about attracting more debt.

A4.3

Comment

A quick 'brainstorm' came up with the following keywords: capital tied up; Pareto; JIT; MRP; review stock levels; surplus stocks; direct from supplier to customer; conclusions – holding costs; stock-out warning; design.

Stocks (inventory of raw materials), work-in-progress, finished goods and fuels represent capital tied up. Stock control aims at keeping stock levels to an acceptable minimum, and in doing so tying up a minimum amount of capital.

How can we reduce the stock levels?

Pareto. The Pareto 80/20 rule can be applied to stock control. For example, 20% of your stock could account for 80% of the value. If the 20% can be identified, and monitored very carefully, a vast proportion of the total value of stock is in fact being controlled.

JIT (just-in-time). Arranging for stock to be delivered just before it is needed reduces the total amount that has to be stocked.

MRP (material requirements planning) is a system that aims at matching the stocks of raw materials with the production requirements.

Frequent reviews of maximum, minimum and reorder levels to take account of changes in demand and seasonal fluctuations can reduce the amount of capital tied up.

Surplus stocks

Searching out and disposing of stock that is *surplus to requirements* frees up space for other purposes, and provides additional cash flow.

Direct from suppliers to customers. It may be possible to order goods from suppliers and then organise delivery direct to the customer, e.g. for large items of furniture and office equipment.

Conclusions

If stock levels are reduced this will tie up less capital and help to reduce expensive holding costs, e.g. insurance, management, heating and lighting, rent. As mentioned above, space could be freed and made available for other purposes, or to sublet. Keeping stocks to an acceptable minimum does pose a threat. If a 'stock-out' occurs, penalties could be incurred for late delivery, and future orders lost.

A4.4

'*Over-trading*' is the description applied to companies that try to carry on a larger volume of business than they are financially equipped to carry on. Some of the possible signs of over-trading are:

☐ Having an overdraft that is up to the limit set by the bank.

☐ Using short-term financing, e.g. short-term loans, hire purchase and creditors.

☐ Being highly geared, e.g. where the ordinary share capital plus reserves is very low compared to any long-term loans.

☐ Making use of 'off-balance-sheet financing', e.g. renting, hiring or leasing fixed assets such as buildings, equipment and motor vehicles.

☐ Employing subcontractors, e.g. for bought-out finished parts. The subcontractor will have to provide the raw materials, and finance the production of these items in terms of labour, overheads and fixed assets.

☐ Performs well in the credit control area, possible because it is desperate for the cash. However, this could have an impact on bottom-line profits as it could have been achieved by offering expensive prompt-payment settlement discounts, i.e. a small percentage discount can have a high APR (annual percentage rate) of interest.

☐ Good inventory control, as it cannot afford to keep high stock levels. It may employ JIT (just-in-time), where the stock arrives just before it is needed. The downside is the risk of running out of stock, causing late deliveries and lost business, e.g. lost future orders or damage to goodwill.

Some of the generally accepted financing rules that tend to be ignored by companies that are over-trading were illustrated above, and were:

☐ Overdrafts. It can be dangerous to rely on the bank overdraft as a long-term source of funds, e.g. where the company experiences serious cash flow difficulties, the banks may call in the overdraft.

☐ Short-term financing. It is dangerous to finance long-term assets from short-term sources, and even more dangerous if finance from trade creditors is being used for this purpose. A certain portion of the working capital (current assets less current liabilities) should be financed from long-term sources. It is a permanent investment, e.g. there will always be a certain amount of capital tied up in stocks.

☐ Gearing. High gearing is dangerous. In bad times, interest on loans still has to be paid. If a compromise has to be reached, this could impact on the company's credit rating.

Although they manage their stock control and credit control well, over-trading companies can quite easily get into difficulties in times of poor trading conditions. High gearing leading to an inability to pay interest on loans and creditors could spell disaster, e.g. creditors may petition the courts to have the company wound up.

A5.1

Capital, whether it be ordinary share capital or loan capital, is an amount owing to the provider on a winding-up. For example, on a winding-up the ordinary shares will have to be repaid if there are sufficient funds available after paying everyone else. Loan capital such as long-term loans and debentures will have to be repaid when due. This is why it is shown with the liabilities under appropriate headings on the balance sheet.

A5.2

The purpose of the profit and loss account is to compute the net profit or loss for the period, and this is illustrated by Figure A5.1.

The other income, i.e. the non-trading income that is added to the gross profit, could consist of items such as rent received, discounts received for prompt payment of amounts owing and investment income.

The expenses could be grouped into administration expenses, selling expenses and distribution expenses. The expenses would include the wages and salaries of employees and directors (other than those that were dealt with in the trading and manufacturing

Profit and loss account
Gross profit
plus
Other income
less
Expenses
equals
Net profit or loss before tax

Figure A5.1 – The profit and loss account

```
┌─────────────────────────────────────────────────────────────────┐
│                  Profit and loss appropriation account            │
│                                                                   │
│                  Net profit before tax (per the P&L)              │
│                  Less Tax                                          │
│                                                                   │
│        equals    Net profit (loss) after tax                      │
│                  Less Dividends and transfers to reserves          │
│                                                                   │
│        equals    Retained profits (loss) for the current period   │
│                  Add Retained profits brought forward from last year │
│                                                                   │
│        equals    Retained profits (P&L account balance)           │
│                  carried forward to next year                     │
└─────────────────────────────────────────────────────────────────┘
```

Figure A5.2 – The profit and loss appropriation account

accounts), loan interest and debenture interest paid, various overhead expenses and the depreciation for the period charged for the use of fixed assets such as plant, machinery, fixtures, fittings, motor vehicles. All the expenses that are not dealt with in the trading or manufacturing account and appropriation accounts are dealt with in the profit and loss account.

The first calculation in Figure A5.2 simply states that net profit before tax less tax equals the net profit after tax. From this figure the appropriations are deducted and could consist of the following:

☐ transfers to reserves, and/or

☐ dividends for the period that have been paid or proposed on ordinary shares (and, preference shares, if any).

Points to note:

☐ Layout and presentation are important.

☐ Key figures are highlighted, e.g. sales, cost of sales, gross profit, net profit.

☐ Directors' fees, loan interest and debenture interest are regarded as charges against income and are therefore included as an expense in the profit and loss section of the statement. They are not treated as appropriations of profit.

☐ The appropriation section shows how the profit earned is shared between the stakeholders, e.g. the tax authorities, the shareholders and the amount ploughed back by the company, i.e. reserves and retained earnings (P&L account balance).

A5.3

The calculation of the gross profit:	£000	£000
Sales		640
Less **Cost of sales:**		
Opening stock	48	
Add Purchases	460	
	508	
Less Closing stock	80	428
Gross profit		**£212**

A5.4

The calculation of the net profit before tax:	£000	£000	
Gross profit		320	
Less **Expenses:**	125		
Depreciation	40		
Loan interest	8		
Directors' fees	50	223	
Net profit before tax			**£97**

Note that tax and dividends are appropriations, and dealt with in the profit and loss appropriation account which takes the net profit before tax as its starting point.

A5.5

The calculation of the retained profit figure:	£000	£000
Net profit before tax		240
Less Taxation		68
Net profit after tax		172
Less:		
Transfers to reserves	100	
Dividends (paid and proposed) (i.e. 20 + 24)	44	144
Retained earnings for the current year		28
Add Retained earnings brought forward from last year		84
Retained earnings carried forward (P&L a/c balance)		**£112**

The directors' fees and loan interest would have already been deducted in computing the net profit before tax.

A6.1 Emmsock plc

CASH FLOW STATEMENT FOR THE YEAR ENDED 31 DECEMBER 20X8
(FRS 1)

		£000	£000
Net cash flow from operating activities	(W1)		80
Returns on investments, and the servicing of finance:			
Dividends received		—	
Dividends paid		(15)	
Interest paid		(22)	(37)
			43
Taxation:			
Tax paid	(W2)		(11)
			32
Investing activities:			
Purchase of tangible fixed assets	(W3)	(65)	
Proceeds from sale of trade investments		—	(65)
			(33)
Financing:			
Proceeds from new share capital	(W4)	271	
Repayment of borrowings	(W5)	(225)	46
Increase in cash and cash equivalents			13

Workings and comments: Emmsock plc

W1 Net cash flow from operating activities:

	£000	£000
Retained profit		25
Increase in general reserve		5
Depreciation: Plant and machinery	16	
Fixtures and fittings	7	23
Profit or loss on the sale of fixed assets		nil
Interest paid on debentures and loans (given)		22
Tax appropriated		15
Dividend appropriated		20
		110
Increase in stocks	(6)*	
Increase in debtors	(13)	
Decrease in creditors	(11)	(30)
		80

* Increases in current assets mean that more cash flow is tied up and decreases in creditors means that cash flow has been used to reduce the amount outstanding. Thus, an increase in current assets and a decrease in creditors will both be deducted in computing the net cash flow from operating activities as illustrated in W1 above.

W2 Tax paid:

			£000
	20X7	Balance b/f	9
Add	20X8	appropriation (P & L a/c)	15
			24
Less	20X8	Balance c/f	13
		therefore Tax paid =	11

The £11,000 was the actual tax paid during the year 31 December 20X8, i.e. the actual cash paid to the tax authorities.

W3 Purchase of tangible fixed assets:

		Cost
		£000
	20X8	659
Less	20X7	594
		65

You can observe that this is made up of an increase in land and buildings of £50,000, an increase in plant and machinery of £10,000 and an increase in fixtures and fittings of £5,000.

W4 Proceeds from new share capital:

		Ordinary Shares	Preference Shares
		£000	£000
	20X8	400	50
Less	20X7	200	nil
		200	50
Total		250	

In addition to the above, there was also the increase in share premium 20X7 £17,000 to 20X8 £38,000, i.e. an additional £21,000, making the total £271,000.

W5 Repayment of borrowings:

		Debentures £000	Loan £000
	20X8	100	nil
Less	20X7	165	160
		(65)	(160)
Total		(225)	

Note

You should appreciate that W1 above could all be computed by reference to the balance sheet. This was designed to help you when you are faced with the situation of only being provided with the balance sheet. However, you were provided with the profit and loss appropriation account, and so should have been able to compute the figure much more quickly, as follows:

		£000
	Net profit before tax (given)	65
Add	Depreciation	23
	Interest paid	22
		110
Less	W1 increase in current assets and decrease in creditors	(30)
		80

Port Peter plc trial balance

(1)				(2)	(3)
Destination	Details	Debit £000	Credit £000	+ or − Adjustment £000	Balance sheet effect £000
B/C	Authorised and issued £1 ordinary shares		400		
T	Sales		375		
T	Purchases	140		Note 4	
T	Stock 1 January 20X4	29		Closing stock	
B/Res	Share premium		25	−20T	20 CA
P&L	Bad debts (written off)	3			
P&L	Wages and salaries	48			
B/FA	Motor vehicles (at cost)	40		Note 1	
−B/FA	Depreciation to date on motor vehicles		16	Depreciation 8 P&L	Depreciation to date −24 FA
P&L	Motor Expenses	9		−4 P&L	4CA
P&L	Overhead expenses	30		Note 2	
B/FA	Freehold land and buildings	437		Prepaid	
B/CA	Debtors	28			
B/CL	Creditors		23		
B/CA	Bank balance	32			
App.	Profit and loss account		11		
B/LTD	10% debentures		50		
P&L	Directors' fees	56			Note 5
-	Taxation	—	—	18 App	18 CL
B/FA	Fixtures, fittings and equipment (at cost)	80			
−B/FA	Depreciation to date on fixtures and fittings and equipment		30	Note 1 Depreciation 8 P&L	Depreciation to date −38 FA (new
B/CA	Provision for bad debts		2		cumulative)
		£932	£932		
	Proposed dividend			Note 3 App 30	30 CL

Port Peter plc profit and loss account for the year ended 31 December 20X4

		£000	£000	£000
	Sales			375
Less:	**Cost of sales**			
	Opening stock		29	
	Add purchases		140	
			169	
Less:	Closing stock		20	149
	Gross profit			226
Less:	**Expenses:**			
	Bad debts		3	
	Wages and salaries		48	
	Motor expenses		9	
	Overhead expenses	30		
	Less rent prepaid	4	26	
	Directors' fees		56	
Depreciation:				
	Fixtures, fittings and equipment	8		
	Motor vehicles	8	16	158
	Net profit before tax			68
Appropriations:				
	Corporation tax			18
	Net profit after tax			50
	Proposed dividend			30
				20
Add	Balance b/f from last year			11
	P&L account balance c/f (Retained earnings)			£ 31

Port Peter plc balance sheet as at 31 December 20X4

Authorised share capital	£000
400,000 £1 ordinary shares	400

	Cost	Depreciation to date	Net
Employment of capital	£000	£000	£000
Fixed assets			
Freehold land and buildings	437	Nil	437
Fixtures, fittings and equipment	80	38	42
Motor vehicles	40	24	16
	557	62	495
Working capital:			
Current assets			
Stock		20	
Debtors	28		
Less Provision for bad debts	2	26	
Prepayments		4	
Bank		32	
		82	
Less **Current liabilities**			
Creditors	23		
Taxation	18		
Less Proposed dividend	30	71	11
			£506
Capital employed:	£000	£000	£000
Capital			
Issued share capital			
Ordinary shares			400
Reserves			
Share premium		25	
Retained earnings (P&L account)		31	56
			456
Long-term debt			
Debentures			50
			£506

A8.1

Intomarkt Consultants Ltd

Earnings per share	£8m/10m = £0.80
Price earnings ratio	£3.60/£0.80 = 4.5 times
Dividend cover	£8m/£2m = 4 times
Dividend yield	£0.20/£3.60 × 100 = 5.55%

A8.2

Holme plc and Colne plc

Financial performance analysis

	Ratio	Holme	Colne	Industry average	Comments
Liquidity Current ratio					
$\dfrac{2}{1.6}$ $\quad$ $\dfrac{3.6}{3.5}$		1.25	1.03	2.00	Both well below industry average, indicating possible liquidity problems. However, they are both above the 'rule of thumb' recommended level of one to one.
Acid test (quick ratio)					
$\dfrac{2-1}{1.6}$ $\quad$ $\dfrac{3.6-2.4}{3.5}$		0.63	0.34	0.90	Colne does have serious liquidity problems, i.e. only 34p's worth of liquid assets for every £1 owing in current liabilities. Holme also has liquidity problems i.e. it has around 63p for every £1 of current liabilities.
Profitability Net profit before tax to sales × 100					
$\dfrac{1}{5} \times 100$ $\quad$ $\dfrac{1.6}{10} \times 100$		20%	16%	20%	Colne has a lower than average net profit margin. It may possibly be using the lower margin to attract a higher volume of sales.

	Ratio	Holme	Colne	Industry Average	Comments
Return on investment (return on assets)	$\dfrac{1}{5.8} \times 100$ $\dfrac{1.6}{6.6} \times 100$	17.24%	24.24%	24%	Colne is making more efficient use of its capital, i.e. making a better return on investment, but just above the industry average. Holme is below the industry average. The industry average could be on the high side if a lot of companies are using 'off-balance-sheet financing'.
Efficiency Average collection period	$\dfrac{0.8}{5} \times 365$ $\dfrac{1.2}{10} \times 365$	59 days	44 days	60 days	Colne is collecting its debts more quickly, i.e. has more efficient credit control. Probably because it is desperate for cash, but this could be at the expense of offering generous prompt-payment discounts.
Credit period taken	$\dfrac{1.4}{5} \times 365$ $\dfrac{2}{10} \times 365$	103 days	73 days	70 days	Holme is taking too long to pay its creditors, and Colne is paying them in line with the industry average.

(No average available for creditors so we had to use the current year's figures. No purchases figure available, so we had to use the sales figure.)

	Ratio	Holme	Colne	Industry Average	Comments
Stock turnover	$\dfrac{5}{1}$ $\dfrac{10}{2.4}$	5 times	4.17 times	7 times	Both are on the low side possibly because they may be carrying stock levels that are too high. This indicates the need for better and more efficient inventory control.
Investment Earnings/shareholders' equity × 100	$\dfrac{0.8}{4.8} \times 100$ $\dfrac{1.2}{2.6} \times 100$	16.67%	46.15%	20%	Holme is not performing too well on these measures. This could have an effect on its share price. Colne's return is very good, possibly due to the high gearing (see below).

	Ratio	Holme	Colne	Industry Average	Comments
Earnings per ordinary share					
	$\dfrac{0.8}{4}$ $\dfrac{1.2}{1}$	0.20	1.20	£0.30	Holme is not performing too well on these measures. This could have an effect on its share price. Colne's return is very good, possibly due to the high gearing (see below).
Gearing Debt/debt plus equity	$\dfrac{1}{5.8} \times 100$ $\dfrac{4}{6.6} \times 100$	17.24%	60.6%	Not given	As mentioned above, Colne is the more highly geared. If there are poor trading conditions in the future, the obligation to pay a lot of interest on the loans could cause severe liquidity problems.

Conclusions and recommendations

Holme is performing better than Colne when it comes to liquidity but could experience some difficulty in meeting its obligations as they arise because it is working at a level that is well below the industry average of 0.9. Colne has very serious liquidity problems, as indicated by the acid test ratio. It only has 34p's worth of liquid assets for every £1 it owes to its current liabilities, and needs to take immediate action.

It would appear that Colne is achieving its higher volume of sales by working on a lower net profit sales margin. Colne's profitability and investment performance is superior to Holme's, i.e. it is getting a better return for its shareholders.

Colne's very good performance on the average collection period is an indication that it has an efficient and effective system of credit control. Holme appears to be taking far too long to pay its creditors, i.e. 103 days, compared to an industry average of 70 days. Thus, there is a possibility that creditors who feel that they are having to wait too long may take them to court and petition to have them wound up. This could damage the company's reputation in the market place.

The stock turnover position for both companies suggests that stocks are moving too slowly through each company and that they may be carrying stock levels that are far too high. This means that capital that could be available for other purposes is being tied up in stocks of raw materials, fuels, finished goods and work-in-progress.

It is recommended that the companies adopt the following courses of action to improve their performance:

	Holme plc	Colne plc
Liquidity and efficiency	Reduce the stock levels	Reduce the stock levels
	(i.e. both to improve their inventory management, e.g. concentrate on getting rid of slow-moving, low-margin lines)	
	Improve credit control (if Colne can do it, why can't Holme?)	Try to keep the credit control at this level, provided it does not involve giving hefty cash discounts for prompt payment
	Reduce the time taken in paying creditors to around the industry average	Could take a few more days to pay creditors, unless this means the loss of generous cash discounts for prompt payment
Profitability and investment	Manage overheads more efficiently and increase gross margins (if possible)	Manage overheads more efficiently and improve gross margins (if possible)

Comment (not part of the answer)

You should be able to observe from your study of the figures that profitability and liquidity do not go hand in hand. Although Colne Ltd is the more profitable, it does have liquidity problems.

Even where a ratio is satisfactory, i.e. around the industry average, this is no reason for inaction. If action can be taken to improve the performance, then it should be. After all, an average is arrived at by combining poor, good and average performances.

A8.3

(a) The information provided by a ratio analysis can be used in the following ways:
- ☐ When you look at comparative figures. For example, this year compared to last year, or company A compared to company B. It is useful to make working notes on each ratio or group of ratios to explain the variances and to highlight the strengths and weaknesses, etc.
- ☐ If a ratio analysis is to be useful, it needs to be based on several years' figures so that trends can be identified and emerging problems detected.
- ☐ The quest for a 'benchmark', i.e. something against which performance can be measured, can be partly solved by using industry figures.

(b) The limitations: Ratio analysis does have limitations, the principal ones being:

- ☐ The inadequacy of the source data, i.e. the final accounts, for example concerning the application of concepts and accounting policies, 'off-balance-sheet financing' and 'window-dressing'/creative accounting.
- ☐ The way in which the ratios are computed, for example the treatment of the bank overdraft as a long- or short-term source of finance; using the sales figure when purchases or cost of sales figures would be more appropriate; the profit figure could be one of many, *for example, net profit before tax, net profit after tax*; the way in which the average debtors, creditors and stocks are arrived at, i.e. taking no account of what happens during the intervening period.
- ☐ The terminology can be very confusing.

(c) Selecting a company with which to compare your own company's financial performance.

If you have to carry out an inter-firm comparison, beware! You cannot just compare with another firm in the same industrial sector. You also need to try to select companies that are in the same industrial sector and that also have some of the following characteristics:

- ☐ Have a similar product portfolio.
- ☐ Are of a similar size, e.g. in terms of turnover and/or number of employees.
- ☐ Have the same year-end.
- ☐ Use similar accounting policies.
- ☐ Finance their assets in a similar manner, i.e. the extent to which they use 'off-balance-sheet financing'.
- ☐ Have revalued their buildings and/or other fixed assets around the same date.
- ☐ Employ the same kind of production or operating methods.
- ☐ Are located in an area where overhead costs are similar.
- ☐ Arrive at the year-end stock valuations using similar methods.

Thus, it is impossible to find a perfect match. All you can do is to find as near a match as you possibly can.

Note

You should note that there were no self-assessments for Chapter 9. However, there were quite a number of tutor-based assignments and projects.

A10.1 (a)

Return on capital employed

Year	1		2		3	
Company	B Ltd	P Ltd	B Ltd	P Ltd	B Ltd	P Ltd
	£m	£m	£m	£m	£m	£m
Net profit before Interest	24	24	36	36	10	10
Capital employed	220	220	220	220	220	220
Return on capital employed	10.91%	10.91%	16.36%	16.36%	4.55%	4.55%

This shows the overall return on capital employed, whether it comes from debt or equity.

Note (not part of the answer): In reality, the capital employed would tend to change every year, e.g. as a result of retained earnings or attracting more share capital or debt.

(b)

Year	1		2		3	
Company	B Ltd	P Ltd	B Ltd	P Ltd	B Ltd	P Ltd
	£m	£m	£m	£m	£m	£m
Net profit before interest	24	24	36	36	10	10
Less interest (@ 12%)	5.76	14.4	5.76	14.4	5.76	14.4
Net profit after interest	18.24	9.6	30.24	21.6	4.24	(4.4)
Earning per share	£0.182	£0.192	£0.302	£0.432	£0.042	£(0.09)

It illustrates clearly that in bad times, e.g. year 3, the more highly geared can have problems because they still have to pay out large amounts of interest, e.g. P Ltd a negative EPS of 9p. In very good times, e.g. year 2, the more highly geared company, P Ltd, has a much higher EPS (earnings per share).

A10.2

'If all the holders of convertible loan stock convert into ordinary shares there will be a dilution of earnings.'

The above statement is not really correct. It is too dogmatic. It should have read: 'there could be a dilution of earnings'.

A dilution of earnings means that the EPS (earnings per share) goes down. It can go down when all the holders of convertible loan stock convert because the profits (the 'cake') grow bigger, because the company no longer has to pay interest on the convertibles. However, as a result of the conversion there will be more ordinary shareholders. More ordinary shareholders sharing a bigger cake could result in a lower EPS, as illustrated by the following example.

Hunwick plc has £10m ordinary shares of £1 each and £12m 10% convertible loan stock (convertible into £1 shares with redemption dates 20X8–20X9). The profit figures for the current year 20X2 and the estimated profit figures for 20X8 are:

	20X2 £m	Converted 20X8 £m	Not converted 20X8 £m
Net profit before interest and tax	9.6	14.4	14.4
Less interest on convertibles	1.2	—	01.2
	8.4	14.4	13.2
Less taxation	3.2	5.2	4.8
Net profit after tax	5.2	9.2	8.4

Undiluted earnings per share 20X2:

$$\frac{£5.2}{10} = \underline{£0.52}$$

Fully diluted earnings per share in 20X8 are:

$$\frac{9.2}{22} = \underline{£0.42}$$

However, if the net profit after tax earnings for 20X8 were greater than 22m × £0.52, i.e. £11.44m, the fully diluted earnings per share would be greater than the current EPS.

If the holders do not convert in 20X8, the EPS would then be:

$$\frac{£8.4m}{10m} = \underline{£0.84}$$

Compared with the current EPS situation, if the holders convert, the compounding of the earnings from the additional funds provided via the retained earnings could be generating much higher profits, leading to an increase in the EPS.

Comment (not part of the answer)

Note that the answer did not accept the initial statement and explained and illustrated why.

A11.1

Worlden Insurance AG

Rather than provide you with just an outline answer, because this is one of the first case studies in the book, a full suggested answer has been provided for question 1.

Question 1   Financial performance

Analysis of the key ratios

The information provided about Worlden, its competitor Davikamp, and its industry average is very limited, but it is possible to assess its financial performance. It would have been useful to have more information, e.g. copies of the annual accounts for the last four years. However, the only way to produce a financial performance analysis from the information given is to make assumptions and speculations.

Return on equity

The return on equity would be computed by expressing the net profit after interest and tax as a percentage of the equity (i.e. ordinary shares plus reserves). Worlden have performed better than Davikamp, 15.2% compared with 10.8%, but this is lower than the industry average of 19.6%. One of the principal reasons for the differences could be the gearing. Worlden is lower geared than the industry average, and more highly geared than Davikamp. The equity to equity plus debt percentage is as follows:

	Worlden	Davikamp	Industry average
(%)	70	80	60

The profit figure used in the calculation could have been significantly affected by the tax factor, e.g. the different tax systems and rates applied in each country.

Return on capital employed (ROCE)

It is assumed that the calculation used was the net profit before interest and tax, as a percentage of the capital employed (i.e. debt plus equity). This takes the effects of interest on debt and taxation out of the ROCE calculation. It provides an indication of the overall productivity of the capital employed, irrespective of whether it comes from debt or equity. Worlden is performing better than Davikamp, 18.6% compared with 16%, but much less than the industry average of 24.3%. It could well be the case that Worlden does not have as much 'off-balance-sheet financing' as other companies in the sector, i.e. fixed assets that are rented, hired or leased, e.g. land and buildings, equipment and motor vehicles. Those companies that have a lot of 'off-balance-sheet financing' will tend to have a lower capital employed figure. If they have similar profit figures, their return on capital employed will be higher. Other possible reasons for differences in profits could be the management and control of overheads, and regional or international differences, e.g. the rent of land and buildings, and the cost of services for lighting and heating, could be much higher than those being paid by other companies in the sector.

Gross profit sales

There is a vast difference between the gross profit sales of Worlden and Davikamp, which could be due to differing product portfolios, or Davikamp's reducing its margins to increase its market share. Worlden is lower than the industry average: 13.4% compared with 16.4%. The 3% difference, when considered in terms of the volume and value of sales, could represent a significant amount running into millions of euros.

Assets utilisation ratio

This ratio would have been arrived at by dividing the sales by the fixed assets. On this measure Worlden is performing worse than Davikamp and worse than the industry average. If Davikamp and numerous other companies in the sector use more 'off-balance-sheet financing' this could be one of the reasons for the differences, e.g. a lower fixed-asset figure divided into a similar sales level would give a higher asset utilisation ratio. Other reasons for differences in the value of fixed assets could be the location, e.g. the cost of land and buildings purchased, and whether or not the fixed assets have been revalued. Worlden really needs to take a more in-depth look at this.

Liquidity – the quick ratio

This ratio should be around one to one, which provides an indication that all of the three sets of figures provided are satisfactory. In practice, companies do tend to manage with a quick (acid test) ratio of less than one to one.

Debtors turnover

Worlden is taking around 17 days longer to collect its debts compared with the industry average and 11 days longer than Davikamp. From this it is clear that it needs to review its credit control system and speed up its debt collection, e.g. by invoicing more promptly, chasing slow payers, etc. However, this should not be at the expense of granting generous discounts for prompt payment. A small percentage settlement discount could have a high APR (annual percentage rate) of interest.

Gearing

As indicated above, Worlden is lower geared when compared to the industry average. Thus, there could be scope for attracting more debt financing in the future, if required. In the event of a recession, because of its low gearing Worlden should be able to survive and be well able to pay the interest on its debt. Its competitor Davikamp is even lower geared.

PE ratio (price/earnings)

The fact that Davikamp's and the industry average are higher is an indication that the market expectations of Worlden are not as high. If Worlden does take over other companies, expectations could change dramatically and the PE may then increase.

Dividend cover

Worlden's is low compared with Davikamp's and the industry average. Maybe it is paying out too much, when it really ought to be ploughing back profits and reinvesting in itself, hence the low market expectations. It needs to review its dividend policy. Why pay out high dividends and then raise more finance via debt or ordinary shares etc. from external sources, which have to be serviced in terms of interest or dividend payments?

Conclusions

With a financial performance analysis, it is not the ratios themselves that are important, but the questions they provoke. Worlden needs to look at the control and management of its overheads – savings may be possible.

They need to review their pricing policy: a small percentage increase could result in millions more euros. If new financing is needed more debt could be attracted which could well increase the wealth of the ordinary shareholders, e.g. once the interest is paid the remainder generated increases the stake of the ordinary shareholders.

Credit policy and credit control systems need to be reviewed and perhaps given a higher priority by the management. Market expectations will only increase when the market is confident that the company is really going places.

Finally, the company needs to carefully review its dividend policy. It could be paying out dividends that are too high, compared to other companies in the sector. However, changing the policy may not be without its problems. The market may not like it, but that is another story.

Comments (not part of the answer)

Where the data are limited and incomplete, assumptions have to be made and stated. In financial performance analysis it is useful to look for interrelationships between the ratios, e.g. the return on equity and the gearing. It is also useful to take account of other factors such as the location, and possible differences in tax systems.

Brief illustrations/explanations of some of the points being made can improve the clarity, e.g. 'off-balance-sheet financing' and its affect on the capital employed and the fixed assets.

To round off the analysis a conclusions section can be used to provide a brief overview of the principal findings and recommendations and the need for further or more in-depth research.

Question 2 Outline answer

The possible financial benefits resulting from the merger

- ☐ 'Synergy', 1 + 1 = 3. The combination can be run more efficiently than the two individual companies, e.g. there could be too much overlap or duplication.
- ☐ Strategic. As part of Worlden's plans to become a global player, e.g. to increase its market share or for horizontal integration purposes, i.e. taking over companies that provide similar services.
- ☐ Marketing and brands. To acquire brands and/or expertise, e.g. marketing and brands.
- ☐ Managerial. To inherit a tried and tested highly regarded managerial team.
- ☐ Tax aspects, e.g. being able to offset tax losses.
- ☐ Technological, e.g. high-tech systems.

Question 3 Outline answer

To become one of the industry's leading players Worlden needs to consider the following:

- ☐ First, concentrating on doing what they are good at, and working towards improving in the areas in which weaknesses have been identified.

☐ Takeovers and acquisitions financed by more debt, and then offering a package of cash plus shares, but taking the control factor into account. This could involve searching for suitable targets, e.g. problem children with lots of growth but short of cash. Synergy, $1 + 1 = 3$.

☐ Searching for new products or opportunities, e.g. diversification, WWW trading.

☐ Paying more attention to marketing, customer retention, operational risk, etc.

☐ Investing in people, e.g. in-company training.

Comments (not part of the answer)

Note that some of the points made in question 3 were also made in question 2. This is quite acceptable, as they are relevant to both questions.

A12.1

'The elements of cost feature in the cost of any product or service.'

The elements of cost consist of direct labour, direct materials, direct expenses and overheads. The overheads are made up of indirect labour, indirect materials and indirect expenses. The cost of any product or service will consist of a combination of the elements of cost. For example, in a manufacturing company the product cost will consist of the manufacturing labour, the raw materials used, direct expenses such as carriage inwards and advertising that is specific to the product and not of a general nature, and the overheads. The overheads could include cleaners' wages or salaries, cleaning materials, heating and lighting, insurance of buildings.

The cost of a service may or may not include a significant amount of raw materials, depending on the type of service. The direct labour would be the labour directly involved in providing the service, e.g. the salary of a management consultant, the salary of a lecturer or tutor at a college, the salaries of maintenance engineers for an equipment servicing company, direct expenses, e.g. *travel costs, special stationery or software, plus overheads*.

By far the most difficult part of costing a product or service is how much to include for the recovery of overheads. There are two approaches that can be used: total absorption costing (including activity-based costing), and marginal costing. To go into greater depth about these here is outside the scope and focus of this question.

A 12.2 (a) and (b)

(a) The insurance brokers

(b) The travel agency

Comment (not part of the answer)

The costs involved in setting up an insurance brokers or travel agency could include the following:

☐ Fixed assets: premises, office furniture, fixtures and fittings; equipment such as computers, fax machines, photocopiers, printers; motor vehicles. These would have to be purchased outright, or rented, hired or leased, as appropriate, taking into account the availability of start-up capital.

☐ Working capital would be needed to finance the holding of stocks of office stationery and outstanding debtors, etc.

☐ Start-up expenditure, such as one-off legal and professional fees, the cost of recruitment and selection of staff.

☐ Other costs would include financing costs. In the case of the travel agency, any finance received from its parent company would have an 'opportunity cost'.

The answers to (a) and (b) could be almost identical: both businesses would need to finance similar types of fixed assets and working capital.

A13.1 What management can do to improve materials management

Stocks (also called inventory) of raw materials, fuels, work-in-progress and finished goods represent capital tied up. To make the most of its capital employed, therefore, management must endeavour to keep stock levels to an acceptable minimum. In addition to the capital tied up in stocks there are also expensive holding costs, e.g. acquisition costs, store keeping costs, insurance, handling. Thus, the real cost of materials will be their purchase cost plus the cost of the capital used to finance their purchase plus the holding costs. The management accounting section should be able to provide a lot of useful information to assist with materials management such as:

☐ Details of maximum, minimum and reorder levels for various stock items so that they can be reviewed and revised according to orders, seasons, etc.

☐ An analysis or printout of slow-moving and/or obsolete stocks.

☐ An analysis of material usage (direct and indirect) by jobs, products, services, departments, etc.

☐ Details of any stocks that are surplus to requirements.

☐ A 'Pareto' analysis of, say, the 20% of the stock items that account for 80% of the value of the stock.

☐ Costings on the employment of subcontractors.

☐ Costings comparing the making or buying of a particular component.

☐ Standard costing (see Chapter 17) – variance analysis.

☐ Budget and actual comparative statements, e.g. for material usage.

Management has a duty of ensuring that there is a sound system of stock (inventory) control within the organisation. Much of the information generated by the management accounting section should assist managers to do this. They should, however, be active in other areas which aim to reduce the value and volume of stock held.

Matching and just-in-time (JIT)

Matching material requirements to the production requirements could involve the scheduling of materials to arrive at the factory, say, a day or so before they are due to enter the production process.

Variety reduction

A variety reduction exercise can reduce costs. Uncalled-for variety is expensive, as variety adds to complexity, e.g. more administrative effort. Nowadays a certain amount of variety can be achieved using differing mixes of standardised components. Management should be aware of this at the product or service design stage so that uncalled-for variety can be eliminated from the outset.

Random stock checks

Providing personnel who are independent of responsibility for the stores or warehouse with the authority to carry out random stock checks should help to detect errors and fraud, and act as a moral deterrent. The staff involved could also carry out investigations into the condition of stock.

Coding and classification systems

Firms have been known to order materials from suppliers when they already have an adequate supply within their stores or other parts of their company. This situation can arise because of poor coding and classification systems.

Monitoring

The environment in which the organisation operates, e.g. social, political, economic, technological, must be monitored on a regular basis to identify changes taking place or about to take place. For example, certain information could reveal that a particular component is about to become obsolete.

Conclusions

Management does not always allocate enough resources to materials management and/or enough time to focus on its problems. There could be enormous savings, e.g. reducing the amount of capital tied up and reducing expensive holding costs. However, if management gets it wrong and there is a 'stock-out', orders and customers could be lost because of late delivery.

A14.1

Overhead absorption

(a) In deciding which basis of apportionment (arbitrary base) to use, the selector has to choose the method that is considered to be the most appropriate for the type of expense that has to be shared out between the departments or cost centres.

(b) A lot of overheads vary more with time than with output; thus time-based methods of overhead absorption tend to be considered more appropriate. However, before the absorption rate can be calculated the machine hours and the direct labour hours have to be estimated for the forthcoming period. The absorption rates can then be computed as follows:

$$\text{Machine hour rate} = \frac{\text{Machine-department overheads}}{\text{Number of machine hours for the department concerned}}$$

$$\text{Direct labour hour rate} = \frac{\text{Overheads for the department}}{\text{Number of direct labour hours for the department concerned}}$$

Both of these methods are time-based.

(c) As jobs or products pass through a department or cost centre, they in effect 'clock up' a share of that particular department's/cost centre's overheads, e.g. at so much per machine hour or so much per direct labour hour. Thus, as a job/product goes from department to department it accumulates a share of the firm's overheads.

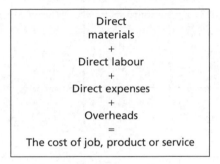

Figure A14.1 – The cost of a job, product or service

(d) A job, product or service cost is made up of the elements shown in Figure A14.1. Some businesses use this cost figure plus a mark-up to fix their selling price or their quotation for a job/product. However, product pricing in practice is not always quite so simple, e.g. notice has to be taken of what competitors are doing.

A14.2

Bonnopia plc

(a) Overhead distribution summary

(All £000)	How it is shared	Total	Machining	Painting	Assembly	Stores	Power
Rent	Area	200	40	70	60	20	10
Repairs to machinery (excluding power plant)	Machine value	144	283	35	18		
Depreciation of machinery (excluding power plant)	Machine value	192 336					
Depreciation of power plant	Allocation	12					
Power	Allocation	108 120					120
Employers liability insurance	No of employees	20	24	19	50	5	2
Supervision	No of Employees	80 100					
		756	**347**	**124**	**128**	**25**	**132**
Power	% estimates		66	26	26		(132) Nil
Stores	% estimates		15	12	12	14 39	
Nil						(39)	
			428	**162**	**166**		

(b) Overhead absorption rates:

	Machining	Painting	Assembly
Machine hours (000)	40		
Direct labour hours		30	12
Rate per machine hour	£10.70		
Rate per direct labour hour		£5.40	£13.83

(b) The cost of Job no 007XL5

		£	£
Direct material			68,200
Direct labour:			
Machining	40 × £10	400	
Painting	20 × £9	180	
Assembly	48 × £8	384	964
Overheads:			
Machining	80 × £10.70	856	
Painting	20 × £5.40	108	
Assembly	48 × £13.83	664	1,628
			£70,792

(c) The validity of the methods used

First, remember that all of the figures used are *predetermined estimates*.

Rent could also have been shared out according to cubic capacity. Using area also is quite acceptable.

The repairs to machinery should have been allocated, i.e. identified with a specific department or service. It should be possible to estimate this per department, based on past performance updated by what is known about the future, e.g. the frequency of routine maintenance, the cost of outside service contracts, major overhauls. Thus, in practice, it should not be necessary to use the value of plant and machinery for sharing out machine repairs.

The depreciation should also be capable of being calculated per department/service. Companies do keep records for financial accounting and management accounting purposes of cost, life, etc. of all their plant and machinery.

Using the number of employees for sharing out employers' liability and supervision does tend to be accepted as being reasonable. However, supervisors can provide records or estimates of where they have spent their time in the past, and details of how this will fluctuate in the future.

A15.1

How activity-based costing works

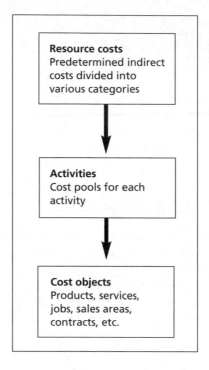

Figure A15.1 – Activity-based costing
Source: L. Chadwick, *Essential Management Accounting for Managers*, Financial Times Prentice Hall, 2001.

As with total absorption costing the indirect costs for the period concerned have to be estimated. Thus, GIGO could apply (i.e. garbage in, garbage out). The figures that are used are only estimates.

The resource costs have to be allocated and apportioned to cost pools, *using resource cost drivers* such as the number of employees, the cubic capacity, the number of computer hours.

The activity cost pools are shared up and charged to cost objects, e.g. products or services *via appropriate activity cost drivers*. For example, purchasing – the number of purchase orders; receiving – the number of received notes; highly merchandised departments – the number of machine hours; highly labour-intensive departments – the number of direct labour hours.

A15.2

Chadus company

Activity cost pools (all £000)

Dept.1	Dept.2	Setting-up	Computing	Purchasing	Total
1,020	820	80	300	100	2,320

Cost drivers (000)

| 340 Machine hours | 410 Direct lab. hours | 80 No. of set-ups | 60 No. of hours | 50 No. of orders | |
| £3 per machine hour | £2 per direct labour hour | £1 per set-up hour | £5 per hour | £2 per order | |

Activity-based costing profit statement

Sales/production (units)		Product R 400,000		Product T 400,000
	£000	£000	£000	£000
Sales		14,400		22,400
Less Prime cost		6,400		14,400
		8,000		8,000
Apportionment of cost pools:				
Dept 1 @ £3 per machine hr	300		720	
Dept 2 @ £2 per direct lab. hr	100		720	
Setting-up @ £1 per set-up	32		48	
Computing @ £5 per hour	200		100	
Purchasing @ £2 per order	80	712	20	1,608
Profit		**£7,288**		**£6,392**

Although product T has a higher selling price, it also has a higher prime cost, and a higher share of the overheads.

A16.1

Should we close one of our services?

(a) The Mainzbonn Leisure Centre

Keeping the swimming pool open

(£000)	Steam room etc	Fitness gym	Swimming pool	Climbing wall	Restaurant	Total
Income	40	60	120	24	36	280
Less Variable costs	10	30	70	8	12	130
Contribution	30	30	50	16	24	150
Less Specific fixed Costs	4	6	25	2	2	39
Contribution after specific fixed costs	**26**	**24**	**25**	**14**	**22**	**111**
Less General fixed costs						85
Profit						26

Closing the swimming pool would result in losing the contribution after specific fixed costs of £25,000:

	£
Profit as above	26,000
Less lost contribution (after deducting specific fixed costs)	25,000
Profit	£ 1,000

The £85,000 general fixed overheads would have to be covered by the contributions after deducting the specific fixed overheads generated by the remaining leisure services.

(b) The other services may lose business, as they are complementary to having a swimming pool. For example, many customers may also use the steam room either before or after they have a swim, and quite a number may make use of the restaurant. Closing down the swimming pool could lead many club members and/or occasional visitors to take their custom elsewhere.

A16.2

Jonbec Ltd

Contribution table

Product	J	O	N
Outputs up to (units)	60	20	24
Per unit:	£	£	£
Selling price	50	40	64
Less Variable cost	30	30	40
Contribution	**20**	**10**	**24**
Time taken to produce one unit	6 mins	10 mins	12 mins
Contribution per minute	**£3.33**	**£1**	**£2**
Ranking	1	5	2
Outputs over (units)	60	20	24
Selling price	40	36	60
Less Variable cost	30	30	40
Contribution	**10**	**6**	**20**
Contribution per minute	**£1.66**	**£0.60**	**£1.66**
Ranking	Joint 3	6	Joint 3

Optimum contribution per day

Product	No of units	Time taken	Cumulative time taken	Contribution per unit	Total contribution
J	60	360 mins	360	20	1,200
N	20	240	600	24	480
					£1,680

Comment

It is useful to draw up a contribution table, as above, and to calculate the contribution per unit of the limiting factor – in this case per minute. If the time available were say 700 minutes, this could then be used to produce J 60 units and N 24 units which would use up to 648 minutes. The remainder could then be used to produce more units of J or N, the joint third-ranked products at the lower-level contributions per minute of £1.66.

A16.3

Calculation of the break-even point

The profit/volume ratio (PV ratio) is:

$$\frac{\text{Contribution}}{\text{Sales}} \times 100 \qquad \frac{16}{40} \times 100 = 40\%$$

The break-even point is:

$$\text{Fixed costs } £336{,}000 \times \frac{100}{40} = £840{,}000$$

A16.4

(Parts 1 & 2)

Part 1 Proof of the break-even point in value:

$$\text{Profit/volume ratio} = \frac{\text{Contribution } £32\text{m}}{\text{Sales } £40\text{m}} \times 100 = 80\%$$

$$\text{Fixed costs } £18\text{m} \times \frac{100}{80} = £22.5\text{m (as above)}$$

Proof of break-even point in units:

$$\frac{\text{Fixed costs } £18\text{m}}{\text{Contribution per unit } £400} = 45{,}000 \text{ units}$$

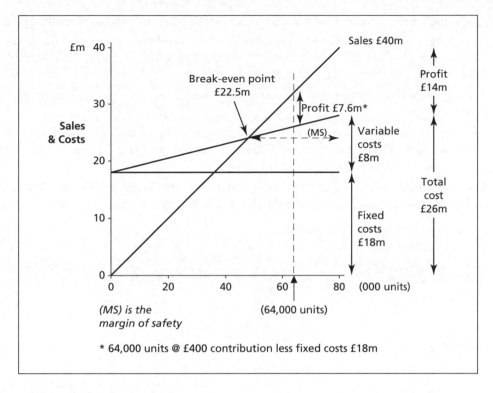

Figure A16.1 – The break-even chart

Part 2

		£m	£m
	Sales (64,000 units)		32.0
Less	Variable costs	6.4	
	Fixed costs	18.0	24.4
	Profit		£ 7.6m

As illustrated by the vertical line in Figure A16.1, drawn on the break-even chart at 64,000 units of output.

Additional points (not part of the answer)

Although it was possible to show all of the information on the break-even chart for parts 1 and 2, in order to produce accurate information it is useful to calculate the break-even point in value and units. Please note that:

☐ Below the break-even point we make a loss, above the break-even point we make a profit.

☐ The margin of safety is the difference between the breakeven point and the selected output or level of activity. This indicates the extent to which the level of activity must fall before a loss-making situation is reached.

☐ The horizontal base line of the chart can be expressed in terms either of output or level of activity.

☐ The logic of the calculations can be followed from a review of the right-hand side of the chart, i.e. sales £40m less total cost of £26m = the profit of £14m. The total cost is made up of fixed costs £18m and variable costs £8m.

☐ We can calculate the effect on profit where output is at 64,000 as above, or 64,000 × contribution per unit of £400, less the fixed costs of £18m = £7.6m.

A16.5

Emmrom plc

(a)

			40,000 units			60,000 units
		per unit £	20 × 8 £000	per unit £	20 × 9 £000
	Sales	320		300	
Less	Variable costs	120		124	
	Contribution	200	8,000	176	10,560
Less	Fixed costs		240		260
	Net Profit		£7,760		£10,300

(b) Break-even points

	20 × 8	20 × 9
Profit/volume ratios	62.5%	58.66%
(£000)		
Break-even point	$240 \times \dfrac{100}{62.5} = £384$	$260 \times \dfrac{100}{58.66} = £443.2$

(c) Contribution required:

			£000
		Fixed cost	260
	plus	Net profit	7,760
			£8,020

(£000)

$$\frac{8,020}{58.66} \times 100 = £136.72 \text{ sales level}$$

	£000
(d) Contribution from 56,000 × £176	9,856
Less Fixed costs	260
	9,596
Less Target profit	8,500
Maximum amount available for additional fixed costs	£1,096

A16.6

Wic Products Ltd

Contribution table

		Product		
		W	I	C
	Outputs up to	30 units	30 units	50 units
		£	£	£
	Selling price	80	120	60
Less	Variable cost	60	108	44
	Contribution	20	12	16
	Contribution per hour	**30**	**36**	**32**
	Ranking	3	1	2
	Outputs above	30 units	30 units	50 units
		£	£	£
	Selling price	75	110	45
Less	Variable cost	60	108	44
	Contribution	15	2	1
	Contribution per hour	**22.5**	**6**	**2**
	Ranking	4	5	6

The maximum contribution per 60-productive-hour day, is:

Rank			Time taken hours	Contribution per unit	Contribution £
1	I	30 units @ 20 mins	10	12	360
2	C	50 units @ 30 mins	25 cum. 35	16	800
3	W	30 units @ 40 mins	20 cum. 55	20	600
4	W	7.5 units @ 40 mins	5* 60	15	112.5 £1,872.5

* 5hrs × 60 = 300 mins divided by 40 mins = 7.5 units.

However, this could have been rounded off to 7 mins, and left 20 unused minutes available to make one more unit of I!

A16.7

(i)

	Vandi	Chungi
(£000)		
Break-even point	$£200 \times \frac{100}{60} = £333.3$	$£160 \times \frac{100}{40} = £400$

(ii)

	Vandi £000	Chungi £000
Fixed costs	200	160
Profit target	160	100
Contribution required	**£360**	**£260**

Sales needed are therefore:
(£000)

$$360 \times \frac{100}{60} = £600 \qquad 260 \times \frac{100}{40} = £650$$

Note (not part of the answer)

We know what the percentage is, as a percentage of the sales, as indicated by the profit/volume ratio. In the case of Vandi, this is 60%.

(a) The principal differences between a cash budget and a cash flow statement

The cash budget is based on *estimated (predetermined) figures*. It excludes non-cash items such as depreciation and accrued expenses (accruals). It takes into account the periods of credit granted to customers and received from the suppliers of goods and services. It does not matter about the time period covered by the receipt or payment, e.g. in the case of dividends or rent, receivable or payable. What does matter is when the cash is estimated to come in or go out (*i.e. when the money moves*).

The cash flow statement is a historic statement, i.e. it looks back over the accounting period under review at where the funds came from and how they have been used. For example, funds can be generated from:

☐ Operating activities (computed by taking into account operating profit plus depreciation and movements in marketable securities and working capital, other than cash and bank balances).

☐ Financing, e.g. new share capital, increases in long-term loans and debentures.

It can then be used to pay dividends, interest on loans, taxation and for acquiring new fixed assets etc.

One quick and simple definition of cash flow is: *net profit plus depreciation* (*Investors' Chronicle*). Thus, in summary, the cash budget is predetermined (about the future) and looks forward, and the cash flow statement is historic and looks backwards at where the money came from and where it went to.

(b) The difference between a cash budget and the budgeted profit and loss account

For the cash budget see part (a).

The budgeted profit and loss account is also predetermined and looks to the future. However, it does treat income and expenditure in a different way from the cash budget. It also uses the *realisation concept*, e.g. it includes all of the cash and credit sales for the period, even though the cash may not have been received, as evidenced by the debtors figure in the balance sheet (and treats purchases in the same way). It takes account of stocks of: raw materials, work-in-progress, finished goods, fuels, etc. (the matching concept) in computing the gross profit.

In the case of other income, e.g. rent received, it includes the amount applicable to the period (*the matching concept*, also called periodicity). In dealing with the expenses it takes *accruals and prepayments* into account, e.g. insurance prepaid, and also includes deprecia-tion of fixed assets. In addition, increases to provisions, e.g. the provision for bad debts, are also included as expenses.

In the appropriation section of the profit and loss the figures include are:

☐ Tax for the year (paid on account and that which is estimated to be still outstanding).

☐ Dividends paid and proposed.

☐ Transfers to reserves.

It must also be remembered that when profit is generated it is used to finance the purchase of fixed assets such as plant and machinery, fixtures and fittings, and to finance increases in the working capital, e.g. stocks and debtors. Thus, profit does not tend to stay cash for long, because the business spends it. Accrued and prepaid items will also be adjusted for in the profit and loss account, but will not be adjusted for in the cash budget.

A17.2

Your answer to the open-ended question 'A cash budgeting system forces management into action' should have been along the following lines:

The cash budget preparation process in itself will dictate that management will have to think about the future. They will have to organise *meetings*, the collection and analysis of relevant data, prepare and ensure that there is a *timetable*, careful *co-ordination*, *co-operation* and good *clear communications*. This should involve the *participation* of appropriate per-sonnel so that their views can be registered and discussed. Budgets are *interrelated* and so they cannot be prepared in isolation. The cash budget will draw on the information pro-vided by the sales budget, the production budget, the purchasing budget, the capital expen-diture and many others, hence the need for meetings and effective co-ordination.

Management will need to *delegate authority and responsibility* for the cash budget and its component parts to various members of staff – '*control by responsibility*'. This would include their roles in the preparation process and their authority, e.g. regarding the implementation and control process.

Management will know at the preparation stage if action is called for in terms of exceeding the overdraft or having surplus cash to invest short-term, or if cash is not avail-able when it is needed and take appropriate corrective action.

The *frequent comparisons and reporting* of budgeted and actual figures provides an '*early warning system*'. Management is forced into action to remedy adverse effects as and when they arise.

Thus, sound cash management which includes making good use of cash budgets will force management into action. Such action is essential if they are to realise the *objectives* that they themselves have set, and if they are to survive and prosper in the long term.

However, such budgets are *only estimates* based on the best available information at the time of their preparation. If the *assumptions* on which they were based change significantly, then the cash budget must also be revised and changed. If this is not done, management may be faced with a number of *behavioural and motivational problems.*

Comment

You should note that this answer has incorporated a significant number of key words, as indicated by italics. If you know and understand the key words of the subject, you can use the appropriate ones in a focused way when it comes to providing an answer to an open-ended written question.

A17.3

(a) Mythical Ltd: Cash budget to 30 June 20X7

Month	Balance b/f	Capital	Sales Time lag 2 months	Purchases Time lag 1 month	Rent	General Exp. & Salaries	Fixed assets c/f	Balance c/f
	£000	£000	£000	£000	£000	£000	£000	£000
Jan	—	2,000	—	—	—	16	200	1,784
Feb	1,784		—	44	—	16	—	1,724
Mar	1,724		20	48	100	16	120	1,460
Apr	1,460		36	36	—	16	—	1,444
May	1,444		54	36	—	16	—	1,446
Jun	1,446		48	36	100	16	—	1,342
			158	200	200	96	320	
			+ Debtors	+ Creditors		Depreciation	32	
			96	36		Net book value	288	
			254	236				
			Total sales	Total purchases				

(b)

Mythical Ltd:

Budgeted profit and loss account
For the half-year to 30 June 20X7

		£000	£000
	Sales		254
Less	Cost of sales:		
	Opening stock	—	
Add	Purchases	236	
		236	
Less	Closing stock	20	216
	Gross profit (25% of sales)		38
Less	Expenses:		
	Rent	200	
	General expenses and salaries	96	
	Depreciation for half-year	32	328
	Net loss		**290**

Budgeted balance sheet as at 30 June 20X7

		£000	£000
	Employment of capital:		
	Fixed assets	320	
Less	Depreciation	32	288
	Working capital:		
	Current assets		
	Stock	20	
	Debtors (two months)	96	
	Cash and bank (per cash budget)	1,342	
		1,458	
	Current liabilities:		
	Creditors (one month)	36	1,422
			1,710
	Capital employed:		
	Issued ordinary share capital	2,000	
	Retained loss	(290)	1,710

The estimated loss should ensure that the management focuses on operating more efficiently and endeavours to increase sales. However, it is a start-up situation, and management may have expected results such as these for the first six months.

(c)

The importance of preparing a cash budget to an organisation is that it forces management to think and plan ahead. It helps management to identify and take appropriate action to combat threats and to take advantage of emerging opportunities. Because it is prepared in advance of the period commencing, it provides management with time to take swift and early action.

The frequent comparisons of actual performance and the budget (e.g. on a monthly basis) enables management to monitor and control what is happening to their cash flow. In effect, it provides management with an early warning system.

It helps them to ensure that cash is available when needed and that shortages are identified well in advance so that appropriate remedial action can be taken. It also helps to show when there will be surplus cash, which could then be invested short-term, e.g. overnight, one week or one month, so as to generate additional income (this activity is often referred to as *treasury management*).

There are a number of other ways in which a cash budget may be useful to management, including:

☐ As a discussion document in obtaining third-party co-operation in project implementation, e.g. with banks and other lending institutions where financing facilities are being sought, or supervisory boards and the like when project approval is being sought.

☐ As an aid to monitoring performance in areas where cash control is an important performance indicator, e.g. credit control. As with all budgets, the comparison of the actual with the budget, together with the relevant variance analysis, should be carried out.

A profitable business can be problematic because of the time lag in collecting the associated cash, which, as a result, puts severe strain on cash flow. It is important, therefore, to know if and when these cash demands may be made on a business – hence the need to forecast.

Cash budgets (cash flow forecasts) may also be needed in support of new business activities or projects, particularly when there is competition for this scarce resource, in order to demonstrate to the appropriate person that:

☐ the project is viable in terms of the ultimate cash returns
☐ the intervening cash demands will not be

— *excessive*
— *impossible to fund*
— *as burdensome as competing projects!*

Thus, a company can be highly profitable, but if it has severe cash flow problems it can, very quickly, go out of business. The preparation of the cash budget is an essential component part of the quest by a company to survive and prosper in the long term.

A17.4

Performance report

Variance	Budget for June 20X5	Actual for June 20X5	
Production (units)	35,000	35,000	
	£	£	£
Indirect labour – variable	43,750	47,600	(3,850)
Consumables – variable	1,750	2,500	(750)
Other variable overheads	9,450	9,000	450
Depreciation – fixed	25,000	25,000	—
Other fixed overheads	15,000	18,000	(3,000)
	94,950	102,100	£(7,150)

Management would also be provided with the reasons for the variances so that they could consider taking appropriate remedial action.

A18.1

Using the discount tables:

(a) The present value of £50,000 in 10 years' time at 10% is:

  £50,000 × 0.386 = £19,300

(b) The present value of £20,000 in 5 years' time, and £20,000 in 10 years' time at 15% is:

		£
	£20,000 × 0.497	9,940
plus	£20,000 × 0.247	4,940
		14,880

(c) £4,000 at the end of each of the next 5 years, at 10% is:

  £4,000 × 3.170 = £12,680

(d) £8,000 at the end of each of the next 4 years, plus £12,000 at the end of year 5, at 12% is:

		£
	£8,000 × 3.037	24,296
plus	£12,000 × 0.567	6,804
		31,100

Note (not part of the answer)

For part (d), we had to use the present value table and the present value of the annuity table.

A18.2

Homedale.com plc

Workings

Year	1	2	3	4	5
	£000	£000	£000	£000	£000
Income	60	80	80	50	30
Expenditure before depreciation	40	40	30	30	20
Net incremental cash flow	**20**	**40**	**50**	**20**	**10**

(a) The payback is:

$$2 \text{ years } plus \frac{40}{50} \times 12 = 9.6 \text{ months}$$

$$= \textbf{2 years, 9.6 months}$$

The cumulative for years 1 and 2 = £60,000, and therefore £40,000 short of initial cost of £100,000.

The payback method simply tells us how long it takes to recover the initial investment. The shorter the payback period, the better, in terms of the risk factor. However, it does not take into account the 'time value of money' unless a discounted payback is used.

(b) Net present value method

Year	Cash flow £000	Average PV 16%	Present value £000
0	(100)	1	(100)
1	20	0.862	17.24
2	40	0.743	29.72
3	50	0.641	32.05
4	20	0.552	11.04
5	30 (including residual value 20)	0.476	14.28
		Net present value	**£ 4.33**

(c) Using a 16% (average risk) discount rate the project is just wealth-creating, having a net present value of £4,330. This does not mean accept the project immediately. It means that the project is worthy of further consideration. For example, there could be other projects that are more wealth-creating. There could also be a number of non-financial factors that need to be considered, e.g. operating considerations, green issues, reliability of servicing.

A18.3

Upgrade v. Replacement

Option 1   Upgrade the existing equipment

	£
Cost Payment at the outset	100,000
Maintenance contract £5,000 × 3.605 (5yrs @ 12%)	18,025
	118,025
Less Disposal end of year 5 (£8,000 × 0.567)	4,536
	£113,489

Option 2 Replace it now

	£
Cost *less* trade-in at the outset	180,000
Maintenance costs £3000 × 3.605	10,815
	190,815
Less Residual value (£20,000 × 0.567)	11,340
	£179,475

Option 2 is much more expensive, even though the maintenance costs for option 1 are higher. It would therefore be appropriate to select option 1.

A18.4

(a) Look before you buy

It may well be worth the time and expense to inspect the equipment in a working environment. The value of taking the opportunity to talk with personnel involved with such equipment should certainly not be neglected, or its benefits underestimated. Reputable suppliers may provide introductions to customers you can contact to discuss the pros and cons of the equipment.

(b) Human, social and environmental factors

Firms that ignore factors such as safety, noise and fumes in today's complex and diverse business environment do so at their peril. The financial consequences of ignoring them could be catastrophic.

The effects of 'people problems' upon an organisation cannot be underestimated. This alone could jeopardise the success of the whole venture, e.g. through resistance to change when introducing new technology, and also as a result of:

☐ *Empire building*, e.g. where sub-unit or personal goals conflict with the organisation's own goals.

☐ *Perceptions* about what the management wants.

☐ *Organisational structure*, e.g. certain personnel may be in control of key information junctions or have direct access to top management.

☐ *The boardroom balance of power*, e.g. finance v. the engineers.

(c) Imported equipment

Exchange rates may have a dramatic effect depending upon the method of payment adopted. How good is the supplier's servicing and spares provision in your country? Do they offer support in your native language? Other considerations under this heading include the additional administration necessary to deal with the documentation and foreign exchange, and delays in delivery of the equipment and spares caused by air and sea transport problems and/or political instability.

Present value tables and annuity tables

Appendix Table 1 Present value of £1 due at end of *n* years

n	1%	2%	3%	4%	5%	6%	7%	8%	9%	10%	n
1	0.99010	0.98039	0.97007	0.96154	0.95238	0.94340	0.93458	0.92593	0.91743	0.90909	1
2	0.98030	0.96117	0.94260	0.92456	0.90703	0.89000	0.87344	0.85734	0.84168	0.82645	2
3	0.97059	0.94232	0.91514	0.88900	0.86384	0.83962	0.81630	0.79383	0.77218	0.75131	3
4	0.96098	0.92385	0.88849	0.85480	0.82270	0.79209	0.76290	0.73503	0.70843	0.68301	4
5	0.95147	0.90573	0.86261	0.82193	0.78353	0.74726	0.71299	0.68058	0.64993	0.62092	5
6	0.94204	0.88797	0.83748	0.79031	0.74622	0.70496	0.66634	0.63017	0.59627	0.56447	6
7	0.93272	0.87056	0.81309	0.75992	0.71068	0.66506	0.62275	0.58349	0.54703	0.51316	7
8	0.92348	0.85349	0.78941	0.73069	0.67684	0.62741	0.58201	0.54027	0.50187	0.46651	8
9	0.91434	0.83675	0.76642	0.70259	0.64461	0.59190	0.54393	0.50025	0.46043	0.42410	9
10	0.90529	0.82035	0.74409	0.67556	0.61391	0.55839	0.50835	0.46319	0.42241	0.38554	10
11	0.89632	0.80426	0.72242	0.64958	0.58468	0.52679	0.47509	0.42888	0.38753	0.36049	11
12	0.88745	0.78849	0.70138	0.62460	0.55684	0.49697	0.44401	0.39711	0.35553	0.31863	12
13	0.87866	0.77303	0.68095	0.60057	0.53032	0.46884	0.41496	0.36770	0.32618	0.28966	13
14	0.86996	0.75787	0.66112	0.57747	0.50507	0.44230	0.38782	0.34046	0.29925	0.26333	14
15	0.86135	0.74301	0.64186	0.55526	0.48102	0.41726	0.36245	0.31524	0.27454	0.23939	15
16	0.85282	0.72845	0.62317	0.53391	0.45811	0.39365	0.33873	0.29189	0.25187	0.21763	16
17	0.84438	0.71416	0.60502	0.51337	0.43630	0.37136	0.31657	0.27027	0.23107	0.19784	17
18	0.83602	0.70016	0.58739	0.49363	0.41552	0.35034	0.29586	0.25025	0.21199	0.17986	18
19	0.82774	0.68643	0.57029	0.47464	0.39573	0.33051	0.27651	0.23171	0.19449	0.16351	19
20	0.81954	0.67297	0.55367	0.45639	0.37689	0.31180	0.25842	0.21455	0.17843	0.14864	20
21	0.81143	0.65978	0.53755	0.43883	0.35894	0.29415	0.24151	0.19866	0.16370	0.13513	21
22	0.80340	0.64684	0.52189	0.42195	0.34185	0.27750	0.22571	0.18394	0.15018	0.12285	22
23	0.79544	0.63414	0.50669	0.40573	0.32557	0.26180	0.21095	0.17031	0.13778	0.11168	23
24	0.78757	0.62172	0.49193	0.39012	0.31007	0.24698	0.19715	0.15770	0.12640	0.10153	24
25	0.77977	0.60953	0.47760	0.37512	0.29530	0.23300	0.18425	0.14602	0.11597	0.09230	25

Note: PV = £1/(1 + r)^n

Appendix Table 1 continued

n	11%	12%	13%	14%	15%	16%	17%	18%	19%	20%	n
1	0.90090	0.89286	0.88496	0.87719	0.86957	0.86207	0.85470	0.84746	0.84034	0.83333	1
2	0.81162	0.79719	0.78315	0.76947	0.75614	0.74316	0.73051	0.71818	0.70616	0.69444	2
3	0.73119	0.71178	0.69305	0.67497	0.65752	0.64066	0.62437	0.60863	0.59342	0.57870	3
4	0.65873	0.63552	0.61332	0.59208	0.57175	0.55229	0.53365	0.51579	0.49867	0.48225	4
5	0.59345	0.56743	0.54276	0.51937	0.49718	0.47611	0.45611	0.43711	0.41905	0.40188	5
6	0.53464	0.50663	0.48032	0.45559	0.43233	0.41044	0.38984	0.37043	0.35214	0.33490	6
7	0.48166	0.45235	0.42506	0.39964	0.37594	0.35383	0.33320	0.31392	0.29592	0.27908	7
8	0.43393	0.40388	0.37616	0.35056	0.32690	0.30503	0.28487	0.26604	0.24867	0.23257	8
9	0.39092	0.36061	0.33288	0.30751	0.28426	0.26295	0.24340	0.22546	0.20897	0.19381	9
10	0.35218	0.32197	0.29459	0.26974	0.24718	0.22668	0.20804	0.19106	0.17560	0.16151	10
11	0.31728	0.28748	0.26070	0.23662	0.21494	0.19542	0.17781	0.16192	0.14756	0.13459	11
12	0.28584	0.25667	0.23071	0.20756	0.18691	0.16846	0.15197	0.13722	0.12400	0.11216	12
13	0.25751	0.22917	0.20416	0.18207	0.16253	0.14523	0.12989	0.11629	0.10420	0.09346	13
14	0.23199	0.20462	0.18068	0.15971	0.14133	0.12520	0.11102	0.09855	0.08757	0.07789	14
15	0.20900	0.18270	0.15989	0.14010	0.12289	0.10793	0.09489	0.08352	0.07359	0.06491	15
16	0.18829	0.16312	0.14150	0.12289	0.10686	0.09304	0.08110	0.07078	0.06184	0.05409	16
17	0.16963	0.14564	0.12522	0.10780	0.09393	0.08021	0.06932	0.05998	0.05196	0.04507	17
18	0.15282	0.13004	0.11081	0.09456	0.08080	0.06914	0.05925	0.05083	0.04367	0.03756	18
19	0.13768	0.11611	0.09806	0.08295	0.07026	0.05961	0.05064	0.04308	0.03669	0.03130	19
20	0.12403	0.10367	0.08678	0.07276	0.06110	0.05139	0.04328	0.03651	0.03084	0.02608	20
21	0.11174	0.09256	0.07680	0.06383	0.05313	0.04430	0.03699	0.03094	0.02591	0.02174	21
22	0.10067	0.08264	0.06796	0.05599	0.04620	0.03819	0.03162	0.02622	0.02178	0.01811	22
23	0.09069	0.07379	0.06014	0.04911	0.04017	0.03292	0.02702	0.02222	0.01830	0.01509	23
24	0.08170	0.06588	0.05322	0.04308	0.03493	0.02838	0.02310	0.01883	0.01538	0.01258	24
25	0.07361	0.05882	0.04710	0.03779	0.03038	0.02447	0.01974	0.01596	0.01292	0.01048	25

Appendix Table 1 continued

n	21%	22%	23%	24%	25%	26%	27%	28%	29%	30%	n
1	0.82645	0.81967	0.81301	0.80645	0.80000	0.79365	0.78740	0.78125	0.77519	0.76923	1
2	0.68301	0.67186	0.66098	0.65036	0.64000	0.62988	0.62000	0.61035	0.60093	0.59172	2
3	0.56447	0.55071	0.53738	0.52449	0.51200	0.49991	0.48819	0.47684	0.46583	0.45517	3
4	0.46651	0.45140	0.43690	0.42297	0.40960	0.39675	0.38440	0.37253	0.36111	0.35013	4
5	0.38554	0.37000	0.35520	0.34111	0.32768	0.31488	0.30268	0.29104	0.27993	0.26933	5
6	0.31863	0.30328	0.28878	0.27509	0.26214	0.24991	0.23833	0.22737	0.21700	0.20718	6
7	0.26333	0.24859	0.23478	0.22184	0.20972	0.19834	0.18766	0.17764	0.16822	0.15937	7
8	0.21763	0.20376	0.19088	0.17891	0.16777	0.15741	0.14776	0.13878	0.13040	0.12259	8
9	0.17986	0.16702	0.15519	0.14428	0.13422	0.12493	0.11635	0.10842	0.10109	0.09430	9
10	0.14864	0.13690	0.12617	0.11635	0.10737	0.09915	0.09161	0.08470	0.07836	0.07254	10
11	0.12285	0.11221	0.10258	0.09383	0.08590	0.07869	0.07214	0.06617	0.06075	0.05580	11
12	0.10153	0.09198	0.08339	0.07567	0.06872	0.06245	0.05680	0.05170	0.04709	0.04292	12
13	0.08391	0.17539	0.06780	0.06103	0.05498	0.04957	0.04472	0.04039	0.03650	0.03302	13
14	0.06934	0.06180	0.05512	0.04921	0.04398	0.03934	0.03522	0.03155	0.02830	0.02540	14
15	0.05731	0.05065	0.04481	0.03969	0.03518	0.03122	0.02773	0.02465	0.02194	0.01954	15
16	0.04736	0.04152	0.03643	0.03201	0.02815	0.02478	0.02183	0.01926	0.01700	0.01503	16
17	0.03914	0.03403	0.02962	0.02581	0.02252	0.01967	0.01719	0.01505	0.01318	0.01156	17
18	0.03235	0.27289	0.02408	0.02082	0.01801	0.01561	0.01354	0.01175	0.01022	0.00889	18
19	0.02673	0.02286	0.01958	0.01679	0.01441	0.01239	0.01066	0.00918	0.00792	0.00684	19
20	0.02209	0.01874	0.01592	0.01354	0.01153	0.00983	0.00839	0.00717	0.00614	0.00526	20
21	0.01826	0.01536	0.01294	0.01092	0.00922	0.00780	0.00661	0.00561	0.00476	0.00405	21
22	0.01509	0.01259	0.01052	0.00880	0.00738	0.00619	0.00520	0.00438	0.00369	0.00311	22
23	0.01247	0.01032	0.00855	0.00710	0.00590	0.00491	0.00410	0.00342	0.00286	0.00239	23
24	0.01031	0.00846	0.00695	0.00573	0.00472	0.00390	0.00323	0.00267	0.00222	0.00184	24
25	0.00852	0.00693	0.00565	0.00462	0.00378	0.00310	0.00254	0.00209	0.00172	0.00152	25

Appendix Table 1 continued

n	31%	32%	33%	34%	35%	36%	37%	38%	39%	40%	n
1	0.76336	0.75758	0.75188	0.74627	0.74074	0.73529	0.72993	0.72464	0.71942	0.71429	1
2	0.58272	0.57392	0.56532	0.55692	0.54870	0.54066	0.53279	0.52510	0.51757	0.51020	2
3	0.44482	0.43479	0.42505	0.41561	0.40644	0.39754	0.38890	0.38051	0.37235	0.36443	3
4	0.33956	0.32939	0.31959	0.31016	0.30107	0.29231	0.28387	0.27573	0.26788	0.26031	4
5	0.25920	0.24953	0.24029	0.23146	0.22301	0.21493	0.20720	0.19980	0.19272	0.18593	5
6	0.19787	0.18904	0.18067	0.17273	0.16520	0.15804	0.15124	0.14479	0.13865	0.13281	6
7	0.15104	0.14321	0.13584	0.12890	0.12237	0.11621	0.11040	0.10492	0.09975	0.09486	7
8	0.11530	0.10849	0.10214	0.09620	0.09064	0.08545	0.08058	0.07603	0.07176	0.06776	8
9	0.08802	0.08219	0.07680	0.07179	0.06714	0.06283	0.05882	0.05509	0.05163	0.04840	9
10	0.06719	0.06227	0.05774	0.05357	0.04973	0.04620	0.04293	0.03992	0.03714	0.03457	10
11	0.05129	0.04717	0.04341	0.03998	0.03684	0.03397	0.03134	0.02893	0.02672	0.02469	11
12	0.03915	0.03574	0.03264	0.02984	0.02729	0.02498	0.02287	0.02096	0.01922	0.01764	12
13	0.02989	0.02707	0.02454	0.02227	0.02021	0.01837	0.01670	0.01519	0.01383	0.01260	13
14	0.02281	0.02051	0.01845	0.01662	0.01497	0.01350	0.01219	0.01101	0.00995	0.00900	14
15	0.01742	0.01554	0.01387	0.01240	0.01109	0.00993	0.00890	0.00798	0.00716	0.00643	15
16	0.01329	0.01177	0.01043	0.00925	0.00822	0.00730	0.00649	0.00578	0.00515	0.00459	16
17	0.01015	0.00892	0.00784	0.00691	0.00609	0.00537	0.00474	0.00419	0.00370	0.00328	17
18	0.00775	0.00676	0.00590	0.00515	0.00451	0.00395	0.00346	0.00304	0.00267	0.00234	18
19	0.00591	0.00512	0.00443	0.00385	0.00334	0.00290	0.00253	0.00220	0.00192	0.00167	19
20	0.00451	0.00388	0.00333	0.00287	0.00247	0.00213	0.00184	0.00159	0.00138	0.00120	20
21	0.00345	0.00294	0.00251	0.00214	0.00183	0.00157	0.00135	0.00115	0.00099	0.00085	21
22	0.00263	0.00223	0.00188	0.00160	0.00136	0.00115	0.00098	0.00084	0.00071	0.00061	22
23	0.00201	0.00169	0.00142	0.00119	0.00101	0.00085	0.00072	0.00061	0.00051	0.00044	23
24	0.00153	0.00128	0.00107	0.00089	0.00074	0.00062	0.00052	0.00044	0.00037	0.00031	24
25	0.00117	0.00097	0.00080	0.00066	0.00055	0.00046	0.00038	0.00032	0.00027	0.00022	25

Appendix Table 2 Present value of an annuity of £1 for n years

n	1%	2%	3%	4%	5%	6%	7%	8%	9%	10%	n
1	0.9901	0.9804	0.9709	0.9615	0.9524	0.9434	0.9346	0.9259	0.9174	0.9091	1
2	1.9704	1.9416	1.9135	1.8861	1.8594	1.8334	1.8080	1.7833	1.7591	1.7355	2
3	2.9410	2.8839	2.8286	2.7751	2.7232	2.6730	2.6243	2.5771	2.5313	2.4868	3
4	3.9020	3.8077	3.7171	3.6299	3.5459	3.4651	3.3872	3.3121	3.2397	3.1699	4
5	4.8535	4.7134	4.5797	4.4518	4.3295	4.2124	4.1002	3.9927	3.8896	3.7908	5
6	5.7955	5.6014	5.4172	5.2421	5.0757	4.9173	4.7665	4.6229	4.4859	4.3553	6
7	6.7282	6.4720	6.2302	6.0020	5.7863	5.5824	5.3893	5.2064	5.0329	4.8684	7
8	7.6517	7.3254	7.0196	6.7327	6.4632	6.2098	5.9713	5.7466	5.5348	5.3349	8
9	8.5661	8.1622	7.7861	7.4353	7.1078	6.8017	6.5152	6.2469	5.9852	5.7590	9
10	9.4714	8.9825	8.5302	8.1109	7.7217	7.3601	7.0236	6.7101	6.4176	6.1446	10
11	10.3677	9.7868	9.2526	8.7604	8.3064	7.8868	7.4987	7.1389	6.8052	6.4951	11
12	11.2552	10.5753	9.9539	9.3850	8.8632	8.3838	7.9427	7.5361	7.1607	6.8137	12
13	12.1338	11.3483	10.6349	9.9856	9.3935	8.8527	8.3576	7.9038	7.4869	7.1034	13
14	13.0038	12.1062	11.2960	10.5631	9.8986	9.2950	8.7454	8.2442	7.7861	7.3667	14
15	13.8651	12.8492	11.9379	11.1183	10.3796	9.7122	9.1079	8.5595	8.0607	7.6061	15
16	14.7180	13.5777	12.5610	11.6522	10.8377	10.1059	9.4466	8.8514	8.3125	7.8237	16
17	15.5624	14.2918	13.1660	12.1656	11.2740	10.4772	9.7632	9.1216	8.5436	8.0215	17
18	16.3984	14.9920	13.7534	12.6592	11.6895	10.8276	10.0591	9.3719	8.7556	8.2014	18
19	17.2261	15.6784	14.3237	13.1339	12.0853	11.1581	10.3356	9.6036	8.9501	8.3649	19
20	18.0457	16.3514	14.8774	13.5903	12.4622	11.4699	10.5940	9.8181	9.1285	8.5136	20
21	18.8571	17.0111	15.4149	14.0291	12.8211	11.7640	10.8355	10.0168	9.2922	8.6487	21
22	19.6605	17.6580	15.9368	14.4511	13.1630	12.0416	11.0612	10.2007	9.4424	8.7715	22
23	20.4559	18.2921	16.4435	14.8568	13.4885	12.3033	11.2722	10.3710	9.5802	8.8832	23
24	21.2435	18.9139	16.9355	15.2469	13.7986	12.5503	11.4693	10.5287	9.7066	8.9847	24
25	22.0233	19.5234	17.4131	15.6220	14.0939	12.7833	11.6536	10.6748	9.8226	9.0770	25

Appendix Table 2 continued

n	11%	12%	13%	14%	15%	16%	17%	18%	19%	20%	n
1	0.0009	0.8929	0.8850	0.3772	0.8696	0.8621	0.8547	0.8475	0.8403	0.8333	1
2	1.7125	1.6901	1.6681	1.6467	1.6257	1.6052	1.5852	1.5656	1.5465	1.5278	2
3	2.4437	2.4018	2.3612	2.3216	2.2832	2.2459	2.2096	2.1743	2.1399	2.1065	3
4	3.1024	3.0373	2.9745	2.9137	2.8550	2.7982	2.7432	2.6901	2.6386	2.5887	4
5	3.6959	3.6048	3.5172	3.4331	3.3522	3.2743	3.1993	3.1272	3.0576	2.9906	5
6	4.2305	4.1114	3.9976	3.8887	3.7845	3.6847	3.5892	3.4976	3.4098	3.3255	6
7	4.7122	4.5638	4.4226	4.2883	4.1604	4.0386	3.9224	3.8115	3.7057	3.6046	7
8	5.1461	4.9676	4.7988	4.6389	4.4873	4.3436	3.2072	4.0776	3.9544	3.8372	8
9	5.5370	5.3282	5.1317	4.9464	4.7716	4.6065	4.4506	4.3030	4.1633	4.0310	9
10	5.8892	5.6502	5.4262	5.2161	5.0188	4.8332	4.6586	4.4941	4.3389	4.1925	10
11	6.2065	5.9377	5.6869	5.4527	5.2337	5.0286	4.8364	4.6560	4.4865	4.3271	11
12	6.4924	6.1944	5.9176	5.6603	5.4206	5.1971	4.9884	4.7932	4.6105	4.4392	12
13	6.7499	6.4235	6.1218	5.8424	5.5931	5.3423	5.1183	4.9095	4.7147	4.5327	13
14	6.9819	6.6282	6.3025	6.0021	5.7245	5.4675	5.2293	5.0081	4.8023	4.6106	14
15	7.1909	6.8109	6.4624	6.1422	5.8474	5.5755	5.3242	5.0916	4.8759	4.6755	15
16	7.3792	6.9740	6.6039	6.2651	5.9542	5.6685	5.4053	5.1624	4.9377	4.7296	16
17	7.5488	7.1196	6.7291	6.3729	6.0472	5.7487	5.4746	5.2223	4.9897	4.7746	17
18	7.7016	7.2497	6.8399	6.4674	6.1280	5.8178	5.5339	5.2732	5.0333	4.8122	18
19	7.8393	7.3658	6.9380	6.5504	6.1982	5.8775	5.5845	5.3162	5.0700	4.8435	19
20	7.9633	7.4694	7.0248	6.6231	6.2593	5.9288	5.6278	5.3527	5.1009	4.8696	20
21	8.0751	7.5620	7.1016	6.6870	6.3125	5.9731	5.6648	5.3837	5.1268	4.8913	21
22	8.1757	7.6446	7.1695	6.7429	6.3587	6.0113	5.6964	5.4099	5.1486	4.9094	22
23	8.2664	7.7184	7.2297	6.7921	6.3988	6.0442	5.7234	5.4321	5.1668	4.9245	23
24	8.3481	7.7843	7.2829	6.8351	6.4338	6.0726	5.7465	5.4509	5.1822	4.9371	24
25	8.4217	7.8431	7.3300	6.8729	6.4641	6.0971	5.7662	5.4669	5.1951	4.9476	25

Appendix Table 2 continued

n	21%	22%	23%	24%	25%	26%	27%	28%	29%	30%	n
1	0.8264	0.8197	0.8130	0.8065	0.8000	0.7937	0.7874	0.7813	0.7752	0.7592	1
2	1.5095	1.4915	1.4740	1.4568	1.4400	1.4235	1.4074	1.3916	1.3761	1.3609	2
3	2.0738	2.0422	2.0114	1.9813	1.9520	1.9234	1.8956	1.8684	1.8420	1.8161	3
4	2.5404	2.4936	2.4483	2.4043	2.3616	2.3202	2.2800	2.2410	2.2031	2.1662	4
5	2.9260	2.8636	2.8035	2.7454	2.6893	2.6351	2.5827	2.5320	2.4830	2.4356	5
6	3.2446	3.1669	3.0923	3.0205	2.9514	2.8850	2.8210	2.7594	2.7000	2.6427	6
7	3.5079	3.4155	3.3270	3.2423	3.1611	3.0833	3.0087	2.9370	2.8682	2.8021	7
8	3.7256	3.6193	3.5179	3.4212	3.3289	3.2407	3.1564	3.0758	2.9986	2.9247	8
9	3.9054	3.7863	3.6731	3.5655	3.4631	3.3657	3.2728	3.1842	3.0997	3.1090	9
10	4.0541	3.9232	3.7993	3.6819	3.5705	3.4648	3.3644	3.2689	3.1781	3.0915	10
11	4.1769	4.0354	3.9018	3.7757	3.6564	3.5435	3.4365	3.3351	3.2388	3.1473	11
12	4.2785	4.1274	3.9852	3.8514	3.7251	3.6060	3.4933	3.3868	3.2859	3.1903	12
13	4.3624	4.2028	4.0530	3.9124	3.7801	3.6555	3.6381	3.4272	3.3224	3.2233	13
14	4.4317	4.2646	4.1082	3.9616	3.8241	3.6949	3.5733	3.4587	3.3507	3.2487	14
15	4.4890	4.3152	4.1530	4.0013	3.8593	3.7261	3.6010	3.4834	3.3726	3.2682	15
16	4.5364	4.3567	4.1894	4.0333	3.8874	3.7509	3.6228	3.5026	3.3896	3.2832	16
17	4.5755	4.3908	4.2190	4.0591	3.9099	3.7705	3.6400	3.5177	3.4028	3.2948	17
18	4.6079	4.4187	4.2431	4.0799	3.9279	3.7861	3.6536	3.5294	3.4130	3.3037	18
19	4.6346	4.4415	4.2627	4.0967	3.9424	3.7985	3.6642	3.5386	3.4210	3.3105	19
20	4.6567	4.4603	4.2786	4.1103	3.9539	3.8083	3.6726	3.5458	3.4271	3.3158	20
21	4.6750	4.4756	4.2916	4.1212	3.9631	3.8161	3.6792	3.5514	3.4319	3.3198	21
22	4.6900	4.4882	4.3021	4.1300	3.9705	3.8223	3.6844	3.5558	3.4356	3.3230	22
23	4.7025	4.4985	4.3106	4.1371	3.9764	3.8273	3.6885	3.5592	3.4384	3.3254	23
24	4.7128	4.5070	4.3176	4.1428	3.9811	3.8312	3.6918	3.5619	3.4406	3.3272	24
25	4.7213	4.5139	4.3232	4.1474	3.9849	3.8342	3.6943	3.5640	3.4423	3.3286	25

Appendix Table 2 continued

n	31%	32%	33%	34%	35%	36%	37%	38%	39%	40%	n
1	0.7634	0.7576	0.7519	0.7463	0.7407	0.7353	0.7299	0.7246	0.7194	0.7143	1
2	1.3461	1.3315	1.3172	1.3032	1.2894	1.2760	1.2627	1.2497	1.2370	1.2245	2
3	1.7909	1.7663	1.7423	1.7188	1.6959	1.6735	1.6516	1.6302	1.6093	1.5889	3
4	2.1305	2.0957	2.0618	2.0290	1.9969	1.9658	1.9355	1.9060	1.8772	1.8492	4
5	2.3897	2.3452	2.3021	2.2604	2.2200	2.1807	2.1427	2.1058	2.0699	1.9352	5
6	2.5875	2.5342	2.4828	2.4331	2.3852	2.3388	2.2936	2.2506	2.2086	2.1680	6
7	2.7386	2.6775	2.6187	2.5620	2.5075	2.4550	2.4043	2.3555	2.3083	2.2628	7
8	2.8539	2.7860	2.7208	2.6582	2.5982	2.5404	2.4849	2.4315	2.3801	2.3306	8
9	2.9419	2.8681	2.7976	2.7300	2.6653	2.6033	2.5437	2.4866	2.4317	2.3790	9
10	3.0091	2.9304	2.8553	2.7836	2.7150	2.6495	2.5867	2.5265	2.4689	2.4136	10
11	3.0604	2.9776	2.8987	2.8236	2.7519	2.6834	2.6180	2.5555	2.4956	2.4383	11
12	3.0995	3.0133	2.9314	2.8534	2.7792	2.7084	2.6409	2.5764	2.5148	2.4559	12
13	3.1294	3.0404	2.9559	2.8757	2.7994	2.7268	2.6576	2.5916	2.5286	2.4685	13
14	3.1522	3.0609	2.9744	2.8923	2.8144	2.7403	2.6698	2.6026	2.5386	2.4775	14
15	3.1696	3.0764	2.9883	2.9047	2.8255	2.7502	2.6787	2.6106	2.5457	2.4839	15
16	3.1829	3.0882	2.9987	2.9140	2.8337	2.7575	2.6852	2.6164	2.5509	2.4885	16
17	3.1931	3.0971	3.0065	2.9209	2.8398	2.7629	2.6899	2.6202	2.5546	2.4918	17
18	3.2008	3.1039	3.0124	2.9260	2.8443	2.7668	2.6934	2.6236	2.5573	2.4941	18
19	3.2067	3.1090	3.0169	2.9299	2.8476	2.7697	2.6959	2.6258	2.5592	2.4958	19
20	3.2112	3.1129	3.0202	2.9327	2.8501	2.7718	2.6977	2.6274	2.5606	2.4970	20
21	3.2174	3.1158	3.0227	2.9349	2.8519	2.7734	2.6991	2.6285	2.5616	2.4979	21
22	3.2173	3.1180	3.0246	2.9365	2.8533	2.7746	2.7000	2.6294	2.5623	2.4985	22
23	3.2193	3.1197	3.0260	2.9377	2.8543	2.7754	2.7008	2.6300	2.5628	2.4989	23
24	3.2209	3.1210	3.0271	2.9386	2.8550	2.7760	2.7013	2.6304	2.5632	2.4992	24
25	3.2220	3.1220	3.0279	2.9392	2.8556	2.7765	2.7017	2.6307	2.5634	2.4994	25

INDEX